D1706110

www.mygrammarlab.com

Contents

Introduction to MyGrammarLab

Welcome to **MyGrammarLab** – a three-level grammar series that teaches and practises grammar through a unique blend of book, online and mobile resources. We recommend that you read this introduction along with the guide on the inside front cover to find out how to get the most out of your course.

What level is MyGrammarLab?

The **MyGrammarLab** series takes learners from elementary to advanced grammar, each level benchmarked against the Common European Framework and providing grammar practice for Cambridge ESOL exams:

	Level description	CEFR level	Grammar practice for exams
Elementary	elementary to pre-intermediate	A1/A2	KET
Intermediate	pre-intermediate to upper intermediate	B1/B2	PET FCE
Advanced	upper intermediate to advanced	C1/C2	CAE IELTS

What is unique about MyGrammarLab?

MyGrammarLab offers every learner of English the opportunity to study grammar in the way that best suits their needs – and provides as much practice as necessary to ensure that each grammar point is learnt and can be used in the context of real communication.

At each level, learners have access to a variety of materials:

book

- **clear and simple explanations** based on the Longman Dictionaries Defining Vocabulary of just 2000 words to ensure full understanding of the grammar
- **natural examples** to illustrate the grammar points, based on the Longman Corpus Network
- a topic-based approach that presents **grammar in context**
- a **variety of exercise types** – from drills to contextualised and personalised practice
- a **review section** at the end of each module to revise the key grammar points
- an **exit test** at the end of each module to check that the grammar has been fully understood
- information on the **pronunciation** of grammar items
- information on **common errors** and how to avoid making them
- a **grammar check section** for quickly checking specific grammar points
- a **glossary** of grammar terms used in the explanations

online

- a **grammar teacher** who explains key grammar points through short video presentations
- a full **diagnostic test** to identify the grammar points that need to be learnt
- **more practice** for every unit of the book
- regular **progress tests** to check that the grammar has been understood
- **catch-up exercises** for learners who fail the progress tests – to ensure that every learner has the opportunity to master the grammar
- a full **exit test** at the end of each module
- automatic marking and feedback
- **pronunciation practice** of grammar items
- the option to **listen and check** the answers for practice exercises from the book
- additional **grammar practice for exams**

mobile

- downloadable exercises for **practice anywhere, any time**
- the ability to **create exercises** from a bank of practice questions
- automatic marking and **feedback** for wrong answers

What is a MyLab?

A MyLab is a Learning Management System – an online platform that enables learners and teachers to manage the learning process via a number of online tools such as automatic marking, the recording of grades in a gradebook and the ability to customise a course.

How can I get the most out of MyGrammarLab?

To the Student:

If you are using MyGrammarLab in class, your teacher will tell you which units to study and which exercises to do.

If you are using MyGrammarLab for self study, you can work through the book from Module 1 to Module 20. Or you can choose a grammar point that you want to study and go to a specific unit. Here is a good way to study a complete module:

The modules in the book start with a text such as an advert, an email or a magazine article. The text introduces the grammar for the module. The grammar is highlighted in the text, and then there is a short exercise. The exercise shows you the units you need to study in order to learn more about the main grammar points.

Go online for a full diagnostic test Look for this instruction at the bottom of the first page of each module. Take the diagnostic test then click on the feedback button to see which unit to go to for more information and practice.

The grammar information is on the left in the book. The practice exercises are on the right. It is therefore easy to check and read the grammar while you are doing the exercises.

For more information about the grammar, go online to watch the grammar videos in each unit and listen to your grammar teacher.

If you would like more grammar and listening practice, you can listen to the correct answers for some of the practice exercises in the book. Look for this symbol: **1.10 Listen and check.** If you have the book with answer key, you can check all the answers at the back of the book.

Go online for more practice Look for this instruction at the end of the practice exercises in the book. All the online exercises are different to the exercises in the book. They are marked automatically. Your grades are recorded in your own gradebook.

Look for this symbol on the grammar information pages in the book: . This means that there is some information on a pronunciation point. Go online to hear the information and practise the pronunciation.

Go online for a progress test Look for this instruction at the end of the practice exercises in the book. The online progress tests show you if you have understood the grammar points in the units that you have studied. If your grade is low, do the catch-up exercises online. If your grade is good, you probably don't need to do these.

For practice away from your computer, download the catch-up exercises questions to your mobile phone. You can create your own practice tests. Go to www.mygrammarlab.com to download.

At the end of each module there is a two-page review section. The review exercises bring together all the grammar points in the module.

Go online for more review exercises Look for this instruction at the end of the review exercises in the book.

At the end of each module, there is also a test. The test shows you how much you know and if you need more practice.

Go online for a full exit test Look for this instruction at the end of the exit test in the book.

To the Teacher:

If you are using MyGrammarLab with a class of students, you can either work through the book from the first to the last module, or you can select the areas that you would like your students to focus on.

You can work through a module as outlined on the previous page – but as a teacher, you are able to assign tests and view all the scores from your class in one gradebook. This will enable you to see at a glance which areas are difficult for your students – and will let you know which of your students are falling behind.

 For pronunciation practice in class, audio CDs are available. The disk and track number for each explanation are given in the book. Look for this symbol: ◀)) 1.10 .

 All tests (diagnostic, progress and exit) are hidden from students. Assign these when you want your class to take the test. Marking is automatic – as is the reporting of grades into the class gradebook.

 Some practice exercises – such as written tasks - require teacher marking. These are hidden from your students so you should only assign these if you want them to submit their answers to you for marking. The grades are reported automatically into the gradebook.

Key to symbols

⚠	This highlights a grammar point that learners find particularly difficult and often gives common errors that students make.
NATURAL ENGLISH	Sometimes a sentence may be grammatically correct, but it does not sound natural. These notes will help you to produce natural English.
GRAMMAR IN USE	This indicates an exercise which practises grammar in a typical context, often a longer passage or dialogue.
◀)) Pronunciation ➤ 1.02	This indicates where you will find pronunciation practice on the audio CDs and in the MyLab.
◀)) 2.10 Listen and check.	This indicates that there is a recorded answer online. You can check your answer by listening to the recording, or, if you are using the edition with answer key, by looking in the key at the back of the book.
short form	Some words in the explanations are shown in green. This indicates that they are included in the glossary on p. ix. Look in the glossary to find out what these words mean.

Glossary

active if a verb or sentence is active, the person or thing doing the action is the subject of the verb. In the sentence *The boy kicked the ball*, the verb *kick* is active.
→ passive

adjective a word that describes a noun, e.g. *big, comfortable, red, pleased*

adverb a word that describes or adds to the meaning of a verb, an adjective, another adverb, or a sentence. There are different types of adverbs: **manner**: *quickly, kindly, beautifully*; **degree**: *completely, definitely*; **frequency**: *always, often, never*; **place**: *here, there*; **time**: *now, then*.

auxiliary verb a verb that we use with another verb to make questions, negative sentences, tenses and the passive. Common auxiliary verbs are *be, do* and *have*.
→ main verb, modal verb

capital letter the large form of a letter of the alphabet, that you use at the beginning of a name or sentence, e.g. *B* not *b*

clause a group of words that contains a verb and usually a subject. A clause may be a sentence or part of a sentence.
→ main clause, relative clause

comparative adjective *nicer, hotter, better, more comfortable*, etc. We use comparative adjectives for comparing two people or things. → superlative adjective

compound adjective an adjective that is made from two or more words, e.g. *high-quality* (*high + quality*), *well-known* (*well + known*)

compound noun a noun that is made from two or more words, e.g. *whiteboard* (*white + board*), *dining room* (*dining + room*)

consonant any of the sounds and letters of the English alphabet, except *a, e, i, o, u* → vowel

continuous the form of a verb in tenses we make with *be* and the *-ing* form. We use the continuous for things we are doing now, or for a temporary period of time: **present continuous**: *I'm using my computer at the moment*; **past continuous**: *They were living in Japan at the time*; **present perfect continuous**: *I've been waiting here for an hour.*

countable a countable noun has a singular and a plural form: *table/tables, man/men.*
→ uncountable

first conditional a sentence with *if* that describes a future situation. We use the present tense after *if* in the first conditional: *If it's sunny tomorrow, we'll go to the beach.*

imperative the form of a verb that you use to tell someone to do something: *Give me that book! | Don't sit there!*

indefinite pronoun *someone, anyone, everywhere, nothing*, etc: *I've looked everywhere for my key.*

indirect question a question that begins with *Could you tell me, Do you know*, etc. We use indirect questions to sound more polite: *Could you tell me when the next bus leaves for London?*

infinitive the base form of a verb, e.g. *be, read, talk, write*. The infinitive with *to* is *to* + the base form: *to be, to read, to talk, to write.*

-ing form the form of a verb that ends in *-ing*: *being, reading, talking, writing*

intonation the way that the level of your voice changes to add meaning to what you say. For example, your voice often goes up at the end of a question.

irregular an irregular verb does not have a past tense and past participle that end in *-ed*, e.g. *go/went/gone*; an irregular noun does not have a plural that ends in *-s*, e.g. *man/men*; an irregular adverb does not end in *-ly*, e.g. *fast/fast* → regular

linking word a word such as *and, but* or *because* that we use to connect one part of a sentence with another, or to show how one sentence is related to another: *We paid the bill and went home. | I like summer because it's warm.*

main clause a group of words that we can use alone or with another clause. In the sentence *It was raining when I went outside*, the main clause is *It was raining*. → clause

main verb a verb that we can use with or without an auxiliary verb, e.g. *cost* in *How much does it cost? It costs $20.*
→ auxiliary verb, modal verb

modal verb a type of auxiliary verb such as *can, should* or *might* that we use with another verb to show ideas such as ability (*can*), advice (*should*) or possibility (*might*): *I can swim. | We should leave now. | You might be right.*

negative a negative sentence contains a word such as *not* or *never*: *Shakespeare wasn't French.* | *I've never liked coffee.* → positive

noun a word for a person, animal, thing, place or idea, e.g. *student, cat, rain, China, happiness*

object a noun or pronoun that usually follows a verb. In the sentence *The boy kicked the ball*, the noun *ball* is the object. → subject

object pronoun *me, him, her, it, us, you, them.* We use object pronouns after the verb. → subject pronoun

passive if a verb or sentence is passive, the subject of the verb does not do the action, but is affected by the action of the verb. In the sentence *The ball was kicked into goal*, the verb *was kicked* is passive. → active

past continuous → continuous

past participle a form of a verb that we use to make perfect tenses and passives. Regular verbs have past participles that end in *-ed*, e.g. *arrive/arrived, call/called.* Irregular verbs have different forms, e.g. *go/gone, speak/spoken, sell/sold.*

past perfect the tense of a verb that we form with *had* and the past participle. We can use the past perfect in reported statements: *He said he'd already seen that film.*

past simple the tense of a verb that we form by adding *-ed* to regular verbs. Irregular verbs have different forms, e.g. *go/went.* We use the past simple for single or repeated actions in the past: *I called you yesterday.* | *I called you twice yesterday.*

phrasal verb a verb that we use with a preposition or an adverb, or both. A phrasal verb has a different meaning from the verb alone: *Please take off your shoes before you enter.* (*take* + *off* = remove)

plural the form of a word that we use for more than one person or thing. *Students* is the plural of *student. They* is a plural pronoun. → singular

positive a positive sentence does not contain a word such as *not* or *never*: *Shakespeare was English.* | *I've always liked coffee.* → negative

possessive adjective *my, your, his, her, its, our, their.* Possessive adjectives show who something belongs to, or who someone is related to: *my house, her brother.*

possessive pronoun *mine, yours, his, hers, ours, theirs.* A possessive pronoun replaces a possessive adjective + noun: *It's hers.* (her car) | *That's mine.* (my mobile)

preposition a word such as *on, at, into* or *by* that we use before a noun to show the position of something, or to talk about time: *Put it on the table.* | *Meet me at six o'clock.* We can use prepositions in other ways, too, e.g. *Please send me your answer by email.*

present continuous → continuous

present perfect the tense of a verb that we form with *have* and the past participle, e.g. *has gone.* The present perfect has many uses; for example, for a situation that started in the past and continues now: *I've been at university for two years now.*

present perfect continuous → continuous

present simple the tense of a verb that uses the base form, or the base form + *s* for *he, she* and *it*: *I live, he lives.* We use the present simple, for example, for regular activities and facts: *I go to work by bus.* | *The Earth goes round the Sun.*

pronoun a word that replaces a noun, e.g. *I, she, they, me, her, them, it* → subject pronoun, object pronoun

question a sentence that needs an answer: *Are you English?* | *What time is it?* → *Wh-* question, *Yes/No* question

question tag *isn't it?, doesn't she?, have you?* etc. We add question tags to the end of a statement to make it a question, or to check that someone agrees with you: *You're from Poland, aren't you?*

reflexive pronoun *myself, yourself, himself,* etc. We use reflexive pronouns when the subject and object of the verb are the same: *Dave looked at himself in the mirror.* (= Dave looked at Dave.)

regular a regular verb has a past tense and past participle that end in *-ed*: *finish/finished*; a regular noun has a plural that ends in *-s*: *book/books*; a regular adverb ends in *-ly*: *quick/quickly.* → irregular

relative clause a group of words that gives information about someone or something in the main part of the sentence. In the sentence *Mary is the woman that I met on holiday*, the relative clause is *that I met on holiday.*

relative pronoun a pronoun that connects a relative clause to the other part of the sentence, e.g. *who, which, that*

reported statement a statement that reports what a person has said. In a reported statement, the sentence *We're going to the shops* becomes *They said they were going to the shops.*

second conditional a sentence with *if* that describes a situation we are imagining in the present or future. We use the past tense after *if* in the second conditional: *If I was rich, I'd buy a Ferrari.*

short answer an answer to a *Yes/No* question that does not repeat the main verb:
Are you waiting for the bus? Yes, I am. | *Did you buy it? No, I didn't.*

short form the form of verbs we usually use when we are speaking, e.g. *I've* (not *I have*), *weren't* (not *were not*)

singular the form of a word that we use for only one person or thing. *Student* is a singular noun. *Am* and *is* are singular forms of the verb *be.* → plural

statement a sentence that is not a question or an imperative: *I'm British.* | *It's three o'clock.* | *The play hasn't started.*

stress the force that we use to say a part of a word. In the word *coffee*, the stress is on the first syllable. If we stress a word or part of a word, we say it with more force.

strong form the way we pronounce a word when we stress the vowel in it: The strong form of *can* is /kæn/ and the weak form of *can* is /kən/. → weak form

subject a noun or pronoun that usually comes before the main verb in the sentence. The subject shows who is doing the action: *The boy* (subject) *kicked the ball* (object). → object

subject pronoun *I, he, she, it, we, you, they.* We use subject pronouns before the verb. → object pronoun

superlative adjective *nicest, hottest, best, most comfortable*, etc. We use superlative adjectives when we compare one person or thing with several others. → comparative adjective

syllable a part of a word that contains a single vowel sound. *Dad* has one syllable and *Daddy* has two syllables.

time expression a word or phrase such as *today, every day, on Mondays, once a week.* Time expressions describe when or how often we do regular activities.

uncountable an uncountable noun does not have a plural form, e.g. *milk, music, information* → countable

verb a word which describes an action or state, e.g. *go, eat, finish* or *live*

vowel one of the sounds that are shown by the letters *a, e, i, o, u* → consonant

weak form the way we pronounce a word when we do not stress the vowel in it: The weak form of *an* /æn/ is *an* /ən/. → strong form

Wh- question a question that begins with a *Wh-* word: *What's your name?* | *How are you?*

Wh- word *who, what, where, when, why, how*

Yes/No question a question which only needs the answer *yes* or *no*: *Are you a student?* | *Do you like pasta?*

Punctuation

'	apostrophe	.	full stop/period *AmE*
( )	brackets	-	hyphen
:	colon	?	question mark
,	comma	' '	quotation marks
!	exclamation mark	;	semicolon

Before you start

1 Read about the market. Look at the <mark>highlighted</mark> grammar examples.

FRENCH MARKET

Try <mark>some</mark> exciting new <mark>food</mark> this weekend!

<mark>A French market</mark> will be in Frampton on Saturday and Sunday. There will be <mark>a lot of</mark> interesting things, including:

- Mediterranean fruit and <mark>vegetables</mark>
- cheese from Normandy
- French bread and cakes
- <mark>chocolate</mark> from Paris
- <mark>a few</mark> clothes and a little jewellery

<mark>All the food</mark> and drink is from France.

<mark>The market</mark> will be in <mark>North Square</mark> on both days from 9.00 to 18.00.

2 Now read the sentences. Choose the correct words in *italics*.
The <mark>highlighted</mark> grammar examples will help you.

1 Do you eat *vegetable / vegetables*? ➤ Unit 1
2 I really like French *food / foods*. ➤ Unit 2
3 *Belgian chocolate / A Belgian chocolate* is delicious. ➤ Unit 3
4 There's *a / an* new restaurant in the town. ➤ Unit 4
5 *A / The* new supermarket in the town centre is really cheap. ➤ Unit 5
6 Let's meet at the food hall in *Sloane Square / the Sloane Square*. ➤ Unit 6
7 There's always *some / any* interesting food at the market. ➤ Unit 7
8 There are *much / a lot of* markets in this area. ➤ Unit 8
9 They sell *a little / a few* clothes at the market, too. ➤ Unit 9
10 It's an Italian shop. *All / Some* the food is from Italy. ➤ Unit 10

3 Check your answers below. Then go to the unit for more information and practice.

1 vegetables 2 food 3 Belgian chocolate 4 a 5 The 6 Sloane Square 7 some 8 a lot of 9 a few 10 All

1 Singular and plural nouns

1 Nouns

A noun is a p erson, a place or a thing:
a waiter   a town   a pizza   a melon
an apple   an egg   a steak

In writing, names of people, places, days, months, etc. begin with a capital letter:
John Smith   Mr Brown
Vancouver   Oxford Street
Saturday   September   May Day

2 Singular and plural nouns

Most nouns can be singular (one) or plural (more than one):

SINGULAR	*a pizza*	*a melon*	*a banana*	*an apple*	*an egg*
PLURAL	*two pizzas*	*three melons*	*four bananas*	*five apples*	*some eggs*

We usually add -*s* to a singular noun to make it plural, but some nouns are different:

NOUNS THAT END IN		PLURAL
s, ss, sh, ch, and *x* (and *potato, tomato*)	add -*es*	*buses, classes, dishes, watches, boxes, potatoes*
consonant (*b, c, d,* etc.) + *y*	change *y* to *i* and add -*es*	*families, babies, countries*
(*ay, ey, oy*)	(add -*s*)	*days, valleys, toys*
f or *fe*	change *f* to *v* and add -*es*	*loaves, wives, scarves*

The plural form of a few nouns is different. We call these irregular nouns:

SINGULAR	*man*	*woman*	*child*	*person*	*foot*	*tooth*	*penny*	*fish*	*sheep*
PLURAL	*men*	*women*	*children*	*people*	*feet*	*teeth*	*pence*	*fish*	*sheep*

Spelling rules ➤ page 316

🔊 Pronunciation ➤ 1.02

3 Noun + verb

We use different verb forms with singular and plural nouns:

singular noun + singular verb
Our teacher is British.
The bus leaves at 8.30.

plural noun + plural verb
Those students are Japanese.
The buses leave from the town centre.

Some nouns are always plural:
clothes
jeans
shorts
scissors
trousers
(reading) glasses

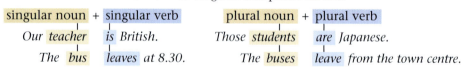

We can also say:
*a **pair of** jeans   a **pair of** shorts   a **pair of** scissors*

Practice

1 Write the plural form of the nouns.

+ -s	+ -es	+ -ies	+ -ves	irregular
		babies		

<del>baby</del> box car child class country day exercise family foot loaf man scarf watch wife

2 Match the two parts of the sentences. ◀)) 2.02 Listen and check.

0   1 My brothers ⟶ A walks to work.
   2 My brother ⟶ B walk to work.
1   1 Our English teacher   A come from London.
   2 Our English teachers   B comes from London.
2   1 The children   A is sick in bed.
   2 Jan's child   B are sick in bed.
3   1 My feet   A are hurting.
   2 My foot   B is hurting.
4   1 Your reading glasses   A is on the table.
   2 Your glass of water   B are on the table.

3 Write the plural form of the nouns in the picture.

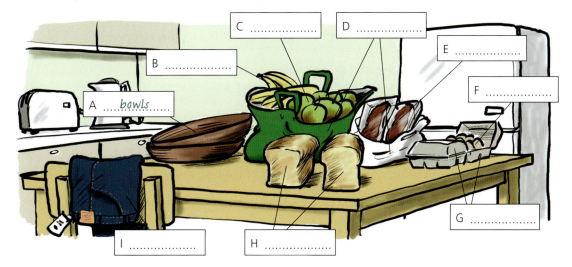

C ....
D ....
E ....
B ....
F ....
A .....bowls......
G ....
I ....
H ....

4 **GRAMMAR IN USE** Complete the note with nouns from Exercise 3 or a form of the verb *be*.
◀)) 2.03 Listen and check.

Sorry, James – I'm going to see Mum because she's not well.
Can you put the shopping away? Thanks.
The steaks (0) ......are........ for dinner tonight, so can you put them in the fridge?
Can you take the eggs out of the (1) .... and put them in the fridge, too?
There are some (2) .... and (3) .... in the green bag – put
them in the two (4) .... on the table. There are two (5) .... of
bread, too – can you put one of them in the fridge, please? The jeans
(6) .... for Simon – can you put them in his room?
See you later – I hope the interview was OK. Maureen

2 Countable and uncountable nouns (1)

ROASTED VEGETABLES

Ingredients
one red onion
two white onions
three potatoes
some carrots
olive oil
salt and pepper

1 Countable nouns

Countable nouns are things we can count, for example, *carrot, onion, potato*.

- they can be singular: *an onion*
  They often have *a/an, the, this/that* in front of them:
  *Is there **a market** here?   Where's **the market**?   **This carrot** is very sweet.*

- they can be plural: *onions*
  They often have *some, the, these/those* in front of them:
  *I'd like **some apples**, please.   **Those apples** look good.   Do you like **apples**?*

2 Uncountable nouns

Uncountable nouns are things we can't count, for example, *salt, oil, water*.

- they don't usually have a plural form: ~~*one oil*~~, ~~*two oils*~~
- they don't usually have *a/an* in front of them: ~~*an oil*~~, ~~*a salt*~~.

 Uncountable nouns often have *some* in front of them:
✗ ~~*Can I have a milk in my coffee?*~~
✓ *Can I have **some milk** in my coffee?*

uncountable noun	+	singular verb

Petrol **is** *expensive.*
This advice **is** *very useful.*

Some common uncountable nouns are:

- food: *bread cheese meat tea coffee sugar*
- materials: *metal wood plastic paper*
- school subjects and languages: *history art music English Russian*
- ideas and feelings: *advice love time education information*
- groups of similar things: *furniture* (chairs, tables, sofas) *luggage* (suitcases, bags)
  money (euros, pounds, dollars)

 ✗ ~~*Do you have some informations about the castle?*~~
✓ *Do you have some **information** about the castle?*

Practice

1 **Is the noun in *italics* in each sentence countable (C) or uncountable (U)? Write C or U.**

0 Is there a *bank* near here? ....C....
1 That *cheese* is delicious. ....
2 Do you have *milk* in your coffee? ....

3 How much *luggage* do you have? ....
4 I need to get some *oil* for the car. ....
5 Can I have some *potatoes*, please? ....

2 **Are the nouns countable or uncountable?**

countable	uncountable
apple	

~~apple~~ art chair
furniture information
man market sugar

3 **Match the pictures with the things on the shopping list.**

0 ....cheese....
1 ....
2 ....
5 ....
4 ....
3 ....

4 steaks
4 potatoes
a melon
bread
cheese
oil

4 **GRAMMAR IN USE** **Choose the correct <u>underlined</u> words in the note from Adam to Rachel.**
 ◀))2.04 Listen and check.

Rachel
Can you buy the food for dinner tonight? Mum and Dad are coming, so can you
get (0) <u>a meat</u> /(<u>some meat,</u>) maybe four nice (1) <u>steak</u> / <u>steaks</u>? We need some
(2) <u>potato</u> / <u>potatoes</u> – four large (3) <u>potato</u> / <u>potatoes</u> for baking. Can you buy
(4) <u>a bread and a cheese</u> / <u>some bread and cheese</u>, too, and maybe
(5) <u>a nice juicy melon</u> / <u>some nice juicy melon</u> to start? Oh, and we need some
(6) <u>oil</u> / <u>oils</u> as well. Thanks.
See you later,
Adam

5 **Correct the mistakes in the <u>underlined</u> parts of the sentences. ◀))2.05 Listen and check.**

0 Do you want <u>a~~ salt~~</u> in your soup? *(some) salt*
1 <u>Education are</u> very important.
2 Can I have <u>two box</u> of eggs, please?
3 Can you give me <u>some informations</u> about the trains?
4 We've got a lot of <u>luggages</u>.
5 I must get <u>a petrol</u> for the car before we start.
6 I haven't got a lot of <u>moneys</u>.

3 Countable and uncountable nouns (2)

> Can I have **a coffee**?

> Sure, I think there's **some coffee** in the machine.

1 Nouns that can be countable or uncountable

Some nouns have a countable meaning and an uncountable meaning:

COUNTABLE	UNCOUNTABLE
I'd like **three teas***, please.* (cups of tea)	*Tea comes from China and India.* (drink)
My uncle has **25 chickens** *on his farm.* (animals)	*I love* **chicken***, it's delicious!* (food)
Would you like **a chocolate***?* (one sweet)	*French* **chocolate** *is very good.* (food)
Can you buy **a paper** *at the shop?* (a newspaper)	*Paper is made from wood.* (material)
There are **four Russians** *in my class.* (people)	*Do you speak* **Russian***?* (language)

2 Ways of counting uncountable nouns

We 'count' uncountable nouns like this:

UNITS
a **piece of** *cake/cheese*
a **piece of** *furniture/luggage/paper*
a **bit of** *information*
a **bar of** *chocolate*
a **slice of** *bread/toast/cake*
a **loaf of** *bread*

CONTAINERS
a **carton of** *milk/juice*
a **can/tin of** *soup*
a **glass of** *orange juice*
a **box of** *chocolates*
a **cup of** *coffee*
a **bottle of** *water*
a **tube of** *toothpaste*

MEASUREMENTS
a **litre of** *milk*
half a kilo of *sugar*
six metres of *cotton*

 We don't use uncountable nouns with *a* or *an*:
✗ ~~Can I have a toast?~~
✓ *Can I have* **a slice of toast***?*

We can say:
Would you like **some chocolate***?* or *Would you like* **a bar of chocolate***?*

When we talk about drinks like tea and coffee we can say:
Would you like **some coffee***? Would you like* **a cup of coffee***? Would you like* **a coffee***?*

Practice

1 Write the correct words from the box under the pictures.

0 .... a paper.   1 ....   2 ....   3 ....

a chicken
chicken
a chocolate
chocolate
a coffee
coffee
a paper
paper

4 ....   5 ....   6 ....   7 ....

2 GRAMMAR IN USE Complete the conversations with *a* or *some* . ◀)2.06 Listen and check.

0 A Would you like ...*a*.... chocolate?

   B Oh, yes. Can I have that white one?

1 A I've got .... luggage in the car.

   B How many bags have you got?

2 A What's on at the cinema tonight?

   B I'm not sure. I'll buy .... paper and check.

3 A We need .... sugar.

   B OK, a kilo or half a kilo?

4 A Can we pay the bill, please?

   B Of course, two coffees and .... tea. That's £4.50.

3 Match the words on the left with the things on the right.

0 a cup of   A toast
1 a tube of   B milk
2 a bit of   C toothpaste
3 a piece of   D soup
4 a litre of   E coffee
5 a can of   F information
6 a slice of   G paper

global comment re lists: all figures/numbers range right except arrowed lists of units on module Openers and Tests

4 GRAMMAR IN USE The <u>underlined</u> words are all in the wrong place. Find and write the correct words. ◀)2.07 Listen and check.

HANNAH Hi, Josie. I'm going to the shops now. Do you want anything?

JOSIE Oh, yes please, just (0) *a bottle of* <u>a piece of</u> water, (1) <u>a kilo of</u> soup and (2) <u>a cup of</u> potatoes.

HANNAH That's no problem. I can get those.

JOSIE That's nice of you. Come in and have (3) <u>a slice of</u> coffee before you go.

HANNAH Oh, lovely. Thanks.

JOSIE Would you like (4) <u>a glass of</u> cake, too?

HANNAH No, thanks. I had (5) <u>two tins of</u> chocolate earlier, but can I have (6) <u>a bottle of</u> water with the coffee? I'm really thirsty.

JOSIE Of course. Now, let me find (7) <u>a bar of</u> paper and make a list of the shopping ...

4 a/an

a banana

an apple

an architect

a dentist

1 Form

We use *a* and *an* before different sounds:

	BEFORE WORDS THAT BEGIN WITH	EXAMPLES
a +	a consonant sound, e.g. *b, c, l, m, p, s, t*	*a cake, a sports teacher, a hat*
	u or *eu*, when they sound like *y*	*a uniform /uː/, a European /ʊə/ city*
an +	a vowel sound: *a, e, i, o, u*	*an apple, an interesting book, an uncle*
	h when you do not pronounce the *h*	*an hour, an honest man*

🔊 Pronunciation ➤ 1.03

2 Use

We use *a/an*

to talk about one person or thing	*We saw **a** good **film** at the cinema on Saturday.* *Do you live in **a house** or **a flat**?*
to describe a person or thing with an adjective	*She's **a nice person**.* *Is that **an interesting book**?*
to talk about jobs	*My uncle is **a dentist**.* *I want to be **an architect**.*
to mean 'one' with fractions and numbers	*one and **a** half, **a** hundred, **a** thousand, **a** million*
to mean 'each' in measurements	*twice **a** day, once **a** month, four times **a** year, 80 kilometres **an** hour*

⚠ ✗ *My uncle is dentist.*
✓ *My uncle is **a dentist**.*

We DON'T use *a/an*

* before plural nouns:
  *I like **books** about other countries.*
  ***Children** are welcome in this restaurant.*
  *Do you like **adventure films**?*
* before uncountable nouns:
  *Do you take **sugar**?*
  ***Furniture** is expensive these days.*
  *Teenagers often listen to **music**.*

Practice

1 Complete the sentences with *a* or *an*.

0 The school is looking for ...*an*... English teacher.

1 They're building .... hospital in the town centre.

2 There's .... hourly train from here to the coast.

3 'What's this?' 'It's .... euro.'

4 I've got .... uncle in Sydney, Australia.

5 We've got enough students for .... new class now.

6 Is there .... university in Manchester?

2 GRAMMAR IN USE Write *a* or *an*. Write – if we don't need *a* or *an*. ◄)) **2.08** Listen and check.

A What shall we do tonight? Shall we go to (0) ...*a*... restaurant? The Star, perhaps?

B No, I'm not keen on (1) .... Chinese food. What about (2) .... Indian restaurant. Or Angelo's? They do fantastic pizzas.

A Yes, but there are always a lot of (3) .... children there and it's very noisy on (4) .... Friday nights.

B That's true. You know, I'd like a kebab. Is there (5) .... Greek restaurant around here?

A Mmm, I love (6) .... kebabs. We don't have (7) .... Greek restaurant, but there's (8) .... new Turkish one in King Street.

B OK, great. Let's go there.

3 Complete the sentences with a nationality from Box A and a noun from Box B. Add *a* or *an* if necessary.

A	American British Chinese Finnish Japanese ~~Swedish~~	B	city businessman ~~cars~~ company motorbikes writer

0 Saabs are .... *Swedish cars* ....

1 Beijing is ....

2 Bill Gates is ....

3 J K Rowling is ....

4 Yamahas are ....

5 Nokia is ....

4 GRAMMAR IN USE There are eight more places in this text where we need *a* or *an*. Write *a* or *an* in the correct places. ◄)) **2.09** Listen and check.

There's *a* fantastic Turkish restaurant in our town. The owners are couple from Istanbul; they came to Britain two years ago. Ayla, the woman, is architect, but she works in the restaurant in the evening. Ocan, her husband, was university lecturer in Istanbul, but he wanted to do something different. They've got Turkish chef, Kemal, and English waiter, Joe. They've got very good menu, with lots of dishes. We go there once or twice month for really delicious meal.

5 the, a/an

Can I have **the sandwich** and **a salad**, please?

1 Pronunciation of *the*

We pronounce *the* with /ə/ before consonant sounds (*b, d, k, t, s*, etc.):
the book, the sports teacher

We pronounce *the* with /iː/ before vowel sounds (*a, e, i, o, u*):
the apple, the English teacher

 Pronunciation ➤ 1.04

2 Use of *the*

We use *the* when there is only one of something:
The sun *is very hot today.* (There's only one sun.)
Jamie's in **the garden**. (We only have one garden.)
Don't forget to lock **the front door**. (There's only one front door on our house.)
Can I see **the manager**? (There's only one manager.)

We DON'T use *the* before plural or uncountable nouns when we talk about things or people in general:
I like children. (children in general)
Milk is good for you. (milk in general)
Compare:
I like the children. (the children in that family)
The milk tastes horrible. (the milk in that bottle)

3 *the* or *a/an*?

We use *the*, not *a* or *an*, when it is clear which person or thing we are talking about.
Compare:

I need to get **a bus** *to the station.* (I don't know which bus.)	**The number 2 bus** *goes to the station.* (We know which bus.)
Let's go to **a restaurant** *this evening.* (There is more than one restaurant.)	*Let's go to* **the restaurant** *in Dean Street.* (We know which restaurant.)
Would you like **a biscuit**? (There is more than one biscuit.)	*Jason had* **the last biscuit**! (We know which biscuit.)

We use *a* or *an* when we use a noun for the first time, and *the* when we use it again:
I bought **a new coat** *and a dress yesterday.* **The coat** *is really warm.*
'There's **a really nice new café** *in the village.'*
'Oh, do you mean **the café** *with tables outside? Yes, it's great.'*

10

Practice

1 Choose the correct sentence, A or B for each picture.

A Shall I open a window?
B Shall I open the window? ✓

A Can I borrow a pen?
B Can I borrow the pen?

A I like a red dress.
B I like the red dress.

A Can you pass me a dictionary?
B Can you pass me the dictionary?

A I'm going to buy an umbrella.
B I'm going to buy the umbrella.

A Would you like a chocolate ice cream?
B Would you like the chocolate ice cream?

2 Write *a*, *an* or *the*. Write – if we don't need *a*, *an* or *the*. 🔊2.10 Listen and check.

0 We're going shopping to buy ....*a*.... new computer.

1 We can't use .... computer in my office. It's not working.

2 Can you answer .... phone? I'm in .... bathroom.

3 Are you going to .... kitchen? Can you get me .... apple?

4 'Do we need .... onions?' 'Yes, and .... pasta. Can you get .... pasta from .... Italian shop near the station?'

5 Look at .... moon. What a beautiful evening!

3 GRAMMAR IN USE Choose the correct words in *italics* in the email. 🔊2.11 Listen and check.

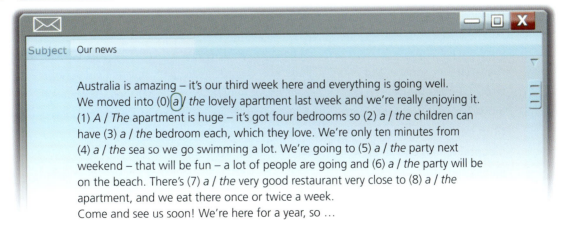

Subject Our news

Australia is amazing – it's our third week here and everything is going well.
We moved into (0) *a* / *the* lovely apartment last week and we're really enjoying it.
(1) *A / The* apartment is huge – it's got four bedrooms so (2) *a / the* children can
have (3) *a / the* bedroom each, which they love. We're only ten minutes from
(4) *a / the* sea so we go swimming a lot. We're going to (5) *a / the* party next
weekend – that will be fun – a lot of people are going and (6) *a / the* party will be
on the beach. There's (7) *a / the* very good restaurant very close to (8) *a / the*
apartment, and we eat there once or twice a week.
Come and see us soon! We're here for a year, so …

6 Uses of *the* and *a/an*

Excuse me, where's the cinema?

It's in Oxford Street. Go along here and turn right.

1 Words with *the*

We usually use *the* with

times of the day	*in the morning, in the afternoon, in the evening* (but *at night*)
musical instruments	*I play the piano. Does she play the guitar?*
names of newspapers	*The Times, The Sun, The New York Times*
the media	*the radio, I saw it on the Internet.*
shops/places in a town	*the bank, the cinema, the post office, the supermarket, the chemist's, the station*
names of museums, cinemas, theatres, hotels	*the Guggenheim Museum, the Odeon Cinema, the Drury Lane Theatre, the Savoy Hotel*
locations	*on the left/right, in the middle, on the coast/border, in the east/north/south/west*
countries with plural names and with Republic, Kingdom	*the Netherlands, the United States, the People's Republic of China, the United Kingdom*
names of oceans, seas, rivers, mountain ranges	*the Pacific Ocean, the Mediterranean Sea, the Thames, the Amazon, the Himalayas, the Andes*

 We don't usually use *the* with *watch TV*:
✓ *I'm **watching TV**.*   ✗ ~~*I'm watching the TV.*~~

2 Words without *the, a* or *an*

We don't use *the, a* or *an* with

times, days and months	*at midday, on Monday, in January*
meals	*What time is breakfast?*
sports	*basketball, tennis, football*
transport and communication	*by train, by bus, by email, by phone*
languages, school subjects	*English, Spanish, Turkish, art, history*
most magazines	*Newsweek, Hello Magazine*
roads, streets, squares and parks	*Park Lane, Oxford Street, Times Square, Central Park*
airports and stations	*Manchester Airport, Victoria Bus Station, Penn Station*
most countries and continents	*Spain, Japan, Turkey, Australia, Asia, Europe, Africa*
cities, towns and states	*Paris, Sydney, Johannesburg, California*
mountains, hills and lakes	*Mount Everest, Lake Ontario*
names and titles	*John, Susan, Mr Smith, Professor Sinclair, Uncle Jack*

 We don't use *the, a* or *an* for: *at home, at work, in bed*

Compare:
*He plays **the** guitar.* but *He plays football.*
*She works at **the** bank.* but *She works at Manchester Airport.*

Practice

1 Find the correct names from the lists on page 12. Include *the* where necessary.

0 a lake in Canada ...*Lake Ontario*.................
1 a newspaper from the US ....
2 a city in Europe ....
3 a hotel in London ....

4 a university teacher ....
5 a river in South America ....
6 a park in New York ....
7 a mountain range in Asia ....

2 Match the two parts of the sentences. ◀)) **2.12** Listen and check.

0 My sister's very musical. She plays the
1 My brother isn't very good at
2 We don't like our children staying out late at
3 I hate getting up early in the
4 The school bell always rings at
5 We usually take our summer holiday in
6 Are there any good films at the
7 On Friday evenings I usually watch

A night.
B July.
C midday every day.
D TV.
E piano and the violin.
F cinema this week?
G football.
H morning.

3 Complete the sentences with the words and phrases from the box. Add *the* if necessary.

0 My favourite newspaper is ......*The Times*.........
1 The highest mountain in the world is ....
2 Juliette Binoche's first language is ....
3 George Bush was president of .... from 2000 to 2008.
4 Cannes is a lovely French town on ....
5 Too many people go to work by ....
6 We always have .... together at eight o'clock.
7 You can buy this medicine at ....
8 There's a really good exhibition on at ....

breakfast
car
chemist's
Guggenheim Museum
Mount Everest
Mediterranean Sea
French
~~The Times~~
United States

4 **GRAMMAR IN USE** There are six more mistakes with *the*, *a* or *an* in the conversation. Find and correct them. ◀)) **2.13** Listen and check.

BRAD   Are you enjoying your time here?

ANNA   Oh, yes. ~~The~~ London is a beautiful city.

BRAD   What have you seen?

ANNA   Well, I've been to a British Museum – that's fantastic – and I really like Regent's Park. It's very peaceful.

BRAD   Mmm, it is, isn't it? Are you studying here?

ANNA   Yes, I'm studying the English and the history.

BRAD   Oh, I see. Where are you living?

ANNA   In an apartment with some friends.

BRAD   When did you come here?

ANNA   In the October, and I'm staying for a year.

BRAD   Do you have much time to travel in United Kingdom?

ANNA   Oh yes, I try to. But everything is so expensive here – every time I go to supermarket I spend about £40.00.

7 *some* and *any*

I'd like **some** Spanish oranges, please.

Sorry, I haven't got **any**. Would you like **some** Californian ones?

1 *some* and *any* with a noun

	+ PLURAL NOUN	+ UNCOUNTABLE NOUN
some	some grapes	some information
any	(not) any bananas	(not) any sugar

🔊 Pronunciation ➤ 1.05

We use *some* and (*not*) *any* for a number (more than one) or an amount of something. The exact number or amount is not important.

	some	*any*	EXAMPLES
in positive sentences	✓	✗	We've got **some** bananas today. 'Shh. I'm doing **some** work.' 'But I want to listen to **some** music.'
in negative sentences	✗	✓	We haven't got **any** melons today. There isn't **any** milk in the fridge. I can't give you **any** advice, I'm afraid.
in most questions	✗	✓	Do you have **any** pears? Is there **any** sugar in the cupboard?
when you ask for something	✓	✗	I'd like **some** Spanish oranges, please. Can I have **some** red grapes?
when you offer something to someone	✓	✗	Would you like **some** strawberries? Do you want **some** tea with your lunch?

2 *some* and *any* without a noun

We can use *some* and *any* without a noun, when it is clear what we are talking about:
*'I'm making some tea. Do you want **some**?'* (some tea)

NATURAL ENGLISH It is possible to repeat the noun after *some* and *any*. But it is more natural NOT to repeat it:
How much bread is there?
*There isn't **any**.* (= There isn't any bread.)

Can I have **some** water?

I haven't got **any**!

Practice

1 **GRAMMAR IN USE** Read the conversation between two teachers. Choose the correct words in *italics*. ◀)) **2.14** Listen and check.

A Let's check that we've got everything for the exam this afternoon.

B OK. I've got (0) *some* / *any* paper and (1) *any* / *some* pens.

A Good. Have you got (2) *any* / *some* pencils?

B No. The students don't need (3) *some* / *any*.

A Oh, OK. What about rulers?

B Oh dear, I haven't got (4) *any* / *some*. Have you?

A Wait a minute. Yes, there are (5) *any* / *some* in the cupboard.

B OK. Everything's ready. Now I'm going to get (6) *some* / *any* food before the students arrive. Would you like (7) *some* / *any*?

A It's nearly two o'clock now. We haven't got (8) *some* / *any* time.

2 **GRAMMAR IN USE** Complete the TV interview with *some* or *any*. ◀)) **2.15** Listen and check.

PRESENTER So, what kind of cake are you going to make?

CHEF It's an orange and lemon cake. It's very easy. You need (0) *some* oranges and (1) .... lemons, and about three eggs.

PRESENTER What about butter?

CHEF You don't need (2) .... butter for this cake – it doesn't contain (3) .... fat!

PRESENTER That's very unusual.

CHEF Yes. Well, I suppose it's not quite true. It contains (4) .... fat because it has nuts in it and nuts contain oil.

PRESENTER I see. And it's very simple, you said.

CHEF Yes, it's very easy and it doesn't take (5) .... time at all because you just mix everything together.

3 Find the mistakes in the sentences and correct them.

0 ~~There's any milk~~ in the fridge. We need to buy some. *There isn't any milk.*

1 I'd like any water, please. ....

2 There aren't some emails for you. ....

3 We've got any nice apples today. ....

4 There are always some horse in the field near our house.

....

5 'Where are your coats?' 'We didn't bring some.' ....

4 Describe what you have in your fridge.

In my fridge there are always bottles of milk and yoghurt.

In my fridge there ....

There aren't ....

And I hate .... so there ....

8 much, many, a lot of

They sell **a lot of** vegetables here but they don't sell **much** fruit.

1 *much*, *many*, *a lot of* with a noun

much	+ uncountable nouns	I don't eat **much sugar**. Hurry up. There isn't **much time**.
many	+ plural nouns	I don't eat **many sweets**. Are there **many students** from Japan?
a lot of	+ plural nouns and uncountable nouns	They sell **a lot of vegetables**. He doesn't earn **a lot of money**. Do you have **a lot of homework** today?

We use *much*, *many* and *a lot of* to talk about a large amount or number. The exact amount or number is not important.

- We can use *a lot of* in positive and negative sentences and questions:
  *Lewis has got **a lot of** friends.*
  *We have**n't** got **a lot of** time.*
  ***Are** there **a lot of** students from Japan?*

- We usually use *much* and *many* in negative sentences and questions:
  *Hurry up! We have**n't** got **much** time.*
  ***Are** there **many** students from Japan?*

  NATURAL ENGLISH In everyday English, we don't use *much* or *many* in positive sentences. We prefer *a lot of*:
  *There are **a lot of** tourists here in the summer.*

2 *much*, *many*, *a lot* without a noun

We can use *much* and *many* without a noun, when it is clear what we are talking about:
*Why don't you buy it? It doesn't cost **much**.*
*'Can I have some of your sweets?' 'No, I haven't got **many**.'*

When we use *a lot* without a noun, we don't need *of*:
*We learned **a lot** in today's lesson.*

3 *how much?* or *how many?*

- We use *how much* and *how many* to ask about an exact amount or number.
  We use *how much* with uncountable nouns:
  ***How much** sugar do I need?*

- We use *how many* with countable nouns:
  ***How many** bedrooms are there in the hotel?*

- We use *how much* to ask about prices:
  ***How much** is it? It's fifteen euros.*
  ***How much** does it cost? It costs ten dollars.*

Practice

1 **GRAMMAR IN USE** Choose the correct words in *italics* in the conversation.
🔊 **2.16** Listen and check.

SAM Where shall we go shopping this afternoon? Shall we just go to the town centre?

ALI I don't know. There aren't (0) *much* / *many* shops in the town centre.
I think the big shopping centre is better – there are (1) *a lot of* / *much* shops there.

SAM Mmm. But we haven't got (2) *much* / *many* time really, and it takes half an hour to drive there.

ALI I know, but I need to buy (3) *many* / *a lot of* presents for my family, and I don't have (4) *much* / *many* money. There are (5) *many* / *a lot of* cheap shops in the shopping centre.

SAM Are there (6) *many* / *much* people in your family, then?

ALI Well, there aren't (7) *many* / *much* adults, but I've got (8) *much* / *a lot of* younger brothers and sisters.

SAM OK, let's go to the shopping centre. But can we go in your car? There isn't (9) *much* / *many* petrol in mine.

2 Use the picture to answer the questions with *much*, *many* or *a lot*.

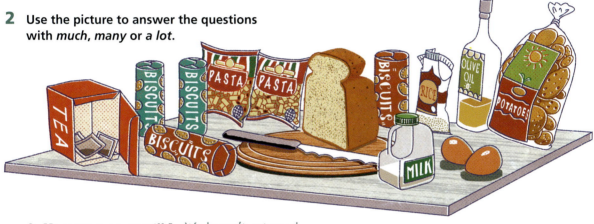

0 Have we got any milk? _We haven't got much._

1 Have we got any rice? ....

2 Have we got any potatoes? ....

3 Have we got any olive oil? ....

4 Have we got any pasta? ....

5 Have we got any bread? ....

6 Have we got any biscuits? ....

7 Have we got any eggs? ....

8 Have we got any tea bags? ....

3 Complete the questions with *How much?* or *How many?* Then write true answers for you.
🔊 **2.17** Listen and check.

0 _How many_ uncles have you got? _I've got three./I haven't got any./I haven't got many._

1 .... aunts have you got? ....

2 .... work have you got at the moment? ....

3 .... good friends have you got? ....

4 .... chocolate do you eat? ....

5 .... exercise do you do? ....

6 .... coffee do you drink? ....

9 *a little, a few, too much, too many, not enough*

Let's go to another café. There are **too many** people and **not enough** tables here!

1 *a little, a few*

a little	+ uncountable nouns	*I think this soup needs **a little salt**.*
a few	+ plural nouns	*There are **a few cafés** near my house.*

We use *a little* to talk about a small amount. The exact amount is not important:
*Food often tastes better when you add **a little salt** to it.*

We use *a few* to talk about a small number. The exact number is not important:
*We've got **a few friends** in the village.*

NATURAL ENGLISH   In everyday English, we don't often use *a little* + noun.
We prefer *a bit of* + noun.
*'Sit down and have a cup of coffee.' 'OK, I've got **a bit of time**.'*

We can use *a little* and *a few* without a noun, when it is clear what we are talking about:
*'Would you like some milk in your coffee?' 'Yes, please, **a little**.'*
*'Have you got any friends on Facebook?' 'Yes, **a few**.'*

2 *too much, too many, not enough*

too much	+ uncountable nouns	*Don't put **too much pepper** in the soup.*
too many	+ plural nouns	*I feel sick. I ate **too many cakes**.*
not enough	+ uncountable nouns + plural nouns	*I haven't got **enough money** to buy a car.* *There aren't **enough eggs** to make a cake.*

Too much and *too many* have a negative meaning. They mean 'more than we want':
*Let's go to another café. There are **too many people** here.*
*We made **too much food** for the party. No one was hungry.*
*It's bad to eat **too many burgers**.*

Not enough is the opposite of *too much/too many*. It means 'less/fewer than we want':
*We can't buy that car. We have**n't** got **enough money**!*
*The party was boring. There were**n't** **enough people** there.*
*We have**n't** got **enough bread**.   We have**n't** got **enough eggs**.*

Practice

1 Do the sentences in each pair have the same (S) or different (D) meanings? Write S or D.

0 A We've got a little luggage.   *...S...*

  B We've got a few bags.

1 A Those children ask too many questions.   ....

  B Those children don't ask enough questions.

2 A The apartment has a little furniture.   ....

  B The apartment has a lot of furniture.

3 A I have a few friends here.   ....

  B I don't have enough friends here.

4 A Let's have a coffee. I've got a bit of time.   ....

  B Let's have a coffee. I've got a few minutes.

5 A We haven't got enough furniture.   ....

  B We've got too much furniture.

2 Choose the correct words in *italics*. 🔊 **2.18** Listen and check.

0 There are only (*a few*)/ *a little* biscuits left in the tin.

1 Would you like *a few* / *a bit of* chocolate?

2 Only add *a bit* / *a bit of* sugar to this drink; it doesn't need much.

3 There were only *a few* / *a little* people at the meeting.

4 I didn't write the report on my own. My teacher gave me *a bit of* / *a few* help.

5 Eggs taste better with *a little* / *a few* salt.

3 Write sentences about the things in the picture. Use *too much*, *too many* or (*not*) *enough*.

Kerry and Michael are having four friends to dinner. They need six chairs, plates, etc.

0 (plates) *...There are enough plates...........*

1 (chairs) ....

2 (bread) ....

3 (water) ....

4 (glasses) ....

5 (burgers) ....

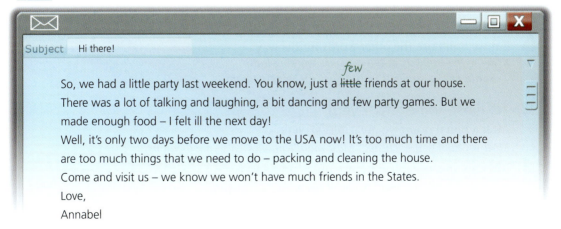

4 **GRAMMAR IN USE** There are six more mistakes in the email. Find and correct them. 🔊 **2.19** Listen and check.

> ✉   ⎯ ⬜ ❌
>
> Subject   Hi there!
>
>   *few*
>
> So, we had a little party last weekend. You know, just a ~~little~~ friends at our house.
> There was a lot of talking and laughing, a bit dancing and few party games. But we
> made enough food – I felt ill the next day!
> Well, it's only two days before we move to the USA now! It's too much time and there
> are too much things that we need to do – packing and cleaning the house.
> Come and visit us – we know we won't have much friends in the States.
> Love,
> Annabel

10 *all, most, some, no/none, both*

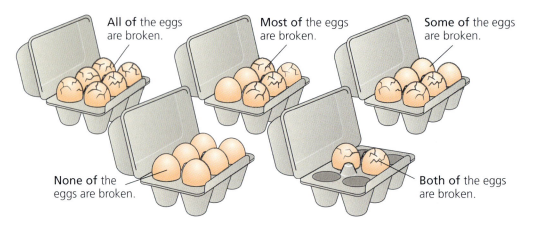

All of the eggs are broken.

Most of the eggs are broken.

Some of the eggs are broken.

None of the eggs are broken.

Both of the eggs are broken.

1 Form

We use *all*, *most*, *some* and *no/none* with plural countable nouns or uncountable nouns. Compare:

WITHOUT *of*	WITH *of*
All fruit is good for you.	*All of the fruit in this shop is local.*
Most vegetables are cheap.	*Most of these vegetables come from my garden.*
Some meat is very expensive.	*Some of the meat in this supermarket is frozen.*
There's no milk in the fridge.	*None of the milk in the shop is fresh.*

We use *both* with plural countable nouns:

Both salads look delicious. = *Both of these salads look delicious.*

2 Use

We use *all*, *most*, *some* and *no* (without *of*) to talk about people or things in general:
***Most people** enjoy going on holiday, but **some people** prefer to stay at home.*

We use *all of, most of, none of* and *both (of)* when we know exactly which people or things we mean:
***All of the teachers at our school** are good.*
***Both (of these) salads** look delicious.*
*Can I have **some of that chocolate cake**?*

We can also use *all the/both the* in the same way as *all of the/both of the*:
✓ ***All (of) the** students in the class are working hard.*

 But we don't use the other words in this way:
✗ ~~*Some the students in the class are working hard.*~~
✓ ***Some of the** students in the class are working hard.*

3 *all, most, some*, etc. + verb

After a plural noun we use a plural verb:
Most vegetables are *cheap.   Most mobile phones* take *photographs.*

After an uncountable noun we use a singular verb:
All fruit is *good for you.   Some of his advice* is *useful.*

 No and *none* mean 'not any'. We use a positive verb after them:
✗ ~~*None of the advice he gave wasn't useful.*~~
✓ *None of the advice he gave **was** useful.*

20

Practice

1 Match the pictures A–E with the sentences below.

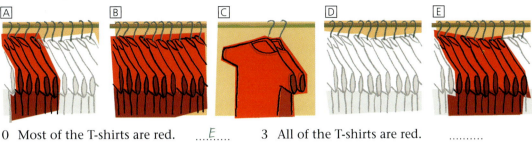

0 Most of the T-shirts are red.   ...E....
1 Some of the T-shirts are red.   ....
2 None of the T-shirts are red.   ....

3 All of the T-shirts are red.   ....
4 Both of the T-shirts are red.   ....

2 `GRAMMAR IN USE` **Look at the information and choose the correct words in *italics*.**
🔊 **2.20** **Listen and check.**

compare our prices

WINTER FRUIT

Samson's Supermarket

has a very good variety of fruit this winter!

Samson's Supermarket

(0) *All* / *Most* / *Some* of the prices are per kilo. (1) *None* / *Some* / *All* the fruit is £1.00 per kilo or more. (2) *Some* / *None* / *Most* of the fruit is over £5.00 per kilo and (3) *most* / *none* / *all* of the items are under £3.00 per kilo. (4) *All* / *Most* / *Some* of the fruit comes from Europe or America, but (5) *some* / *all* / *none* of the tropical fruit comes from Africa. (6) *All* / *None* / *Both* of the European countries provide a lot of fruit.

FRUIT	FROM	£ PER KILO
apples	France	1.50
bananas	Africa	1.00
pears	UK	1.70
oranges	USA	1.30
melons	UK	2.50
pineapples	Africa	3.60
grapes	France	4.00
strawberries	UK	4.80

3 **Use the words below to write sentences. Add *of the* if necessary.** 🔊 **2.21** **Listen and check.**

0 some / spiders / poisonous *Some spiders are poisonous.*

00 all / spiders / in my garden / harmless *All of the spiders in my garden are harmless.*

1 all / fruit / contain / vitamins ....

2 none / fruit / in the bowl / ready to eat ....

3 some / clothes / in this shop / very expensive ....

4 most / tea / comes from / India and China ....

5 no / cakes and biscuits / healthy ....

6 most / food / in my fridge / fresh ....

4 **Complete these sentences with *all*, *most*, *some* or *no/none* so they are true for you.**

0 ...*All*... American films are fantastic.

1 .... exercise is fun.

2 .... English grammar is very difficult.

3 .... of my classmates are really friendly.

4 .... travel is bad for the environment.

5 .... of the TV programmes in my country are really interesting.

Review MODULE 1

1 UNITS 1, 2 AND 3 **Find the mistake(s) in the sentences and correct them.**

0 Look at those chicken/in the yard.

1 All the farmers take their sheeps to the market in August.

2 Could you make an appointment for me to see mr hawkins while I'm in paris?

3 How many slices of luggage are you taking?

4 Would you like a bread with your soup?

5 All the teachers in this school is from England.

6 We need some more furnitures in our new house.

2 UNITS 4, 5 AND 6 **Write *a*, *an* or *the*. Write – if you don't need *a*, *an* or *the*.**

Is *chocolate* really *good* for you?

PEOPLE STARTED MAKING (0) ....—.... chocolate centuries ago in (1) .... South America, and people have always told stories about how healthy chocolate is. (2) .... stories tell us that it can make us happy, too, and that may be true. A little chocolate may be good for our hearts, but (3) .... fruit and vegetables are much better for us than chocolate.

Chocolate contains a lot of (4) .... fat and sugar – but some people argue that (5) .... fat in chocolate is good fat because it comes from a particular type of butter. That's true, but most chocolate doesn't contain much of it.

So, the answer to (6) .... question above is really 'no'. It's good to have (7) .... bar of chocolate occasionally, but we all really know that if (8) .... type of food tastes good, it's probably bad for us!

3 UNITS 7, 8 AND 9 **Complete the conversation with some of the phrases from A–J.**
🔊 **2.22** **Listen and check.**

A Good morning. I'm looking for some red apples.
B We (0) ...B.... today, I'm afraid.
A Oh, what about green apples, then?
B Yes, we (1) .... of those.
A And (2) .... Spanish oranges?
B Yes, I've got (3) ....
A OK. (4) ....
B They're £1.50 a kilo.
A And the apples?
B They're £2.20 a kilo.
A £2.20? (5) .... I'll just have a kilo of the oranges, please.
B OK ... one, two, three oranges – that's just a kilo.
A (6) .... Can you give me another one, please?
B Here you are. That's £1.95, please.

A How much are they?

B ~~haven't got any~~

C 've got any

D 've got some

E a few, but not many

F That's not enough!

G 've got no

H That's too much!

I a little but not much

J have you got any

22

4 UNITS 8, 9 AND 10 **Look at the information below about two English colleges. Decide whether the statements below are true (T) or false (F). Correct the false ones.**

College	Location	Teachers (full-time)	Levels	Average class no.	Computers in media centre	Cost for four weeks
Abbey	*Oxford, UK*	*5*	*Beginner–Intermediate*	*8*	*8*	*£800.00*
Carnegie	*Cambridge, UK*	*100*	*Beginner–Advanced*	*30+*	*2*	*£200.00*

0 Abbey College has a lot of full-time teachers. ....F....
   Abbey College hasn't got many full-time teachers..................................

1 Carnegie College doesn't have many full-time teachers. ....

   ....

2 There are too many students in the Carnegie College classes. ....

   ....

3 There aren't enough computers in the Carnegie College media centre. ....

   ....

4 Carnegie courses cost a lot of money. ....

   ....

5 Both colleges offer courses for beginners. ....

   ....

6 One of the colleges is in the UK. ....

   ....

5 ALL UNITS **Complete the second sentence so it means the same as the first. Use one, two or three words.**

0 How much paper do you need?
   How many .....*pieces of paper*...... do you need?

1 Let's talk about your problems. I've got a few minutes.
   Let's talk about your problems. I've got .... time.

2 Stop! That's more salad than I want.
   Stop! That's ....·

3 This camera is really expensive, and that camera is really expensive, too.
   .... are really expensive.

4 All of my friends are away this weekend.
   .... my friends are here this weekend.

5 We've got less time than we need for this project.
   We haven't got .... for this project.

6 I'd like about a kilo of potatoes, please.
   I'd like .... potatoes, please. About a kilo.

Test MODULE 1

Using nouns

Choose the correct answer, A, B or C.

1 How many .... do you have?
   A child B children C childs
   ➤ Unit 1

2 I like your jeans. .... new?
   A Are they B Is it C Is they
   ➤ Unit 1

3 I'd like .... apples, please.
   A an B some C that
   ➤ Unit 2

4 Could you give me .... about courses?
   A an advice B some advices C some advice
   ➤ Unit 2

5 Can I have ...., please?
   A two toasts B two slice of toast C two slices of toast
   ➤ Unit 3

6 Do you read .... newspaper every day?
   A one B a C an
   ➤ Unit 4

7 Our children like riding so we keep ....
   A an horse B horses C a horses
   ➤ Unit 4

8 Don't look at .... It can hurt your eyes.
   A a sun B sun C the sun
   ➤ Unit 5

9 'Would you like .... chocolate biscuit?'
   A a last B last C the last
   ➤ Unit 5

10 'You've got a lot of books.' 'Oh, ... all belong to my husband.'
   A the books B books C a book
   ➤ Unit 5

11 The plane arrives at .... Airport.
   A Gatwick B a Gatwick C the Gatwick
   ➤ Unit 6

12 Marcia started to play .... when she was fifteen.
   A a tennis B the tennis C tennis
   ➤ Unit 6

13 We haven't got .... milk left.
   A some B any C a
   ➤ Unit 7

14 'How .... the bus ticket to the town centre?'
   A much is B many is C much are
   ➤ Unit 8

15 I can't come out this evening. I've got .... homework.
   A much B a lot of C many
   ➤ Unit 8

16 Can you pay for the drinks? I haven't got .... money.
   A many B too much C enough
   ➤ Unit 9

17 I don't have a lot of time to help you, but I have .... time on Friday.
   A a bit of B a few C much
   ➤ Unit 9

18 Most .... here have at least four weeks' holiday from work a year.
   A of people B the people C of the people
   ➤ Unit 10

19 None of the furniture in the flat .... new.
   A is B isn't C are
   ➤ Unit 10

20 I like .... her brothers. They are nineteen and twenty-one.
   A most of B both of C all of
   ➤ Unit 10

Pronouns and possessives

Before you start

1 Read the information on the website. Look at the <mark>highlighted</mark> grammar examples.

www.myfriends.net

myfriends.net

Home   Browse   Find people   Forums   Music   Video   More▼   Log in   Sign up

about me

My name's Jaz. I'm nineteen. Here I am with my classmates. We all study at the London Fashion School. <mark>Those</mark> are my friends Clare, Alice, Lucy and Mel behind <mark>me</mark>. Lucy and Mel are next to <mark>each other</mark>. <mark>Mel's</mark> sister is a famous actress. Do you like <mark>my</mark> grey jacket? I designed it! I've got <mark>another one</mark> at home in dark red. Everyone <mark>loves</mark> my clothes. In my free time I like playing sports and enjoying <mark>myself</mark>.

16:45

2 Now read the sentences. Choose the correct words in *italics*.
The <mark>highlighted</mark> grammar examples will help you.

1 Clare's standing next to *I / me* in the photo.   ➤ Unit 11
2 Can you see *Lucys' / Lucy's* brother in the photo?   ➤ Unit 12
3 I design some of *me / my* clothes.   ➤ Unit 13
4 *Those / This* are my friends from college.   ➤ Unit 14
5 Did you enjoy *you / yourself* at the show?   ➤ Unit 15
6 Clare sits next to Anna in class. I think they like *themselves / each other*.   ➤ Unit 15
7 Everyone *is / are* happy in this photo.   ➤ Unit 16
8 Do you like this photo? I've got *another / more* one on my phone.   ➤ Unit 17

3 Check your answers below. Then go to the unit for more information and practice.

1 me 2 Lucy's 3 my 4 Those 5 yourself 6 each other 7 is 8 another

⏻ Go online for a full diagnostic test

11 Subject and object pronouns

1 Form

	SINGULAR					PLURAL		
subject pronouns	I	you	he	she	it	we	you	they
object pronouns	me	you	him	her	it	us	you	them

2 Use

We use the pronouns *I/me, you/you, he/him, she/her, we/us* and *they/them* for people.
We use subject pronouns before the verb. We use object pronouns after the verb.

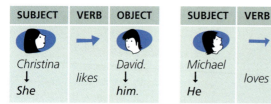

SUBJECT	VERB	OBJECT
Christina↓*She*	*likes*	*David.*↓*him.*

SUBJECT	VERB	OBJECT
Michael↓*He*	*loves*	*the children.*↓*them.*

 Here's the postman.   ✗ ~~Comes every day at this time.~~
                       ✓ **He** *comes every day at this time.*

What do you think of our new teacher?   ✗ ~~I like.~~
                                           ✓ *I like* **her**.

3 Things and animals

We use the pronouns *it, they* and *them* for things and animals:
'Can I put these 5p coins in the ticket machine?' *'No, **it** doesn't accept **them**.'*
*There's a fox in our garden. **It** eats the food from the bins.*

But if we know the sex of an animal we can also use *he/she/him/her*:
*Jack has a cat called Fluffy. **She** is three years old.*

it for weather, time, distance, etc. ➤ Unit 76.1

4 Object pronouns after prepositions and *be*

We also use object pronouns

- after prepositions (e.g. *near, to, of*):
  *Mr and Mrs Jenson live **near us**.*
  *Can you give this letter **to him**?*
  'Which colour do you prefer?' *'I like both **of them**.'*
- after the verb *be*:
  'Who's that?' *'**It's me**.'*
  *That's **us** in the photo.*

Practice

1 Who/what is Clara talking about? Match the sentences.

0 'I like him.' ⟶
1 'He likes me.' ⟶ B
2 'We like them.'
3 'They like us.'
4 'He likes them.'
5 'They like them.'
6 'She likes it.'

A George likes Tiggles and Fluffy.
B Clara likes Martin.
C Helen likes her mobile phone.
D Helen and George like Clara and Martin.
E Martin likes Clara.
F Tiggles and Fluffy like George and Helen.
G Clara and Martin like Helen and George.

2 Choose the correct words in *italics*. ◀)) **2.23** Listen and check.

0 'Hello. Is that you, Jane?' 'Yes, it's *me* / *I*.'
1 Have you seen my keys? I can't find *they* / *them*.
2 Do you live near *him* / *he*?
3 Every Tuesday *me* / *I* go to an exercise class.
4 There's too much pasta on my plate. I can't eat all of *it* / *them*.
5 Is that *they* / *you* in the photograph?
6 *We* / *Us* walk to college. It's not very far.
7 She's got two computers. She uses both of *them* / *they*.
8 Who's that in the photo? It's *we* / *us*.
9 Juana gave *I* / *me* a fantastic present.
10 I told *you* / *we* to be quiet!

3 GRAMMAR IN USE Replace the underlined words with pronouns. ◀)) **2.24** Listen and check.

JEMMA Have you got any brothers and sisters? Can you tell me about (0) ~~your brothers and sisters~~? *them*

HILAL Well, I've got one sister – her name is Meena.

JEMMA Is (1) Meena older than you? ....

HILAL No, (2) Meena is the same age as me. (3) Meena and I are twins. ....

JEMMA And have you got any brothers?

HILAL Yes, I've got one brother. (4) My brother is called Ali. ....
(5) Ali is older than my sister and me. ....

JEMMA Do you live with your parents?

HILAL No, I don't. (6) My parents live in Salford. I live in a student flat in London. ....

JEMMA Where is (7) the flat? ....

HILAL (8) The flat is near the university. ....

JEMMA Do you see your brother and sister very often?

HILAL Yes, I see my brother once a week. I go to football with (9) my brother .... every Saturday. But I don't see my sister very often. I only see (10) my sister .... when I visit my parents.

4 Answer the questions about you. Use pronouns and full sentences.

0 What's your job? *I'm a student.* ....
1 How old are you? ....
2 Where was your mother born? ....
3 Where do your parents live? ....

Go online for more practice

12 Possessive forms of nouns

Where can I find **Mr Ridley's** art class?

It's in Room 10, at the end **of the corridor.**

1 Noun + 's or '

We use noun + 's or ' to show that something belongs to someone.

singular nouns	add 's	John → John's (car) James → James's (phone) my mother → my mother's (garden)
plural nouns that end in s	add '	boys → boys' (school) birds → birds' (eggs) parents → parents' (house)
plural nouns that don't end in s	add 's	children → children's (books) men → men's (clothes) people → people's (names)

We use noun + 's or ' for people and animals:
*I'm using my **friend's** mobile phone.* (the phone belongs to my friend)
***Clara's** brother is **Marco's** teacher. What is your **cat's** name? This is my **parents'** car.*

We can use noun + 's or ' alone

- when the meaning is clear:
  *'Is this Lucy's mobile phone?' 'No, it's **Amanda's**.'* (Amanda's phone)
  *That isn't our cat. It's our **neighbours'**.* (our neighbours' cat)
- for people's homes:
  *Shall we go to **Sally's**?* (Sally's house)
- to talk about some shops and services:
  *I need to go to the **doctor's**.*
  *Are you going to the **butcher's**?*

2 *of* + noun

We usually use *of* + noun for things and places:
*We visited the centre **of Madrid**. What happens at the end **of the film**?*
*What's the size **of the screen** on your TV? What's the height **of Mount Everest**?*

 We don't usually use *of* + noun for people:
✗ *He is the brother of Clare.* ✓ *He is **Clare's** brother.*

 We don't usually use noun + 's or ' for things:
✗ *I didn't see the film's end.* ✓ *I didn't see the end **of the film**.*

Practice

1 **GRAMMAR IN USE** **Complete the sentences with noun +** **'s or '.** 🔊 **2.25** **Listen and check.**

Ann and Frank are married.

Ann is (0) ...*Frank's*... wife. Frank is (1) .... husband.

Ann has two children, Mike and Lucy.

Lucy is (2) .... daughter. Mike is (3) .... brother.

Ann has brown hair but the children have blond hair.

(4) .... hair is brown but the (5) .... hair is blond.

The family has two cats called Spike and Susie.

The (6) .... names are Spike and Susie.

2 **GRAMMAR IN USE** **Choose the correct words in** *italics* **in the text.** 🔊 **2.26** **Listen and check.**

The oldest student in the world?

IF YOU VISIT (0) *London's University /* (*the University of London*) you'll have a surprise. This university has a student who is 250 years old! The student's name is Jeremy Bentham. He sits in a box at the (1) *main building's end / end of the main building*. He can watch the other students and listen to the lecturers through the (2) *box's glass front / glass front of the box*. Of course, he isn't a real student because he died in 1832.

Jeremy Bentham was a famous writer who believed in free education for everybody. (3) *Bentham's ideas / The ideas of Bentham* encouraged people to start new universities. After he died, they put (4) *Jeremy's body / the body of Jeremy* in a glass box in the (5) *college's centre / centre of the college*, so he can be a student forever.

3 **Find five more mistakes in the sentences and correct them. Tick (✓) the correct sentences.**

0 I am interested in ~~the Scotland geography~~. *the geography of Scotland* ....

1 I live eight kilometres from the Paris's centre. ....

2 My mother's name is Alice. ....

3 I like watching womens' sports events on TV. ....

4 We sometimes have lunch at Carol's. ....

5 What is the computer's size? ....

6 Do you know the age of Diana? ....

7 Where is the bowl of your cat? ....

4 **Write sentences 1–4 from Exercise 3 so they are true for you. Use possessive forms.**

0 *I am interested in the history of my country.* ....

1 ....

2 ....

3 ....

4 ....

13 Possessive adjectives and pronouns

Excuse me. Is this **your** homework?

Oh, yes. It's **mine**. Thanks.

1 Form

	SINGULAR					PLURAL		
subject pronouns	*I*	*you*	*he*	*she*	*it*	*we*	*you*	*they*
possessive adjectives	*my*	*your*	*his*	*her*	*its*	*our*	*your*	*their*
possessive pronouns	*mine*	*yours*	*his*	*hers*	*–*	*ours*	*yours*	*theirs*

2 Possessive adjectives

Possessive adjectives tell us who things belong to. We put them before a noun:
*Jenny is **Christina and Michael Brown's** daughter.* → *Jenny is **their** daughter.*
***Jenny's** brother is called David.* → ***Her** brother is called David.*

⚠ The possessive adjective depends on the noun it replaces, NOT the noun that follows it:
***John's** father = **his** father*
***John's** mother = **his** mother (✗ ~~her mother~~)*

***Mary's** father = **her** father (✗ ~~his father~~)*
***Mary's** mother = **her** mother*

We also use possessive adjectives with parts of the body:
*The children closed **their** eyes and listened to the story.*
*I'm tired and **my** legs hurt.*

Look at the difference between *its* and *it's*:
*I like Thailand. **It's** a beautiful country.* (it is)
*Thailand is famous for **its** beautiful beaches.* (the beaches of Thailand)

3 Possessive pronouns

We can use possessive pronouns instead of a possesssive adjective + noun:
*Is that **your mobile phone**?* → *Is that **yours**?*
*No, it isn't **my mobile phone**.* → *No, it isn't **mine**.*
*It's **Clara's mobile phone**.* → *It's **hers**.*
*Can we borrow **your umbrella**? We forgot to bring **ours**.* (our umbrella)

⚠ We don't use *a, an, the* or apostrophes (') with possessive adjectives and pronouns:
✗ ~~That pen is her's.~~   ✓ *That pen is **hers**.*
✗ ~~This bedroom is the mine.~~   ✓ *This bedroom is **mine**.*

4 *Whose?*

We often use *Whose?* instead of 'Who does it belong to?':
*'**Whose** phone is this?' 'It's Clara's.'*
*'**Whose** are these?' 'I don't know – they aren't mine.'*

Practice

1 Complete the questions in each line so they have the same meaning.

0 Does this book belong to you?   Is this ..your.. book?   Is this ..yours.?
1 Is this Mary's book?   Is this .... book?   Is this ....?
2 Is this the children's book?   Is this .... book?   Is this ....?
3 Does this book belong to me?   Is this .... book?   Is this ....?
4 Does this book belong to us?   Is this .... book?   Is this ....?
5 Is this Peter's book?   Is this .... book?   Is this ....?
6 Who does this book belong to?   .... book is this?   .... is this?

2 **GRAMMAR IN USE** Choose the correct words in *italics* in the text.

I live next door to (0) *my*/ *me* friend David and (1) *his / her* sister, Fiona. David is in (2) *ours / our* class at college; he's taller than Fiona and (3) *the / his* hair is darker. Fiona's two years older than (4) *his / her* brother. She's an art student and she's always got paint on (5) *the / her* fingers! (6) *Theirs / Their* house is small but (7) *it's / its* garden is beautiful, and (8) *their / theirs* barbecues are always great fun!

3 **GRAMMAR IN USE** Complete the conversation with the correct words from the box. 2.27 Listen and check.

A Is this your suitcase, Sir?
B Yes. It's (0) ....mine......

hers ~~mine~~ my our ours whose your yours

A Can you open it for me, please? OK. Are these (1) .... clothes?
B Some of them are (2) .... clothes, but some of them belong to my wife.
A Is this dress (3) ....?
B Yes, she bought it in Thailand.
A There are a lot of toys here. (4) .... are they?
B They belong to (5) .... daughter.
A What about all this money. Is it (6) ....?
B Oh, no, it isn't (7) ....!

4 Write questions and answers. Use possessive adjectives and pronouns. 2.28 Listen and check.

0 that / you / phone? / No / it / not me / she   *Is that your phone? No, it isn't mine, it's hers.*
00 who / pens / these? / They / she   *Whose pens are these? They're hers.*
1 this / he / book? / No / it / not he / she
.... ?   ....
2 who / drinks / these? / They / they
.... ?   ....
3 that / she / iPod? / It / not she / me
.... ?   ....
4 who / ticket / this? / It / you
.... ?   ....

14 *this, that, these, those*

1 Form

	ADJECTIVE (BEFORE A NOUN)	PRONOUN (WITHOUT A NOUN)
singular	*This coat is expensive.* *That building is beautiful.*	*This is expensive.* *That is beautiful.*
plural	*These coats are expensive.* *Those buildings are beautiful.*	*These are expensive.* *Those are beautiful.*

We use a singular verb after *this/that* and a plural verb after *these/those*.

2 Near or far?

We use *this* and *these* to talk about things that are near us:
*Excuse me. Is **this** seat free?* (the seat near us)
*I need some new glasses – **these** are broken.* (the glasses I am holding)

We use *that* and *those* for things that are not near us:
*Look at the sky – **that**'s the North Star.*
*I'd like some pens – how much are **those** on the top shelf?*

3 Now or then?

We also use *this/these* to talk about now or a time that is near us:
***This** lesson is interesting.* (the lesson we are in now)
*I hate **these** cold winter days.* (the winter days we have now)
*I'm doing a lot of exercise **these** days.* (at the present time)
*What are you doing **this** evening?* (It's the morning or afternoon now.)

We use *that/those* to talk about a situation in the past:
*What did you think of **that** lesson yesterday?*
*There were no cars in **those** days.* (at a time in the past)

4 *this is / is that … ?*

We use *this is …* to introduce someone:
*Peter, **this is** Jane.*

We use *this is …* and *is that … ?* on the phone:
*'Hello, can I speak to Joan?' '**This is** Joan speaking.'*
*'**Is that** Angela?' 'No, she isn't here at the moment.'*

Practice

1 Look at the picture and tick (✓) the things which belong to Darren.

2 Match the sentences 1 and 2 with A and B in each group.

0 1 What's your opinion of that film?   A The film we are watching now.
   2 What do you think of this film?   B The film we watched yesterday.

1 1 I don't like this car.   A The car we are in now.
   2 I don't like that car.   B The car in the garage window.

2 1 Do you like those flowers?   A The flowers in my hand.
   2 Do you like these flowers?   B The flowers in my neighbour's garden.

3 1 Are these phones expensive?   A The phones we are looking at.
   2 Are those phones expensive?   B The phones we looked at last week.

3 Complete the sentences. Use *this*, *that*, *these* or *those*. ◀◢ 2.29 Listen and check.

0 .....*Those*..... phones in the window look really smart.

1 Do you like .... ring? My sister gave it to me.

2 What did you think of .... DVD we saw yesterday?

3 I'd like two of .... cakes – the ones on the top shelf.

4 Theatre tickets are very expensive .... days.

5 Could you help me? .... books are very heavy.

6 In .... days, children often worked in factories.

4 GRAMMAR IN USE Complete the conversations with *this*, *that*, *these* or *those* and the correct form of the verbs in brackets (). ◀◢ 2.30 Listen and check.

1 A Let me introduce my colleagues. (0) ..*These are*.. (be) my assistants, Sue and Joe.

  B Pleased to meet you.

  A And (1) .... (be) our office manager, Mike.

  B Hello, Mike. So, where is your boss?

  A (2) .... (be) my boss, Eleanor, over there in the corner of the room.

2 A Hello. Can I speak to Mrs Hargreaves?

  B (3) .... (be) Mrs Hargreaves speaking. Can I help you?

3 A Here are the two keys. (4) .... (open) the front and back doors.

  B What about the keys for the balcony door and the car?

  A Oh, (5) .... (be) in the cupboard in the kitchen.

  B And where's the key for the garage?

  A Oh, (6) .... (not have) a lock, so there's no key.

15 Reflexive pronouns; *each other*

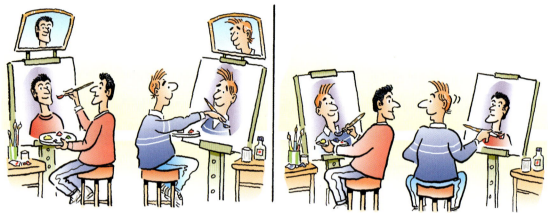

The students are painting **themselves**.   They are painting **each other**.

1 Form

subject pronoun	*I*	*you*	*he*	*she*	*it*	*we*	*they*
object pronoun	*me*	*you*	*him*	*her*	*it*	*us*	*them*
reflexive pronoun	*myself*	*yourself* (singular) *yourselves* (plural)	*himself*	*herself*	*itself*	*ourselves*	*themselves*

2 Use

We use reflexive pronouns when the subject and object are the same person or thing:

Daniel is painting Daniel. = **He** is painting **himself**.

*Have **you** hurt **yourself**?*
*I hate watching **myself** in videos.*
*My **computer** turns **itself** off at night.*

We often use reflexive pronouns with these verbs:

enjoy: *We **enjoyed ourselves** at the party.* (we had fun)

help: ***Help yourself** to some pizza.* (take some)

behave: *The children **behaved themselves** at the restaurant.* (behaved well)

We often use *by myself, by himself,* etc. It means 'alone' or 'without help'.
*I live **by myself**.* (= I live alone.)
*Don't help him. He wants to do it **by himself**.* (without your help)

3 *each other*

We use *each other* (not *themselves* or *ourselves*) when the subject and object are different:

✓ *Maria and Suzanna like **each other**.* (= Maria likes Suzanna and Suzanna likes Maria.)
✗ *Maria and Suzanna like themselves.*

✓ *We meet **each other** for lunch every Tuesday.*
✗ *We meet ourselves for lunch every Tuesday.*

Practice

1 Complete the sentences with reflexive pronouns or *each other*.

'My phone turns .... on when I open it.'

Jan and Maritza are always arguing with ....

'I've hurt ....!'

2 GRAMMAR IN USE Complete the information with the correct words from the box. 2.31 Listen and check.

each other   himself   itself   ourselves   ~~themselves~~   yourself

The Danger of Power Tools

 power saw   nail gun   safety goggles

WHAT CAN HAPPEN?

Did you know that each year power tools cause more than 100,000 accidents in the United States? The most dangerous tools are power saws. Last year 40,000 people cut (0) *themselves* using them. Another dangerous tool is the nail gun. On average, an American man injures (1) .... with a nail gun every twenty minutes – that's 28,600 accidents per year!

WHAT TO DO?

So, how can we protect (2) .... from these dangerous machines?

- You should always wear suitable clothes – you can protect (3) .... by wearing safety goggles and strong gloves.
- Make sure your power tool has a safety device. Then, if something goes wrong, the machine will turn (4) .... off immediately.
- Never use power tools near water or when it is raining.

And remember, if you are working with another person, make sure you don't stand too close to (5) ....

3 Write a sentence with the same meaning. Use reflexive pronouns or *each other*. 2.32 Listen and check.

0 I wrote this song without any help. *I wrote this song by myself.* ....

1 Karen is looking in the mirror. ....

2 You must fill in this form without any help. ....

3 Derek is talking to Kim and Kim is talking to Derek. ....

4 My aunt lives alone in a small flat. ....

5 My brother hurt his leg when he was playing football.

....

6 Selma doesn't like Emma and Emma doesn't like Selma.

....

Mum. I'm getting **something** to eat. Do you want **anything**?

16 Indefinite pronouns

1 Form

PEOPLE	someone/somebody	anyone/anybody	everyone/everybody	no one/nobody
THINGS	something	anything	everything	nothing
PLACES	somewhere	anywhere	everywhere	nowhere

We use a singular verb with all these pronouns.
*Everything **is** expensive in Switzerland. Nobody **lives** on the moon.*

⚠ ✗ *Everybody make mistakes.* ✓ *Everybody **makes** mistakes.*

2 Indefinite pronouns with *some/any*

We use indefinite pronouns to talk about a person, object or place. The exact person, object or place is not important:

	some	*any*	EXAMPLES
in positive sentences	✓	✗	*I'll ask **someone** for help.* *He needs **something** for his computer.*
in negative sentences	✗	✓	*I can't find **anywhere** to sit.* *There isn't **anything** on TV tonight.*
in most questions	✗	✓	*Did you see **anyone** in town?* *Is there **anything** you want at the shop?*
when you ask for or offer something	✓	✗	*Can I have **something** to drink?* *Would you like **something** to eat?*
when you suggest something	✓	✗	*Let's go **somewhere** nice for a meal tonight.*

some/any ➤ Unit 7

3 Indefinite pronouns with *no*

We use *no one/nobody*, *nowhere* and *nothing* with positive verbs, but the meaning is negative:
*There's **nowhere** to sit.* (= There isn't anywhere to sit.) ***No one** answered the phone.*

⚠ We don't use two negatives in English:
✗ *I didn't eat nothing.* ✓ *I **didn't** eat **anything**.*
✗ *Nobody isn't here.* ✓ ***Nobody** is here.*

4 Indefinite pronouns with *every*

We use *everyone/everybody*, *everything* and *everywhere* when we mean 'all people', 'all things' or 'all places':
***Everyone** in the room stopped speaking. **Everybody** was very happy with the results.*
*Is **everything** all right? I want to visit **everywhere** on the island.*

Practice

1 **Choose the correct words in *italics*.** 🔊 **2.33** **Listen and check.**

0 I'm thirsty. I need *anything* / (*something*) to drink.
1 Everybody on my course *has* / *have* a university degree.
2 We don't have *something* / *anything* in the fridge.
3 The shop was expensive so I didn't buy *nothing* / *anything*.
4 She looked *anywhere* / *everywhere* but she couldn't find her key.
5 Be quiet! Everyone *are* / *is* asleep.
6 They're on holiday so nobody *is* / *isn't* at home.
7 No one *like* / *likes* unfriendly people.
8 We don't know *somebody* / *anybody* who speaks Turkish.

2 **GRAMMAR IN USE** **Complete the conversation with indefinite pronouns.**
🔊 **2.34** **Listen and check.**

A I'm hungry. I haven't eaten (0) ...*anything*... today.
  Let's find (1) .... for lunch.
B But there's (2) .... to eat near here.
A I'm sure there is. Let's ask (3) ....
B Excuse me. Is there (4) .... to eat
  around here – a café or a restaurant?
C There's a hotel on Grange Street, but it's
  quite expensive.
B Oh. Are there any cheaper places to eat?
C Mmm, not really. I'm afraid (5) .... in this
  town is expensive.
A What about (6) .... like a sandwich?
C Well, there's a supermarket near here. I think it sells sandwiches.

3 **Write the sentences again. Change the <u>underlined</u> word(s) to an indefinite pronoun and / or a different form of the verb.**

0 There is <u>no food</u> in the fridge. *There is nothing in the fridge.*..........................
1 <u>All the students</u> in my class <u>are</u> friendly. ....
2 There <u>are no students</u> in the classroom. ....
3 I didn't eat <u>any food</u> yesterday. ....
4 <u>All the things</u> here <u>are</u> dirty. ....
5 I've got <u>no clothes</u> to wear to the wedding. ....
6 There isn't <u>a place</u> to sit on this train. ....

4 **Find four more mistakes in the sentences and correct them. Tick (✓) the correct sentences.**

0 Nobody in my class likes classical music. ✓   00 ~~Somewhere~~ is busy at this time of year.   *Everywhere*
1 We didn't get nothing at the supermarket today.
2 Somebody was talking, but I don't know who.
3 The restaurant was empty; there wasn't nobody there.
4 Everyone use the Internet these days.
5 In my town there are cafés everywhere.
6 I think anything is expensive in this shop.

17 one/ones, another one

Which one would you like?

I'd like that one.

1 Replacing a noun

We use *one* to replace a singular countable noun:
*I'm making **a cup of coffee**. Would you like **one**?* (a cup of coffee)

We use *ones* to replace a plural countable noun:
*Shall I wear brown **shoes** or black **ones**?* (shoes)
*'Which **jeans** do you want to buy?' 'The **ones** on the right.'* (jeans)

We can use *a/an/the/some* + adjective + *one(s)*:
*I don't like the blue shirt. I like **the red one**.* (the red shirt)
*Those are really bad photos but here are **some good ones**.* (good photos)
*That pen's very expensive. I only want **a cheap one**.* (a cheap pen)

 We can't use *one* or *ones* to replace an uncountable noun.
✗ *I prefer folk music to classical one.* ✓ *I prefer folk music to classical music.*

2 *Which one/ones?*

We can ask people to say which thing they want or mean with *Which one(s)?*:
*'**Which one** do you want?' 'I want the red one.'*
*'I've got some Tom Cruise films on DVD.' '**Which ones?**'* (= Which films?)

We use *this/that/these/those* + *one(s)* to say which thing we want or mean:
*'Which pen would you like?' 'I'd like **that one**.'*
*Can you pass me some plates? **Those ones** on the top shelf.*

Countable/uncountable nouns ➤ Unit 2

3 *another one*

We use *another one*
- for an extra thing:
  *Sara hasn't got a student book. Have you got **another one**?* (an extra book)
- for a different thing:
  *She doesn't like that jumper. She wants **another one**.* (a different jumper)

Practice

1 Choose the correct words in *italics*.

0 I prefer plain food to spicy *one* / (*food*.)

1 Do you have a gas cooker or an electric *one* / *ones*?

2 We've got three litres of milk but we need *another* / *other* one for tomorrow.

3 Can we have a blue pen and a *black* / *black one*, please?

4 I don't want the cotton trousers, I want the wool *ones* / *one*.

5 I'm still hungry. I'd like *sandwich another* / *another sandwich*.

6 Would you like brown sugar or white *one* / *sugar*?

2 Complete the sentences with *one*, *ones* or *another*. ◀》**2.35** Listen and check.

0 I'd like two red peppers and a green ....*one*......... .

1 I don't like modern films, I prefer old ....

2 Do you have any more euros? We need .... one for the drinks machine.

3 Do you have these .... in a smaller size?

4 There are a lot of things to take; I think we need .... suitcase.

5 James sold his old car and bought a new ....

6 That dress is nicer than the .... you were wearing yesterday.

3 GRAMMAR IN USE Improve this conversation by replacing some more words with *one* or *ones*. ◀》**2.36** Listen and check.

A Can I help you?

B Yes. I'd like that coffee pot.

A Which ~~coffee pot~~ *one*?

B The coffee pot on the top shelf.

A Oh, I see. That coffee pot?

B Yes, that's it.

A Anything else?

B Yes. I'd like some cups.

A Do you mean the cups next to the coffee pot?

B No, not those cups. The blue and white cups on the other shelf.

A These cups?

B Yes.

4 Answer the questions with full sentences. Do not use the <u>underlined</u> words in your answer.

0 Do you prefer plain <u>biscuits</u> or chocolate <u>biscuits</u>? *I prefer chocolate ones.*

1 What colour <u>shoes</u> are you wearing? ....

2 What colour <u>pen</u> do you usually use? ....

3 Do you prefer hot <u>drinks</u> or cold <u>drinks</u>? ....

4 Do you prefer old <u>houses</u> or new <u>houses</u>? ....

Review MODULE 2

1 UNITS 11, 12 AND 13 **Choose the correct answer, A, B or C below.**

Subject | My first term

Dear Mum and Dad
(0) .... 'm really enjoying (1) .... first term at college. The lessons are really interesting and (2) .... have lots of friends. (3) .... best friend is Simon. (4) .... is doing the same course as (5) .... Simon lives with (6) .... family in a flat near the university. I visited them yesterday. The flat is much nicer than (7) .... (8) .... is in an expensive area and (9) .... are quite rich. By the way, we did (10) .... first project last week and I got an A!

Lots of love, Dan

0 A Me (B) I C Myself
1 A mine B my C me
2 A me B mine C I
3 A Mine B Me C My
4 A He B Him C His
5 A me B I C mine

6 A her B him C his
7 A me B mine C my
8 A He B It C Their
9 A the parents of Simon B Simons' parents
   C Simon's parents
10 A us B our C we

2 UNITS 12 AND 13 **Complete the second sentence so it means the same as the first. Use one, two or three words.**

0 Does this belong to you?   Is *this yours* ....?
1 Does this belong to the children? Is ....?
2 We went to college in the car David owns. We went to college in ....
3 Caroline lives in Moscow – near the centre. Caroline lives near the ....
4 Does this book belong to him?   Is ....?
5 You can't have that, it belongs to me. That's ...., you can't have it.
6 I love these old teacups, they belonged to my grandmother. I love these old teacups, they were ....

3 UNITS 14 AND 15 **Find five more mistakes in the text and correct them.**

This ~~are~~ *is* a photograph from last summer. Look, that's my little brother and those is my two sisters. It was the day we went to the funfair. We had a lot of fun this day, we really enjoyed myself. We went into the hall of mirrors and looked at ourselves – we laughed so much! Then we went on the rollercoaster. It was really frightening. My brother hates heights but he made he go on it – he was very brave! But the best part was seeing the animals in the circus tent – these animals were fantastic to watch!

4 UNITS 16 AND 17 **Choose the correct words in *italics* in the conversation.**
2.37 **Listen and check.**

A Can I help you?
B Yes. I'm going to a college interview next month and I need (0) *anything /*(something)
   to wear.
A Well, these dresses are very nice.
B Mmm, I'm not sure. Have you got (1) *anything / anyone* in a lighter colour?
A How about this (2) *one / ones*?
B I'd prefer one in blue – (3) *no one / everyone* says blue suits me.
A OK. What about this dress?
B I think that's a bit big. Have you got (4) *other / another* one in a smaller size?
A Yes, we have. That's £125.
B Oh, that's a bit expensive. Have you got (5) *everything / anything* under £100?
A No. I'm afraid (6) *there's / there isn't* nothing under £100 here.
B Oh, dear. Is there (7) *anything / anywhere* I can find cheaper clothes near here?
A Well. There's a clothes market around the corner …

5 ALL UNITS **Complete the crossword.**

ACROSS
2 Excuse me. Is … your bag over there?
5 We took the wrong suitcase. It wasn't ours, it was … .
8 … house is this? Your uncle's?
9 My son painted that picture by … .
12 That cake was delicious. Can I have … one?
13 Our teacher gives … a lot of homework every day.

DOWN
1 I've looked … but I can't find my phone.
2 I don't like … shoes – I prefer those ones over there.
3 Does … in this class speak Russian?
4 The heating in my house turns … off at midnight.

6 I'm hungry. I'd like … to eat.
7 My best friend and I send text messages to each … every day.
10 That isn't your book, it's … !
11 I prefer happy films to sad … .

6 ALL UNITS **Complete the text with the correct words from the box. There are two extra words.**

'Good morning, everyone. (0) ……*My*…… name is Roger Downley and I am the head teacher of this college. It is a great pleasure for (1) ……………… to welcome you all personally to Crandon. First, I'd like to tell (2) ……………… about the fantastic facilities we have here. There are two libraries. The main library is in the Shelton building and the smaller (3) ……………… is behind the history department. So there is plenty of space for (4) ………………. Your education is the most important thing for (5) ……………… here. But we also want you to enjoy (6) ………………, so we have plenty of social and sporting activities, too. You probably saw the sports fields outside (7) ……………… building. We are very proud of (8) ……………… fields – not many colleges have so much open space … '

everyone itself
me ~~my~~ one
ones this those
us you yourselves

Test MODULE 2

Pronouns and possessives

Choose the correct answer, A, B or C.

1 George likes me but I don't like ....
   A him B he C his
   ➤ Unit 11

2 That's a nice mobile phone. Does .... take photos?
   A he B she C it
   ➤ Unit 11

3 'Who's that in the photo?' 'It's ....'
   A we B us C I
   ➤ Unit 11

4 Do you like ....?
   A Anna's cooking B the cooking of Anna C Anna' cooking
   ➤ Unit 12

5 David is ....
   A brother of Alan B Alan's brother C Alans' brother
   ➤ Unit 12

6 She lives in the ...., near the Empire State building.
   A New York's centre B New York centre C centre of New York
   ➤ Unit 12

7 I feel sick and .... head hurts.
   A the B mine C my
   ➤ Unit 13

8 This dictionary doesn't belong to me. It's ....
   A her B hers C her's
   ➤ Unit 13

9 Don't touch that. It's ....
   A the mine B my C mine
   ➤ Unit 13

10 I'd like some apples. How much are .... behind you?
    A these B those C them
    ➤ Unit 14

11 What did you think of .... film we saw last week?
    A this B those C that
    ➤ Unit 14

12 'Can I speak to the manager?' 'Yes, ... is the manager speaking.'
    A that B this C these
    ➤ Unit 14

13 We enjoyed .... at the concert.
    A themselves B yourselves C ourselves
    ➤ Unit 15

14 I don't have any family so I live ....
    A myself B by me C by myself
    ➤ Unit 15

15 I phone Miranda every day; we spend a long time talking to ....
    A ourselves B each other C themselves
    ➤ Unit 15

16 Where are my keys? I can't find them ....
    A anywhere B nowhere C somewhere
    ➤ Unit 16

17 Caroline wasn't hungry so she didn't eat ....
    A something B nothing C anything
    ➤ Unit 16

18 Everybody in my town .... friendly.
    A are B aren't C is
    ➤ Unit 16

19 I don't like black jeans. I prefer blue ....
    A one B ones C them
    ➤ Unit 17

20 We need two phones. Do you have ....?
    A other one B another one C more one
    ➤ Unit 17

Prepositions

Before you start

1 Read the information in the article. Look at the <mark>highlighted</mark> grammar examples.

THE STRATFORD SHAKESPEARE FESTIVAL

THE STRATFORD SHAKESPEARE FESTIVAL is one of the major theatre festivals in the world. It takes place <mark>in</mark> Stratford, Ontario, <mark>near</mark> the town of Kitchener. It starts <mark>in</mark> the spring and runs from April <mark>to</mark> November <mark>every</mark> year.

Some of the world's best actors appear on stages <mark>in front of</mark> crowds of thousands of fans who travel <mark>to</mark> the festival from all parts of the world. Transport to the festival is good: you can reach Stratford <mark>by</mark> plane, train, bus or car. There are special buses from Toronto and Kitchener on some Saturdays <mark>during</mark> the summer.

Tickets for this year's festival are <mark>for sale</mark> now, on the festival website.

2 Now read the sentences. Choose the correct words in *italics*.
The <mark>highlighted</mark> grammar examples will help you.

1 Our closest theatre festival takes place *on / at / in* Burnham. ➤ Unit 18
2 Sometimes you can't get *close / near / by* the stage. ➤ Unit 18
3 Some actors don't like to play *opposite / behind / in front of* a big crowd. ➤ Unit 19
4 A lot of people go *at / in / to* the Burnham Theatre festival. ➤ Unit 20
5 The Burnham Theatre Festival starts *in / on / at* August. ➤ Unit 21
6 Most summer festivals here are from July *up / in / to* September. ➤ Unit 21
7 We try to see a play at the festival *in every / on every / every* week. ➤ Unit 21
8 Festivals don't usually take place *while / during / from* the winter. ➤ Unit 22
9 Most people travel to the festival *in / with / by* car or train. ➤ Unit 23
10 Tickets are usually *to sale / by sale / for sale* two months before the start. ➤ Unit 24

3 Check your answers below. Then go to the unit for more information and practice.

1 in 2 near 3 in front of 4 to 5 in 6 to 7 every 8 during 9 by 10 for sale

18 Prepositions of place (1)

1 Main uses

at		There's someone **at** the door. She's **at** her desk by 9.00 every day. Write your name **at** the top of the paper.
in		There are some books **in** the cupboard. There was no one **in** the house.
on		The computer is **on** the desk. The poster is **on** the wall.
above		There's a poster on the wall **above** the desk. He lives in the flat **above** the shop.

below		Adrian is standing **below** the clock. The coats are in the cupboard **below** the stairs.
under		The rubbish bin is **under** the desk. I keep my old school books **under** the bed.
next to by beside		The cupboard is **next to/by/beside** the desk. He lives in the house **next to/by/beside** the school.
near		Adrian is standing **near** the door. She works at the shop **near** the station.

2 Other uses

We use *at* with

- home and places of study/work:
  at home, at school, at university, at work, at the office
- other places in a town:
  at the doctor's, at the cinema, at the station

We use *in* with

- towns and countries:
  in Milan, in Italy, in Europe

 ✗ ~~I live at Buenos Aires.~~ ✓ *I live **in** Buenos Aires.*

Practice

1 **Match the two parts of the sentences.**

0 There were some really good bands   A on the desk in my office.
1 Your coats and scarves are   B on the bedroom wall?
2 Who painted that lovely picture   C in the cupboard by the front door.
3 Can you put your old papers in the bin   D at her best friend's wedding.
4 You'll find the tickets   E under the sink?
5 At the moment Meral is living   F at the festival last year.
6 Louisa met her husband   G in Izmir, but she comes from Ankara.

2 **GRAMMAR IN USE** **Complete the conversation with the correct phrases from the box.**
🔊 **2.38** **Listen and check.**

> beside the park   in the office block   in the park   near the festival   ~~near the station~~   next to our house

A How are you getting to the festival on Saturday?
B I'm going by train. We live quite (0) ...*near the station*... – it's only about a
   fifteen-minute walk.
A That's too far with luggage!
B No, I'll take a taxi to the station. The taxi office is (1) .... next door.
A That'll be expensive. Why don't you drive here and we can go by bus? The bus stops
   (2) ...., just outside really.
B Does it stop (3) ...., then?
A Quite near, it's only about a five-minute walk.
B But the station is (4) .... You can walk straight into the festival.
A Why don't we just drive? There's parking for the festival (5) ....·
B That's true! Let's do that.

3 **GRAMMAR IN USE** **Look at the picture. Complete the text with prepositions.**
🔊 **2.39** **Listen and check.**

Hi Melissa!
About Saturday – let's meet at the station. You can't miss it – there's a huge clock
(0) ....on........ the wall at the front and there's a car park (1) .... the station.
I'll meet you at the taxi stop (2) .... the station – it's just outside. There are some
nice shops (3) .... the station and we can have lunch at the café (4) .... the
department store. The cinema is right (5) .... the store, so we can go straight there
after lunch. Maggie can't meet us for lunch so she'll just meet us (6) .... the cinema
at 2.30. See you then! Jackie

⏻ Go online for more practice

19 Prepositions of place (2)

1 in front of, behind, opposite, between

in front of		*Joanne is **in front of** Simon.* *Annie sits **in front of** me in the class.*
behind		*Simon is **behind** Joanne.* *There's a police car **behind** our car.*
opposite		*The snack bar is **opposite** the ticket office.* *My house is **opposite** the post office.*
between		*Simon is **between** Joanne and Mariella.* *That's me in the photo – **between** mum and dad.*

 ✗ ~~The snack bar is opposite to the ticket office.~~
✓ *The snack bar is **opposite** the ticket office.*

2 Describing a picture

We use prepositions to describe where things are in a picture.
Read this description of the picture at the top of the page.

The picture shows the entrance to a festival.
***At the front** we can see the ticket office. Three people are waiting for tickets.*
*There's a festival stage **at the back**.*
*The ticket office is **on the left** of the picture and the snacks are **on the right**.*
***In the centre** there's a group of people.*
***At the top** we can see the sky and **at the bottom** we can see some children.*

Practice

1 Look at the plan below. Then choose the correct words in *italics*. 🔊**2.40** Listen and check.

0 A is on the *right* / *left* of B.
1 C is *opposite* / *between* B and E.
2 D is *in front of* / *behind* E.
3 F is *opposite* / *between* A and B.
4 G is *between* / *in front of* H.

5 G is *opposite* / *in front of* C.
6 I is on the *right* / *left* of H.
7 E is *behind* / *opposite* I.
8 C is on the *right* / *left* of E.

A	B .....*hotel*......	C	D ....
			E ....

Shopping Centre – Main Street

| F .... | You are here 🚶 | G .... | I .... |
| | | H .... | |

2 GRAMMAR IN USE Now read the text. Write the correct places in the plan.

The biggest building in the shopping centre is the department store. It's opposite the supermarket and a small hotel. The hotel is on the right of the supermarket. On the right of the hotel is a cinema, and opposite that is the café, which has a lot of tables and chairs in front of it. The café is on the left of the bus station, which is opposite the sports centre. That has a small area behind it with a tennis court.

3 GRAMMAR IN USE Look at the photo. Complete the text with the correct words from the box. 🔊**2.41** Listen and check.

back ~~front~~ left right top

The picture shows a scene from Chinese New Year in London. At the (0) ....*front*...... we can see people holding models of a dragon and a bird. There are some old buildings and shops on the (1) .... and (2) .... of the picture. It is a nice day because we can see blue sky at the (3) .... Behind all the people, at the (4) .... , there are more colourful things that are part of the festival.

4 Now look at a picture in the room you are in, or find a picture from this book. Write three sentences with prepositions to describe it.

At the front I can see ... .

....

....

20 Prepositions of movement

From the ticket office, you go **through** the main gate and **along** the path. Go **past** the toilets and follow the path **to** the food court. Then go **round** the fountain and **across** the bridge. The main stage is in front of you.

1 *along, past, across, over, through, round, from, to*

along	→	Walk **along** the path.	round		Go **round** the fountain.
past		Go **past** the toilets.	from		You go **from** the ticket office ...
across over		Go **across** the bridge. Go **over** the bridge.	to		Follow the path **to** the food court.
through		Go **through** the main gate.			

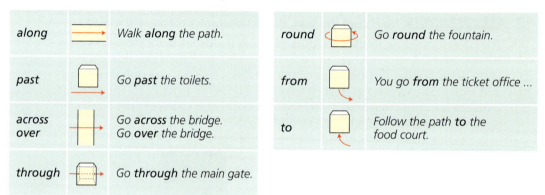

We also use *from* in this way:
*Our English teacher **comes/is from** New Zealand.* (= New Zealand is her country.)

2 *into, out of, onto, off*

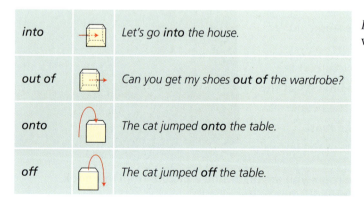

into		Let's go **into** the house.
out of		Can you get my shoes **out of** the wardrobe?
onto		The cat jumped **onto** the table.
off		The cat jumped **off** the table.

Into is similar to *in*, but we use *into* for movement.

in for position/place ➤ Unit 18

We *get into/out of* a car or taxi, but *get on/off* a bus, plane, train, ship, bike:
Get into the car. We're ready to go. I felt ill when I **got off** the ship.

 ✗ I got into the bus. ✓ I **got on** the bus.

Practice

1 GRAMMAR IN USE **Read these directions to an arts festival.
Then choose the correct words in *italics*.** ◀)**2.42** **Listen and check.**

How to find us

If you are coming by train, follow these directions from the station to the Arts Centre:
when you leave the station, go (0) *across* / *through* the railway bridge. (1) *To* / *From*
the bridge, turn right and walk (2) *along* / *past* the path by the river for about
200 metres, then go (3) *along* / *through* the small park on your left.
Go (4) *across* / *round* the statue in the middle and (5) *from* / *past* the park café.
Follow the path (6) *to* / *along* the main gate and go (7) *across* / *through* the gate.
Go (8) *along* / *across* the main road and you'll see the Arts Centre in front of you.

| Tickets | Cars & Parking | Food and drink | Train times | Contact us |

2 **Complete the sentences with prepositions.** ◀)**2.43** **Listen and check.**

0 You have to turn your lights on when you go ...*through*... the tunnel.
1 I always walk .... the bridge to get to work. It's quicker.
2 'Is this Kew Gardens?' 'No. You need to get .... the bus at the next stop.'
3 The doors open at 6.00 p.m. and then people can go .... the cinema.
4 Turn right and go .... the post office – it's the next building on the right.
5 Walk .... the lake. The café is on the other side.

3 GRAMMAR IN USE **Complete the description below with prepositions.
Use the map to help you.**

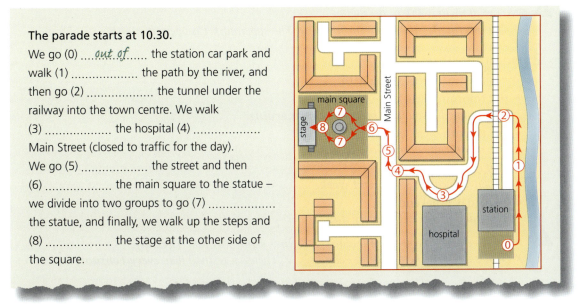

The parade starts at 10.30.
We go (0) ...*out of*..... the station car park and
walk (1) .... the path by the river, and
then go (2) .... the tunnel under the
railway into the town centre. We walk
(3) .... the hospital (4) ....
Main Street (closed to traffic for the day).
We go (5) .... the street and then
(6) .... the main square to the statue –
we divide into two groups to go (7) ....
the statue, and finally, we walk up the steps and
(8) .... the stage at the other side of
the square.

4 **Describe your route to school/work every day.**

I always walk to work. I go out of my apartment and turn left. I walk along the street,
past some shops ...

....

21 Prepositions of time (1)

THEATRE! DANCE! MUSIC! COMEDY!   **Brighton festival**

England's biggest, busiest festival is back –
it starts **on** 5 May and continues **until** 27 May.

Events **at** lunchtime **on** most days and **in** the evening every day.

The ticket office is open **from** 10.00 a.m. **to** 6.00 p.m. every day.

1 at, in, on

at +	an exact time	*The train arrives **at 6.00**.* *The film starts **at 9.00**.*
	special days or occasions	*Lucy met an old friend **at her sister's wedding**.*
	times of meals and the weekend	*The concert is **at lunchtime**.* *What are you doing **at the weekend**?*
in +	parts of the day	*There are events **in the evening** every day.* *It gets cooler **in the afternoon**.*
	months, seasons, years, centuries	*The festival is **in May**.* *He was born **in 1994**.* *They built the castle **in the eleventh century**.*
on +	dates and days	*The festival starts **on 5 May**.* *My interview is **on Thursday afternoon**.*

 We say *at night*, NOT *in the night*:
✗ ~~The supermarket is open in the night~~   ✓ *The supermarket is open **at night**.*

2 No preposition

We don't use a preposition with

- *this* (morning, week, etc.):
  *What time did you have breakfast **this morning**?*
- *last* (month, year, etc.):
  *The new theatre opened **last month**.*
- *next* (week, year, etc.):
  *My English course starts **next week**.*
- *every* (day, weekend, etc.):
  *There are special events **every day**.*

 ✗ ~~Kevin's exam was on last Tuesday.~~   ✓ *Kevin's exam was **last Tuesday**.*
✗ ~~There's a festival here in every February.~~   ✓ *There's a festival here **every February**.*

3 in, until, from ... to/until

*My birthday is **in five days**.* (five days from now)
*The festival continues **until 12 May**.* (it ends on this date)
*The festival lasts **from 9 May to/until 12 May**.*
(from the beginning to the end of this time)

Use of prepositions in American English ➤ page 317

Practice

1 Match the two parts of the sentences. 🔊 **2.44** Listen and check.

0 The first men walked on the moon in   A 9 June, 1963.
1 Americans usually have family parties in   B Saturdays.
2 World War Two lasted from   C the morning.
3 People usually do their best work in   D 1969.
4 Johnny Depp was born on   E November.
5 Children don't usually go to school on   F 1939 until 1945.

2 Look at the notices. Complete the sentences below them. Use the correct prepositions.

Knightley Manor
~ OPEN TO PUBLIC ~
SATURDAY & SUNDAY ONLY

NEXT TRAIN TO
WINCHESTER
ARRIVES – 10.25
DEPARTS – 10.28

HOLIDAY
SORRY – WE'RE CLOSED
FOR ALL OF JULY

0 Knightley Manor is only open to the public _at the weekend_ .

1 The train to Winchester arrives .... and leaves ....

2 The shop is closed ....

DATES FOR NEXT TERM
5 SEPTEMBER 10 DECEMBER

MONDAYS
ALL TICKETS HALF PRICE

NEXT PERFORMANCE
2 p.m. 23 April

3 The next term starts ....

4 The cinema tickets are half price ....

5 The next performance of the play will be ....

3 Complete/write the second sentence so it means the same as the first. Use the words in brackets (). 🔊 **2.45** Listen and check.

0 I usually go to the gym at 10.00. (in) _I usually go to the gym in the morning._
1 I went to the gym at 10.30 today. (this)
   I went ....
2 It's Monday 15 June now. I have a doctor's appointment for Monday 22 June. (next)
   I'm going ....
3 At the moment I'm working from Monday to Sunday. (every)
   ....
4 It's Monday. The report will be ready on Thursday. (in)
   ....
5 The builders are starting on Wednesday and working until Saturday. (from ... to)
   ....

4 Complete the sentences about you. Use the information in brackets ().

0 (year) I was born _in 1986_ .
1 (year) I was born ....
2 (day, month) My birthday is ....
3 (time) I usually get up .... and go to bed ....
4 (period) I usually work / study from ....
5 (day) I often take exercise / play a sport ....

22 Prepositions of time (2)

London FILMFESTIVAL

Classic films of the 1920s:

The Hunchback of Notre Dame

Wednesday 10 March at 7 p.m.

- Drinks **before** the film
- Neil Brand plays the piano **during** the film
- Talk **after** the show by the Director of the National Film Theatre

1 before, after

We use *before* and *after* with

- times:
  *Let's meet **before 7.00**. The film starts then.*
  *Train tickets are cheaper **after 9.30** in the morning.*

- events/situations:
  *There will be drinks **before the film**. Let's watch TV **after dinner**.*
  *My grandmother was born **before the war**. I can meet you **after work**.*

before and *after* + *-ing* form ➤ Unit 95.1

2 by, for, during

We use *by* to mean 'not later than':
*Please give me your homework **by Friday**. (on or before Friday)*
*The holiday will be cheaper if we book it **by 30 April**. (on or before 30 April)*
*The meeting is on Wednesday so I'll finish the report **by then**.*

We use *for* + a period of time:
for an hour, two days, three weeks
It means 'the whole time':
*We waited for the bus **for an hour**.*

12 o'clock   1 o'clock
FOR AN HOUR

We use *during* + an event or situation:
during the flight, the winter, the war
*Neil Brand plays the piano **during the film**.*
*Uncle Andy called us **during supper** with some bad news.*

Compare *during* and *for*:
*I only slept **for** half an hour **during** the flight.*
*It rained **for** two days **during** our holiday.*

 ✗ I go to classes during three hours in the afternoon.
✓ *I go to classes **for three hours** in the afternoon.*

for with present perfect ➤ Unit 53.1

Practice

1 `GRAMMAR IN USE` **Look at the flight information board. Use the information below to complete it.**

DEPARTURES			ARRIVALS		
	08.55	(0) BC218 Edinburgh	09.05	LT079	FRANKFURT
	09.10	AC1525 MONTREAL	(5)	AF1062	PARIS
	09.15	DA729 MADRID	09.15	(6)	
	09.25	PA1921 (1)	09.30	BA9193	JOHANNESBURG
	09.35	LT200 FRANKFURT	09.35	DA738	MUNICH
	09.45	DA1910 MILAN	09.55	AA0107	TANGIER
	09.50	PA8310 MONTEVIDEO	10.10	(7)	
(2)	(3)		10.25	(8)	
	10.20	(4)	10.35	DA661	ATHENS

Only one flight leaves the airport before 9 o'clock in the morning, the BC218 to Edinburgh.
There are two flights for North America before 9.30, for Montreal and New York.
Only two flights leave between 10.00 and 10.30, the AF1063 to Paris, and ten minutes before that the SAS202 to Stockholm.

Two flights arrive from Paris after 9.00: BA5634 arrives five minutes after the Air France flight.
There are two arrivals from the United States: BA4242 from Miami first at 10.10, then PA2190 from Dallas fifteen minutes after that.

2 **Choose the correct words in *italics*.** `2.46` **Listen and check.**

0 If you aren't doing anything this evening, let's go to the cinema *during* / (*after*) work.
1 The flight's at 8.00 a.m. so we'll have to get up *after* / *before* 6.00 to get to the airport.
2 The last date for your project is 25 March. Please give it to your teacher *by* / *after* then.
3 Mike had a bad accident *during* / *for* his holiday and was in hospital *during* / *for* two weeks.
4 Everything smells very fresh *before* / *after* rain.
5 Please don't talk *for* / *during* the exam.
6 We'll send out the interview letters *by* / *after* the weekend, so you'll hear early next week.

3 `GRAMMAR IN USE` **Complete the text with the correct words from the box.** `2.47` **Listen and check.**

after before by during during ~~for~~ for

The Rocks Hotel
has welcomed visitors (0) ...*for*... 25 years.

The following information will help you to have an enjoyable stay:

• The restaurant is open from 6.30 until 9.30 p.m. If you would like an evening meal (1) .... this time, please call 135.
• Breakfast is served between 6.30 and 9.00 a.m. If you would like breakfast in your room, please hang the menu card on your door (2) .... 2.00 a.m.
• Reception is closed from 11.30 p.m. to 6.00 a.m. If you need a doctor (3) .... the night, please call 100.
• We ask guests to leave their rooms by 11.00 a.m. If you wish to keep your room later than this, please let us know (4) .... 9.00 a.m.

** SPECIAL SPRING OFFER** (5) .... the months of March and April, stay (6) .... two nights and have dinner here, get the third night FREE!

23 Prepositions with other meanings

Last year I went to the Hay-on-Wye book festival. I went **with** my two best friends, and we went **by** bus. It was great — we went to a really funny and interesting talk **by** Charlie Higson. He wrote the *Young James Bond* books.

1 by

We use *by* to talk about

* a way of travelling:
  *We went to Hay **by bus**.*
  *Dave goes to work **by bike**.*

* a way of communicating:
  *I keep in touch with all my friends **by email**.*

* a way of paying for something:
  *I pay for my shopping **by credit card**.*
  (But we pay for something **in cash** or **by cash**.)

 ✗ ~~Amanda goes to work by foot.~~ ✓ *Amanda goes to work **on foot**.*

We also use *by* to say who wrote or produced something:
*The 'Young James Bond' books are **by Charlie Higson**.*
*'Guernica' is a famous painting **by Pablo Picasso**.*
*The play 'Macbeth' was written **by Shakespeare**.*

by with passive form of verb ➤ Unit 96.3

2 with

We use *with* to mean 'together':
*I went to Hay **with my two best friends**.*
*My parents are on holiday **with my brother** at the moment.*

We can also use *with* to say what we use to do something:
*He pushed the door open **with his foot**.*

3 as, like

We use *as* for a person's job, or to say what something is used for:
*Martin works **as a waiter** in the evenings.*
*You can use the side of a book **as a ruler**.*

We use *like* when we mean 'similar to':
*Debbie's very beautiful – she looks **like** a model.* (She isn't a model.)
*This tastes **like** chocolate.* (It isn't chocolate.)

 We don't use *like* when we talk about someone's job. We use *as*:
✗ ~~Alex works like a builder.~~ ✓ *Alex works **as** a builder.* (This is his job.)

Practice

1 Match the sentences 1–5 with the meanings A–F.

0 That picture is by Karen, when she was at college.
1 That picture is of Karen, when she was at college.
2 Karen usually goes to work on foot.
3 Karen catches the bus if she's late.
4 Karen works as a photographer.
5 Karen looks like a photographer.

A She is a photographer.
B She walks to work.
C She is in the picture.
D She painted the picture.
E She isn't a photographer.
F She sometimes goes to work by bus.

2 **GRAMMAR IN USE** Complete the conversation with the phrases A–H below. 🔊 **2.48** Listen and check.

SUE   Did you go to any festivals last year?
AMY   Yes, we went to one – a film festival in Liverpool.
SUE   Really? Did you go (0) ...*H*...?
AMY   Yes. We went to a wonderful talk (1) .... about Indian films.
SUE   How did you go – (2) ....?
AMY   No, we didn't drive. We went (3) ....
      But it was quite expensive – we had to pay for the train fares (4) ....
SUE   Mmm, but did you enjoy the festival?
AMY   Yes, it was great – but Justin fell and hurt his foot and he had to walk (5) .... for weeks afterwards!
SUE   Oh, no! Is he OK now?
AMY   Yes. He got a book (6) .... with exercises in, and he did those. He's fine now.
SUE   Good. Oh, I nearly forgot. When is the Ely festival this year?
AMY   Mmm, I've got the information at home. I'll send it to you (7) ....
SUE   Great. Thanks.

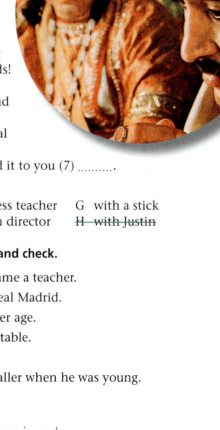

A by email   C by car   E by a famous fitness teacher   G with a stick
B by train   D by credit card   F by an Indian film director   H with Justin

3 Complete the sentences with *as* or *like*. 🔊 **2.49** Listen and check.

0 Robert spent years ...*as*... a carpenter before he became a teacher.
1 Your brother really looks .... that footballer in Real Madrid.
2 Marina loves going to parties, ... most girls of her age.
3 You can use this sofa .... a bed. It's really comfortable.
4 Mmm, your perfume smells .... roses. It's lovely.
5 The TV chef Gordon Ramsay trained .... a footballer when he was young.

4 Change the sentences so they are true for you.

0 I pay for most things by cheque. *I pay for most things in cash.*
1 I look like my father. ....
2 I live with two other students. ....
3 I love music by Mozart. ....
4 I always go to work by car. ....

24 Common phrases with prepositions

1 Phrases of place

	PHRASE	EXAMPLE
at	at home at school at work	I'm usually **at home** in the evenings. The children are **at school** next week so we can't come. Robert's **at work** now – why don't you call him there?
in	in bed	Teenagers often stay **in bed** till late.
on	on holiday on business	Where are you going **on holiday** this year? Melissa's in Rome **on business** this week. (working there)

 We don't use *to* with *home, here* or *there*:

✗ ~~I'm tired. I want to go to home now.~~   ✓ I'm tired. I want to **go home** now.

2 Phrases of time

	PHRASE	MEANING	EXAMPLE
at	at first at last at once at the same time	in the beginning after a long time immediately together	**At first** I was unhappy at college but now I really like it. **At last** it stopped raining so we went outside. The ambulance arrived almost **at once**. You can't watch TV and study **at the same time**.
in	in a hurry in the end in time	have to do something quickly finally early enough for something	I can't talk now. I'm **in a hurry**. We solved the problem **in the end**, after a lot of work. Make sure you get home **in time** for dinner.
on	on time	at the right time	The plane left **on time**.

In time means 'early enough for something':
*I didn't arrive at the station **in time** for the six o'clock train, so I had to wait for the next one.*

On time means 'at the correct time':
*Last year 92 percent of South-East trains left **on time**.*

3 Other common phrases

	PHRASE	MEANING	EXAMPLE
by	by chance	you did not plan or expect it	We found this wonderful restaurant **by chance**.
	by mistake	you did not intend to do it	I sent that email **by mistake** – I didn't want you to read it.
in	in love	loving someone in a romantic way	My father says that he's still **in love** with my mother after twenty-five years!
	in public	where everyone can see / hear	I was very nervous the first time I spoke **in public**.
	in private	where other people can't see / hear	Can we discuss your work **in private**?
on	on fire	burning	The motorway was closed because a car was **on fire**.
	on purpose	deliberately	I didn't get wet **on purpose** – I fell in the water.
for	for sale	you can buy it	The house at the end of the road is **for sale**.
out of	out of order	not working	The lift is **out of order**. We'll have to use the stairs.

Practice

1 **Complete the sentences with prepositions. ◄))2.50 Listen and check.**

0 Which languages do you study ...*at*.... school in your country?

1 Can I talk to you .... private after the class?

2 It's dangerous to drive and talk on a mobile phone .... the same time.

3 I really like the handbag in the window. Is it .... sale?

4 The police found the money .... chance when they searched the apartment.

5 Ahmed travels to Switzerland every month .... business.

6 After nearly an hour, our bus arrived .... last!

2 `GRAMMAR IN USE` **Complete the story with the correct words and phrases from the box.**

> at first   at once   home   ~~in a hurry~~   in the end   in time   on fire

We had a terrible experience a few weeks ago. One evening, a friend of ours had dinner with us, and we drove him to the station after our meal. We were quite late for his train so we left the house (0) .*in a hurry*., and I forgot to turn off the cooker. When we got (1) .... from the station, the kitchen was (2) ....! We were shocked (3) .... but then we called the fire service. They arrived almost (4) ...., and put the fire out. We were lucky that they put the fire out (5) .... to save our kitchen – there wasn't much damage, so everything was OK (6) ....

3 **Write the sentences again. Replace the underlined words with a common phrase.**

0 I'm really sorry I took your coat – I didn't do it underlined{deliberately}.
   I'm really sorry I took your coat – I didn't do it on purpose.

1 The film seemed very boring in the beginning, but then it got better.

   ....

2 I'm going to be in Prague for work next week.

   ....

3 Please make sure that you arrive at the correct time for your appointment.

   ....

4 If you hear the bell, go to your class immediately.

   ....

5 The coffee machine isn't working again.

   ....

4 `GRAMMAR IN USE` **There are five more mistakes with prepositions in the conversation. Find and correct them. ◄))2.51 Listen and check.**

A Did you get tickets for Radiohead?

B Yes, I did. I had to phone the box office about ten times but I got through *in* ~~on~~ the end.

A That's great!

B I've got tickets for Friday 15th – I'll be on work that day, so I'll go straight from the office to Wembley Stadium.

A Well, I'm actually by holiday from work that day. I'll meet you to there.

B Can you meet me at 6.30? It starts at 8.00 and I want to be there by time – at least an hour before it starts.

A Yes, that's fine. I'll drive and park nearby, then I can drive you to home afterwards.

B Thanks. That's great.

Review MODULE 3

1 UNITS 18, 19 AND 20

Look at the map and read the instructions. Then:

- draw the way to the language school
- find the places A–K and write them below.

A *bus station* ....
B ....
C ....
D ....
E ....
F ....
G ....
H ....
I ....
J ....
K ....

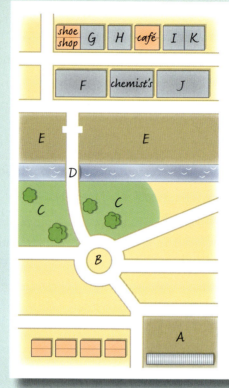

HOW TO FIND US
From the bus station, take the road to the roundabout. Go round the roundabout and along the path through the park to the river. Go across Brook Bridge to a car park. Go straight across the car park; you come out opposite a cinema. Take the road next to the cinema and go past the cinema on the right. Turn right and go past the shoe shop and the bookshop opposite the cinema. Go past the police station and an Italian café opposite the chemist's. Our language school is on your left, opposite the hospital and between the café and a clothes shop.

2 UNITS 21 AND 22 **Replace the underlined words in the conversation with the phrases A–F.**
🔊 **2.52** **Listen and check.**

ANDY When's your brother coming back from his trip round Europe?
JANE It's Monday now. He'll be here (0) <u>by the middle of the week</u>. ....*C*........
ANDY And how long is he going to stay with us?
JANE Well, (1) <u>until the weekend</u>, at least. Then he's going back to New York. ....
ANDY Is he going to see your parents while he's here?
JANE No, they're coming here to see him. They'll be here (2) <u>in three days</u>. ....
ANDY I see. And are they going to stay (3) <u>for three days</u>? ....
JANE Yes, but they'll leave (4) <u>after breakfast</u>. ....
ANDY You know I'm in a golf competition (5) <u>at the weekend</u>, don't you? ....
JANE Oh, Andy! You told me that wasn't until next weekend!

A on Thursday   C ~~on or before Wednesday~~   E on Saturday and Sunday
B in the morning   D from then to Saturday or Sunday   F until Sunday

3 UNITS 23 AND 24 **Choose the correct words in *italics*.**

0 Joe works *by / like /* (as) a builder in the college holidays.
1 I'm sorry I stepped on your foot. I didn't do it *by / on / with* purpose.
2 We can let you know the football results *by / with / on* text message.
3 What time did you get *at home / home / to home* last night?
4 Wait a minute. I can hold the door open *with / by / for* my foot.
5 This is a photo *by / from / of* my daughter when she was at college.
6 Swiss trains always arrive *in / on / at* time – they're never late.
7 Gosh! You really look *as / like / to* your older brother.
8 I can't stop and talk now – I'm *on / at / in* a hurry.

4 ALL UNITS **Complete the text with prepositions or – (no preposition).**

Last year we were (0) ......*on*........ holiday in Spain and we went to an amazing festival – the running of the bulls in Pamplona. The festival starts (1) .... 7 July and the bulls run every day (2) .... 14 July. The bulls run from outside the town centre, (3) .... the town's streets (4) .... the bullring, and people – often young men – can run (5) .... the bulls until they get (6) .... there. Lots of people watch the bulls run; you just stand (7) .... special fences. We stood (8) .... the museum, where there is a very good view, but we had to be there (9) .... 6.30 in the morning to get a place! The festival started hundreds of years ago, but it only became famous in the 1920s when it appeared in a book (10) .... Ernest Hemingway. It was great fun – very exciting but also quite scary!

5 ALL UNITS **Complete the word puzzle. Use the sentences 1–6 below to help you. Then answer 7.**

0 I got ... the bus at the wrong stop.
1 The cat's sleeping ... the bed.
2 Let's wait ... a few minutes.
3 The main door is locked – walk ... it and go in the next door.
4 We usually have coffee ... dinner.
5 My brother looks ... a famous film star!
6 My parents have a house ... the sea in Italy.
7 The phrase in the green squares is

....·

	7		
0	O	F	F
1			
2			
3			
4			
5			
6			

6 ALL UNITS **Complete the second sentence so it means the same as the first. Use one, two or three words.**

0 It's Tuesday today. The festival lasts until Friday.
   The festival finishes *in three days.*..........................·

1 We often drive to France.
   We often go to France ....·

2 Our office is on the floor above the dentist's.
   The dentist's is on the floor ....·

3 Hal writes books in his free time.
   Hal works .... in his free time.

4 The museum is always open on Saturday and Sunday.
   The museum is always open ....·

5 Lucas sits behind Magda in class.
   Magda sits .... Lucas in class.

6 They won't let us in if we arrive after the show has started.
   We have to arrive .... for the start of the show.

Test MODULE 3

Prepositions

Choose the correct answer, A, B or C.

1 I've got an appointment .... the doctor's in the morning.
  A in B at C by
➤ Unit 18

2 Arnold Schwarzenegger was born .... Austria.
  A in B at C from
➤ Unit 18

3 Gary lives .... the airport. It takes about 20 minutes to get there.
  A beside B near C next to
➤ Unit 18

4 My house is .... the red house and the grey one.
  A in B by C between
➤ Unit 19

5 Look at this picture. Can you see the building .... the back?
  A in B at C on
➤ Unit 19

6 You can have a lovely walk .... the path beside the river.
  A under B past C along
➤ Unit 20

7 It takes about three hours to walk .... the lake.
  A round B across C through
➤ Unit 20

8 Hurry up and get .... the car! We want to leave now.
  A on B onto C into
➤ Unit 20

9 Is the supermarket open .... Sunday morning?
  A on B in C at
➤ Unit 21

10 There was a terrible crash on the motorway .... week.
  A last B in last C on last
➤ Unit 21

11 There's a great fitness class .... lunchtime here.
  A in B on C at
➤ Unit 21

12 Please leave the building quietly .... the concert.
  A on B after C before
➤ Unit 22

13 The bus will leave at 9.00 a.m. Please be at the bus station .... 8.45.
  A after B by C during
➤ Unit 22

14 That photo is .... Rachel. She's a great photographer.
  A from B of C by
➤ Unit 23

15 I've marked the interesting points in the article .... a red pen.
  A with B by C of
➤ Unit 23

16 Sally's very beautiful – she's .... a princess.
  A as B for C like
➤ Unit 23

17 Did you do anything interesting .... holiday?
  A on B for C by
➤ Unit 24

18 Is the bus coming .... to pick up the tourists?
  A here B to here C at here
➤ Unit 24

19 Don't try to read .... the same time as watching TV.
  A with B by C at
➤ Unit 24

20 We discovered this hotel .... chance – we intended to stay at a different one.
  A on B with C by
➤ Unit 24

Adjectives and adverbs

Before you start

1 Read the information on the website. Look at the <mark>highlighted</mark> grammar examples.

> ◄ ► ▼ | www.myfriends.net | ▼
>
> **myfriends.net**
>
> Home Browse Find people Forums Music Video More▼ Log in Sign up
>
> **my hobbies and interests**
> I love sport, especially cycling. On Saturdays I sometimes go to the market to buy new sports clothes – it's <mark>cheaper</mark> than the shops in town – those fashionable shops are <mark>too expensive</mark> for me! On Sundays I go cycling with my friends. I think it's a <mark>brilliant hobby</mark>. It's a good way to get healthy and it is<mark>n't as expensive as</mark> going to a gym. There's some beautiful countryside outside my town and we <mark>usually go</mark> there. There are a lot of hills and it's <mark>really exciting</mark> when you cycle down them! My friend Zak is <mark>younger than me,</mark> but he cycles <mark>well</mark>. In fact he's <mark>the fastest</mark> cyclist in our group.

2 Now read the sentences. Choose the correct words in *italics*.
The <mark>highlighted</mark> grammar examples will help you.

1 I love diving; I think it's a *sport fantastic / fantastic sport*.	➤ Unit 25
2 Life under the sea is very *interesting / interested*.	➤ Unit 26
3 You have to swim *good / well* to be a successful diver.	➤ Unit 27
4 I *swim often / often swim* when I'm on holiday.	➤ Unit 28
5 My sister likes diving. She's only fourteen, so I'm older than *her / she*.	➤ Unit 29
6 Diving in the sea is *more good / better* than diving in a swimming pool.	➤ Unit 30
7 The North Sea is the *most cold / coldest* place in England to swim.	➤ Unit 31
8 The Mediterranean isn't as *cold / colder* as the North Sea.	➤ Unit 32
9 My grandfather was a good diver but now he's *too much old / too old* to dive.	➤ Unit 33
10 I like diving because it's *really / a lot* exciting.	➤ Unit 34

3 Check your answers below. Then go to the unit for more information and practice.

> 1 fantastic sport 2 interesting 3 well 4 often swim
> 5 her 6 better 7 coldest 8 cold 9 too old 10 really

25 Types of adjective

That green silk dress looks nice.

Yes, it's beautiful.

1 Form

Adjectives describe people, things and places. There are many different types of adjectives, for example:

OPINION	SHAPE	COLOUR	NATIONALITY
nice beautiful difficult fantastic	square long short	red yellow black blue	Russian British French

 Adjectives do not have a plural form:
✗ ~~two blues dresses~~   ✓ one **blue** dress, two **blue** dresses

Forming adjectives from nouns/verbs ➤ Unit 106.1

2 Before nouns

 Adjectives always come before a noun:
✗ ~~a dress blue~~   ✓ a **blue** dress

 We can put two or more adjectives before a noun. We don't usually use *and* between the adjectives:
✗ ~~a beautiful and red dress~~   ✓ a **beautiful red** dress

We put opinion adjectives (e.g. *beautiful, fantastic, friendly*) BEFORE other adjectives:
a **fantastic** red dress, a **friendly** French student, a **beautiful** old painting

We put nationality adjectives (e.g. *Spanish, Russian*) AFTER most other adjectives:
an expensive **Italian** car, a young **Russian** student, a blue **Chinese** plate

We always put material words (e.g. *cotton, silk*) next to the noun:
a Chinese **silk** dress, some old **cotton** sheets, a red **leather** handbag

3 After verbs

We can use adjectives after the verb *be*:
That dress **is beautiful**. (= It is a beautiful dress.)

We can also use adjectives after verbs like *appear, feel, look, taste* and *seem*:
I **feel happy** today! That dress **looks beautiful**. Her new neighbours **seem nice**.

We use *and* between two adjectives after a verb:
That maths exam was **long and difficult**.

Practice

1 Write adjectives from the box under the pictures. Use two adjectives for each description.

Chinese cotton friendly fur ~~old~~ red Russian ~~wooden~~

0 an *old wooden* chair   1 a .... shirt   2 a .... hat   3 a .... student

2 Use the words below to write sentences. ◀))2.53 Listen and check.

0 long boring book / (be) *This book is long and boring.*...

1 beautiful suit / (look) ....

2 delicious salad / (taste) ....

3 interesting film / (look) ....

4 soft pullover / (feel) ....

5 new exciting project / (be) ....

6 small dark apartment / (seem) ....

3 **GRAMMAR IN USE** Complete the text with the words in brackets (). ◀))2.54 Listen and check.

In a recent questionnaire 60% of people said shopping was their

(0) ...*favourite hobby*... (hobby, favourite). They preferred it to going to

restaurants, playing sport or visiting friends. One reason may be the

(1) .... (huge, number) of shopping centres which are now open.

With (2) .... (parking, free) and long opening hours, shopping

at these places (3) .... (easy, seems, enjoyable, and).

But 20% of people say they buy things on the Internet at least once a month.

The most popular things are (4) .... (electronic, products) such

as DVD players and digital TVs. The Internet never closes, so shopping this way

(5) .... (convenient, is) for people who work long hours.

4 **GRAMMAR IN USE** There are six more mistakes in the advertisement. Find and correct them.

Cheap prices

Carleon Discount Stores
summer sale

PRICES CHEAP!

Buy some new clothes and you will fantastic look!

• black and wool suits £20!   • cotton white T-shirts £1.50!
• leather Italian shoes £25!   • Americans jeans £10!

OPEN FROM 9 A.M. – 10 P.M. SATURDAY AND SUNDAY.

And parking at our store free is!

26 Adjectives with *-ed* and *-ing*

Carlos and his grandfather are very **excited**.
They are watching an **exciting** football
match on TV. They are **pleased**
their team is winning.

1 Form

-ed (OUR FEELINGS)	*-ing* (THE THING THAT CAUSES OUR FEELINGS)
We're **excited**.	The film is **exciting**. It's an **exciting** film.
I'm **bored**.	The test is **boring**. It's a **boring** test.

2 *-ed* adjectives

We often use adjectives that end in *-ed* to say how people or animals feel:
*Carlos and his grandfather are very **excited**.*
*There's nothing to do here – we're **bored**.*
***Tired** children often behave badly.*

3 *-ing* adjectives

We use adjectives that end in *-ing* to describe something that causes our feelings:
*They are watching an **exciting** football match on TV.* (the football match excites them)
*The end of the film was very **surprising**.* (the end of the film surprised me)
*We've had a very **tiring** day.* (the day made us tired)

We often use *-ing* adjectives to ask about something or to give an opinion:
*Do you think English grammar is **interesting**?*
*Amanda's sister is really **boring**.*

⚠ We don't use *-ing* adjectives to talk about how we feel:
✗ *I'm very interesting in sport.*
✓ *I'm very **interested** in sport.*

 Pronunciation ➤ 1.06

Practice

1 `GRAMMAR IN USE` **Choose the correct words in** *italics*. ◀)) **2.55 Listen and check.**

ANNA   How was the football match?

PEDRO   Fantastic. It was really (0) *excited* /(*exciting.*) We won!

ANNA   Really?

PEDRO   You seem (1) *surprised / surprising*!

ANNA   Well, yes. I am a bit. Anyway, I'm (2) *pleased / pleasing* you won.

PEDRO   What about you? How was your day?

ANNA   Oh, it was (3) *bored / boring*. I spent all day working on the new website.

PEDRO   But yesterday you said it was (4) *interested / interesting*!

ANNA   I know. But now I feel (5) *bored / boring* with it.

PEDRO   Well, I'm quite (6) *tired / tiring* now, I don't feel like cooking.
Shall we order a pizza or something? And watch *Dracula* on TV?

ANNA   Oh, no! I feel (7) *frightening / frightened* when I watch that kind of film.

2 **Write adjectives from the box under the pictures.**

excited / exciting   frightened / frightening   pleased / pleasing   surprised / surprising   ~~tired~~ / tiring

0 He feels ......*tired*.......

1 They are ....·

2 The letter has some
.... news.

3 It was a very ....
film.

4 The race was
...................·

5 She's ....·

3 `GRAMMAR IN USE` **There are three more mistakes in the email. Find and correct them.**
◀)) **2.56 Listen and check.**

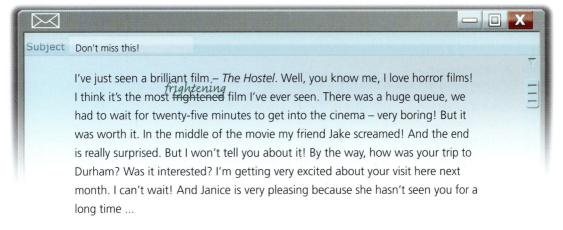

Subject   Don't miss this!

I've just seen a brilliant film – *The Hostel*. Well, you know me, I love horror films!
I think it's the most ~~frightened~~ *frightening* film I've ever seen. There was a huge queue, we
had to wait for twenty-five minutes to get into the cinema – very boring! But it
was worth it. In the middle of the movie my friend Jake screamed! And the end
is really surprised. But I won't tell you about it! By the way, how was your trip to
Durham? Was it interested? I'm getting very excited about your visit here next
month. I can't wait! And Janice is very pleasing because she hasn't seen you for a
long time ...

27 Types of adverb

Harry Royston repairs beautiful old watches in **his free time**. He works **slowly** and **carefully** because the watches are valuable.

1 Form

Adverbs describe how, when or where someone does something. There are many different types of adverbs, eg:

manner (how)	quickly slowly carefully well	Harry works **slowly** and **carefully**.
frequency (how often)	often sometimes never	Teresa **never** works.
time (when)	today soon in his free time last week yesterday	Matthew didn't work **yesterday**.
place (where)	here upstairs in	Linda works **in a bank**.
direction (which way)	left right straight on	Turn **right** at the end of the street.

Adverbs of degree ➤ Unit 34

Most adverbs of manner add *-ly* to the adjective:
careful → *careful**ly**, slow* → *slow**ly**, perfect* → *perfect**ly**, bad* → *bad**ly***

But adjectives ending in *-y*, change *y* to *i* and add *-ly*:
easy → *eas**ily**, happy* → *happ**ily***

 The words *friendly*, *lovely*, *silly* and *lonely* end in *-ly* but they are adjectives, not adverbs. We can't make them into adverbs, so we say '*in a … way*':
✗ *She smiled at me friendly.*
✓ *She smiled at me **in a friendly way***.

2 Irregular adverbs

Fast, *hard*, *late* and *early* are adverbs and adjectives. We don't add *-ly* to them:
*Sven owns a **fast** car.* (*fast* = adjective)

 ✗ *He drives fastly.*
✓ *He drives **fast**.* (*fast* = adverb)

 Good is an adjective. The adverb for *good* is *well*:
✗ *She plays tennis good.*
✓ *She **plays** tennis **well**.*

Practice

1 Complete the sentences. Use the correct words and phrases from the box. ◀)**2.57** Listen and check.

> always   at the end   carefully   early   fast   in a friendly way
> in the bedroom   ~~last week~~   never   right   ~~slowly~~   upstairs

0 My grandmother fell over ....*last week*.......... . She hurt her leg so now she can only
   walk ....*slowly*............ .

1 I always get up .... so I am .... late for work.

2 Remember to answer the questions .... and stop writing
   .... of the test.

3 I went .... with the electrician and we looked at the broken
   light ....

4 Our teacher is nice; she .... talks to us ....

5 Go to the end of the road and turn .... at the traffic lights. If you walk
   ...., you'll get there in about five minutes.

2 GRAMMAR IN USE Complete the story using a form of the words in brackets ().
Be careful, one of the words you need is not an adverb.

When he was a small boy, Zack loved cars. So, as soon as he was seventeen, he began
taking driving lessons. He learned (0) ...*quickly*.... (quick) and became a
(1) .... (good) driver. After ten lessons he took his driving test. During the test
he drove (2) .... (perfect) and he passed it (3) .... (easy). Zack's parents
were very pleased and decided to buy him a car. Zack always drove (4) .... (good)
and he usually drove (5) .... (slow). But Zack had a problem. He always woke up
(6) .... (late) in the mornings. He hated being late for college. Now he had a car,
Zack was sure he was (7) .... (never) going to be late for college again. But, of
course, the very first day he had his new car Zack was late again. So he got up
(8) .... (quick), rushed to his car and drove to college very (9) .... (fast).
But there was a police car on the road and the police officer stopped him for driving
(10) .... (bad). As a result, he lost his driving licence just one week after passing
his test!

3 Change the adjectives to adverbs and write the sentences again. ◀)**2.58** Listen and check.

0 Clare is a slow driver *Clare drives slowly.*..

1 Michael is a hard worker. ....

2 My parents are frequent travellers. ....

3 Denise is a fast runner. ....

4 Antonio is a skilful painter. ....

5 My aunt is a quiet speaker. ....

6 Emelda and Maureen are brilliant cooks. ....

4 Complete the sentences so they are true for you.

0 I ....*never drive*.... fast.   2 I .... badly.   4 I can .... easily.

1 I .... well.   3 I .... late.

28 Adverbs and word order

Chrissie **usually** watches football **on Saturdays**. She shouts **loudly** when her team plays **well**.

1 After the verb

We usually put adverbs of manner (e.g. *well, badly, quickly, slowly, quietly, loudly, easily, happily, carefully, perfectly*) after the verb:
*Chrissie **shouts loudly** when her team **plays well**.*

If there is an object after the verb, we put the adverb after the object:

SUBJECT	VERB	OBJECT	ADVERB
He	*plays*		*well.*
He	*plays*	*football*	*well.*

2 Before the verb

We use adverbs of frequency to say how often we do something:

100%			HOW OFTEN				0%
always	*usually*	*often*	*sometimes*	*not often*	*hardly ever*	*rarely*	*never*

We put these adverbs BEFORE present simple and past simple verbs:
*I **never eat** toast for breakfast. She **hardly ever plays** tennis. We **always walked** to school.*

But we put them AFTER:

- the verb *be*:
  *She **is always** late for work. We **are often** very busy.*
- an auxiliary verb or modal verb (e.g. *have, will, can* or *must*):
  *I **have never** watched a football match. You **can usually** get tickets on the Internet.*

3 At the end of the sentence

We usually put adverbs of place (e.g. *here, there, at the café*) and time (e.g. *yesterday, on Saturday, immediately, last week, every day, twice a month*) at the end of the sentence:
*Do you have your lunch **at the café**? We go to the cinema **twice a month**.*
*Chrissie watches football **on Saturdays**.*

Word order with more than one adverb ➤ Unit 72.3

Practice

1 GRAMMAR IN USE Choose the correct words in *italics* in the text. ◀)) 2.59 Listen and check.

In my free time I like playing sports and using the Internet. I (0) *play often /* (often play)
tennis at the weekend and I (1) *sometimes play / play sometimes* football on Tuesday
evenings. My team (2) *wins never / never wins* and I don't (3) *play well / well play*,
but I enjoy it very much. I think I use the Internet every day – my computer
(4) *is always / always is* on! I like websites like YouTube and Facebook. I can
(5) *type quickly / quickly type* so it is easy for me to send lots of emails to my friends.
I also like music. My Internet connection is really fast so I can download
(6) *easily songs / songs easily*. Then I can listen to them on my iPod.

2 Look at the information about watching TV. Complete the sentences below.

	HOW OFTEN DO YOU WATCH TV?				WHEN?	
	sometimes	every day	once a week	never	in the evenings	at the weekends
Cilla			✓			
David				✓		
Marion		✓				
Eduardo			✓			
Monty	✓					
Caroline						✓
Max					✓	

0 Cilla and Eduardo *watch TV once a week* .

1 David.. .

2 Marion.. .

3 Monty ....

4 Caroline ....

5 Max ....

3 Put the adverbs in brackets () in the correct position in each sentence.
◀)) 2.60 Listen and check.

0 I *often* watch TV in the evenings. (often)

1 Does your best friend speak Spanish?
   (perfectly)

2 We go to the beach in the summer. (usually)

3 Hilary is late. (always)

4 Where do you go? (at the weekends)

5 When I play football I feel really happy. (well)

6 I have been to Australia. (never)

7 She was frightened so she opened
   the door. (slowly)

8 My family has lived on a farm. (always)

9 I talk when I'm excited. (loudly)

10 You should go to the dentist.
    (every six months)

4 Write true sentences about the hobbies in brackets (). Use an adverb in each sentence.

0 I .... *never play football* .... (play football)

1 I .... (sing songs I like)

2 I .... (read magazines)

3 I .... (play computer games)

4 I .... (write stories)

5 I .... (go to the cinema)

6 I .... (cook meals for friends)

29 Comparative adjectives (1)

> I love playing computer games. Modern machines are **smaller than** old ones and the games are **more exciting**.

1 Form

To make comparative adjectives:

ADJECTIVE	→	COMPARATIVE ADJECTIVE
most short adjectives (1 syllable)	add -er	*small → smaller, young → younger, short → shorter, new → newer*
adjectives that end in -e	add -r	*late → later, nice → nicer, wide → wider*
adjectives that end in vowel + consonant, e.g. -ig, -at, -ot, -in	add another consonant + -er	*big → bigger, fat → fatter, hot → hotter, thin → thinner*
adjectives that end in -y	change y to i and add -er	*dry → drier, easy → easier, friendly → friendlier*

For most adjectives with two syllables we use *more* + adjective:
*This new computer is **more useful** than my old one.*
*My mobile is **more modern** than Emily's.*

For adjectives with three or four syllables we always use *more* + adjective:
*Modern computer games are **more exciting**. Gold is **more expensive** than silver.*

 We don't add -er to these adjectives.
✗ *Mobile phones are usefuller than cameras.* ✓ *Mobile phones are **more useful** than cameras.*

 We don't use *more* with an adjective that is already comparative:
✗ *Charlotte is more taller than Susie.* ✓ *Charlotte is **taller** than Susie.*

🔊 Pronunciation ➤ 1.07

2 Use

We use comparative adjectives when we compare two people/things.

 We usually use *than* after comparative adjectives:
✓ *Modern machines are **smaller than** old ones.*
✗ *Modern machines are smaller old ones.* ✗ *Modern machines are smaller of old ones.*

 We use me, her, etc., not *I*, *she*, etc. after *than*:
Maria is taller than Anna. ✗ *Maria is taller than she.*
 ✓ *Maria is taller than **her**.*

But we can use *I*, *he*, *she*, etc. if we put *am/is/are* after the subject pronoun:
*Maria is taller than **she is**.*

Practice

1 **Use the information to complete the sentences.**
Use the comparative form of an adjective from the box.

0	AVERAGE TEMPERATURE IN JULY London 17°C Madrid 25°C

1	**hotels4you.com** Cost of a one night stay in a double room with shower: THE REGAL HOTEL $350.00 THE PARK HOTEL $85.00

2	In a recent survey British people chose their favourite drink – 56% voted for coffee and 44% voted for tea.

3	**Airport to central London** Heathrow 24km Gatwick 45km

4	**LENGTH OF CAR** Toyota Auris 4.22m Toyota Prius 4.45m

5	**FANTASTIC PRICES FOR PAINTINGS!** 'Sunflowers' by Van Gogh sold for $40 million and 'Nympheas' by Monet sold for $37 million.

near   expensive   ~~warm~~   valuable   long   popular

0 Madrid *is warmer than London* ....

1 The Regal Hotel ....

2 In the UK, coffee ....

3 Heathrow Airport .... central London .... Gatwick Airport.

4 The Toyota Prius ....

5 *Sunflowers* by Van Gogh ....

2 **Choose the correct words in *italics*.** ◀)) **2.61** **Listen and check.**

0 My brother is taller than (I am) / me am.
1 I'm eighteen but my best friend is younger than *me / I* – she's seventeen.
2 Do you like Lucy? I think Mariela is nicer than *she / her*.
3 I don't like horror films; I think action films are more interesting than *them / they*.
4 Our neighbours are richer than *us / we*.
5 My uncle is forty-five but my aunt is older than *he is / him is*. She's forty-seven.

3 **Write the sentences again so they are true. Use a different comparative adjective.**
◀)) **2.62** **Listen and check.**

0 It's warmer in London than Madrid.
   It's colder in London than Madrid. ....

1 The mobile phone is a newer invention than the iPod.
   ....

2 A car is faster than a jet plane.
   ....

3 Five-star hotels are cheaper than four-star hotels.
   ....

4 The Pacific Ocean is smaller than the Atlantic Ocean.
   ....

5 It's wetter in the summer than the winter.
   ....

30 Comparative adjectives (2)

Janie loves shopping. But she doesn't go to shops, she uses the Internet.
She thinks the service is **better** and the prices are **cheaper**.

1 Comparatives without *than*

We can use comparative adjectives without *than* when it is clear what or who we are
talking about:
*The first exam was easy but the second was **more difficult**.* (more difficult than the first exam)
*She thinks the service is **better** and the prices are **cheaper**.* (better and cheaper than shops)
*Don't take the car. It's **quicker** to go by train.*
*I'm tall but my brother's **taller**.*

2 Irregular adjectives

Some comparative adjectives are irregular:

adjective	*bad*	*good*	*far*	*well* (= healthy)
comparative adjective	*worse*	*better*	*further/farther*	*better*

*My exam results are **worse** than yours.*
*The Chinese restaurant is nice, but I think the food is **better** in the Italian one.*
*The flight to Seattle is longer because it's **further**.*
*Jenny is **better** than she was before the operation.* (healthier)

3 *more* and *less*

The opposite of *more* is *less*. We can use *less* with adjectives with two or more syllables:
*Gold is **more expensive** than silver.* (= Silver is **less expensive** than gold.)
*Books are **less exciting** than films.*

 We don't use *less* with adjectives with only one syllable (e.g. *old, tall, nice, young*):
✗ ~~My mother is less old than my father.~~
✓ *My mother is **younger** than my father.*

We can also use *not as* + adjective + *as* (e.g. *not as old as*) (➤ Unit 32.1).

 We don't use *more* or *less* with an adjective that is already a comparative adjective:
✗ ~~People in Argentina are more friendlier than people here.~~
✓ *People in Argentina are **friendlier** than people here.*

 We don't use *more* with irregular adjectives:
✗ ~~I think television is more good than radio.~~
✓ *I think television is **better** than radio.*

Practice

1 GRAMMAR IN USE Complete the conversation with the correct words and phrases from the box. ◀)2.63 Listen and check.

~~better~~ easier further more expensive nicer worse

A Where shall we eat tonight? The Indian restaurant?
B No, I think the Chinese place is (0) .... *better* ....
A I'm not sure. It's (1) .... and I haven't got much money.
B Well, we can try the Italian place. It isn't expensive, and it's very nice.
A Yes, I know it's nice, but the Indian restaurant is (2) ....
B But it's not very close to us. It's (3) .... than the Italian restaurant – on the other side of town. What about the burger place near the library?
A Oh, no. That place is terrible. It's (4) .... than the others in every way!
B It's really difficult to decide! I know – let's stay at home and phone for a pizza.
A Great. That's (5) .... than going out. We can eat in front of the TV and watch a DVD.

2 GRAMMAR IN USE Choose the correct words in *italics* in the email.

Subject Optron Computers

Dear Mr Danby
Thank you for your email asking for information on our two new laptop computers, the Optron X1 and the Optron X23.
The X23 is £1,350, so it is (0) *expensiver* / (more expensive) than the Optron X1, but it is (1) *powerfuller / more powerful* – it is (2) *faster / more fast* and it has a (3) *larger / more large* memory. I know that you want to carry the laptop with you when you travel so a light machine is (4) *more good / better* than a heavy one. The X1 is less (5) *heavy / heavier* than the X23, in fact it only weighs two kilos. You asked about the size of the screen. The X23's screen is (6) *biger / bigger* so it will give a (7) *better / gooder* picture if you want to play computer games, and the games will be (8) *excitinger / more exciting*. The X1 is less (9) *expensive / expensiver*, but I think the X23 is (10) *more good / better* value for money.

3 Find the grammar mistakes in each sentence and correct them. ◀)2.64 Listen and check.

0 New York is bigger ~~of~~ Rome. ......*than*......
1 The River Nile is more long than the River Thames. ....
2 Meat is less healthier than vegetables. ....
3 Which is more worse – cold weather or rainy weather? ....
4 Leather shoes are more good than plastic shoes. ....
5 It's more warmer in Spain than in England. ....
6 Life in the countryside is less excitinger than life in the city. ....
7 People say TV programmes are badder than they used to be. ....
8 I think Sally is more nicer than her husband. ....
9 Which is more far from London – Moscow or New York? ....
10 Harry took some medicine so he feels weller now. ....

31 Superlative adjectives

Kingda Ka
USA
height: 139 metres
speed: 206 kph

Eejanaika
Japan
height: 79 metres
speed: 126 kph

Silver Star
Germany
height: 73 metres
speed: 130 kph

Lots of people enjoy going on roller coasters. Kingda Ka is **the highest** and **the fastest**. But many people think Eejanaika is **the most exciting** roller coaster in the world.

1 Form

To make superlative adjectives:

ADJECTIVE	→	SUPERLATIVE ADJECTIVE
most short adjectives (1 syllable)	add -est	*small → smallest, young → youngest, high → highest, fast → fastest*
adjectives that end in -e	add -st	*late → latest, nice → nicest, wide → widest*
adjectives that end in vowel + consonant, e.g. -ig, -at, -ot, -in	add another consonant + -est	*big → biggest, fat → fattest, hot → hottest, thin → thinnest*
adjectives that end in -y	change y to i and add -est	*dry → driest, happy → happiest, early → earliest*

Spelling rules ➤ page 317

 Pronunciation ➤ 1.08

For most adjectives with two or more syllables (e.g. *useful, difficult, expensive*) we use *the most* + adjective:
*Eejanaika is **the most exciting** roller coaster. My mobile phone is **the most useful** thing I own.*

The opposite of *the most* is *the least*. We usually use *the least* with adjectives with two or more syllables: *Excuse me. Which is **the least expensive** phone you sell?*

 These adjectives have irregular superlative forms:
bad → worst, good → best, far → farthest/furthest
✗ *He's the most good student in the class.* ✓ *He's **the best** student in the class.*

2 Use

We use superlative adjectives when we compare one person/thing with several others.

 We use *the* before superlative adjectives:
✗ *Kingda Ka is fastest roller coaster.* ✓ *Kingda Ka is **the fastest** roller coaster.*

 After superlative adjectives we use *in* before the names of places and groups:
✗ *Eejanaika is the most exciting roller coaster of the world.*
✓ *Eejanaika is the most exciting roller coaster **in the world**.*

We can also use *my/your/his,* etc. before superlative adjectives:
*Jenny is **my oldest** friend. What is **your happiest** memory?*

We often use superlative adjectives + *I've ever …, you've ever …,* etc. to talk about our experiences:
*That was **the best** book **I've ever read**. What's **the most expensive** thing **you've ever bought**?*

4

Practice

1 Write the missing words in the box. Then complete the sentences below. Use some of the words from the box. 🔊 2.65 Listen and check.

adjective	fast	friendly	happy		late	dry		bad	far
superlative	*fastest*			*nicest*			*best*		

Complete these sentences.

0 That was the ....*worst*.... meal I've ever eaten. It was disgusting!
1 July is usually the .... month in my country. It never rains then.
2 Milo is the .... student in my class. He talks to everybody.
3 Neptune is the .... planet from the sun.
4 The .... time you can arrive is six o'clock. We close the doors after that.

2 **GRAMMAR IN USE** Read the information about three British castles. Complete the questions with a superlative form of the adjectives in brackets (). Then answer the questions.

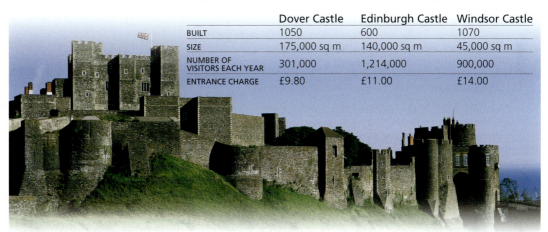

	Dover Castle	Edinburgh Castle	Windsor Castle
BUILT	1050	600	1070
SIZE	175,000 sq m	140,000 sq m	45,000 sq m
NUMBER OF VISITORS EACH YEAR	301,000	1,214,000	900,000
ENTRANCE CHARGE	£9.80	£11.00	£14.00

0 Which is .*the most expensive*. (expensive) castle to visit?   ...*Windsor Castle*...
1 Which is .... (old) castle?   ....
2 Which castle is .... (popular)?   ....
3 Which castle is .... (small)?   ....
4 Which castle is .... (big)?   ....
5 Which castle has .... (low) entrance charge?   ....

3 **GRAMMAR IN USE** Choose the correct words in *italics* in the conversation. 🔊 2.66 Listen and check.

LOUIS So, Carol. Did you enjoy your holiday?
CAROL Yes. It was the (0) *better* / *best* holiday I've ever had!
LOUIS Really? What was the (1) *most good* / *best* part?
CAROL Well, the hotel was fantastic, but the coast was really beautiful.
LOUIS And what was the (2) *most beautiful* / *beautifulest* place?
CAROL Definitely the beach. It was the (3) *most warm* / *warmest* water I've ever swum in. And there were some good restaurants in the town. The Thai restaurant was (4) *nicest* / *the nicest* one, although it was the (5) *furthest* / *most far* from the hotel.
LOUIS Was that the best one (6) *in* / *of* the town?
CAROL Yes, and it was the (7) *less* / *least* expensive one there! The Italian restaurant was the (8) *most* / *more* expensive one, but it wasn't very nice.

32 *not as ... as, the same (... as)*

1 *not as* + adjective + *as*

We use *not as … as* to say that one thing is less difficult, interesting, expensive, etc. than another thing:

The blue jeans are £75. The white jeans are £40.	The blue jeans are**n't as cheap as** the white jeans. The white jeans are**n't as expensive as** the blue jeans.

Compare these examples. They have the same meaning:
*Paris is**n't as big as** London. = London **is bigger than** Paris.*
*Spanish is**n't as difficult as** Arabic. = Arabic **is more difficult than** Spanish.*

bigger, smaller, more difficult, less easy, etc. ➤ Units 29 and 30

2 *the same* + noun (+ *as*)

We use *the same … as* to compare two things that are equal:
*The black jeans are **the same price as** the blue ones.*
*My mobile phone is **the same type as** yours.*

 We use nouns after *the same (… as)*, not adjectives:
✗ ~~The jeans are the same expensive.~~
✓ *The jeans are **the same price**.*

We can also say *the same as + mine, yours, this one, that one*, etc:
*Jane's car is **the same as mine**. We both have Toyotas.*
*This bicycle is exactly **the same as that one**.*

3 *as* + adverb + *as*

We can also use *not as* + adverb + *as*:
*I don't wear jeans **as often as** Ben.*
*Danny doesn't play **as well as** Boris.*

🔊 Pronunciation ➤ 1.09

Practice

1 Do sentences A and B have the same (S) or different (D) meanings? Write S or D.

0 A My sister isn't as tall as me.   B I'm taller than my sister.   *S*
1 A I'm twenty-one. My sister is eighteen.   B I'm not as old as my sister.   ....
2 A The price of tea and coffee is the same.   B Tea is not as expensive as coffee.   ....
3 A I visit my grandfather once a month and I visit my cousins twice a month.   B I don't visit my grandfather as often as I visit my cousins.   ....
4 A American football isn't as popular as soccer.   B Soccer is less popular than American football.   ....

2 **GRAMMAR IN USE** Read the information. Then write sentences comparing the two apartments. Use *not as … as* or *the same* (*… as*) and the words in brackets (). Write your own opinions for sentences 5 and 6. **2.67** Listen and check.

Turley Street

Salford Road

location	TURLEY STREET	SALFORD ROAD
distance from bus stop	100 metres	400 metres
price	£350 per month	£500 per month
size	100 sq m	100 sq m
distance from centre	6 km	2 km
age of building	2002	1920

0 (near the bus stop) *Salford Road isn't as near the bus stop as Turley Street.*
1 (expensive) ....
2 (size) ....
3 (far from the centre) ....
4 (new) ....
5 (beautiful) *I think* ....
6 (comfortable) *I think* ....

3 **GRAMMAR IN USE** The words in the box are missing from the conversation. Put them in the correct positions. **2.68** Listen and check.

SILVIE What do you think of these jeans?
CLAUDE They aren't as nice *as* the ones you bought last winter.

     as   the   as   same   as

SILVIE Really? I think they're exactly same as those.
CLAUDE No. They're a much darker colour.
SILVIE Yes, perhaps you're right.
CLAUDE Did they cost the as the other pair?
SILVIE No. They weren't expensive as those. I bought them in the sale.
CLAUDE Do they have any Calvin Klein jeans in the sale?
SILVIE No, but they have some that are nearly the same Calvin Klein jeans – they look like them but they're cheaper.
CLAUDE You mean they're copies. I always think they look completely different from the real ones!

33 *too, enough*

1 too

We use *too* + adjective if something is bigger or more than we want or like.
We use *too* + adverb if something is faster, later, etc. than is good or safe.

too + ADJECTIVE	*too* + ADVERB
*This jacket's **too big**.* (bigger than I want) *£75 is **too expensive**!* (more expensive than I want)	*You'll be sick if you eat **too quickly**.* (faster than is good or safe) *I got up **too late** and missed the bus.*

too much, too many ➤ Unit 9.2

Compare *too* and *very*:
*It's **very hot** today.* (This is a fact.)
*It's **too hot** today.* (It's hotter than I want or like.)

2 (not) enough

If something is *enough*, it is the correct size, amount, speed, etc. for what we want:

ADJECTIVE + *enough*	ADVERB + *enough*
*This jacket isn't **big enough**.* (smaller than I want) *Are these jeans **long enough**?* *He can learn to drive now. He's **old enough**.*	*I can't understand the teacher.* *She doesn't speak **slowly enough**.* (= She speaks too quickly.)

 ✗ *Our car isn't enough big for six people.*
✓ *Our car isn't **big enough** for six people.*

We can also use (*not*) *enough* before a plural or uncountable noun:
*Do we have **enough plates** for fifteen people?*
*Can you pay for this? I don't have **enough money**.*

3 too/not enough to do something

We use *too/not enough to do something* to say why something isn't possible:

	too + ADJECTIVE	*not* + ADJECTIVE + *enough*
My sister can't vote because she's too young.	*My sister's **too young** to vote.*	*My sister isn't **old enough** to vote.*

Practice

1 Match the sentences. 🔊2.69 Listen and check.

0 This mobile phone is too old. ⟶
1 That table is too small.
2 The air conditioning is too warm.
3 Your hair is too long.
4 My suitcase is too heavy.
5 Our car is too slow.

A It isn't big enough.
B It isn't cold enough.
C It isn't fast enough.
D It isn't light enough.
⟶ E It isn't new enough.
F It isn't short enough.

2 GRAMMAR IN USE Complete the advertisement with *too* or *enough*.

Supersizestores.com
Visit our website now.

Do you find that the clothes in the stores are always (0) ....*too*.... small for you?
Perhaps the waist is (1) .... tight or the legs aren't long (2) ....
Of course, there are shops that sell larger sizes, but people often find their designs aren't
fashionable (3) .... They don't change their designs often (4) .... so
there isn't (5) .... choice. And for many people their clothes are much
(6) .... expensive. Well, now your problems are over!

At **Supersizestores.com** we offer a range of fashionable clothes in extra large and extra
tall sizes. Our range is wide (7) .... to satisfy even the most fashionable customer!

3 Esther wants to buy a small dark blue jumper. She has €35 to spend.
Write sentences with *too* or *enough*, and use the adjectives in brackets ().

0 A ......*is too big*........ (big)
1 A .... (small)
2 B .... (light)
3 B .... (dark)
4 C .... (expensive)
5 C .... (cheap)

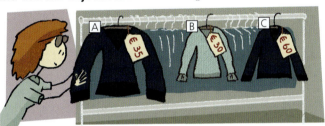

4 Complete the second sentence so it means the same as the first.
Use *too* or *enough* and the words in brackets (). Use short forms. 🔊2.70 Listen and check.

0 I don't want to go in the garden because it's cold. (cold)
   It *'s too cold to go in the garden* ....
1 We can't go into the theatre because the play has already started. (late)
   It ....
2 The baby can't eat adult food because she is very young. (young)
   She ....
3 He can't rent a car because he is only seventeen. (old)
   He ....
4 I can't carry this bag because it's extremely heavy. (heavy)
   This bag ....
5 I can't use this bed because it's uncomfortable. (comfortable)
   This bed ....

34 Adverbs of degree

> Those shoes are **really** beautiful.

> Yes. But they're **a lot** more expensive than most shoes.

1 Form

	WEAKER	STRONGER
with verbs	*a bit a little*	*a lot (very) much*
with adjectives/adverbs	*quite fairly*	*very really extremely*
with comparative adjectives	*a bit a little*	*much a lot*

2 With verbs

We use (*very*) *much* and *a lot* to make verbs stronger:
*She **loves** her children **very much**.*
*Kristin **complains a lot**.* (= She often complains.)

We use *a little* and *a bit* to make verbs weaker:
*I can **play** the piano **a little**.* (not very well)
*It **annoys** me **a bit**.* (= It annoys me but not a lot.)

 We put these adverbs after the verb and object.
✗ ~~I like very much skiing.~~ ✓ *I like skiing **very much**.*

3 With adjectives/adverbs

We use *really*, *very* and *extremely* to make adjectives and adverbs stronger:
*Those shoes are **really beautiful**.*
*Diego Maradona was a **very good** footballer.*
*My new car goes **really fast**.*
*She worked **extremely hard** before her exams.*

We can use *fairly* or *quite* to make them weaker:
*That meal was **quite expensive**.*
*My father drives **quite slowly**.*
*I speak Italian **fairly well**.*

4 With comparative adjectives

To describe a big difference between things we use *much* or *a lot*:
*Those shoes are **a lot more expensive** than most shoes.*
*Canada is **much larger** than England.*

To describe a small difference between things we use *a little* or *a bit*:
*Charlotte is **a little taller** than Susie.*
*DVDs are **a bit more expensive** than CDs.*

Practice

1 Match the sentences A–F with the pictures.

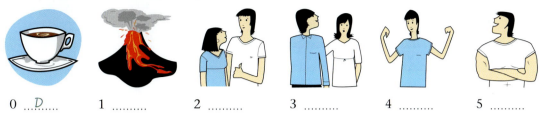

0 ..D.. 1 .... 2 .... 3 .... 4 .... 5 ....

A He's a bit taller than his sister.
B It's extremely hot.
C He only exercises a little.
(D) It's quite hot.
E He exercises a lot.
F He's much taller than his sister.

2 Match the two parts of the sentences. ◆）2.71 Listen and check.

0 There was no snow last winter because the weather was quite
1 The heating isn't turned on so the house is fairly
2 We stayed in that hotel because it was quite
3 She didn't buy it because it was really
4 My Spanish isn't very good; I only speak
5 I like studying English

A a lot.
B expensive.
C warm.
D a little.
E cold.
F cheap.

3 Write the sentences again with the words in brackets (). ◆）2.72 Listen and check.

0 Cooking is more interesting than cleaning. (much)
  Cooking is much more interesting than cleaning.

1 Some Italian clothes are beautiful. (really)

....

2 The silk in the market is expensive. (quite)

....

3 Lisa can cook. (a little)

....

4 This winter is colder than last winter. (much)

....

5 The film was more exciting than the book. (a lot)

....

6 That exam was hard. (fairly)

....

7 Emelda loves her children. (very much)

....

8 We watch action films. (a lot)

....

4 Change the underlined phrases so the sentences are true for you.

0 I am ~~a bit shorter~~ *a lot taller* than my mother.
1 My country is a little smaller than Scotland.
2 I am much older than my best friend.
3 In my country, going to the cinema is extremely expensive.
4 My home town is fairly small.
5 The winter is quite warm in my country.

Review MODULE 4

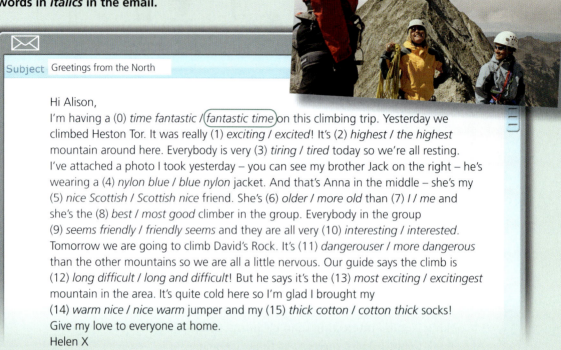

1 UNITS 25, 26, 29 AND 31 **Choose the correct words in *italics* in the email.**

Subject Greetings from the North

Hi Alison,

I'm having a (0) *time fantastic /* fantastic time on this climbing trip. Yesterday we climbed Heston Tor. It was really (1) *exciting / excited*! It's (2) *highest / the highest* mountain around here. Everybody is very (3) *tiring / tired* today so we're all resting. I've attached a photo I took yesterday – you can see my brother Jack on the right – he's wearing a (4) *nylon blue / blue nylon* jacket. And that's Anna in the middle – she's my (5) *nice Scottish / Scottish nice* friend. She's (6) *older / more old* than (7) *I / me* and she's the (8) *best / most good* climber in the group. Everybody in the group (9) *seems friendly / friendly seems* and they are all very (10) *interesting / interested*. Tomorrow we are going to climb David's Rock. It's (11) *dangerouser / more dangerous* than the other mountains so we are all a little nervous. Our guide says the climb is (12) *long difficult / long and difficult*! But he says it's the (13) *most exciting / excitingest* mountain in the area. It's quite cold here so I'm glad I brought my (14) *warm nice / nice warm* jumper and my (15) *thick cotton / cotton thick* socks! Give my love to everyone at home.
Helen X

2 UNITS 27 AND 28 **Use the words below to write questions and answers.**
🔊 **2.73** **Listen and check.**

A How's your new job going?

B (0) well it's going   *It's going well.* ....

A Are you busy at the moment?

B (1) busy always I am!   ....

A (2) you every day work do?   ....

B Yes, from Monday to Friday.

A And what do you do there?

B (3) my emails I in the mornings answer   ....

A What about the afternoons?

B (4) often I clients meet   ....

A And what do you do with them?

B (5) look usually at their tax documents we   ....

A Do you ever visit your clients at their offices?

B (6) do no, never I that   ....

A Do you ever go out for lunch?

B (7) go yes, sometimes to Starbucks I   ....

A (8) work you in the evenings do?   ....

B No, I always go home at six o'clock.

3 UNITS 32, 33 AND 34 **Complete the second sentence so it means the same as the first. Use one, two or three words.**

0 I am taller than my brother. My brother isn't ......*as tall as*...... me.

1 I haven't got enough money for that dress. That dress .... expensive for me.

2 I got 75 percent in the test and Dave got 75 percent. Dave's test result was .... mine.

3 Mr Grant is thirty-five. Mrs Grant is thirty-two. Mrs Grant .... old as her husband.

4 We need some more tickets. We haven't got ....

5 That jacket is too small for me. That jacket isn't .... for me.

6 I don't play the guitar very well. I play .... little.

7 The burger is $4 and the tuna salad is $3.80. The tuna salad is .... cheaper than the burger.

8 Carlos is too young to vote. Carlos can't vote because he isn't old ....

4 ALL UNITS **There are seven more mistakes in the advertisement. Find and correct them.**

You will have a ~~holiday fantastic~~ *fantastic holiday* at the

Sunset Beach Hotel

Our clients often describe us as

66 the most good hotel on Miranda Beach 99

Our facilities include a swimming pool large and a fitness centre.
We offer every afternoon exercise classes.
The Sunset Beach Hotel is more near to the town than any
other beach hotel, so you can explore the local area.
But if the weather is hot too for you, you can stay cool by
the pool (comfortable sun beds always are available) or you
can eat in one of our restaurants beautiful.

Sunset Beach Hotel

Contact your travel agent for more details.

5 ALL UNITS **Complete the text with the correct phrases, A, B or C below.**

PEOPLE HAVE ALWAYS loved games and puzzles. Until recently word games were (0) .... type of puzzle, and games with numbers were much (1) .... Many people thought that number games were (2) .... and not (3) .... word games. Sudoku is a new kind of number game. You have to fill (4) .... so that each row and column contains the numbers 1 to 9. Howard Garns invented the game in 1979. He (5) .... Garns called the game 'Number Place'. In the 1980s a (6) .... gave the game the name Sudoku.

Sudoku became very popular around the world. Everyone can play it because it isn't (7) .... for ordinary people and it's a lot of fun!

0 A more popular (B) the most popular C most popular
1 A the less popular B popular less C less popular
2 A bored B boring C a boring
3 A as interesting than B more interesting as C as interesting as
4 A the squares carefully B careful the squares C carefully the squares
5 A an American architect was B was an architect American C was an American architect
6 A large Japanese company B company large Japanese C Japanese large company
7 A enough difficult B too difficult C difficult enough

Test MODULE 4
Adjectives and adverbs

Choose the correct answer, A, B or C.

1 I'm reading .... at the moment. ➤ Unit 25
   A a book interesting   B an interesting book   C a book is interesting

2 Misha is wearing a ....   ➤ Unit 25
   A cotton green T-shirt   B T-shirt green cotton   C green cotton T-shirt

3 The ice cream ....   ➤ Unit 25
   A tastes delicious   B delicious tastes   C delicious

4 I never watch TV. I think it ....   ➤ Unit 26
   A boring is   B is boring   C is bored

5 John's very .... because it's his birthday tomorrow. ➤ Unit 26
   A excited   B exciting   C excitement

6 Make sure you answer these questions ....   ➤ Unit 27
   A careful   B carefuller   C carefully

7 Lewis Hamilton can drive ....   ➤ Unit 27
   A good   B goodly   C well

8 The children .... in the garden. ➤ Unit 28
   A hardly ever play   B play hardly ever   C hardly play ever

9 Did you ....? ➤ Unit 28
   A last week see the game   B see last week the game
   C see the game last week

10 The weather is usually .... in London than in Edinburgh. ➤ Unit 29
    A dryer   B drier   C dryly

11 Carlo's watch was .... than Silvia's. ➤ Unit 29
    A expensiver   B more expensive   C expensive more

12 I think beach holidays are .... than skiing holidays. ➤ Unit 30
    A better   B good   C more good

13 Mr Davidson is the .... person in our street. ➤ Unit 31
    A more friendly   B friendliest   C friendlyest

14 Who is .... footballer in your team? ➤ Unit 31
    A the most good   B the better   C the best

15 This exercise isn't as difficult .... the last one. ➤ Unit 32
    A like   B as   C than

16 Jeans aren't as .... as suits. ➤ Unit 32
    A much expensive   B expensively   C expensive

17 Terry can't vote yet. He's fifteen so he's ....   ➤ Unit 33
    A young enough   B young too   C too young

18 I don't like swimming in the sea. The water isn't ....   ➤ Unit 33
    A warm enough   B too warm   C enough warm

19 I loved that film; it was .... exciting. ➤ Unit 34
    A a bit   B a lot   C really

20 I like ....! ➤ Unit 34
    A very much chocolate   B chocolate very much
    C very chocolate much

Present tenses

Before you start

1 Read the magazine article about Kate Winslet. Look at the <mark>highlighted</mark> grammar examples.

Kate Winslet

Who <mark>is</mark> she?

Kate Winslet is one of Britain's most successful actresses. Her most famous film <mark>is</mark> *Titanic* with Leonardo DiCaprio. She<mark>'s got</mark> two children, Mia and Joe. Kate <mark>has</mark> a house in the west of England.

What <mark>is she doing</mark> now?

Kate <mark>usually works</mark> in Europe but she <mark>is living</mark> in the United States at the moment. She's making a film in Hollywood – she <mark>likes</mark> the weather there, and Kate <mark>prefers</mark> films to theatre.

2 Now read the sentences and questions below about Leonardo DiCaprio.
Choose the correct words in *italics*. The <mark>highlighted</mark> grammar examples will help you.

1 Leonardo's other name *be / is* Leo. ➤ Unit 35
2 How old *he is / is he*? ➤ Unit 36
3 He *speak / speaks* a little German because his mother is German–American. ➤ Unit 37
4 He *usually works / works usually* in Hollywood. ➤ Unit 38
5 Leonardo *works / 's working* with Kate Winslet again now. ➤ Unit 39
6 Where *is he living / lives he* now? ➤ Unit 40
7 He *is loving / loves* the weather in California. ➤ Unit 41
8 He *'s got / have got* one step-brother called Adam. ➤ Unit 42
9 He *has / have* a house in Los Angeles. ➤ Unit 43

3 Check your answers below. Then go to the unit for more information and practice.

1 is 2 is he 3 speaks 4 usually works
5 's working 6 is he living 7 loves 8 's got 9 has

35 Present simple of *be*

This is Kevin Spacey. He's an actor.
But he **isn't** British, he**'s** American.
His shows **are** very popular.

1 Form

POSITIVE			SHORT FORM	
I	*am*		*I'm*	
He/She/It	*is*		*He's/She's/It's*	
We	*are*	*English.*	*We're*	*from Cuba.*
You	*are*		*You're*	
They	*are*		*They're*	

NEGATIVE			SHORT FORM	
I	*am not*		*I'm not*	
He/She/It	*is not*		*He/She/It **isn't*** *He's/She's/It's **not***	
We	*are not*	*British.*	*We **aren't**/We're **not***	*French.*
You	*are not*		*You **aren't**/You're **not***	
They	*are not*		*They **aren't**/They're **not***	

 NATURAL ENGLISH We use short forms (*I'm, I'm not, You're*, etc.) when we are speaking to someone and in informal writing.

🔊 Pronunciation ➤ 1.10

2 Use

We use the verb *be*

● to describe people and things:
  *This **is** my brother. We **aren't** teachers, we**'re** students.*
  *My car **is** Japanese. My sisters **are** both married.*

 ✗ ~~I not married.~~ ✓ I**'m not** married.

● to talk about our feelings or ideas:
  *We**'re** all tired and hungry. This book **is** boring. His shows **are** very popular.*

● to describe position and time:
  *My flat**'s** close to the city centre. It**'s** two o'clock.*

 Use *be* not *have*
  ✗ ~~I have cold.~~ ✓ I**'m** cold.
  ✗ ~~I have hungry.~~ ✓ I**'m** hungry.
  ✗ ~~He has six years old.~~ ✓ He**'s** six years old.

there+ be ➤ Unit 75   *it + be* ➤ Unit 76.1

Practice

1 Write sentences with forms of *be*. Use the words below. ◀)) 2.74 Listen and check.

0 Angela not a student *Angela isn't a student.*
1 My brother married ....
2 Our house near the bus stop ....
3 I very hungry ....
4 We not Canadian ....
5 The bank close to the station ....
6 I not an English teacher ....
7 It time for lunch now ....
8 Those magazines not very interesting ....

2 Read the information. Write sentences about these famous people. Use short forms where possible. ◀)) 2.75 Listen and check.

comedian
not American
from Ontario, Canada
not married
1.71 metres tall
very funny

actors
very rich
American
not from New York

0 Mike Myers is a *comedian* .
1 He's ....
2 ....
3 ....
4 ....
5 ....

6 Jennifer Aniston and Courteney Cox
....
7 ....
8 ....
but ....

3 GRAMMAR IN USE There are six more mistakes in the text. Find and correct them.

> Michael Mason ~~are~~ *is* my best friend. He's Australian and he am an actor.
> He's a very good actor – but he not very famous. He's twenty-six and
> he married. Michael and his wife not are very rich, but they is happy.
> Michael's very friendly and funny. He a really nice person is!

4 Write about your best friend. Write three or four sentences like the examples in Exercise 3.

....
....
....

36 Questions with *be*

Who **is** he?

He's Andrea Bocelli.

Is he British?

No, he **isn't**. He's Italian.

1 Form

Yes / No QUESTIONS			SHORT ANSWERS	
Am	I		Yes, I am.	No, I'm not.
Is	he/she/it		Yes, he/she/it is.	No, he/she/it isn't. No, he's/she's/it's not.
Are	we	late?	Yes, we are.	No, we aren't/we're not.
Are	you		Yes, you are.	No, you aren't/you're not.
Are	they		Yes, they are.	No, they aren't/they're not.

Wh- QUESTIONS		
Where	am	I?
Who	are	you?
What	is ('s)	your job?
How old	is ('s)	your brother?

 Pronunciation ➤ 1.11

2 Use

We use *be* to ask about

- names, nationality, jobs and family:
  What's your name? **Is** *Sandra Canadian?* **Are** *they doctors?* **Is** *she married?*
- feelings:
  Are *you hungry?* *How* **are** *you?* **Is** *she happy?*
- position and time:
  Where **is** *it?* **Is** *your house near here?* *What time* **is** *it?* **Am** *I late?*

 In questions, we put the verb *be* before the subject of the sentence:
✗ ~~You are hungry?~~ ✓ **Are you** *hungry?*
✗ ~~What your job is?~~ ✓ *What's your job?*

3 Short answers

We usually use the short form of the verb in short answers with *no*:
Is he British? No, he **isn't**.

 We don't use the short form of the verb in short answers with *yes*:

Are those people students?   ✗ ~~Yes, they're.~~
✓ *Yes, they* **are**.

 We use pronouns, not nouns, in short answers:

Is your house near here?   ✗ ~~Yes, my house is.~~
✓ *Yes,* **it** *is.*

Are Carrie and Karl married?   ✗ ~~Yes, Carrie and Karl are.~~
✓ *Yes,* **they** *are.*

Practice

1 **Write questions. Use the words below.**

0 you / English / or / Scottish *Are you English or Scottish?*

00 where / your / house *Where is your house?*

1 Maria / a / student ....

2 your / brothers / married ....

3 where / the / post office ....

4 I / early ....

5 who / your / teacher ....

6 the / station / near / here ....

2 GRAMMAR IN USE **Complete the conversation with forms of *be*.** ◄)) 2.76 **Listen and check.**

A What a lovely family photo. (0) ..Are.. they your children?

B No, they (1) .... They (2) .... my sister's children.

A The girl (3) .... pretty. How old (4) .... she?

B She (5) .... four.

A (6) .... she at school?

B No, she (7) .... She (8) .... very young!

A Who (9) .... the two people at the back?

B They (10) .... my parents.

3 **Write true short answers.**

0 Are you American? ..No, I'm not..

1 Are you a student? ....

2 Are you Polish? ....

3 Are you married? ....

4 Are your parents teachers? ....

5 Is your house in a town? ....

6 Is Eminem Australian? ....

7 Are Mercedes cars German? ....

8 Is it winter now? ....

4 **Complete the questions and give true answers. Write complete sentences.** ◄)) 2.77 **Listen and check.**

0 What .....is..... your surname?

My surname is Lopez.

1 What nationality .... you?

....

2 How old .... your brother/sister?

....

3 Where .... your parents at the moment?

....

4 What .... the name of your home town?

....

5 Who .... your favourite singer?

....

37 Present simple (1)

> I **live** in Los Angeles but my mother **lives** in the Mojave desert. She **prefers** the countryside.

1 Form

POSITIVE		
I/We/You/They	*live*	*in São Paulo.*
He/She/It	*lives*	*in the countryside.*

We add *-s* or *-es* to the verb after *he/she/it*:
go → goes, teach → teaches, wash → washes, relax → relaxes

Sometimes the spelling changes:
carry → carries, fly → flies

NEGATIVE				SHORT FORMS	
I/We/You/They	*do not*	*like*	*big cities.*	I/We/You/They *don't live*	*here.*
He/She/It	*does not*		*the countryside.*	He/She/It *doesn't live*	

 After *he/she/it*, we use *doesn't*:
✗ ~~He don't like cities.~~ ✓ He **doesn't like** cities.

Spelling rules for *he, she, it* forms ➤ page 316

 Pronunciation ➤ 1.12

2 Use

We use the present simple
- for facts that are always true:
  *Water **boils** at 100°C and **freezes** at 0°C. The Sun **doesn't go** round the Earth. Some trees **don't lose** their leaves in winter.*
- for things that we don't expect to change:
  *I **don't live** in the country; I **live** in the city. My sister **doesn't work** in an office; she **works** in a hospital.*
- for feelings (e.g. *feel, hate, like, love, prefer, want*):
  *My grandfather **likes** the countryside. He **doesn't like** the city. I **prefer** ballet to opera.*
- for thoughts and ideas (e.g. *agree, believe, know, mean, remember, think, understand*):
  *'I **think** New York is exciting.' 'Yes, I **agree.**' A red light **means** 'Stop'. You **don't understand**.*

Verbs that don't use the continuous form ➤ Unit 41.2

Practice Use the spelling rules to help you complete these exercises. ➤ page 316

1 Write the *he/she/it* form of these verbs below.

+ -s	+ -es	(-y) + -ies
		carries

carry enjoy fly
go hurry know
live relax take
try wash watch

2 Complete the sentences about famous people. Use the verbs in brackets () and short forms. ◄》2.78 Listen and check.

0 The actor Colin Farrell is Irish but he ......doesn't work...... in Ireland; he
   ....works........... in Hollywood. (not work, work)

1 Film star Alicia Silverstone .... meat; she's a vegetarian. (not eat)

2 Brad Pitt and Angelina Jolie .... in Hollywood but they
   .... there. (work, not live)

3 Phil Collins is a famous musician but he .... painting and acting. (prefer)

4 The actor Russell Crowe also .... and .... the guitar in
   an Australian band. (sing, play)

5 Nicole Kidman .... fruit but she .... strawberries.
   (love, not eat)

6 Catherine Zeta-Jones .... chocolate or sweets. (not like)

7 Antonio Banderas .... from Spain but he .... films in
   Europe these days. (come, not make)

8 Businessman Bill Gates is a very rich man but he .... his children a lot
   of money. (not give)

3 **GRAMMAR IN USE** Read about Carmen Salandras. Complete the
text with the correct verb forms. ◄》2.79 Listen and check.

My name is Carmen Salandras. I come from Puerto Rico
but I don't live there now. I live in Florida. I work at
a big hospital in Miami. It's a fantastic job and I love
it. Like a lot of people in Florida, I speak English and
Spanish. I'm married and my husband's name is Juan
Antonio. We don't live near the beach, we live in an
apartment in the centre of the city. In my free time, I
enjoy cooking – I try to cook healthy food for my family.

Carmen Salandras (0) .....comes..... from Puerto Rico but she (1) .... there now.
She (2) .... in Florida. She (3) .... at a big hospital in Miami. She
(4) .... her job. Carmen (5) .... English and Spanish. She is married and
her husband's name is Juan Antonio. They (6) .... near the beach, they live in an
apartment in the centre of the city. In her free time, Carmen (7) .... cooking and
she (8) .... to cook healthy food for her family.

⏻ Go online for more practice

38 Present simple (2)

Do you **come** to the studio every day?

Yes, I **do**. We **usually** **start** at eight o'clock.

1 Form

Yes / No QUESTIONS			SHORT ANSWERS	
Do	I/we/you/they	**work** here?	Yes, I/we/you/they **do**.	No, I/we/you/they **do not (don't)**.
Does	he/she/it		Yes, he/she/it **does**.	No, he/she/it **does not (doesn't)**.

Wh- QUESTIONS			
When/What time How often	**do**	I/we/you/they	**get up?** **come?**
What	**does**	he/she/it	**do** on Sundays?

 We don't add -s to the main verb in questions and negatives.
✗ ~~Where does he works?~~ ✓ Where **does** he **work?**

2 Use

We use the present simple for things that happen regularly:
*David **goes** to work by bus.   The bus **stops** outside his house.*
*'**Do** you **drink** a lot of coffee?' 'Yes, I **do**, but my parents only **drink** tea.'*

When we talk about *when* or *how often* we do regular activities we can use

- time expressions (e.g. *every day/evening/weekend, at the weekend, on Mondays/Sundays, once a week/month/year*):
  *Do you come here **every day**? I go on holiday **once a year**.*

 Look at the word order:
✓ **On Sundays**, *we go to our grandparents' house for lunch.*
✓ *We go to our grandparents' house for lunch* **on Sundays**.
✗ ~~We go on Sundays to our grandparents' house for lunch.~~

- adverbs of frequency (e.g. *never, often, always*). We usually put these BEFORE the verb:
  *We **usually** start at eight o'clock.*
  *'Do you drive to work?' 'No, we **always** take public transport. We **never** drive.'*

 With the verb *be* we put the adverb AFTER the verb:
✗ ~~She often is late.~~ ✓ *She's **often** late.*

Adverbs and word order ➤ Unit 28

 Pronunciation ➤ 1.13

Practice

1 GRAMMAR IN USE **Choose the correct words in *italics* in the text.**

A DAY IN THE LIFE

I (0) *get up always* / (always get up) at seven o'clock. My husband (1) *work* / *works* in a restaurant so he (2) *get up* / *gets up* much later. I (3) *don't eat* / *doesn't eat* breakfast, I just drink a cup of coffee. I drive to the office and I (4) *usually am* / *am usually* at my desk by nine o'clock.

When I arrive, I (5) *check* / *checks* my email messages. After that, my assistant and I (6) *visit* / *visits* one of our buildings and (7) *talks* / *talk* to the builders. Then we (8) *go* / *goes* for lunch. We (9) *doesn't eat* / *don't eat* very much, just a salad or a sandwich. In the afternoon I work at the computer and my clients often (10) *calls* / *call* me on the phone.

I (11) *finishes* / *finish* work at six. In the evenings I like to relax by watching TV – I (12) *work never* / *never work* at home. But my husband (13) *doesn't finish* / *don't finish* before ten o'clock. So we (14) *don't see* / *doesn't see* each other very much! ∎

Alexandra Wilson is an architect in Sydney, Australia.

She tells us about a typical day in her busy life.

2 GRAMMAR IN USE **Complete the conversation with the correct words from the box.** 🔊 2.80 **Listen and check.**

A Do you (0) .....*watch*..... TV during the day?

B No, I (1) ....; I work during the day.

A What about the evenings? Do you watch TV then?

B Yes, I (2) ....·

A What programmes (3) .... you like?

B I (4) .... films and comedy shows best. But I (5) .... watch the news – it's boring.

A (6) .... you watch TV on your own or with members of your family?

B Well, I (7) .... watch TV with my sister, but not very often. She (8) .... dramas and music programmes.

A (9) .... she watch the news?

B No, she (10) ....·

> do (x3) does doesn't
> don't like likes never
> sometimes ~~watch~~

3 **Use the verbs below to write questions. Then write true answers.** 🔊 2.81 **Listen and check.**

0 what time / you / get up *What time do you get up? I usually get up at 7.30.*

00 you / work / in an office *Do you work in an office? No, I'm a student.*

1 what / you / have / for breakfast ....

2 how often / you / watch TV ....

3 you / visit / friends / at the weekend ....

4 your family / go to the beach / in summer ....

5 you / often / go to bed / late ....

6 how often / your best friend / phone you ....

39 Present continuous (1)

1 Form

We form the present continuous with *am, is* or *are* + the *-ing* form of the main verb
e.g. *watching, going, eating.*

POSITIVE			SHORT FORM
I	*am*	*watching TV.*	*I'm watching TV.*
He/She/It	*is*	*leaving.*	*He's/She's/It's leaving.*
We/You/They	*are*	*practising.*	*You're/We're/They're practising.*

NEGATIVE			SHORT FORM	
I	*am not*		*I'm not*	
He/She/It	*is not*	*watching TV.*	*He isn't/He's not* *She isn't/She's not* *It isn't/It's not*	*watching TV.*
We/You/They	*are not*		*You aren't/You're not*	

Sometimes the spelling of the main verb changes, eg:
take → *taking*
lie → *lying*
swim → *swimming*

Spelling rules for *-ing* forms ➤ page 316

 Pronunciation ➤ 1.14

2 Use

We use the present continuous

- to describe something that is happening while we are speaking:
  *Hurry up. The taxi's **waiting** outside right now.*
  *Can you help me? I**'m looking for** the post office.*
  *James can't come to the door – he's **having** a bath.*

- to talk about something that is happening around now, for a limited period of time:
  *I'm using my brother's computer today because mine **isn't working**.*
  *We're on holiday this week. We**'re staying** in a hotel near the beach.*

We often use time expressions (e.g. (*right*) *now, at the moment, today, this week*):
This year *we**'re studying** the history of the theatre.*

Practice
Use the spelling rules to help you complete these exercises. ➤ page 316

1 Write the continuous form of these verbs below.

+ -ing	double consonant + -ing	(-e) + -ing
		living

~~live~~ happen
make run
sit sleep
stop swim
take use
visit wait

2 What are they doing? Complete the sentences about the people in the pictures. Use verbs from Exercise 1. ◀)) 2.82 Listen and check.

0 Susy ..'s running.. in the park.

1 They .... in the garden.

2 Jenny .... a cake.

3 The children .... on the sofa.

4 Pedro .... in a river.

5 They .... for a bus.

3 Complete the sentences. Use forms of the phrases in the box. ◀)) 2.83 Listen and check.

play in the garden   not have a lunch break   eat in a restaurant today   wear a pullover   ~~have a shower~~
not go to work today   computer not work   taxi wait outside   not dance at the moment

0 Fernando can't come to the phone because he 's having a shower.

1 It's cold today so I ....

2 Jane's cooker isn't working so she ....

3 The weather is nice today so the children ....

4 Dave can't send you an email because his ....

5 Carla has hurt her leg so she ....

6 Hurry up! It's time to leave. The ....

7 We have a lot of work in the office today so we ....

8 It's a bank holiday so most people ....

40 Present continuous (2)

What **are** they **doing** now?

They**'re running** away.

Is that man **phoning** the police?

Yes, he **is**.

1 Form

Yes / No QUESTIONS			SHORT ANSWERS	
Am	I		Yes, I am.	No, I'm not.
Is	he/she/it	sitting here?	Yes, he/she/it is.	No, he/she/it isn't.
Are	we/you/they		Yes, we/you/they are.	No, we/you/they aren't.

Wh- QUESTIONS			
What	am	I	doing?
Where	is	he/she/it	going?
Why	are	we/you/they	running?

In questions, we put *am/is/are* before the subject of the sentence.
We put the *-ing* form after the subject:
*What **are** you **studying** this term?*
*Is she **listening** to the radio?*

 ✗ ~~Are waiting you for me?~~
✗ ~~Waiting are you for me?~~
✓ **Are** you **waiting** for me?

 We don't usually repeat the main verb when we answer questions:
*Is that man **phoning** the police?*   ✗ ~~Yes, he is phoning.~~   ✓ *Yes, he **is**.*
   ✗ ~~No, he isn't phoning.~~   ✓ *No, he **isn't**.*

 We don't use the short form of the verb in short answers with *yes*.

Is she sleeping?   ✗ ~~Yes, she's.~~
   ✓ *Yes, she **is**.*

2 Use

We often use the present continuous to talk about what is happening in pictures and photos:
*What **are** they **doing**?*
*– They**'re watching** a film.*

That's an interesting painting. **Is** that woman **writing** something?

No, she **isn't**. She**'s reading** a letter.

96

Practice Use the spelling rules to help you complete these exercises. ➤ page 316

1 a GRAMMAR IN USE **Complete the text. Use the present continuous forms of the verbs in brackets (). ◀)) 2.84 Listen and check.**

It's a lovely summer afternoon in the park. Robert and Mick (0) ......*are playing*...... (play) football. Miranda (1) .... (listen) to some music and Carlos (2) .... (run). My friends Isabel and Rashid (3) .... (have) a picnic – Isabel (4) .... (eat) a sandwich and Rashid (5) .... (drink) a cola. Over there I can see my neighbours, Mr and Mrs Berenson – they (6) .... (take) their dog for a walk.

b Now put the correct names by the letters in the picture.

B ....
C ....
D ....
A ...*Isabel*.....
F ....
E ....

2 Complete these questions and answers about the picture in Exercise 1.

0 ......*Is*......... Miranda ...*listening*... to music? Yes, she ......*is*.........

1 .... Robert and Mick .... tennis? No, they ....

2 .... Carlos ....? No, he .... walking, he's ....

3 What .... Isabel ....? She .... a sandwich.

4 What .... Mr and Mrs Berenson .... ? They .... their dog for a walk.

5 .... Rashid .... a burger? No, he ....

3 Write the questions and short answers. ◀)) 2.85 Listen and check.

0 it / rain / today? / No, *Is it raining today? No, it isn't.* ....

1 you / do / your homework? / Yes, ...

2 Steven / cook lunch? / No, ...

3 the / children watch TV? / Yes, ...

4 we / wait / for somebody? / No, ...

5 Elizabeth / stay / with her grandparents / this week? / Yes, ...

....

4 Write true answers.

0 What are you doing at the moment? *I'm doing my homework.*..

1 What are you studying this year? ....

2 Where are you sitting right now? ....

3 What are you looking at? ....

41 Present simple or present continuous?

1 Use

PRESENT SIMPLE	PRESENT CONTINUOUS
to talk about things we do regularly:	to talk about things that are happening at the time we are speaking:

Carla **dances** for the Euro Ballet Company every evening.

STAGE DOOR

Right now, Carla**'s dancing** in *Swan Lake*.

with time expressions:	with time expressions:
usually, often, every day, once a month	*right now, at the moment*

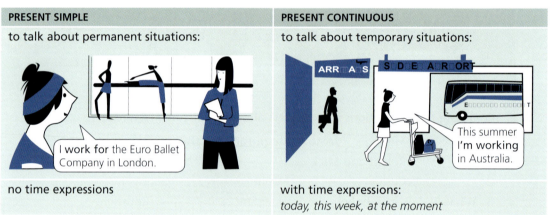

PRESENT SIMPLE	PRESENT CONTINUOUS
to talk about permanent situations:	to talk about temporary situations:

I **work for** the Euro Ballet Company in London.

ARRAS   SDE ARORT

This summer I'm working in Australia.

no time expressions	with time expressions:
	today, this week, at the moment

2 Verbs that don't use the continuous form

 We don't normally use the continuous with these verbs:

- feeling verbs (*like, love, hate, prefer, need, want*):
  - ✗ ~~I am liking music.~~
  - ✓ I **like** music.
- thinking verbs (*agree, believe, forget, know, mean, remember, think, understand*):
  - ✗ ~~My brother is agreeing with me.~~
  - ✓ My brother **agrees** with me.
- sense verbs (*hear, see, smell, taste*):
  - ✗ ~~That coffee is smelling delicious!~~
  - ✓ That coffee **smells** delicious!
- the verbs *be, belong, contain, cost, own*:
  - ✗ ~~That bag isn't belonging to me.~~
  - ✓ That bag **doesn't belong** to me.

The verb *think* has a different meaning in the present simple and the present continuous:
*What **do** you **think** of the show?* (= What is your opinion?)
*What **are** you **thinking** about?* (= Tell me your thoughts now.)

Practice

1 Match the two parts of the sentences. 🔊 **2.86** Listen and check.

0 Davina's computer isn't working so
1 Caroline misses her family so
2 Lucy likes to be clean so
3 I'm afraid Maria can't speak to you right now;
4 Melissa isn't in the office today;
5 As part of Anne's job
6 When Judy goes to the sea
7 Stephanie has a headache so

A she visits clients once a week.
B she stays with her grandparents.
C she's staying at home today.
D she's sending her emails from an Internet café.
E she's having a bath.
F she's visiting some clients.
G she sends them emails every day.
H she has a bath every day.

2 GRAMMAR IN USE Choose the correct words in *italics* in the text.

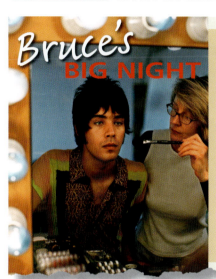

Bruce's BIG NIGHT

BRUCE LAURENCE (0) *is* / *is being* a young actor. He is very excited because right now he (1) *acts* / *is acting* in a professional show for the first time. He (2) *loves* / *is loving* the theatre and this is his first proper job. It's 7.15 and he (3) *waits* / *'s waiting* in his dressing room. His assistant (4) *puts* / *'s putting* on his make-up and Bruce (5) *practises* / *is practising* his words.

Tonight's show is at the Theatre Royal in Edinburgh. Bruce (6) *lives* / *is living* in London but while he is in the show he (7) *stays* / *is staying* at a small hotel in Edinburgh. It isn't very comfortable but single rooms (8) *don't cost* / *aren't costing* very much and two other actors (9) *stay* / *are staying* at the same place. Bruce (10) *thinks* / *is thinking* the show will be a big success.

3 GRAMMAR IN USE Complete the conversation. Use forms of the words in brackets () and short forms. 🔊 **2.87** Listen and check.

CLARA Hi, Josie. How are things?

JOSIE Busy. We moved into our new flat last week.

CLARA That's great. Where is it?

JOSIE (0) *Do you remember* (you remember) the garage on Old Street? It's next to that.

CLARA Oh, yes. I (1) .... (know) that place. It's quite old, isn't it?

JOSIE Yes. So we're in the middle of painting it at the moment.

CLARA (2) .... (you use) professional painters?

JOSIE No, they (3) .... (cost) too much. We (4) .... (do) it all ourselves. It's very hard work!

CLARA Well, I (5) .... (not do) much at the moment. Would you like me to help?

JOSIE That's kind of you but we (6) .... (not need) any help really.

CLARA OK. How's your little baby?

JOSIE Oh, she (7) .... (be) fine. My mother (8) .... (look after) her today.

42 *have got*

Gwyneth Paltrow**'s got** two children.
They**'ve got** a house in London.

1 Form

POSITIVE			NEGATIVE		
I/We/You/They	**'ve (have) got**	a garden.	I/We/You/They	**haven't (have not) got**	a garden.
He/She/It	**'s (has) got**		He/She/It	**hasn't (has not) got**	

Yes/No QUESTIONS				SHORT ANSWERS					
Have	I/we/you/they	got	a garden?	Yes,	I/we/you/they	have.	No,	I/we/you/they	haven't.
Has	he/she/it				he/she/it	has.		he/she/it	hasn't.

Wh- QUESTIONS			
What kind of car	**have**	you	
What colour hair	**has**	she	got?
How many children	**have**	they	

NATURAL ENGLISH We usually use the short forms of *have got* (*'ve got/'s got*).

 Pronunciation ➤ 1.15

2 Use

We use *have got*

- to talk about possessions (things that belong to you):
  *I**'ve got** a good camera. He**'s got** two cars. **Have** they **got** a lot of money?*
- to talk about your family or friends:
  *I**'ve got** two sisters. **Has** she **got** any friends at her new school?*
- to describe what somebody looks like:
  *I**'ve got** dark hair and brown eyes.*
- to talk about illnesses:
  *I**'ve got** a cold/headache/stomachache. **Has** the baby **got** a temperature?*

 ✗ *I got brown hair.*
✓ *I**'ve got** brown hair.*
✗ *He got a good job.*
✓ *He**'s got** a good job.*

have got and *have* British/American English ➤ page 317

Practice

1 Complete the sentences with a form of *have got*. Use short forms.

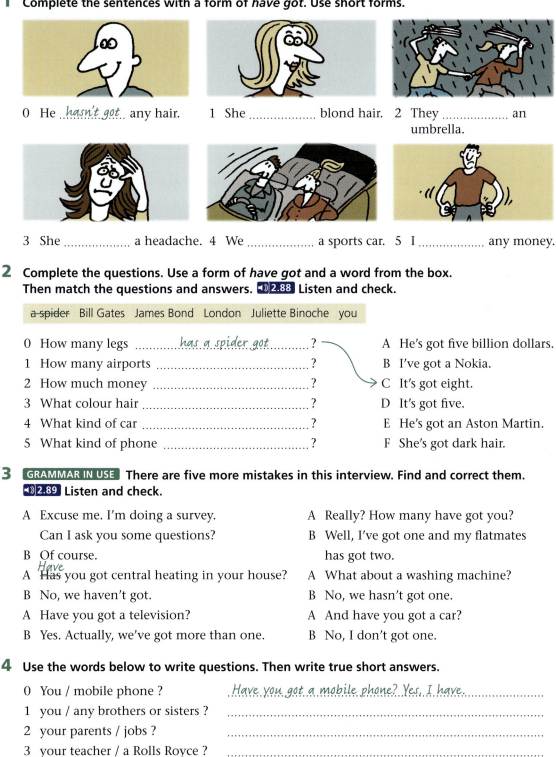

0 He _hasn't got_ any hair. 1 She .... blond hair. 2 They .... an umbrella.

3 She .... a headache. 4 We .... a sports car. 5 I .... any money.

2 Complete the questions. Use a form of *have got* and a word from the box.
Then match the questions and answers. ◄))2.88 Listen and check.

| a spider Bill Gates James Bond London Juliette Binoche you |

0 How many legs ...._has a spider got_.........?   A He's got five billion dollars.
1 How many airports ....?   B I've got a Nokia.
2 How much money ....?   C It's got eight.
3 What colour hair ....?   D It's got five.
4 What kind of car ....?   E He's got an Aston Martin.
5 What kind of phone ....?   F She's got dark hair.

3 GRAMMAR IN USE There are five more mistakes in this interview. Find and correct them.
◄))2.89 Listen and check.

A Excuse me. I'm doing a survey.
 Can I ask you some questions?
B Of course.
A *Have* ~~Has~~ you got central heating in your house?
B No, we haven't got.
A Have you got a television?
B Yes. Actually, we've got more than one.

A Really? How many have got you?
B Well, I've got one and my flatmates has got two.
A What about a washing machine?
B No, we hasn't got one.
A And have you got a car?
B No, I don't got one.

4 Use the words below to write questions. Then write true short answers.

0 You / mobile phone ?   *Have you got a mobile phone? Yes, I have.* ....
1 you / any brothers or sisters ?   ....
2 your parents / jobs ?   ....
3 your teacher / a Rolls Royce ?   ....
4 your best friend / any pets ?   ....
5 you / a headache ?   ....
6 your mother / dark hair ?   ....

43 *have*

ACTOR FACTFILE

MOVIE STAR NICOLAS CAGE **has** an island in the Caribbean, a castle in England and a twelve-bedroom house in Middleton, Rhode Island. He **has** a son called Kal-El. Nicolas and Kal-El **have** a good time together.

1 Form

POSITIVE			NEGATIVE		
I/We/You/They	**have**	*dark hair.*	*I/We/You/They*	**don't** (do not) **have**	*any hair.*
He/She/It	**has**		*He/She/It*	**doesn't** (does not) **have**	

Yes/No QUESTIONS				SHORT ANSWERS		
Do	*I/we/you/they*	**have**	*a camera?*	*Yes,*	*I/we/you/they*	**do.**
				No,		**don't.**
Does	*he/she/it*			*Yes,*	*he/she/it*	**does.**
				No,		**doesn't.**

Wh- QUESTIONS			
What kind of car	**do**	*you*	**have?**
What colour hair	**does**	*she*	**have?**

2 *have = have got*

We can use *have* in the same way as we use *have got* (➤ Unit 42.2)

- to talk about possessions:
  *Nicolas Cage **has** an island in the Caribbean. **Do** you **have** a lot of money?*
  *Switzerland **doesn't have** a coast.*

- to talk about your friends or family:
  *Nicolas **has** a son. How many children **do** you **have**?*

- to describe what somebody looks like:
  *I **have** dark hair and brown eyes.*

- to talk about illnesses:
  *I **have** a cold/headache. **Do** you **have** a temperature?*

 ✗ I have eighteen years old. ✓ *I am eighteen years old.*

 When *have = have got*, we don't use it in continuous tenses:
✗ I'm having two sisters. ✓ *I **have** two sisters.*

3 *have* for doing things

We also use *have* to talk about things we do. We cannot use *have got* in this way:

have +	*a shower/a bath/a wash/a shave/a haircut*
	breakfast/lunch/dinner/a meal/a snack/a drink/a cup of coffee
	fun/a good time/a party/a holiday/a celebration
	an argument/an accident/a bad time

We can use *have* for doing things in the present continuous or the present simple:
*Listen to that noise! The neighbours **are having** a party! I always **have** a good time at parties.*

Practice

1 GRAMMAR IN USE **Complete the conversation with words from the box.**
🔊 **3.01** **Listen and check.**

do (x3)   does   doesn't   don't   have (x2)   has (x2)   you

OFFICER   (0) .... _Do_ .... you have your tickets?

STEVEN   I think my wife (1) .... them.

JACKIE   Here they are.

OFFICER   Thank you. (2) .... you (3) ....
any metal objects in your luggage?

STEVEN   No, we (4) ....

OFFICER   Are you sure, Sir? Do (5) .... have a
mobile phone or a laptop?

JACKIE   He (6) .... a mobile phone.

STEVEN   Oh, yes. I forgot about that.

OFFICER   Put it in the tray please, Sir. (7) .... it have a battery?

STEVEN   No, it (8) ....

OFFICER   (9) .... you have anything else with metal?

STEVEN   No. Oh, I (10) .... some coins in my pockets.

OFFICER   OK. Please put those in the tray as well, Sir.

2 **Look at the information about Nicolas Cage (on page 102).**
Complete the questions and answers.

0   .... _Does_ ..... Nicolas Cage ..... _live_ ..... in Australia? No, he ... _doesn't_ ...

1   .... Nicolas Cage .... a castle in England? Yes, he ....

2   Where .... he .... a house? He .... a house in Middleton.

3   How many bedrooms .... his house ....? It .... twelve bedrooms.

4   .... he .... a daughter? No, he .... He .... a son.

5   .... Nicolas Cage and his son .... a good time together?
Yes, they ....

3 **Complete the sentences with a form of _have_ and a word or phrase from the box.**
Use short forms. Some sentences need a negative verb. 🔊 **3.02** **Listen and check.**

a headache   fun   a king   a driving licence   ~~any brothers or sisters~~
a temperature   lunch   any mountains   a cup of coffee

0   I _don't have any brothers or sisters_, I'm my parents' only child.

1   I think she .... – she's very hot.

2   Holland is very flat – it ....

3   This is a great party! We ....!

4   When I ...., I go and lie down.

5   Clare can't drive because she ....

6   I always .... and a biscuit at eleven o'clock in the morning.

7   France has a president, so it .... or queen.

8   The office is very busy today, so I .... at my desk – just a sandwich.

Review MODULE 5

Use the spelling rules to help you complete these exercises. ➤ page 316

1 UNITS 36, 37, 38, 39, 40, 41 AND 42 **Match the two parts of the sentences.**

0 We always have	A often listen to the radio.
1 Sally is having	B stay with their grandparents in August.
2 I think I've	C English magazines?
3 This week the children	D got flu.
4 The children usually	E a party again. It's really noisy.
5 Be quiet. I	F are staying with their grandparents.
6 On Sunday mornings I	G am listening to the radio.
7 Are you reading	H fun at Miranda's parties.
8 How often do you read	I a good book at the moment?

2 UNITS 35, 36, 39, 40, 41, 42 AND 43 **Choose the correct words in *italics* in the telephone conversation.** ◀》 **3.03** **Listen and check.**

A Good morning. University Accommodation Office.
B Hi. I'd like to use the accommodation service.
A OK. (0) *Are* / *Be* you a full-time student here?
B Yes, (1) *I'm* / *I am*.
A What (2) *name have you* / *is your name*?
B Jason Brien.
A Jason Brien. OK. And what course
    (3) *do you study* / *are you studying* this year?
B History and politics.
A Do you (4) *have* / *have got* your student number?
B No, I'm afraid not.
A Mmm. Let me check on the computer …
    Yes. Here it is: 67567. OK. Now, (5) *do* / *are* you want
    accommodation for this year or for next year?
B Next year.
A And (6) *are* / *is* you in student accommodation now?
B Yes, (7) *I live* / *I'm living* in the flats in George Street at
    the moment.
A OK. (8) *Have you* / *Do you have* got a mobile phone?
B Yes, but it (9) *doesn't* / *isn't* working.
A Well, (10) *got you* / *have you got* an email address?
B Yes, of course.

3 UNITS 35 AND 43 **There are five more missing forms of *be* and three missing forms of *have* in this text. Put the missing verbs in the correct positions.**

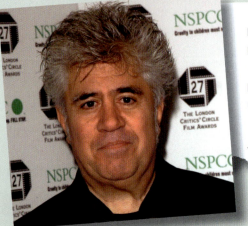

                                    is
Pedro Almodovar/a famous Spanish film director.
His most famous films *Talk to Her* and *Bad Education*.
His films popular in Spain and many other countries
but they not in English; they in Spanish. Pedro grey
hair and brown eyes. He lives in Madrid and he not
married. He doesn't any children but he a brother,
Agustin Almodovar.

4 ALL UNITS Use the words below to write questions and answers. Use short forms.

  0 Mike Myers / be / a famous singer / ? *Is Mike Myers a famous singer?*

      No, / he / be / a famous comedian *No, he's a famous comedian.*

  00 Jennifer Aniston / live / in San Francisco / ? *Does Jennifer Aniston live in San Francisco?*

      No, / she / not. She / live / in Los Angeles *No, she doesn't. She lives in Los Angeles.*

  1 Gwyneth Paltrow / have / six children / ?

      No, / she / not. She / has / two

  2 New York / be / the capital of the USA / ?

      No, / it / not. Washington / be / the capital

  3 London / have got / four airports / ?

      No, / it / have got / five

  4 you / watch / TV / at the moment / ?

      No, / I / not. I / do / an exercise

  5 Red Square and the Kremlin / be / in St Petersburg / ?

      No, / they / be / in Moscow

  6 your family / live / in a house / ?

      No, / we / not. We / live / in an apartment

  7 you / have got / a cold / ?

      No, / I / have got / headache

5 ALL UNITS Complete the second sentence so it means the same as the first.
Use one, two or three words and short forms.

  0 There are two bathrooms in my apartment.

      My apartment *has two bathrooms*.

  1 My daughter lives in Spain and my son lives in Portugal.

      My children .... in different countries.

  2 There are five English dictionaries in Harry's room.

      Harry .... five English dictionaries.

  3 My pen friend only speaks English.

      My pen friend .... Italian or Spanish.

  4 I can't find my key. Can you help me look for it?

      Can you help me? I'm .... my key.

  5 Armand and Justine don't come from France.

      Armand and Justine .... French.

  6 Jane usually stays with us but this week she is at her grandmother's.

      Jane .... with her grandmother this week.

  7 There are no theatres in my home town.

      My home town .... any theatres.

  8 What is their address?

      Where .... live?

Test MODULE 5

Present tenses

Choose the correct answer, A, B or C.

1 1 My friend .... American.
   A not is   B are not   C isn't   ➤ Unit 35

2 The women in my family .... very tall.
   A have   B are   C am   ➤ Unit 35

3 .... hungry?
   A Have you   B Are you   C Do you have   ➤ Unit 36

4 What time .... it?
   A is   B are   C has   ➤ Unit 36

5 Maria .... the answer to that question.
   A know   B knows   C is know   ➤ Unit 37

6 Jane is a nurse; she .... in a hospital.
   A works   B work   C working   ➤ Unit 37

7 Laptop computers .... batteries.
   A are using   B uses   C use   ➤ Unit 37

8 My uncle .... near here.
   A not lives   B doesn't lives   C doesn't live   ➤ Unit 37

9 .... coffee in the mornings?
   A Do you drink   B Does you drinks   C Drink you   ➤ Unit 38

10 I .... a big breakfast.
   A am having always   B always have   C have always   ➤ Unit 38

11 I'm afraid the baby .... very well.
   A isn't sleeping   B not sleeps   C is sleeping not   ➤ Unit 39

12 My mobile isn't working so I .... my sister's phone.
   A using   B 'm using   C use   ➤ Unit 39

13 What .... right now?
   A do you do   B are doing you   C are you doing   ➤ Unit 40

14 Carol usually .... to work but this week she is taking the bus.
   A is driving   B drives   C isn't driving   ➤ Unit 41

15 You are wrong. I .... with you.
   A don't agree   B 'm not agreeing   C 'm not agree   ➤ Unit 41

16 .... the tickets and passports?
   A Got you   B Have you got   C Do you have got   ➤ Unit 42

17 Dave isn't very well; he .... a bad cold.
   A is having   B 's got   C 've got   ➤ Unit 42

18 My parents .... a car.
   A don't have   B do have not   C have not   ➤ Unit 43

19 Isabel .... dark hair and brown eyes.
   A is   B has   C is having   ➤ Unit 43

20 Every morning I .... before breakfast.
   A make shower   B am showering   C have a shower   ➤ Unit 43

Past tenses

Before you start

1 Read about James Dean.
Look at the <mark>highlighted</mark> grammar examples.

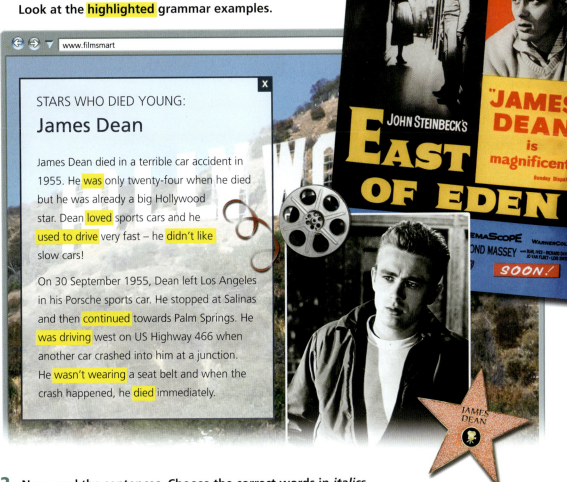

STARS WHO DIED YOUNG:
James Dean

James Dean died in a terrible car accident in 1955. He <mark>was</mark> only twenty-four when he died but he was already a big Hollywood star. Dean <mark>loved</mark> sports cars and he <mark>used to drive</mark> very fast – he <mark>didn't like</mark> slow cars!

On 30 September 1955, Dean left Los Angeles in his Porsche sports car. He stopped at Salinas and then <mark>continued</mark> towards Palm Springs. He <mark>was driving</mark> west on US Highway 466 when another car crashed into him at a junction. He <mark>wasn't wearing</mark> a seat belt and when the crash happened, he <mark>died</mark> immediately.

JOHN STEINBECK'S
EAST OF EDEN

"JAMES DEAN is magnificent"
Sunday Dispatch

CINEMASCOPE WARNERCOLOR
...OND MASSEY with BURL IVES • RICHARD DAVALOS
JO VAN FLEET • LOIS SMITH

SOON!

JAMES DEAN

2 Now read the sentences. Choose the correct words in *italics*.
The <mark>highlighted</mark> grammar examples will help you.

1 My grandfather *was / were* a student in the 1950s. ➤ Unit 44
2 He *loves / loved* his years at university. He studied physics. ➤ Unit 45
3 But he didn't *like / liked* physics so he changed to chemistry. ➤ Unit 46
4 He finished university and then he *lived / living* in London. ➤ Unit 46
5 He *was working / worked* in London when he met his wife. ➤ Unit 47
6 He *wasn't / didn't* earning much money when he married my grandmother. ➤ Unit 47
7 When my father was born, they *moved / were moving* to the country. ➤ Unit 48
8 I *used / use* to visit him every summer when I was young. ➤ Unit 49

3 Check your answers below. Then go to the unit for more information and practice.

1 was 2 loved 3 like 4 lived 5 was working 6 wasn't 7 moved 8 used

44 Past simple of *be*

Deborah Kerr and Ingrid Bergman **were** film stars in the 1950s, but they **weren't** American. Deborah Kerr was British and Ingrid Bergman **was** Swedish.

1 Form

We make the past tense of the verb *be* with *was* and *were*:

POSITIVE		
I/He/She/It	**was**	*French.*
We/You/They	**were**	

There are no short forms of *was* and *were* in positive sentences.

NEGATIVE		SHORT FORM	
I/He/She/It	**was not**	*(wasn't)*	*there.*
We/You/They	**were not**	*(weren't)*	

NATURAL ENGLISH We use the short forms *wasn't* and *weren't* when we are speaking to someone and in informal writing.

QUESTIONS	SHORT ANSWERS
Was I/he/she/it there?	*Yes, I/he/she/it* **was**. *No, I/he/she/it* **wasn't** *(was not).*
Were we/you/they there?	*Yes, we/you/they* **were**. *No, we/you/they* **weren't** *(were not).*
Where **were** *you?* *How much* **was** *it?* *What* **was** *the name of the film?*	

 Pronunciation ➤ 1.16, 1.17

2 Use

We use the past simple tense of *be* to talk about people and situations in the past. We often use dates and times with *was* and *were*:
Deborah Kerr and Ingrid Bergman **were** *film stars* **in the 1950s**.
Was *he in the beginners' class* **last year?**
It **wasn't** *very cold* **in December**.

Compare *was/were* with *is/are*:
The weather **was** *hot yesterday but it's cooler today.*
1920s films **were** *in black and white but now most films* **are** *in colour.*

Present simple of *be* ➤ Unit 35   To talk about actions in the past ➤ Unit 47

Practice

1 **GRAMMAR IN USE** Choose the correct words in *italics* in the text.

Leslie Howard

Leslie Howard (0) *is* / *was* a famous film star in the 1930s in Hollywood. But he (1) *wasn't* / *didn't* American – he (2) *were* / *was* British. In those days there (3) *not be* / *weren't* a lot of British actors in Hollywood, most of the film stars (4) *was* / *were* American. Leslie Howard (5) *be* / *was* a very good actor and his films (6) *was* / *were* very successful, but he (7) *wasn't* / *weren't* happy in Hollywood and he went back to England. His most famous film (8) *did* / *was* 'Gone With The Wind' in 1939.

2 Write questions and short answers. ◀)) **3.04** Listen and check.

0 Thomas Edison / a famous inventor ? (✓)
   Was Thomas Edison a famous inventor? Yes, he was. ....

1 Christopher Columbus / Spanish ? (✗)
   ....

2 Grace Kelly / a famous scientist ? (✗)
   ....

3 Gustave Eiffel / French engineer ? (✓)
   ....

4 Michelangelo and Raphael / film directors ? (✗)
   ....

5 the Wright brothers / American ? (✓)
   ....

6 John F Kennedy and Winston Churchill / actors (✗)
   ....

3 **GRAMMAR IN USE** Complete the conversations with *was*, *were*, *wasn't* or *weren't* and the word(s) in brackets (). ◀)) **3.05** Listen and check.

1 A Where (0) ....*were you*......... last night? (you)
   B (1) .... at that new Chinese restaurant in Dover Street. (I)
   A (2) .... good? (it)
   B No, (3) .... terrible. (the food)

2 A (4) .... a doctor? (your grandfather)
   B No, (5) .... He was a dentist. (he)
   A (6) .... successful? (he)
   B Yes, (7) .... very rich. (he)

3 A (8) .... at home yesterday morning? (you)
   B No, (9) .... at home – we were at the supermarket. (we)
   A (10) .... with you? (the children)
   B No, (11) .... with our neighbours. (they)

45 Past simple (1)

Daniel Craig **made** his first James Bond film **in 2006**.

1 Form

We add *-ed* to most verbs to make the past simple:

watch → *watch**ed***, *finish* → *finish**ed***

I/You	
He/She/It	**finished** yesterday.
We/You/They	

Study these spellings:

die → *die**d***, *live* → *live**d***, *like* → *like**d***

stop → *stop**ped***, *plan* → *plan**ned***, *travel* → *travel**led***

carry → *carr**ied***, *study* → *stud**ied***

Spelling rules for regular verbs ➤ page 316

⚠ The pronunciation of the *-ed* ending depends on the sound that comes before it.

 Pronunciation ➤ 1.18

Some verbs are irregular. They do not form the past simple with *-ed*:

buy → **bought**, *do* → **did**, *have (got)* → **had (got)**,

go → **went**, *hit* → **hit**, *leave* → **left**,

make → **made**, *put* → **put**, *say* → **said**, *take* → **took**,

see → **saw**, *tell* → **told**, *win* → **won**

Irregular verbs ➤ page 314

2 Use

We use the past simple to talk about

- a single finished action in the past:
  *I **went** to the dentist yesterday.*
  *I **passed** my exam last week.*
- a repeated action in the past:
  *I **called** your mobile five times yesterday.*

We often use time expressions (e.g. *yesterday*, *in 2002*, *last year*) to say when something happened:

Daniel Craig **made** his first Bond film	*in 2006.*
*I **started** work*	*last month.*
*It **rained** all day*	*yesterday.*
*My English course **started***	***two months ago**. (two months before now)*

We can also use *when* + past simple:

*My father played football **when he was young**.*

***When she left college**, Isabel had no money.*

Practice Use the spelling rules to help you complete these exercises. ➤ page 316

1 In each group, one past form is made in a different way from the others.
Find the ones that are different.

0 talked asked (made) passed
1 walked played went visited
2 stopped robbed planned listened

3 died smiled phoned cried
4 watched told took had
5 carried worried studied enjoyed

2 Write the past form of the verbs in the box below.

+ -ed	repeat the consonant and add -ed	+ -d	(-y) + -ied	irregular verbs
happened	robbed	phoned	hurried	told

~~happen~~ ~~hurry~~ ~~phone~~ ~~rob~~ ~~tell~~ carry enjoy go live make plan smile stop study watch

3 **GRAMMAR IN USE** Choose past forms from Exercise 2 to complete the text.
🔊 **3.06** Listen and check.

DANIEL CRAIG – the new James Bond

Daniel Craig was born in Chester, England in 1968. When he was young, he
(0) ....*lived*.... in the Wirral, near Liverpool. At school he (1) .... sport
and he was in several teams. When he was a child, he (2) .... *Star Trek* on
television and he says it is his ambition to appear in a *Star Trek* film. He (3) ....
to London when he was sixteen and joined the National Youth Theatre. He then
(4) .... acting at the Guildhall School of Music and Drama. He
(5) .... his first film for the BBC in 1996 – *Our Friends in the
North*. In 2006 he got the part of James Bond. Many people were
surprised when this (6) ...., because Craig has blond hair
and all the other actors who have played Bond have dark hair.

4 Complete these sentences. Put the verbs in brackets () in the past tense.
Then put the underlined words in the correct position. 🔊 **3.07** Listen and check.

0 Jane (start) a new job month. <u>last</u> *Jane started a new job last month.*

1 I (play) football all the time I was young. <u>when</u>

2 Europeans (see) potatoes for the first time about five hundred years. <u>ago</u>

3 Somebody (rob) our local bank Wednesday. <u>on</u>

4 My father (have) an American motorbike he was young. <u>when</u>

5 April I (win) a bicycle in a magazine competition. <u>in</u>

6 Six months my brother (stop) smoking. <u>ago</u>

46 Past simple (2)

What **did** you do last night?

We **went** to the cinema.

Then we **had** dinner at Frankie's.

We **didn't get** home until midnight …

1 Form

NEGATIVE	Yes/No QUESTIONS	SHORT ANSWERS
I/He/She/It/We/You/They **did not (didn't) arrive**.	**Did** I/he/she/it/we/you/they **arrive?**	Yes, I/he/she/it/we/you/they **did**. No, I/he/she/it/we/you/they **didn't**.

WH- QUESTIONS				
What	**did**	you	**do**	on Saturday?
Where	**did**	you	**go**	for dinner?
How much	**did**	the meal	**cost?**	

 ✗ ~~What you did on Saturday?~~
✓ What **did** you **do** on Saturday?

2 Use

We use the past simple

- when one thing happens after another in the past:
  We **arrived** at the airport at eleven o'clock and **took** a taxi to the hotel.
  Then we **went** to the café and **had** a drink, but we **didn't eat** anything.

- to talk about a situation that finished in the past:
  I **lived** with my grandparents last summer.
  Did men **have** long hair in the 1960s?
  MP3 players **didn't exist** when I was a child.

Linking words for describing events in the past ➤ Unit 95.1

3 Words we use with the past simple

- We use *then* to say that one action happened after another one:
  'I finished school in 2006. **Then** I went to university.'
  'And what did you do **then**?' (after university)

- We use *from … to* to say when a past situation started and finished:
  James Dean lived **from 1931 to 1955**.
  I waited for you **from eight o'clock to half past nine**!

- We use *for + ten minutes, two hours, a week*, etc. to say how long a past situation lasted:
  Daniela stayed with her cousins **for two weeks** last summer.

More about:
from ➤ Unit 21.3   *for* ➤ Unit 22.2

Practice

1 **Use the words below to write questions and short answers.**

0   die / President Kennedy / 1963 ? (✓)   *Did President Kennedy die in 1963? Yes, he did.*

1   fly / Neil Armstrong / to Mars ? (✗)

....

2   win / Tony Curtis / an Oscar ? (✗)

....

3   invent / Alexander Graham Bell / the telephone ? (✓)

....

4   paint / Michelangelo / the *Mona Lisa* ? (✗)

....

5   write / Ian Fleming / the James Bond books ? (✓)

....

6   exist / computers / in the 1990s ? (✓)

....

2   GRAMMAR IN USE   **There are five more mistakes in the conversation. Find and correct them.**
🔊 **3.08 Listen and check.**

TOM   Did you ~~went~~ *go* to the cinema
        yesterday?

SILVIA   Yes, we do.

TOM   What did you saw?

SILVIA   We didn't saw anything.

TOM   What do you mean?

SILVIA   Well. There was a queue when we got to
         the cinema, so we don't wait.

TOM   So, what did you done?

SILVIA   We went to Video City and rented a DVD.

3   GRAMMAR IN USE   **Look at the pictures. Then describe what Janice did yesterday evening.
Use the words and phrases in the box with the verbs in the past simple.**
🔊 **3.09 Listen and check.**

brush her teeth   ~~go home on the bus~~   go to bed at   have a shower
make a snack   send some emails   watch television from   and then   then

Janice went home on the bus at six o'clock. She

....

....

....

....

47 Past continuous

> What **were** you **doing** at nine o'clock yesterday evening?

> I was watching TV.

1 Form

POSITIVE
I/He/She/It **was working**.
We/You/They **were working**.

NEGATIVE
I/He/She/It **was not (wasn't) working**.
We/You/They **were not (weren't) working**.

QUESTIONS	SHORT ANSWERS	
Was I/he/she/it **working?**	Yes, I/he/she/it **was**.	No, we/you/they **weren't**.
Were we/you/they **working?**	Yes, we/you/they **were**.	No, we/you/they **weren't**.

We form the past continuous with *was/were* + the *-ing* form of the verb.

Spelling rules for *-ing* forms ➤ page 316

2 Use

We use the past continuous

- to describe an action at or around a time in the past:
  *At seven o'clock Marek **was making** the dinner and Isabella **was putting** the children to bed.*
  *I **was watching** TV at nine o'clock.*

watching TV

The action started before nine o'clock and can continue after it.

- for temporary situations in the past:
  *Sally **was living** in Paris when she had her first baby.*

| 2006 | had her first baby | 2008 |
moved to Paris —— living in Paris —— left Paris

- to describe a scene in the past, especially when you are telling a story:
  *When we arrived at the beach, the sun **was shining**.*
  *They **were cleaning** the swimming pool when we got to the hotel.*

- to describe something you did until an event interrupted you and stopped you:
  *I **was watching** TV when the phone **rang**.*

the phone rang
watching TV

  *James Dean **was driving** a Porsche when he **died**.*
  *Gerald **was playing** football when he **hurt** his arm.*

 We don't usually use verbs, such as *like, see, hear, think, agree* in the past continuous.

Verbs that don't use the continuous form ➤ Unit 41.2

Practice   Use the spelling rules to help you complete these exercises. ➤ page 316

1 GRAMMAR IN USE **Complete the text. Use past continuous forms of the verbs in brackets ()
and short forms.** 🔊 3.10 **Listen and check.**

A few years ago we (0) ......_were living_...... (live) in France at the time of the Cannes film
festival. My wife (00) ...._wasn't working_.... (not work) that weekend so we decided to
drive to Cannes to see some of the new films. The sun (1) .... (shine)
when we arrived and the town looked beautiful. It was very busy – lots of people
(2) .... (walk) in the streets. But it wasn't very hot that day so people
(3) .... (not sunbathe) on the beach. We got to our hotel and went
to the restaurant. We had a big surprise – Juliette Binoche (4) .... (sit)
at the back of the restaurant! But she (5) .... (not have) lunch, she
(6) .... (talk) to some other famous film stars. It was so exciting!

2 **Complete the questions and short answers below. Use information from Exercise 1.**
🔊 3.11 **Listen and check.**

0 ......_Was_...... the sun ...._shining_.... when they arrived? – Yes, it was.
1 .... lots of people .... in the streets? – Yes, they were.
2 .... people .... on the beach? – No, they weren't.
3 Who .... at the back of the restaurant? – Juliette Binoche
4 .... she .... lunch? – No, she wasn't.

3 GRAMMAR IN USE **Last night there was a robbery at the Denmore Hotel. The police want
to know what everybody was doing at five past eight. Look at the photos from the hotel
cameras. Read all the questions before you answer them.**

Mr Denby

Steve Burton

Mr and Mrs Grant

Maria

Marco

Alfredo and Alex

0 Was Mr Denby carrying some suitcases? _No, he wasn't. He was swimming in the pool._
1 Was Steve Burton eating in the restaurant? ....
2 Were Mr and Mrs Grant paying the bill? ....
3 Was Maria swimming in the pool? ....
4 Were Alfredo and Alex using the Internet? ....
5 Was Marco cooking in the kitchen? ....

🔘 Go online for more practice

48 Past simple or past continuous?

At the end of the film the bridge **collapsed** while the truck **was crossing** it.

1 Use

PAST SIMPLE	PAST CONTINUOUS
to describe one or more finished actions in the past: *We **arrived** at the hotel at three o'clock and went to our room.* *I **called** you about four times yesterday afternoon.*	to describe an unfinished action at and around a time in the past: *When we arrived at the hotel, the maid **was cleaning** our room.* (The cleaning was not finished when we arrived.) *I couldn't answer the phone because I **was speaking** to some clients.*
when one action happened after another: *When Isabel **came**, we **watched** a DVD.* (= Isabel came and then we watched a DVD.) 6.00 8.00 Isabel came ━━━ we watched a DVD ━━▶	to describe something you were doing at the time when another thing happened: *When Isabel **came**, we **were watching** a DVD.* (= We were watching a DVD at the time Isabel came.) 6.00 8.00 Isabel came ├ we were watching a DVD ━━▶

2 *when* and *while*

We can use either *when* or *while* before the past continuous:
*The bridge collapsed **when/while** the truck **was crossing** it.*
*The post came **when/while** I **was having** my breakfast.*

 We don't use *while* before the past simple, but we can use *when*:
✗ ~~While the post came I was having my breakfast.~~
✓ ***When** the post **came**, I was having my breakfast.*

Practice

1 Choose the correct words in *italics*. 🔊3.12 Listen and check.

0 After I brushed my teeth I(went)/ *was going* to bed.
1 I *went* / *was going* to the dentist five times last year.
2 My computer *broke down* / *was breaking down* yesterday.
3 Hilary fell on the ice last winter and *broke* / *was breaking* her arm.
4 We were relaxing in the garden *when* / *while* we suddenly heard a loud noise.
5 Karl didn't hear the doorbell because he *listened* / *was listening* to his iPod.
6 After I left university, I worked in a bank and then I *moved* / *was moving* to an insurance company.
7 My cousin couldn't visit us in August because she *did* / *was doing* a summer course.
8 I was having a shower *when* / *while* the phone rang.

2 Match the sentences 1 and 2 with A and B.

0 1 When my father arrived, we looked at his photos.   A We started looking at the photos before my father arrived.
2 When my father arrived, we were looking at his photos.   B My father brought the photos with him.

1 1 My aunt worked for Mr O'Reilly.   A She was his assistant.
2 My aunt was working for Mr O'Reilly when she heard the news.   B She was speaking to a client on the phone.

2 1 I was having a party when she told me the news.   A I had a party after she told me the news.
2 When she told me the news I had a party.   B The party started before she told me the news.

3 1 Paul travelled a lot in his last job.   A He was on a plane to Rio.
2 Paul was travelling when the accident happened.   B He was an international salesman.

3 `GRAMMAR IN USE` Complete the text. Use the correct form of the verbs in brackets (). 🔊3.13 Listen and check.

The sinking of the
TITANIC

ON THE NIGHT of 14 April 1912 the cruise ship *Titanic* (0) ...... *was* ...... (be) in the middle of its first journey between England and New York. It (1) .... (travel) across the north Atlantic, south of Greenland. As usual, a sailor (2) .... (watch) the sea in front of the ship; he (3) .... (look) for icebergs. But it was dark and there was no moon, so he couldn't see anything. Suddenly, at exactly 11.40, the ship (4) .... (hit) a huge iceberg. The ship quickly began to sink. At the time of the accident many of the passengers (5) .... (sleep).The sailors

(6) .... (tell) everybody to leave the ship, but there (7) .... (not be) enough boats for all the people. In the end more than 1,500 people (8) .... (die).

49 *used to*

Hollywood actor Russell Crowe **used to work** in a restaurant in Sydney.

1 Form

	POSITIVE	NEGATIVE	
I/He/She/It/We/You/They	**used to work**	**did not (didn't) use to work**	*in a shop.*

QUESTIONS	SHORT ANSWERS	
Did *I/he/she/it/we/you/they* **use to work** *here?*	*Yes, (he)* **did.**	*No, (we)* **didn't.**

 There is no present form of *used to*:
✗ *I use to go to work by bus.*
✓ *I usually* **go** *to work by bus.*

2 Use

We use *used to*

- for actions that happened regularly in the past but do not happen now:
  People **used to write** *a lot of letters.* (but now they send emails)

- to say how often we did things in the past (with *always, once a week, every year*, etc.):
  I **always used to swim** *before breakfast.*
  We **used to go** *to the beach* **every summer***.*

- for past situations that are different now:
  Russell Crowe **used to be** *a waiter.* (but now he is an actor)
  My parents **didn't use to** *live in the city.* (but now they live in the city)
  When I was a child I **used to have** *a pet rabbit.*
  Where **did** *you* **use to go** *on holiday when you were young?*

We pronounce the *s* in *used to* as /s/ not /z/. We do not pronounce the final *d*: /juːstə/.

🔊 Pronunciation ➤ 1.19

3 Past simple or *used to*?

 We use the past simple, *NOT used to*

- for single actions in the past:
  ✗ *I used to have a driving lesson last week.*
  ✓ *I* **had** *a driving lesson last week.* (a single action = past simple)

- for repeated actions in the past with a number:
  ✗ *I used to have a driving lesson twice last week.*
  ✓ *I* **had** *a driving lesson twice last week.* (a repeated action = past simple)

- to talk about a period of time with *for*:
  ✗ *He used to be in the army for two years.*
  ✓ *He* **was** *in the army for two years.*

Practice

1 **Read the information. Then complete the answers below.**

	IN THE PAST	NOW
0 films	in black and white	in colour
1 cameras	big and heavy	small and light
2 phones	attached to wires	mobile
3 transport	ride horses	drive cars
4 work	work on farms	work in factories and offices
5 children	finish school at 12	finish school at 16
6 location	live in the country	live in towns
7 entertainment	go to the cinema	watch TV and DVDs

0 How are films different?
   Films used to be in
   black and white but
   now they are in colour.

1 What about cameras? Cameras ....

2 What about phones? Phones ....

3 How is transport different? People ....

4 Do people work in the same places as in the past?
   No, most people ....

5 What about schools? Children ....

6 Do people live in the same places as in the past?
   No, most people ....

7 What about entertainment? People ....

2 **Find the mistakes in the sentences and correct them. ◀))3.14 Now listen and check.**

0 ~~Were~~ *Did* people use to smoke inside cinemas in the 1950s?

1 Films didn't used to have sound but now they do.

2 Did use to be cameras very expensive?

3 Harrison Ford used to being a carpenter before he became a film star.

4 Glenda Jackson use to be a film actress but now she is a politician.

5 Did Bruce Willis used to have a lot of hair?

6 It wasn't use to be expensive to go to the cinema but now it is.

3 **GRAMMAR IN USE** **Choose the correct words in *italics* in the text. ◀))3.15 Listen and check.**

The politician who used to be a film star

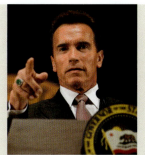

Arnold Schwarzenegger's life is very different today. He (0) *use /* (*used*) to be an actor but now he is a politician. These days he lives in California but he (1) *didn't live / didn't use to live* there, he used to (2) *live / living* in Austria. He (3) *had / use to have* an Austrian passport for many years but he (4) *got / used to get* an American passport in 1983 when he (5) *became / used to become* a US citizen.

When he was young he (6) *wasn't use to be / didn't use to be* interested in politics – his main interest was exercise and he (7) *used to spend / used spend* hours in the gym every day, building his muscles. He was very successful and he (8) *won / used to win* the Mr Universe competition five times. ∎

Review MODULE 6

Use the irregular verb list to help you complete these exercises. ➤ page 314

1 UNITS 44, 45 AND 46 **Complete the text with past simple forms of the verbs in brackets () and no short forms.**

Alfred Hitchcock

ALFRED HITCHCOCK (0) ......was...... (be) one of the most famous and successful film directors of the 20th century. He was born in London in 1899 and he (1) .... (die) in Los Angeles in 1990. Hitchcock (2) .... (begin) his career at Gainsborough Studios in London in 1920. In those days films (3) .... (not have) sound and Hitchcock (4) .... (not be) a director; he (5) .... (be) a designer. But Hitchcock (6) .... (do) a good job and they (7) .... (ask) him to direct a film in 1925.

Hitchcock (8) .... (make) his first film in Germany. He (9) .... (use) a lot of interesting ideas from German cinema in this film. After that he (10) .... (direct) many films in England. But at the end of the 1930s he (11) .... (move) to Hollywood to make his first American film.

That film was called *Rebecca* and it (12) .... (win) the best film Oscar in 1940. After that success he (13) .... (direct) many more movies in Hollywood, including *Psycho*, *Rear Window* and *The Birds*, but he (14) .... (not win) any more Oscars.

Hitchcock (15) .... (become) famous because his films were very exciting and sometimes frightening.

2 UNITS 47, 48 AND 49 **Choose the correct words in *italics* in the conversation.**
◀))3.16 **Listen and check.**

ALAN   Hi, Sadie. What's wrong with your arm?

SADIE   Oh, I (0) *burnt* / *was burning* it while I (1) *cooked* / *was cooking* yesterday.

ALAN   Does it hurt?

SADIE   Not really. I (2) *bought* / *was buying* some special cream at the chemist's. That helps.

ALAN   Mike usually does the cooking in your house, doesn't he?

SADIE   Well, he (3) *used to do* / *was doing* it, but these days he's too busy.

ALAN   His new job?

SADIE   Yes. He (4) *wasn't* / *didn't* use to work full-time, but now he has to work until seven every evening.

ALAN   So do you have to do everything in the house?

SADIE   Yes. He (5) *started* / *was starting* the new job about two weeks ago, so now I'm really tired!

ALAN   I'm sorry to hear that. But (6) *had you* / *did you have* time to go to the music festival on Sunday?

SADIE   Yes, I (7) *go* / *did*. But when we (8) *got* / *were getting* there, it (9) *used to rain* / *was raining*.

ALAN   So what did you (10) *do* / *done* ?

SADIE   It (11) *was* / *were* OK. They (12) *had* / *used to have* a big tent and all the bands played in there.

3 UNIT 49 **Complete the second sentence so it means the same as the first. Use one, two or three words and short forms.**

0 Jake lived in the Far East when he was young.

Jake ...... *used to live* ...... in the Far East.

1 Long flights used to be expensive.

Long flights .... to be cheap.

2 I had short hair when I was young.

I .... to have long hair.

3 Was Sweden a republic in the 19th century?

Did Sweden .... a republic?

4 Most people didn't have cars before 1900.

Before 1900, most people .... to have cars.

4 ALL UNITS **There are four more mistakes in the text. Find and correct them.**

When I was a child, there were only a few TV channels and the programmes
were
~~was~~ in black and white. So I use to love going to the cinema. The colour pictures
were very exciting. We were used to eat sweets and drink lemonade while we
are watching the films. But my parents stopped taking us to the cinema when
I was twelve because they used to buy a colour TV.

5 ALL UNITS **Complete the text with the correct words or phrases, A, B or C below.**

CINEMA

– Early history
The first movies were made in the United States, France and Britain in the
late 19th century. In the early days films (0) .... very new and you used to
look at strange machines to see them. But in 1905 the first cinema (1) ....
in Pittsburgh, USA. This was possible because Thomas Edison and the Lumière
brothers (2) .... film projectors – that make films appear on screens.

– Silent movies
The early films (3) .... sound. Cinema owners (4) .... silence while the
film (5) .... so they employed musicians to play the piano during the film.
Some large cinemas even (6) .... bands. To help people understand what was
happening, directors (7) .... words on the screen called 'intertitles'. The most
popular films (8) .... comedies and there were many famous stars.

0 A was   B did   (C) were
1 A opened   B was opening   C used to open
2 A used to invent   B invented   C did already invent
3 A didn't have   B hadn't   C didn't had
4 A not wanted   B didn't wanted   C didn't want
5 A was playing   B did play   C were played
6 A were having   B had   C having
7 A did put   B used to put   C use to put
8 A were   B were being   C was

Test MODULE 6

Past tenses

Choose the correct answer, A, B or C.

1 George Washington .... the first president of the USA.   ➤ Unit 44
   A was   B were   C be

2 .... your grandparents Polish?   ➤ Unit 44
   A Was   B Did   C Were

3 The children .... at school yesterday.   ➤ Unit 44
   A wasn't   B weren't   C didn't be

4 My watch .... working yesterday; it needs a new battery.   ➤ Unit 45
   A stoped   B stop   C stopped

5 I .... my little sister to the zoo last Saturday.   ➤ Unit 45
   A take   B took   C taked

6 My sister started her first job ....   ➤ Unit 45
   A has two months   B two months ago   C ago two months

7 The letter isn't here because the post .... this morning.   ➤ Unit 46
   A didn't arrived   B didn't arrives   C didn't arrive

8 .... to Rebecca's party last night?   ➤ Unit 46
   A Did you go   B Went you   C Did you went

9 Those shops are new; they .... here ten years ago.   ➤ Unit 46
   A did not be   B weren't   C wasn't

10 We .... dinner at eight o'clock last night.   ➤ Unit 47
    A were eating   B was eating   C did eating

11 I .... living there in October.   ➤ Unit 47
    A weren't   B didn't   C wasn't

12 When we got there, it was cold but it ....   ➤ Unit 47
    A wasn't raining   B not rain   C rained

13 The children were having breakfast when the postman ....   ➤ Unit 48
    A did arrive   B was arriving   C arrived

14 Jeremy .... his car to the garage six times last year.   ➤ Unit 48
    A took   B taking   C was taking

15 We ran to the station and .... the first train we saw.   ➤ Unit 48
    A were getting on   B got on   C was getting on

16 I got a text message while I .... for the bus.   ➤ Unit 48
    A was waiting   B waited   C were waiting

17 When I was a child I .... stay up late.   ➤ Unit 49
    A didn't used to   B used to not   C didn't use to

18 .... go to the same school as my sister?   ➤ Unit 49
    A Did you use to   B Did you used to   C Did use you

19 My best friend .... to a fantastic concert last Saturday.   ➤ Unit 49
    A was going   B used to go   C went

20 My aunt .... in an international bank for fifteen years.   ➤ Unit 49
    A use to work   B worked   C used to work

Present perfect

Before you start

1 Read the letter. Look at the highlighted grammar examples.

ABBOTTS
HEALTH & FITNESS CLUB

Dear member

We've now finished our work on the new ABBOTTS – the difference is amazing! Six weeks ago we closed the club, and since then we've been working hard to improve all the public areas. We've added several new machines to the gym and we've increased the length of the swimming pool to 25 metres.

Many of you have been members of our club for several years – to thank you for staying with us, we have reduced gym, pool and class prices for you.

And we have some new classes! Have you ever tried judo? Now's your chance!

If you haven't visited our new website yet, go to www.abbotts.co.uk.

2 Now read the conversation. Choose the correct words in *italics*. The highlighted grammar examples will help you.

CARLA	Look, Abbotts is opening again. (1) *Have you ever been / Were you* there?	➤ Unit 50
KIM	Yes, and it wasn't very good.	
CARLA	But (2) *they improved / they've improved* the club. It looks fantastic!	➤ Unit 51
KIM	Really? Have they got a sauna now?	
CARLA	Yes, they've got one, but they haven't opened it (3) *yet / already*.	➤ Unit 52
KIM	Are you going to join the new Abbotts?	
CARLA	I'm already a member actually – (4) *I've been / I am* a member for months.	➤ Unit 53
KIM	Oh, right. (5) *I've joined / I joined* a different health club about three years ago and only went twice!	➤ Unit 54
CARLA	I think that often happens. Why don't we go now? You can have a look at it.	
KIM	I don't think so. (6) *I'm studying / I've been studying* hard all day. I'm tired.	➤ Unit 55
CARLA	Well, I've (7) *cleaned / been cleaning* six houses today, but I'd like to go!	➤ Unit 56

3 Check your answers below. Then go to the unit for more information and practice.

1 Have you ever been 2 they've improved 3 yet
4 I've been 5 I joined 6 I've been studying 7 cleaned

50 Present perfect for past experiences

Have you visited the gym before?

No, I haven't.

1 Form

We form the present perfect with
have + the past participle form of the verb.
The regular past participle ends in *-ed*.

SUBJECT	POSITIVE	NEGATIVE	PARTICIPLE
I/We/You/They	*have ('ve)*	*have not (haven't)*	*finished.*
He/She/It	*has ('s)*	*has not (hasn't)*	

Yes/No QUESTIONS			SHORT ANSWERS
Have	*I/we/you/ they*	*finished?*	Yes, *I/we/you/they* **have.** No, *I/we/you/they* **haven't.**
Has	*he/she/it*		Yes, *he/she/it* **has.** No, *he/she/it* **hasn't.**

Wh- QUESTIONS			
What	*have*	*you*	*finished?*
Where	*has*	*she*	*worked?*

Irregular past participles (e.g. *gone*, *stolen*) ➤ page 314

2 Use

We use the present perfect to talk about past experiences in our lives. It is not important when they happened:
*John **has worked** in several gyms. I've **travelled** a lot.*

We can use *before, once, twice, several times,* etc. to say how often:
*I **haven't visited** the gym **before** but I've **stayed** at this hotel **several times**.*
*My parents **have visited** the United States **once**.*

We often use *ever* to ask about past experiences. It means 'in your life':
*'Have you **ever** played golf?' 'Yes, several times.'*
*'Has she **ever** tasted Japanese food?' 'Only once.'*

We use *never* in negative sentences. It means 'not in your life':
*I've **never** played golf. She's **never** cooked Italian food.*

⚠ We put *ever* and *never* BEFORE the past participle:
✗ *'Have you stayed ever in a Hilton Hotel?'*
✓ *'Have you **ever** stayed in a Hilton hotel?'*
✗ *'I've stayed never in any hotels!'*
✓ *'I've **never** stayed in any hotels!'*

3 Superlatives

We often use the present perfect with superlative adjectives (➤ Unit 31):
*That was **the best food I've ever tasted**!*

Practice All the past participles in these exercises are **regular**.

1 Choose the correct words in *italics*. ◀)**3.17** **Listen and check.**

0 I (have)/ *has* worked in several different companies.
1 They haven't *live / lived* in the city before now.
2 Have you *played / play* baseball before?
3 'Have you finished your homework?' 'Yes, I *do / have*.'
4 We *have / did* watched all of Quentin Tarantino's films.
5 'Has Maria called the shop?' 'No, she *hasn't / haven't*.'
6 The cat *has / have* never tasted real steak before!

2 GRAMMAR IN USE **Read the advertisement and the email. Then complete them with words from the box.**

ever has Have have
haven't stayed visited

HOME to HOME
the special holiday experience

Have you (0) .....*ever*...... wanted to experience real Spanish life?

(1) .... you always wanted to be more than a tourist in a hotel?

WELL, HOW ABOUT A HOUSE EXCHANGE?
We organise exchanges of two to four weeks – you live in a Spanish family house here in Spain, and the Spanish family lives in your house in the UK.

Contact us for more information.

Subject House exchange

Dear Sir / Madam
I'm writing about your advert for a 'house exchange'. My family and I have
(2) .... Spain on holiday many times but we've only (3) ....
in hotels before so we (4) .... experienced 'real Spanish life'. We
would like a house for four weeks in the south of Spain. My daughter is learning
Spanish at school but she (5) .... never talked to Spanish people, so
four weeks in the country will be perfect for her.
We (6) .... never invited other people to live in our house, so could
you tell me ...

3 **Write the words in the correct order to make questions. Then write true answers.**
◀)**3.18** **Listen and check.**

0 you visited Have another country ever ?
Have you ever visited another country? Yes, I have. I've visited the USA.

1 Have worked ever in a shop you ?
....

2 watched ever film the best you have What's ?
....

3 your parents Have lived in a foreign country ever ?
....

4 ever you stayed in Have a luxury hotel ?
....

5 you the most interesting What's tasted have food ever ?
....

51 Present perfect with present results

I can't play today because **I've broken** my arm.

1 Form

	REGULAR VERBS			IRREGULAR VERBS			
infinitive	*visit*	*play*	*want*	*break*	*come*	*eat*	*have*
past participle	*visited*	*played*	*wanted*	*broken*	*come*	*eaten*	*had*

Past participles are either regular (infinitive + *-ed*) or irregular.

Spelling rules ➤ page 316   Irregular past participles ➤ page 314

2 Use

We use the present perfect

- to talk about things that happened a short time ago and that have a result now:
  I've broken my leg. (It's broken now.)
  Your sister has arrived. (She's here now.)
  The post has come. (There's a letter for you.)
  They've gone out. (They aren't here.)

  With the past simple, the results are also in the past:
  I broke my leg last year and didn't play football from August to October.
  My sister arrived late and missed the beginning of the film.

- to introduce new information:
  'Julian has passed his driving test.' 'Oh, that's good news!'
  The US President has arrived in London.

  When we give more details about these events, we use the past simple:
  Julian has passed his driving test. He took it yesterday.
  The US President has arrived in London. He flew here from Washington last night.

3 *been* and *gone*

Been is the past participle of *be*. *Gone* is the past participle of *go*:
I've been tired all day. (And I'm still tired now.)
Fran has gone to the doctor's. (And she's still there now.)

⚠ But we use *been* as the past participle of *go* when it means 'has gone and come back':
My parents have been to New Zealand. (They have visited it in the past and have returned.)
My parents have gone to New Zealand on holiday. (They are there now.)

Practice

1 Write the past participles of these verbs. Use the list on page 314 to help you.

0 break ...*broken*...   3 buy ....   6 eat ....   9 read ....

1 take ....   4 have ....   7 run ....   10 see ....

2 go ....   5 be ....   8 lose ....

2 Complete these conversations with participles from Exercise 1. ◀ᴏ 3.19 Listen and check.

0 A Hi, you look happy!

   B Yes, we've just ....*been*.... on holiday. We had a great time!

1 A What's wrong with Jake? He wasn't at school today.

   B Well, he's .... some bad food, I think. He feels ill and he's .... to bed!

2 A Jenny's unhappy because she's .... her bike.

   B I know. Don't tell her yet, but I've .... her a new one.

3 A How good are your computer skills?

   B Well, I've .... several lessons and I've .... two exams.

4 A Hi, Sam, it's me. Is something wrong? You weren't at the gym yesterday.

   B Yes, I've .... my leg, I'm afraid.

3 Match the sentences with the pictures. Then complete them with the verbs in brackets (). ◀ᴏ 3.20 Listen and check.

0 I ...*'ve been*... to the dentist. (go)   *E*

1 Harry .... his arm. (break)   ....

2 Pat .... the door. (paint)   ....

3 I .... ten kilometres. (run)   ....

4 Louisa .... her pen. (lose)   ....

5 Alex .... too much! (eat)   ....

4 Write two sentences for each set of words below.

0 famous footballer / buy / a royal palace / pay £2 million for it

   A famous footballer has bought a royal palace. He paid £2 million for it.

1 US President / arrive / in Moscow / plane / land / two hours ago

   ....

2 TV star David Walliams / swim / English Channel for charity / take eleven hours

   ....

3 J K Rowling / write / a new book / finish it / twenty-four hours ago

   ....

52 Present perfect with *just, already, yet*

> Has the match finished yet?

> Yes, it**'s just finished**. Federer won.

1 *just*

We use *just* with the present perfect to talk about things that happened a short time ago:
*The plane **has just landed**.* (a few minutes ago)
*The play **has just started** – you can't go in now.*

 We put *just* before the past participle:
✗ *The match has finished just.*
✗ *The match just has finished.*
✓ *The match **has just finished**.*

2 *already, yet*

We can use *already* and *yet* with the present perfect.

- *Already* means 'before now'. We use it in positive sentences when something happens before you expect it:
*You've missed the match. It**'s already finished**.*

  We usually put *already* before the past participle:
*Graham's train **has already arrived**.*
*You don't need to wash the dishes. I**'ve already done** them.*

- *Yet* means 'by now'. We use it in questions to ask about something we are expecting to happen:
***Has** the six o'clock train **arrived yet**? It's five past six and I haven't seen it.*

  We also use *yet* in negative sentences when we expected something to happen before now:
*Our burgers **haven't come yet**. We ordered them nearly half an hour ago!*

  We usually put *yet* at the end of a question or negative statement:
*Has the match finished **yet**?*
*I haven't read this book **yet**.*

 We don't use *yet* in positive sentences or *already* in negative sentences:
✗ *I've paid for the meal yet.*   ✓ *I've **already** paid for the meal.*
✗ *The parcel hasn't arrived already.*   ✓ *The parcel hasn't arrived **yet**.*

Practice

1 Write a sentence after each statement. Use *just* + the present perfect form of the verbs in brackets (). Use short forms. ◄❱ **3.21** Listen and check.

0 Her hair's wet. (wash) She's *just washed her hair.* ....

1 He hasn't got any money. (spend) He's ....

2 There's no one at home. (leave) They ....

3 There aren't any crisps left. (eat) I ....

4 They're giving him a prize. (win) He ....

5 She's watching TV now. (turn on) She ....

6 Lorenzo is here now. (arrive) He ....

2 Write the words again in the correct order. ◄❱ **3.22** Listen and check.

0 has landed yet plane Their not *Their plane has not landed yet.* ....

1 fed cat I already have the ....

2 Have phone bill the you yet paid ? ....

3 arrived post The just has ....

4 We yet had any not have news ....

5 already shopping done I the have all ....

6 Keira yet Has new job her started ? ....

3 **GRAMMAR IN USE** Write *just*, *already* or *yet* in the text below.

Paula Radcliffe

WITH SEVERAL EUROPEAN and World records, Paula Radcliffe has (0) *already* achieved a lot in long-distance running. It's true that she hasn't won an Olympic race (1) ...., but she has won almost everything else, including the 5,000 metres at the Commonwealth Games and the 10,000 metres at the European events. But she is most famous for the longest race – the marathon. She has (2) .... won the London Marathon three times. She had a baby earlier this year and has (3) .... returned to competitions – only a month ago – but she has (4) .... won an important race, the New York Marathon. Is she the greatest ever female long-distance runner? Well, perhaps she hasn't proved that (5) ...., but she has (6) .... become one of the most popular sportswomen in the United Kingdom.

NOVEMBER 2007

4 Write three sentences about what you have done or not done today.

1 What have you just done? *I've just* ....

2 What have you already done? ....

3 What haven't you done yet? ....

53 Present perfect with *for*, *since*, etc.

1 for/since

We use the present perfect with *for* or *since* to talk about situations that started in the past and continue now:

5 YEARS AGO	NOW
(John left school and started work here.)	(John still works here.)

⊢ *John has worked here for five years.* ───────→
⊢ *John has worked here since he left school.* ───────→

For and *since* both answer the question *How long?*
'**How long** have you worked here?' '**For** five years.'
'**How long** have you known Sami?' '**Since** 2000.'

Use *for* + a period of time	five minutes, an hour, two weeks, for years, a long time, etc.	*Sami's been my best friend for* **many years**.
Use *since* + an exact time, day, date or event	five o'clock, Monday, March, he left school	*Sami's been my best friend* **since 2000**. *Sami's been my best friend* **since we** **started school**.

 ✗ *I know Alan for thirty years.* ✓ *I've known Alan for thirty years.*

Present perfect continuous ➤ Unit 55

2 this morning, this week, etc.

We use the present perfect with time expressions (e.g. *today, this morning, this week, this year*) when the time is still continuing:
Have you **seen** Jan **this morning**? (It is still morning.)
I've worked forty hours **this week**. (The week has not finished.)

Compare the present perfect and past simple
- present perfect:
  I've made several phone calls this morning. (It is still morning.)
- past simple:
  I made several phone calls this morning.
  (It is now afternoon/evening – the morning has finished.)

 After *when* or *what time* in questions, we use the past simple not the present perfect:
✗ *When have you bought your car?* ✓ *When* **did you buy** *your car?*
✗ *What time have you arrived?* ✓ *What time* **did you arrive**?

Practice

1 Write *for* or *since* below.

0 ....*for*........ about 200 years   4 .... one year

00 .....*since*...... 1810   5 .... July

1 1987   6 .... I was eighteen

2 .... ten minutes   7 .... nearly three months

3 .... quarter past three   8 .... about twenty-five years

2 Complete each sentence in two ways. Use the phrases from Exercise 1.

0 They built that school a long time ago.

It's been there *for about 200 years* / ...... *since 1810* ....

1 It's 3.25 and I've been at the dentist's .... / ....

2 My parents have been married .... / ....

3 I'm nineteen. I started college when I was eighteen.

I've been at college .... / ....

4 It's October and the weather has been lovely .... / ....

3 Match the two parts of the sentences. ◀)) **3.23** Listen and check.

0 I haven't heard from my sister this   A we had that meal at the airport.
1 This film's so long! It's already   B my holiday – two weeks by the beach!
lasted for   C two hours and there's still another
2 We haven't felt very well since   hour to go.
3 I haven't seen my parents for   D morning and I haven't finished
4 I'm really sorry but I've been   the report.
very busy this   E week, but she usually phones on Fridays.
5 I've felt more relaxed since   F two months because they live abroad now.

4 **GRAMMAR IN USE** For 1–6, write the present perfect or the past simple of the verbs in brackets (). For A–D, write *for*, *since* or *How long*. ◀)) **3.24** Listen and check.

DOCTOR (0) ..*How long*... have you had this cold?

PATIENT Well, I (00) ....*'ve had*.... (have) it for nearly two weeks, but I've had a cough for longer.

DOCTOR How long have you had that?

PATIENT I've had it (A) .... October, so more than a month. The thing is, I (1) .... (have) about five colds (B) .... the spring.

DOCTOR That is a lot. (2) .... (you / have) a lot of colds last year, too?

PATIENT No, not really. I think I (3) .... (have) only two all last year.

DOCTOR Mmm, (4) .... (you / change) anything about your life this year?

PATIENT Well, yes, my job. I work in a gym now. I'm a fitness trainer.

DOCTOR I see. (C) .... have you worked there?

PATIENT I (5) .... (start) the job in March, so I've been there (D) .... eight months. We've had a few customers with colds I suppose …

DOCTOR I see. And what was your job before?

PATIENT I was a gardener. I worked by myself.

DOCTOR Well, that's it. You (6) .... (spend) a lot of time close to people with colds, and you've caught their colds. Now, I think you should …

54 Present perfect or past simple?

We've lived here for ten years.

I lived there in the 1960s when I was a child.

1 Use

PRESENT PERFECT	PAST SIMPLE
to talk now about finished actions in the past, when we don't know the time or it isn't important: *I've been to that beach before.* before ——→ NOW	to talk now about finished actions that happened at a definite time in the past: *I went to that beach last summer.* —— last summer —— NOW
to talk now about situations that started in the past and are still continuing: *James has worked at the gym for two years.* —— 2 years ——→ NOW = He is working there now.	to talk now about situations that started and finished in the past: *James worked at the gym for two years.* —— 2 years —— NOW = He isn't working there now.
to talk about one or more finished actions in a time period that is still continuing: *We've had three yoga lessons this month.* —— this month ——→ NOW	to talk about finished actions in a time period that is past: *We had three yoga lessons in July.* —— July —— August —→ NOW
with time expressions: *ever, never, just, yet, already, since, for, this week/month/year*	with time expressions: *yesterday, in the summer/June/2007, ago, last week/month/year, for*

⚠ It is sometimes difficult to hear /v/ in *I've, we've, you've, they've* and /s/ in *he's* and *she's*.

PAST SIMPLE   *I finished work.*   *He started early.*   *We carried the bags.*
PRESENT PERFECT *I've finished work.*   *He's started early.*   *We've carried the bags.*

The other words around the verb can usually help you to understand which form you hear:
*I finished work **an hour ago**.*
I've finished my work.

 Pronunciation ➤ 1.20

132

Practice

1 Match each sentence 1–4 with A or B.

0 Emma has lived with us for two years. ——→ A She's still living with us.
   B She doesn't live with us anymore.

1 Kieran lived in Tokyo for six months.
   A He still lives there.
   B He doesn't live there now.

2 I didn't go to the Tutankhamun exhibition when it was on.
   A It's finished and I missed it.
   B I am planning to visit it soon.

3 I haven't seen Alex this morning.
   A It's too late to see him now.
   B I hope I will see him before the morning ends.

4 Lucy has been to Toronto.
   A She's still in Toronto.
   B She went there for a holiday in 2007.

2 **GRAMMAR IN USE** Choose the correct words in *italics* in the text. ◀》**3.25** Listen and check.

ACTION TOURS is a small, friendly company and we (0) *have provided* / *provided* many different specialist activity holidays for people since we started. We (1) *have begun* / *began* in 2006 with only two types of holiday, but we (2) *have grown* / *grew* every year since then and can now offer a wide range of tours.

Our most popular holidays are skiing and cycling. Our main ski trainer, Jules, (3) *has taught* / *taught* skiing for nearly twenty years. Suraya is our cycling tour leader – she (4) *has taken* / *took* part in the National Championships three times and she (5) *has finished* / *finished* fifth last year.

This year we (6) *have organised* / *organised* over twenty activity holidays – already more than we (7) *have done* / *did* last year, when we (8) *have provided* / *provided* a total of eighteen. Take a look at our website ...

3 **GRAMMAR IN USE** Complete the conversation. Use the verbs in the correct tense. ◀》**3.26** Listen and check.

OFFICIAL Here are the details. Now, (0) ..*have you entered*.. (you / enter) a long-distance swimming race before?

DARRYL Yes, (1) .... (I / have). (2) .... (I / do) two.

OFFICIAL When (3) .... (you / do) those?

DARRYL In 2005 and 2008.

OFFICIAL And (4) .... (you / complete) both of them?

DARRYL Yes, (5) .... (I / do). I (6) .... (finish) them both easily.

OFFICIAL Good. Now, let's talk about your training for this race ...

4 Use the words below to write information about yourself.

1 join a club? / kind of club? / member since? / why join?
I've joined a tennis club. I've been a member since July. I joined it because I love tennis!

2 go on an activity holiday? / kind of holiday? / when? / where to?
....

3 ever visited a foreign country? / how many? / where?
....

55 Present perfect continuous

They look tired!

Well, they**'ve been running** for more than two hours.

1 Form

SUBJECT	POSITIVE	+ *been* + *-ing* verb	NEGATIVE	+ *been* + *-ing* verb
I/We/You/They	*have ('ve)*	*been waiting.*	*have not (haven't)*	*been waiting.*
He/She/It	*has ('s)*		*has not (hasn't)*	

QUESTIONS			SHORT ANSWERS
Have	*I/we/you/they*	*been waiting?*	*Yes, I/we/you/they **have**.* *No, I/we/you/they **haven't**.*
Has	*he/she/it*		*Yes, he/she/it **has**.* *No, he/she/it **hasn't**.*

We form the present perfect continuous with *have* + *been* + the *-ing* form of the verb.

2 Use

We use the present perfect continuous to talk about an action or situation that started in the past and is still happening now. We often use *for* and *since* with the present perfect continuous:
I've been waiting in this queue for three hours!

It is different from the present perfect because we usually use the continuous for a temporary action or situation, not for a situation that we think is permanent.

Compare:
present continuous → present perfect continuous (temporary)
I'm training for the race. I've been training for it for six months.
Are you waiting for the bus? Yes. I've been waiting for it for an hour/since three o'clock.

present simple → present perfect (permanent)
I live in Istanbul. I've lived there for twenty years.
'Do you know Alan?' 'Yes, I've known him all my life.'

We often use the present perfect continuous to explain a present situation:
'They look tired.' 'Well, they've been running for more than two hours.'
'Your Spanish is good.' 'Thanks, I've been studying it for two years now.'

 ✗ ~~I live here for five months.~~ ✓ *I've been living here for five months.*

 Pronunciation ➤ 1.21

Practice

1 Use the words below to write sentences. Use the present perfect continuous and short forms.

0 I / drive / for three hours   *I've been driving for three hours.*

1 We / wait / since two o'clock   ....

2 Carola / not / sleep / well   ....

3 you / revise / for your exam ?   ....

4 They / build / a new gym   ....

5 How long / he / work there ?   ....

6 You / not / listen / to me !   ....

2 Look at the pictures. Complete the conversations with verbs from the box. Use short forms. **3.27** Listen and check.

cook shop talk ~~travel~~ wait work

0 'We haven't seen Michael for some time.'
'No, he *'s been travelling* .'

1 'The kitchen's a bit untidy!'
'Mmm, I .... all afternoon.'

2 'You look really tired.'
'I .... all night.'

3 'The buses are terrible these days, aren't they?'
'Yes, I .... for forty minutes.'

4 'Can I have some money for the cinema?'
'Sorry, I .... I haven't got any!'

5 'You've been on the phone for hours!'
'I .... to my friends.'

3 Write sentences about the situations. Use the present perfect continuous and *for/since*. **3.28** Listen and check.

0 They started playing tennis at two o'clock. It's now five-thirty and they're still playing the same game! (since)
They've been playing the same game of tennis since two o'clock!

1 I started learning Chinese when I was fifteen. Now I'm seventeen. (for)
....

2 Our friends came to stay with us on Sunday, and they're still here. (since)
....

3 It started raining yesterday afternoon and it still hasn't stopped. (since)
....

4 Graham started looking for a new job six months ago. He still hasn't found one. (for)
....

⏻ Go online for more practice   135

56 Present perfect or present perfect continuous?

We've been playing since nine o'clock this morning. We're excited because we've won the competition!

1 General uses

PRESENT PERFECT	PRESENT PERFECT CONTINUOUS
for an action that happened a short time ago and has a result now: *He's broken his leg* (and can't play football today).	to explain a present situation: *He's muddy because he's been playing football.*
for a finished action in the past, to answer *How much/many?*: *We've played six games.*	for an action that is still continuing or has just finished, to answer *How long?*: *We've been playing since nine o'clock.*
for a situation that is still continuing, and that we think is permanent, usually with *for* or *since*: *The castle has stood here for 800 years.*	for a situation that is still continuing, and that we think is temporary, usually with *for* or *since*: *I've been standing in this queue for forty minutes!*

2 Uses with some verbs

We can use some verbs (e.g. *live, work, teach, study* with *for* or *since*) in the present perfect or present perfect continuous. They mean almost the same:
We've lived in this house since we got married.
or *We've been living in this house since we got married.*

Philip has taught geography at Durham University for fifteen years.
or *Philip has been teaching geography at Durham University for fifteen years.*

 We don't use the present perfect continuous with some verbs (e.g. *understand, know, want, be*). We use the present perfect:
✗ *Carly has been knowing Jason for two years.*
✓ *Carly has known Jason for two years.*
✗ *I've been being much happier recently.*
✓ *I've been much happier recently.*

Verbs that don't use the continuous form ➤ Unit 41.2

Practice

1 **Match the question to the correct answer, A or B.**
For one question, both answers are correct. 🔊 **3.29 Listen and check.**

0 Where's the bus? ⟶
   A No idea. We've waited for over an hour!
   B No idea. We've been waiting for over an hour!

1 These cookies are delicious! Do you make them yourself?
   A Yes, I've made about 50 of them today!
   B Yes, I've been making about 50 of them today!

2 Where does your brother live?
   A In New York at the moment. He's lived there for nearly two months.
   B In New York at the moment. He's been living there for nearly two months.

3 Have you met Teresa?
   A Yes, we've known each other all our lives.
   B Yes, we've been knowing each other all our lives.

4 What's wrong with your feet?
   A They're really sore. I've walked all day.
   B They're really sore. I've been walking all day.

5 Was this an Oxfam charity event?
   A Yes, I've just walked 20 kilometres to raise money.
   B Yes, I've just been walking 20 kilometres to raise money.

2 **GRAMMAR IN USE** **Choose the correct words in *italics* in the interview.** 🔊 **3.30 Listen and check.**

INTERVIEWER I'm terribly sorry I'm late, Ms Drake. Have you (0) (*been*)/ *been being* here long?
MS DRAKE No, I've only just (1) *arrived* / *been arriving*. My train was late.
INTERVIEWER OK, let's start. Why do you want to work with Camp America next summer?
MS DRAKE Well, I've just (2) *finished* / *been finishing* a course in sports science and since then I've (3) *looked* / *been looking* for a job with young people. And I've always (4) *wanted* / *been wanting* to go to the United States, so this is a perfect opportunity.
INTERVIEWER Right. Have you (5) *had* / *been having* any experience of this sort of work?
MS DRAKE Not exactly, but I have three younger brothers, and I've (6) *looked* / *been looking* after them a lot in the past.
INTERVIEWER That sounds good. Now, have you (7) *chosen* / *been choosing* your main sport?
MS DRAKE To teach, you mean? Yes, I'm a good cyclist, but I think my best sport is swimming.
INTERVIEWER That's fine, Ms Drake. I think you've (8) *told* / *been telling* me everything …

3 **Complete the conversations with verbs from the box.**
Use the present perfect or present perfect continuous and short forms.

call make play put read ~~swim~~ think

0 A Your hair's wet.
   B Yes, I 've been swimming in the lake.

1 A What's wrong? You look very sad.
   B I .... about my pet rabbit. It died yesterday.

2 A Have you heard from Sara?
   B No, I .... her twice today – there's no answer.

3 A Where's the car?
   B It's OK. I .... it in the garage.

4 A Why are the children so tired?
   B They .... with their cousins all day.

5 A Would you like to read this book?
   B Thanks, but I .... it before.

6 A Mmm, lovely smell!
   B Yes, Phil .... cakes all morning.

Review MODULE 7

Use the irregular verb list to help you complete these exercises. ➤ page 314

1 UNITS 50, 51 AND 54 **Choose the correct form in *italics* in the conversations.**

1 A I'm afraid I *broken /('ve broken)* the DVD player.
  B Oh, no! What has *happen / happened*?
  A I *dropped / 've dropped* it.

2 A I've just *had / have* a call from Shona.
  B Is everything OK?
  A Yes. Her plane *has landed / landed* early and she got the eleven o'clock train, so she'll be home soon.

3 A What's the most difficult exam you *ever took / 've ever taken*?
  B That's easy! My driving test.
  A When *have you taken / did you take* it?
  B A long time ago, when I *was / 've been* twenty.

4 A Can I speak to David?
  B Sorry, he isn't here now.
  A Oh, where's he *been / gone*?
  B He*'s took / has taken* Mum to the station.

2 UNITS 51 AND 52
**Complete the text with the words in brackets ().
Use the present perfect without short forms.**

Spurs sign Croatian Modric

TOTTENHAM HOTSPUR (0) *have just announced* (just / announce) that (1) .... (they / agree) to pay over 20 million euros for Croatian Luka Modric. The 22-year-old joined Dinamo Zagreb in 2005, and played his first international match a year later.

(2) .... (He / already / play) over 20 matches for Croatia, and was part of the team that beat England in the race for Euro 2008. Modric (3) .... (recently / have) talks with other teams, for example Newcastle and Barcelona, but Spurs (4) .... (beat) the others to an agreement. Spurs (5) .... (agree) the contract with the player, but (6) .... (they / not / sign / it / yet) because Modric needs permission to work in the UK.

3 UNITS 53, 54, 55 AND 56 **Choose words and phrases from the box to complete the conversation. There are four extra phrases.** 🔊3.31 **Listen and check.**

> been painting   chose   painted   didn't   did you do   haven't
> have you been choosing   have you chosen   ~~have you been doing~~
> 's been helping   's been studying   've chosen   helped

A What (0) *have you been doing* ? There's paint everywhere!

B I've (1) .... Look, I've (2) .... three walls in the living room.

A But they're pink! Who (3) .... that awful colour?

B I did. And I (4) .... these colours for the bedrooms, too.
  Look – what do you think?

A Oh, dear, they're ... Hey! Is that Justin in the other room? Why isn't he at school?

B Because (5) he .... me since lunchtime.

A But he should be at school.

B No, they've got some time to study at home before their exams.
  (6) He .... really hard all week, so he needed a break from it.

A I see. What about the bathroom, (7) .... the colour for that, too?

B No, I (8) .... Maybe you'd like to choose that one?

4 ALL UNITS **Complete the text with the correct word or phrase, A, B or C below.**

Lewis Hamilton

LEWIS HAMILTON WAS born in January 1985 in a town in the south of England. He (0) .... cars of one type or another since he was eight years old, and he (1) .... since then that one day he'll be a success.

The motor racing team McLaren noticed him when he was a young teenager, and he (2) .... part of their young driver programme when he was thirteen. Since then he (3) .... for McClaren teams.

Hamilton (4) .... successful in all the main motorsport events, including the Formula 1 World Championship. He (5) .... that in 2008. He (6) .... a lot of special motorsport prizes – he (7) .... three at the end of his first year in Formula 1. Hamilton moved from the UK to Switzerland in 2007 and he (8) .... there since then.

0 A a is racing   B has raced   C has been racing
1 A has known   B knows   C has been knowing
2 A has become   B has been becoming   C became
3 A has always driven   B always drives   C always drove
4 A has been yet   B has already been   C has just been
5 A won   B has been winning   C won yet
6 A also received   B also receives   C has also received
7 A won   B has been winning   C has won
8 A lived   B lives   C has been living

5 ALL UNITS **Write a sentence about each situation. Use the past simple, present perfect or present perfect continuous form of the verbs in brackets ().**

0 Harry started his essay at 5.30. It's now 11.30 and he still hasn't finished it. (write)
   Harry's been writing his essay for six hours. / Harry's been writing his essay since 5.30.

1 Becky moved to Milan in 2006, and she came back to England in 2008. (live)

2 Irina visited Athens in 2008 and 2009. She wants to go back there. (be)

3 Jack starts work at 8.30. It's 9.30 now and Jack isn't at work. (arrive)

4 I started cleaning the house two hours ago and I haven't finished it yet. (clean)

5 Ginny's been driving for a month. Her driving test was four weeks ago. (pass)

6 Adrian bought his car in November. It's now June. (have)

6 ALL UNITS **Find the mistakes in the sentences and correct them.**

0 Selina ~~has~~ hurt her arm and can't play tennis tonight.
1 Kevin has just been to the doctor's. I don't know when he'll be back.
2 Sit down – you don't need to do the dishes. I've done them yet.
3 Brian and Sally are married for thirty years and they have thirteen grandchildren.
4 Is the dentist free yet? I've been waiting since an hour.
5 I've been having three job interviews this week.
6 Mario doesn't speak much English – he's only learning it for six weeks.

Test MODULE 7

Present perfect

Choose the correct answer, A, B or C.

1 Kerry .... never stayed in a hotel.
   A is B was C has
   ➤ Unit 50

2 They .... by sea several times this year.
   A travelled B have travelled C is travelled
   ➤ Unit 50

3 Have you .... the the British Museum in London?
   A ever visited B ever visit C never visit
   ➤ Unit 50

4 That's the biggest cat I .... !
   A see B have ever seen C saw
   ➤ Unit 50

5 Carl says he's never .... Indian food.
   A ate B eats C eaten
   ➤ Unit 51

6 Louisa has .... to the shops. She isn't back yet.
   A gone B been C went
   ➤ Unit 51

7 Hey! I .... the competition! I've just had a letter in the post!
   A won B 've won C win
   ➤ Unit 51

8 Two trains have crashed near London. They .... each other at 150 kph.
   A have hit B were hitting C hit
   ➤ Unit 51

9 Don't feed the dog. I've ....
   A done it yet B already done it C done already it
   ➤ Unit 52

10 'Is Mary here?' 'No, she ....'
   A hasn't arrived yet B yet hasn't arrived C has arrived yet
   ➤ Unit 52

11 Oliver hasn't seen his daughter ....
   A since two years B two years ago C for two years
   ➤ Unit 53

12 'Do you know Portugal?' 'Well, we .... to Lisbon. We went there last year.'
   A went B 've been C 've gone
   ➤ Unit 54

13 I .... on a farm during the summer last year.
   A worked B have worked C work
   ➤ Unit 54

14 Have you had breakfast ....?
   A yesterday B an hour ago C this morning
   ➤ Unit 54

15 We've been .... in this house for six months.
   A lived B living C live
   ➤ Unit 55

16 The weather's awful. It .... all morning, and it's still raining.
   A rained B 's raining C 's been raining
   ➤ Unit 55

17 I .... English for five years so I'm in the advanced class now.
   A study B 've been studying C 'm studying
   ➤ Unit 55

18 I have to finish my history homework! I .... all evening but it's still not ready.
   A 'm writing B 've written C 've been writing
   ➤ Unit 56

19 I .... you five times to clean your room! Now do it!
   A 've asked B ask C 've been asking
   ➤ Unit 56

20 Come back, Beth! You .... your mobile phone.
   A 've forgotten B 've been forgetting C forget
   ➤ Unit 56

Before you start

1 Read the telephone conversation. Look at the <mark>highlighted</mark> grammar examples.

MANAGER	I'm in a traffic jam so I think <mark>I'm going to be</mark> late for work. Have I got a lot of appointments this morning?
SECRETARY	Yes. You<mark>'re seeing</mark> the sales director at ten o'clock.
MANAGER	<mark>I don't think I'll be</mark> there in time.
SECRETARY	OK. I<mark>'ll phone</mark> him and change the appointment.
MANAGER	What about the marketing meeting?
SECRETARY	It<mark>'s</mark> at eleven-thirty and everyone<mark>'s having</mark> lunch afterwards.
MANAGER	OK. Is there anything else?
SECRETARY	Yes. The managing director wants to see you.
MANAGER	OK. I'll phone him <mark>when I get</mark> to the office. What about the problem with my laptop computer?
SECRETARY	Don't worry. I<mark>'m going to see</mark> the technician tomorrow.

Monday 12 April
8.00
9.00
10.00   sales director
11.30   marketing meeting
13.00   lunch with marketing team

2 Now read the sentences. Choose the correct words in *italics*. The <mark>highlighted</mark> grammar examples will help you.

1 The sky is very dark. I think it's *raining / going to rain* later.   ➤ Unit 57
2 'What are your plans for the weekend?'   ➤ Unit 57
   '*I'll see / I'm going to see* my cousins in Cambridge.'
3 'It's very dark in here.'   ➤ Unit 58
   'OK. *I'll / I'm going to* turn on the light.'
4 Sorry, Clare. I *don't think I'll / think I will not* have time to see you today.   ➤ Unit 58
5 Hurry up! The meeting *will be / is* at 11.00 and it's already 10.55.   ➤ Unit 59
6 We want to be in town early tomorrow so *we're taking / we take* the early   ➤ Unit 59
   train to London Bridge.
7 I'll phone you when I *get / will get* to the airport.   ➤ Unit 59
8 I've got the tickets. We *'ll sit / 're sitting* in the front row!   ➤ Unit 60

3 Check your answers below. Then go to the unit for more information and practice.

1 going to rain 2 I'm going to see 3 I'll
4 don't think I'll 5 is 6 we're taking 7 get 8 're sitting

57 Future with *going to*

> I'm not going to finish this copying by three o'clock!

1 Form

POSITIVE			NEGATIVE		
I	am ('m)		I	am not ('m not)	
He/She/It	is ('s)	going to win.	He/She/It	is not (isn't)	going to win.
We/You/They	are ('re)		We/You/They	are not (aren't)	

QUESTIONS			SHORT ANSWERS	
Am	I		Yes, I am.	No, I'm not.
Is	he/she/it	going to win?	Yes, he/she/it is.	No, he/she/it isn't.
Are	we/you/they		Yes, we/you/they are.	No, we/you/they aren't.

2 Future plans

We use *going to* to talk about our future plans:
*I**'m going to** apply for a new job.*
*Carol **isn't going to be** at the meeting.*
***Are** you **going to come** to the party?*

We often use time expressions (e.g. *tomorrow, next week, on Monday*) with *going to*:
*I'm going to see Manchester United **on Saturday.***
*They're not going to have a summer holiday **this year.***
*What are you going to do **this evening?***

NATURAL ENGLISH It is possible to use *going to* + *go/come*:
*I**'m going to go** shopping this afternoon.*

But the present continuous (➤ Unit 59) is more common:
*I**'m going** shopping this afternoon.*
*I**'m coming** to London on Tuesday.*

3 Things we expect to happen

We also use *going to* to talk about things we expect to happen in the future because of
something we know or can see NOW:
*I**'m not going to finish** this copying by three o'clock!* (because it's 2.51 and there's a lot to do)
*I**'m going to be** late for work.* (because I'm in a traffic jam now)
*It**'s going to rain**.* (because the sky is dark and full of clouds now)

Future with *will* ➤ Unit 58

In informal conversation and in songs we often pronounce *going to* as 'gonna' /ɡənə/.

Pronunciation ➤ 1.22

Practice

1 Complete the sentences with a form of *going to* and a verb from the box. Use short forms.
🔊 **3.32** Listen and check.

be~~ break down eat hit

0 'When I grow up, I *'m going to be* a singer.'

1 'Watch out! We .... that tree!'

2 'I .... here – it's too expensive.'

3 'Everyone uses this photocopier – it ....'

2 Write the words in the correct order. 🔊 **3.33** Listen and check.

0 going to are see that new film you ? *Are you going to see that new film?*

1 not at anything the shops going to buy today I'm

....

2 visit us your sister is going to next weekend ?

....

3 the exam take the children going to aren't this year

....

4 they our party are going to to some friends bring ?

....

5 tonight isn't rain it going to

....

3 **GRAMMAR IN USE** Read Debbie's email and the statements below. Do you think the statements are true (T) or false (F)?

> **Subject** Work is boring!
>
> Hi Tess,
> I'm writing this from work. As usual there's nothing for me to do. It's so boring here. I know this company isn't making very much money at the moment so I don't think it has a very good future. The manager doesn't like me very much, and I really don't like any of my colleagues. In fact I think I might look on the Internet and see if there are any other jobs around here.
> See you soon,
> Debbie

0 Debbie's going to stay in this job for several years. *F*

1 The manager is going to give Debbie a pay increase. ....

2 Debbie's going to look for another job. ....

3 The company is going to be successful in the future. ....

4 Debbie's going to make some good friends in the office. ....

⏻ Go online for more practice 143

58 Future with *will*

In the future people **will live** and work in space.

1 Form

POSITIVE	I/He/She/It/We/You/They **will** (**'ll**) **win**.
NEGATIVE	I/He/She/It/We/You/They **will not** (**won't**) **win**.
QUESTIONS	**Will** I/he/she/it/we/you/they **win**?
SHORT ANSWERS	Yes, I/he/she/it/we/you/they **will**. No, I/he/she/it/we/you/they **will not** (**won't**).

2 Certain/possible future

We use *will* to talk about things that are certain to happen in the future:
*My mother **will be** fifty in May.*
*There **will be** elections next year.*
*China **will** soon **be** the world's richest country.*

We also use *will* to say what we think will happen in the future:
*In the future people **will live** and work in space.*
*Clare **won't be** late, she's always on time.*

We can use *probably* and *definitely* to say how sure we are:
*I'**ll definitely pass** the test.* (I'm sure this will happen.)
*We'**ll probably go** to Spain next summer.* (I think this will happen, but I'm not sure.)

We usually put these adverbs after *will* but before *won't*:
*We'**ll probably** go to Spain.   We **definitely won't** go to Portugal.*

3 Decisions, offers, promises and warnings

We use *will* when we decide to do something while we are speaking – something that we didn't plan:
*'Mr Baxter isn't here at the moment. Can I take a message?' 'No thanks. I'**ll call** again later.'*
*'Do you want to watch the midnight movie?' 'No, I'm tired. I think I'**ll go** to bed now.'*

NATURAL ENGLISH   We often use *I (don't) think + will*:
*I'm tired. I **think** I'**ll go** to bed now.*
*It's quite early. I **don't think** I'**ll go** to bed yet.*

We also use *will* to make offers, promises and warnings:
*We'**ll take** you to the hospital.   I'**ll work** harder next year.   Don't eat so much – you'**ll get** fat!*
*Leave now or you'**ll miss** the train.*

 Pronunciation ➤ 1.23

4 *shall*

It is possible to use *shall* to mean *will* after *I* and *we*. But in everyday English we only use *shall* to offer or suggest something:
*It's hot in here. **Shall I open** a window?   **Shall we get** the earlier train?*

Practice

1 **Complete the sentences with *will* and words from the box.**

0   My grandfather ....*will be*.... ninety years old next April.

1   This year the summer sales .... a week earlier than usual.

2   .... the same course next year?

3   Next year the school holiday .... for seven weeks instead of six.

4   I'm afraid the library .... open during the holiday.

5   .... a certificate when you pass the exam.

> not be
> last
> ~~be~~
> start
> you get
> you take

2 **The words in brackets () are missing from the sentences. Put them in the correct position.** ◀)) **3.34** **Listen and check.**

0   Do you/Clare will win the race? (think)
     think

1   Miss Watts, we have any homework tonight? (will)

2   I will start a diet next month. (definitely)

3   I think I'll have any ice cream today. (don't)

4   Manchester United will win the cup this year. (probably)

5   Don't buy any food at the airport – it cost a fortune. ('ll)

6   You can try phoning her this evening but I don't she will be at home. (think)

3 **Match the two parts of the sentences. Then complete the sentences with *will*, *'ll* or *won't*.** ◀)) **3.35** **Listen and check.**

0   Don't eat so many cakes – you   A .... have a snack.

1   I'm really hungry – I think I   B .... be cold there.

2   Eat lots of salads – they   C .... make you fat.

3   The sun's shining and it definitely   D .... rain today.

4   I don't think people   E .... have a lemonade.

5   Take a warm pullover; it   F ...*'ll*... get fat.

6   I'm thirsty so I think I   G .... ever live on the moon.

4 **What would you say in these situations? Complete the sentences with suitable forms of the words and phrases in the box. There are two extra words / phrases.**

> close   carry   ~~get~~   open   phone   ~~some more~~   the door   the technician   the window   them for you

0   I don't think there's any coffee left. I *'ll get some more* ....

1   It's too hot in here. I ....·

2   Those books look heavy. I ....·

3   There's something wrong with my computer. I think I ....·

59 Future with present continuous and present simple

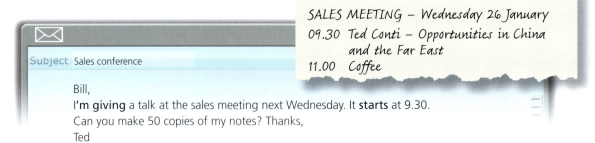

SALES MEETING – Wednesday 26 January
09.30 Ted Conti – Opportunities in China
        and the Far East
11.00 Coffee

Subject: Sales conference

Bill,
I'm giving a talk at the sales meeting next Wednesday. It starts at 9.30.
Can you make 50 copies of my notes? Thanks,
Ted

1 Present continuous

We use the present continuous to talk about things that we have already arranged to do:
I'm giving a talk at the sales meeting next Wednesday.
David sent me a text message. He's meeting us at six o'clock.
'What are you doing this weekend?' 'I'm going to the theatre.'

We usually give the time/period or date:
I'm seeing the dentist at half-past eleven on Thursday.

NATURAL ENGLISH We often use the present continuous to give the reason why we can't do something in the future:
'Can you come to lunch on Sunday?'
'I'm afraid I can't come. I'm working on Sunday.'

Form and use of the present continuous ➤ Unit 39

January
26 WEDNESDAY
talk at sales meeting

27 THURSDAY
11.30 dentist

28 FRIDAY

29 SATURDAY
theatre

30 SUNDAY
working

2 Present simple

We can use the present simple with a time or date to talk about future events that are on a timetable or programme:
The train leaves London at 10.25 and arrives in Bristol at 11.50. It stops in Swindon at 11.15.

'When do your classes finish?'
'They finish on December the 5th.'

London	Swindon	Bristol
10.25	11.15	11.50
11.50	12.35	13.05

 We don't use the present simple for things we have arranged to do; we use the present continuous or *going to*:
✗ *We meet our friends this evening.* ✓ *We're meeting our friends this evening.*

Form and use of the present simple ➤ Unit 37

3 *after, when, as soon as*, etc.

We use the present simple not *will* to talk about the future after *when, as soon as, before, after* and *until*:

 ✗ *As soon as I will get there I'll phone you.* ✓ *As soon as I get there, I'll phone you.*
✗ *I'll see you when I'll arrive.* ✓ *I'll see you when I arrive.*

Linking words for future time ➤ Unit 94.2

Practice

1 GRAMMAR IN USE **Look at Lucy's business diary for next week.**
Complete the conversation with the present continuous of the verbs in brackets ().
Then write the missing information, A–C in Lucy's diary. 🔊3.36 **Listen and check.**

JAN   Hi, Lucy. Can we arrange a meeting for next week?

LUCY Of course. How about Tuesday morning?
      I (0) *'m not doing* (not do) anything then.

JAN   That's no good for me, I'm afraid.
      Are you free in the afternoon?

LUCY No. We (1) .... (have) a special sales
      meeting then.

JAN   Well, I'm free on Thursday morning.

LUCY Sorry, I (2) .... (go) to the dentist then.
      How about Thursday afternoon?

JAN   No, our office manager (3) .... (give) a
      talk. (4) .... (you do) anything on Friday?

LUCY I'm afraid I'm busy. I (5) .... (fly) to
      Stockholm to meet some clients. Look, I
      (6) .... (not work) on Monday. But I can
      come into the office if it's important.

JAN   Yes, it's quite important. The accounts manager (7) .... (come) to
      see me in the morning but I (8) .... (not do) anything in the afternoon.

LUCY OK. Let's meet on Monday afternoon then.

> 23 MONDAY
> am   one-day holiday
> pm   A
> 24 TUESDAY
> am
> pm   B
> 25 WEDNESDAY
> am   ? visit new factory
> pm
> 26 THURSDAY
> am   C
> pm
> 27 FRIDAY
> am
> pm   ? trip to Sweden

2 **Read the information about Lucy's trip to Sweden on Friday. Complete the questions and
answers. Use only one word or a short form in each space.** 🔊3.37 **Listen and check.**

08.30	departure flight SA109 from London Heathrow, Terminal 4
11.40	arrival flight SA109 in Stockholm
12.00	start of meeting at Svenska Hotel
15.00	give talk to clients

1 When ......*does*...... Lucy's flight leave? It .... at half past ....

2 .... the flight go from Terminal one? No, it ....

3 .... does it .... in Stockholm? It .... at 11.40.

4 Is Lucy .... at the Hilton Hotel? No, she ....

5 What .... Lucy doing at three o'clock? She is .... a talk.

3 **Find four more mistakes in the sentences and correct them. Tick (✓) the correct sentence.**

0 After the film ~~will finish~~ *finishes*, we'll go for a snack.

1 Jane can't come to the meeting because she goes on holiday tomorrow.

2 The timetable says that the train arrives in Edinburgh at 10.30.

3 We meet some friends at a restaurant this evening. Would you like to come, too?

4 I'll send you a text message when we'll arrive at the hotel.

5 We stay in a beach house in Greece next summer.

60 Comparing future forms

1 Possible/certain future

will	*going to*
for talking about what we think will happen:	for talking about something we are sure will happen because we can see it now:
I don't think Kirsty **will stay** here long. She doesn't like her job.	Jack**'s going to talk** to the manager. Do you know what it's about?

2 Plans and arrangements

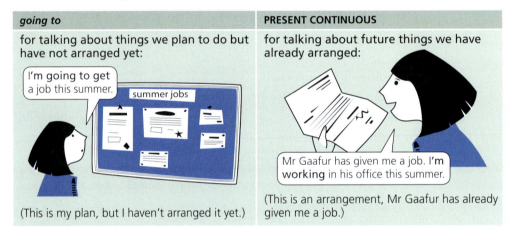

going to	PRESENT CONTINUOUS
for talking about things we plan to do but have not arranged yet:	for talking about future things we have already arranged:
I'm going to get a job this summer.	Mr Gaafur has given me a job. I'm working in his office this summer.
(This is my plan, but I haven't arranged it yet.)	(This is an arrangement, Mr Gaafur has already given me a job.)

NATURAL ENGLISH When we ask someone about their plans for the evening or the weekend (the near future), it is more common to use the present continuous than *going to*:
*What **are you doing** this weekend?*
***Are you doing** anything tonight?*

3 Immediate decisions

⚠ We use *will* for immediate decisions, not the present simple or *going to*:

	✗ ~~OK. I get the torch.~~
The light isn't working.	✗ ~~OK. I'm going to get the torch.~~
	✓ OK. I**'ll get** the torch.

Compare *going to* for plans and *will* for immediate decisions:
'My football shirt's dirty.'
*'Don't worry. I**'m going to do** some washing this afternoon so I**'ll put** your shirt in the machine.'*
(I've already planned to do some washing.)

Practice

1 **Match the sentences 1 and 2 with A and B.**

0 1 It will probably stop working soon. ⟶   A I can see smoke coming from it.
    2 That machine's going to stop working. ⟶   B It was very cheap.

1 1 It'll rain today.   A I can see lots of dark clouds.
    2 It's going to rain today.   B It always rains on my birthday!

2 1 Marco will be the manager one day.   A I've just had an email from the office.
    2 Marco's going to be our new manager.   B He's a very good worker.

2 **GRAMMAR IN USE** **Complete the conversation. Use the verbs in the box with *will* or *going to*. Use short forms. 🔊 3.38 Listen and check.**

| answer look open phone |
| rain show spend ~~wait~~ |

CARRIE Have you got any plans for the weekend?

ZACK Not really. I (0) *..'m going to wait..* until my sister arrives. I'm not sure what she wants to do.

CARRIE She (1) .... the weekend here, isn't she?

ZACK Yes. She (2) .... me all her holiday photos.

CARRIE Well, if the weather's good tomorrow, you can go for a nice walk.

ZACK Yes, but look at those dark clouds. It (3) .... tonight.

CARRIE Maybe. I (4) .... on the Internet and see what they say about tomorrow's weather. Oh, what's that noise?

ZACK I think there's someone at the door.

CARRIE I (5) .... it. ... It's a letter for you. What is it?

ZACK I (6) .... it now. Oh, it's our concert tickets. Marek's ticket is here as well. I (7) .... him now and tell him.

3 **GRAMMAR IN USE** **Complete the email. Use the verbs in brackets () with *will* or in the present continuous. 🔊 3.39 Listen and check.**

✉

| Subject | Our Highlands tour |

Hi Danny,

I'm so excited that you (0) *..'re coming..* (come) with us on the Highlands tour tomorrow! The bus (1) .... (pick us up) at eight, so make sure you're up in time. Don't worry about breakfast because we (2) .... (stop) at a motorway café at nine o'clock, so we can eat then. I don't know exactly what is included in this tour, but I think we (3) .... (probably / see) at least three or four castles – they're on the website. I know we (4) .... (visit) Loch Ness because I saw it on the programme. We might see the monster! In fact, according to the programme, we (5) .... (spend) half an hour at the Loch Ness Monster exhibition in the afternoon. It often rains in the Highlands at this time of year so it (6) .... (probably / rain) tomorrow, but I (7).................. (not take) an umbrella – I don't want to carry it around all day! I don't know what time the tour ends but it (8) .... (be) dark by seven o'clock, so I think we (9) .... (be) home by then.

See you tomorrow. Michaela X

Review MODULE 8

1 UNITS 57, 58 AND 60 **Complete the conversations with *will* or *going to* and the verbs in brackets (). Use short forms.**

0 A It's getting really cold.   B Yes. I'm sure it ...*'s going to snow*... (snow).

1 A Do you have my mobile number?

   B I'm not sure. I .... (check).

2 A Look at that beautiful blue sky!

   B Yes. It .... (be) a lovely day.

3 A I'm terribly thirsty. I'd love a glass of water.

   B I .... (get) you one from the kitchen.

4 A Have you found a new flat yet?

   B No, but we .... (look) at a few more next week.

5 A Excuse me. Is this jacket in the sale?

   B I'm not sure. I .... (ask) the manager.

2 UNITS 57, 58 AND 59 **Match the sentences 1–5 with A or B.**

0 I think we're going to buy a new car.   A We've already chosen the model.
                                               (B) We haven't chosen the model yet.

1 Kristin arrives at six o'clock.   A She is walking here.
                                               B She is coming by train.

2 Look, Xavier's going to win the race!   A He's in front of the other runners.
                                               B He's a good runner.

3 Debbie's taking her guitar onto the plane.   A The airline has given her permission.
                                               B She's going to ask for permission.

4 The sale ends on January 25th.   A I think this is true, but I'm not sure.
                                               B This is a fact.

5 Petro's coming to the opera with us.   A I've bought a ticket for him.
                                               B He loves opera.

3 UNITS 58 AND 59 **Choose the correct words in *italics* in the text.**

At 9 a.m. next Monday an exciting exhibition called 'The Office of the Future' (0)(*opens*)/ *is going to opening* at the Brighton Conference Centre. The exhibition (1) *is show* / *will show* hundreds of new inventions that could change the way people work.

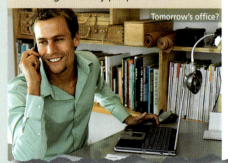

Tomorrow's office?

The office of the future?

DOUG STEVENSON, THE EXHIBITION ORGANISER, says that large offices full of hundreds of workers (2) *probably won't exist* / *won't probably exist* in the future. Many people work at home but they go into the office for meetings. In the future this (3) *will not be* / *not will be* necessary because you will be able to do everything from your own living rooms. With new technology it (4) *is being* / *will be* possible to have meetings on your computer. Your computer (5) *is going to show* / *will show* moving images of your colleagues and business partners. As soon as you (6) *will turn* / *turn* it on, you will see your colleagues, and you will think they are standing in the room next to you!

If you want to find out more about these developments, Mr Stevenson (7) *gives* / *is giving* a talk in the exhibition hall on Wednesday. After the talk (8) *will finish* / *finishes*, you will be able to look at the newest computer software from California.

4 ALL UNITS **Complete the second sentence so it means the same as the first. Use one, two or three words.**

0 I want to visit Venice sometime in the future.
   One day I'm ....*going to visit*.... Venice.

1 My birthday is on 26 September.
   I .... 25 years old on
   26 September next year.

2 Which hotel did you book for us?
   Which hotel .... at?

3 Do you plan to take the car to the garage?
   Are .... take the car to
   the garage?

4 Gerald won't win that race – that's my opinion.
   I .... Gerald will win that race.

5 It's usually very sunny at this time of year.
   It .... rain today.

6 You will receive an email tomorrow. Please contact us when this happens.
   You should contact us as soon as .... the email.

5 ALL UNITS **There are five more mistakes in the conversation. Find and correct them.**
🔊 **3.40** **Listen and check.**

CUSTOMER Excuse me. Do you give a discount to business customers?
ASSISTANT I'm afraid I don't know. ~~I'm asking~~ *I'll ask* the manager. Mr Davies, can you help?
MANAGER Of course. What do you want to know, sir?
CUSTOMER Yes. I work for DataFlow and we open a new branch near here soon. We're going need lots of office equipment. Can you give us a good discount?
MANAGER Well, it depends on how much you spend each month.
CUSTOMER Well, we'll spend probably about 500 euros a month.
MANAGER Oh, that's fine – we're giving you a 20% discount. As soon as you will fill in this form, we'll open a business account for you.

6 ALL UNITS **Read the information. Then complete the email. Use forms of the verbs in the box.**

~~come~~ do finish phone sit start want

ROYAL THEATRE COMPANY
presents
Othello
at the Lakeside Theatre
Monday 12 May – Sunday 18 May at 7.30 p.m.
Tickets £10 – £50
book online at www.ticketcentre.org

Subject: Petrov Ballet

Hi Alison
Great news! I know you love the theatre. Well, the Royal Theatre Company
(0) ..*is coming*.. here next month. I looked at their website this morning and
booked three tickets for Wednesday 14th – they're really good seats –
we (1) .... in the third row. (2) .... you .... anything on that day?
Would you like to come with me and Bob? The show (3) .... at 7.30 so
you could meet us outside the theatre after work. Of course Bob is always hungry
so he (4) .... probably .... to get something to eat after the show
(5) .... We could try that new Chinese place near the theatre.
I (6) .... them and see if I can book a table.
Let me know if you want to come.
Hedda x

Test MODULE 8

Future forms

Choose the correct answer, A, B or C.

1 Are you .... her a present?
   A going buy   B going to buy   C going to buying
   ➤ Unit 57

2 The children .... come with us this year.
   A going not   B aren't going   C aren't going to
   ➤ Unit 57

3 When I grow up I .... an artist.
   A will being   B am   C 'm going to be
   ➤ Unit 57

4 The floor is very wet. He ....
   A falls over   B 's going to fall over   C is falling over
   ➤ Unit 57

5 The train is delayed so I .... late for work.
   A 'm going to be   B 'm being   C can be
   ➤ Unit 57

6 There's no moon so it .... very dark tonight.
   A 'm going to be   B will being   C 's going to be
   ➤ Unit 57

7 My father .... fifty next Wednesday.
   A is being   B will to be   C will be
   ➤ Unit 58

8 I'm not hungry. I .... have any lunch today.
   A think I not will   B don't think I'll   C don't think to
   ➤ Unit 58

9 'It's very cold in here.' 'OK, I .... the heating.'
   A 'm going to turn on   B 'll turn on   C will turning on
   ➤ Unit 58

10 Don't touch the cooker. You .... yourself.
   A 'll burn   B are going to   C burn
   ➤ Unit 58

11 'Do you want to go out this evening?'
   'No, I can't. I .... Steve with his homework.'
   A will help   B 'm helping   C help
   ➤ Unit 59

12 The flight to New York .... at 17.05.
   A leaves   B is going to leave   C will leaving
   ➤ Unit 59

13 I'm so excited. We .... our cousins from Canada tomorrow.
   A see   B seeing   C 're seeing
   ➤ Unit 59

14 As soon as I .... any news, I'll phone you.
   A hear   B will hear   C am going to hear
   ➤ Unit 59

15 Don't start eating until I .... there.
   A will get   B am getting   C get
   ➤ Unit 59

16 This queue is enormous. We .... here for a long time!
   A 're going to be   B are being   C are
   ➤ Unit 60

17 When we get to the top of the hill, I .... some photos.
   A 'm taking   B 'm going to take   C take
   ➤ Unit 60

18 Thanks for booking a restaurant for Dad's birthday. Where ....?
   A do we go   B will we go   C are we going
   ➤ Unit 60

19 'What's the dentist's phone number?'
   'I don't know, I .... in the phone book.'
   A 'll look   B 'm going to look   C look
   ➤ Unit 60

20 'Look, my suit's dirty!' 'OK, I .... it to the dry cleaner's this afternoon.'
   A am taking   B 'll take   C 'm going to take
   ➤ Unit 60

Modal verbs

Before you start

1 Read the information and Ethan's conversation with his teacher.
Look at the highlighted grammar examples.

All-UK Schools'
Swimming Championships

TWELVE COMPETITIONS
FOR ALL AGES OF STUDENT

Does your school have a brilliant swimmer? Can he/she swim like a fish?
This might be your chance to win a place at the European Schools' Championships.

ALL SCHOOLS OF 500+ STUDENTS CAN ENTER. SCHOOLS SHOULD ENTER TEAMS OF TWELVE SWIMMERS.
APPLICATIONS MUST ARRIVE BY 31 JANUARY.

ETHAN	Mr Hawkins, can I be in the school swimming team?
MR HAWKINS	I'm not sure, Ethan. I haven't chosen the team yet.
ETHAN	But could you remember me when you choose it, please?
MR HAWKINS	But you're doing important exams this year. Will you be able to spend enough time at the pool?
ETHAN	Yes, I'll have to go early in the morning, but that's fine.
MR HAWKINS	Well, you are a good swimmer, Ethan, but I need to think carefully about it. You mustn't get too excited.

2 Now read the sentences. Choose the correct words in *italics*.
The highlighted grammar examples will help you.

1 My brother *can / cans* play football really well. ➤ Unit 61
2 Will I *can / be able to* speak French after the course? ➤ Unit 62
3 It's a great club. *Can / Do* we join it, please? ➤ Unit 63
4 Good morning, Mr Leigh. *May / Could* you leave your keys with me, please? ➤ Unit 63
5 Justin has a lot to do tomorrow. He *needs / needs to* get up early. ➤ Unit 64
6 Visitors *must / must to* leave their bags in the cloakroom. ➤ Unit 65
7 I won't have a lot of money at college so I *'ll have to / had to* be careful. ➤ Unit 66
8 You *should to / should* complete the form carefully. ➤ Unit 67
9 That film *will / might* be interesting, but I'm not sure. ➤ Unit 68

3 Check your answers below. Then go to the unit for more information and practice.

1 can 2 be able to 3 Can 4 Could 5 needs to 6 must 7 'll have to 8 should 9 might

61 *can/can't*

Usain Bolt will win. He **can run** really fast!

And we **can watch** the race on my mobile phone.

1 Form

SUBJECT	POSITIVE	NEGATIVE
I/He/She/It/We/You/They	*can run.*	*cannot (can't) run.*

QUESTIONS	SHORT ANSWERS
Can I/he/she/it/we/you/they run?	*Yes, I/he/she/it/we/you/they can.* *No, I/he/she/it/we/you/they can't.*

Modal verbs are different from main verbs.

 We use the infinitive without *to* after them:
✗ ~~We can to come to your party.~~ ✓ We **can come** to your party.

 We don't add -*s* after *he/she/it*:
✗ ~~Marek cans swim.~~ ✓ Marek **can swim**.

 We do not use *do/don't* to form questions and negatives:
✗ ~~Do you can drive?~~ ✓ **Can** you **drive**?
✗ ~~I don't can speak Spanish.~~ ✓ I **can't speak** Spanish.

Past and future forms of *can/can't* ➤ Unit 62

🔊 Pronunciation ➤ 1.24

2 Use

We use *can/can't*

- to talk about ability in the present:
  *Usain Bolt **can run** really fast.*
  *I **can speak** Spanish perfectly.*
  *Young children **can't understand** difficult ideas.*

- to say if something is possible or allowed in the present:
  *We **can watch** the race on my mobile phone.* (= It is possible for us to watch the race.)
  ***Can** I **use** this mobile phone in the USA?* (= Is it possible for me to use it?)
  *Students **can use** dictionaries in the exam.* (= It is allowed.)
  *You **can't drive** in the UK until you are seventeen.* (= You are not allowed to drive.)

- for making an arrangement:
  *The doctor **can see** you tomorrow at 10.30.*
  ***Can** you **meet** me here at nine o'clock on Sunday?*

Practice

1 GRAMMAR IN USE **Complete the text with *can* or *can't*.** ◀))3.41 **Listen and check.**

YOUNG PEOPLE WANTED FOR COMPETITION!

(o) ..*Can*.. you sing? (1) .... you play a musical instrument? (2) .... you tell jokes?

Do you watch competitions and think 'They (3) .... sing very well.

I (4) .... do better than that!'?

Whatever you do, you (5) .... find a way to become famous on the stage.

You (6) .... enter the competition by phone or by email.

Just contact us and tell us what you (7) .... do.

We will then invite the lucky people to perform for us.

Please note: we (8) .... answer every email or phone call, so if you don't

hear from us in three weeks, it means we haven't chosen you this time.

2 **Find five more mistakes in the sentences and correct them. Tick (✓) the correct sentence.**

0 I ~~don't can~~ open my suitcase without the key.   *can't*

1 Jack cans come with us to the cinema.

2 Ms Wilkes can to see you tomorrow afternoon at two.

3 We can get tickets for the concert online.

4 Does Sue can speak Spanish well?

5 Can you to stay after the class for a few minutes?

6 My grandfather doesn't can see very well.

3 **Write questions or positive (+)/negative (–) sentences with *can* or *can't*.**
Use the words below to help you. ◀))3.42 **Listen and check.**

0 I / leave my suitcase here / for an hour (?)   *Can I leave my suitcase here for an hour?*

00 I / come with you tomorrow (–) *I can't come with you tomorrow.*

000 your friend / stay at my house (+) *Your friend can stay at my house.*

1 Sarah / call me later (?) ....

2 you / use dollars / in this store (–) ....

3 you / call the doctor from my office (+) ....

4 you / use mobile phones here (–) ....

5 I / speak to the manager (?) ....

6 Fran / make a really good curry (+) ....

7 Sandy / afford a new car (–) ....

8 Owen / speak Welsh (?) ....

4 **Write four sentences about what you can and can't do.**

0 *I can't drive a car.* ....   3 ....

1 ....   4 ....

2 ....

⏻ Go online for more practice   155

62 could, will be able to

> **Could** my great-grandmother **run** really fast?

> She **could**, but women **couldn't enter** competitions like the Olympics in those days.

1 Past form and use

SUBJECT	POSITIVE	NEGATIVE
I/He/She/It/We/You/They	could run.	could not (couldn't) run.

QUESTIONS	SHORT ANSWERS
Could I/he/she/it/we/you/they run?	Yes, I/he/she/it/we/you/they **could**. No, I/he/she/it/we/you/they **couldn't**.

We usually use *could/couldn't*

- to talk about ability in the past:
  *Mozart **could write** beautiful music when he was a child.*
  ***Could** my great-grandmother **run** really fast?*

- to say if something was possible in the past:
  *Children **could play** in the streets years ago.*
  *Women **couldn't enter** competitions like the Olympics then.*

2 Future form and use

SUBJECT	POSITIVE	NEGATIVE
I/He/She/It/We/You/They	will be able to run.	will not (won't) be able to run.

QUESTIONS	SHORT ANSWERS
Will I/he/she/it/we/you/they be able to run?	Yes, I/he/she/it/we/you/they **will**. No, I/he/she/it/we/you/they **won't**.

We use *will/won't be able to*

- to talk about ability in the future:
  *Karen **will be able to speak** Russian after two years in Moscow.*
  *I've broken my leg – I **won't be able to drive** for weeks.*

- to say if something will be possible in the future:
  *We**'ll be able to swim** every day at the hotel.*
  ***Will** you **be able to get** a good job after your technology course?*

Practice

1 GRAMMAR IN USE **Choose the correct words in *italics* in the interview.** 🔊3.43 **Listen and check.**

A So you're interested in the translation job. Can you speak Spanish perfectly?

B Well, I (0) *able to* / *could* when I was at university, but that was a long time ago. I'm taking a course so I (1) *will be able to* / *can* speak it very well again soon.

A OK. I'll give you our test, but I (2) *couldn't* / *won't be able to* recommend you for the job if you don't pass it.

B I understand that. Will I (3) *can* / *be able to* take the test soon?

A Let's see ... (4) *will you be able* / *can you* to come back next Tuesday at four o'clock?

B No, I'm afraid I (5) *will* / *won't*. I collect the children from school at that time.

A That's OK, we can arrange another time. Now, how are your computer skills?

B Well, I (6) *can't* / *couldn't* use a computer six months ago, but I've learnt now. I (7) *could* / *can* type really fast when I was a student, and I'm sure I (8) *can* / *will be able* to learn the other things really quickly.

2 GRAMMAR IN USE **Complete the text with phrases from the box.** 🔊3.44 **Listen and check.**

could dive   could enter   could practise   ~~could walk~~   couldn't dive   couldn't surprise

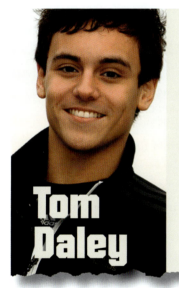

NOT LONG AGO Tom Daley (0) ......*could walk*...... through the streets in his town and no one stopped him – but it's different now because he is a member of the Great Britain Olympic team.

Tom's the best diver in Europe now, but he (1) .... at all a few years ago. He saw a diving board at his local swimming pool when he was seven and in a few months he (2) .... really well. People in the sport started to notice him, and told him that he (3) .... in the best diving centre in the UK.

Before he (4) .... the Beijing Olympics, Tom needed to finish in the first eight at the competitions in Beijing. He finished seventh, so at the age of fourteen, he returned to Beijing as part of the Olympic team. Although Tom (5) .... everyone by winning in Beijing, he finished seventh out of twelve divers in one event. Tom will be an amazing diver when he's older!

3 **Put the words in brackets () in the correct order. Then complete the sentences.**

0 (paint pictures Picasso amazing could) when he was very young.
    Picasso could paint amazing pictures .... when he was very young.

1 (be use to gas or coal we able won't) in the future.
    .... in the future.

2 (you name write could your) before you went to school?
    .... before you went to school?

3 (will store you able to be) about 70 films on this DVD recorder.
    .... about 70 films on this DVD recorder.

4 (could we not a hotel find) near the beach.
    .... near the beach.

5 (to able we the match won't watch be) because it's on TV too late.
    .... because it's on TV too late.

63 *can, could, may*

1 Asking for permission

	ASKING FOR PERMISSION	GIVING PERMISSION	REFUSING PERMISSION
informal	*Can I use* your pen?	*Yes, you **can**.* *Yes, of course (you **can**).* *Yes, sure.*	*No, you **can't**.* *No, I'm sorry.*
formal/ polite	*Could I use* your bathroom? *May I make* a suggestion?	*Yes, you **can/may**.* *Yes, of course/certainly.*	*No, you **can't/may not**.* *No, I'm sorry/I'm afraid not.*

We use *can I/we* to ask for permission to do something:
'**Can I have** a shower here?' '**No**, I'm sorry, **you can't**! It's for women.'
'Dad, **can we borrow** the car this evening?' '**Yes, you can.** I don't need it.'

If we want to be very polite or formal, we use *could* or *may*:
'**Could I use** your bathroom, please?' 'Of course **you can**. It's over there.'
'**May I make** a suggestion?' '**Certainly.**'

 Pronunciation ➤ 1.25

NATURAL ENGLISH We only use *may* or *may not* in written instructions or very formal situations:
*Students **may not take** bags into the exam.*
*You **may start** writing now.*

2 Making a request

	MAKING A REQUEST	REPLYING
informal	*Can you lend* me some money?	*Sure, how much do you need?* *No, I'm sorry. I don't have enough.*
formal/ polite	*Could you pass* me the salt?	*Yes, of course.* *Certainly.*

We use *can you* to make a request in an informal way:
'**Can you help** me with these bags?' '**Yes, of course.**'
'**Can you tell** Tom I called?' '**Yes, sure.**'

If we want to be more polite or formal, we use *could*:
'**Could you pass** me the water, please?' '**Yes, here you are.**'

NATURAL ENGLISH We use *please* with *can* or *could* to ask for something or make a request in a polite way:
'**Please could you** be quiet?'
or '**Could you** be quiet, **please**?'

Practice

1 **Match the questions 1–5 with the answers A–F.** 🔊 **3.45** **Listen and check.**

0 Can I use your phone, please?
  I haven't got my mobile.
1 Please may I leave the room for
  a few minutes?
2 Can we go to the cinema this evening?
3 Could I ask you for some advice?
4 Could we leave our bags here?
5 Can I take photos?

A No, you may not leave during the
  examination.
B Yes, of course you can. I'll try to help.
C Yes, you can leave them at reception.
D Yes, of course. It's on the table.
E No, you can't use cameras in the
  museum.
F Yes, you can, but be back by 10.30.

2 **Write a request for each picture. Use the words under the pictures and *can* or *could*.**

1	2	3	4
open the window	turn the TV on	close the door	take a photo of us

1 ....
2 ....
3 ....
4 ....

3 **Choose the correct words in *italics*.**

0 Wife to husband: Adam, (*can*)/ *may* I use your laptop computer this weekend?
1 Notice in library: Students *can* / *may* borrow DVDs from the library.
2 Woman in café: *Could I* / *Could I to* sit over there?
3 Two colleagues: 'Could I use your desk tomorrow?' 'Yes, of course you *could* / *can*.'
4 Two friends: '*Can you* / *may you* lend me five pounds?' 'Sure.'
5 Notice in train: Passengers *can't* / *may not* open the doors while the train is moving.

4 **GRAMMAR IN USE** **Complete the conversation about people doing a race.**
   Use words from the box. 🔊 **3.46** **Listen and check.**

can Can I ~~Can we~~ can't Could you you can

A OK. Are there any questions?
B Yes, my friends and I are in different groups. (0) ...*Can we*... run together, please?
A No, I'm afraid you (1) .... You're in different groups because you run at
  different speeds.
C (2) .... stop while I'm running – to buy a drink or something?
A Ah, no. I'm afraid not. The rules say (3) .... only have drinks that the organisers
  provide. There will be tables at the side of the road with drinks on – you (4) ....
  take as many of those as you want.
D (5) .... give us a copy of the rules, please?
A Yes, of course. Here you are.

64 have to, need to

Come on! You **have to put** a card down.

Wait! I **need to think**.

1 Form

SUBJECT	POSITIVE	NEGATIVE
I/We/You/They	*have to/need to pay.*	*do not (don't) have to/need to pay.*
He/She/It	*has to/needs to pay.*	*does not (doesn't) have to/need to pay.*

QUESTIONS	SHORT ANSWERS	
Do I/we/you/they **have to/need to** *pay?*	*Yes, I/we/you/they* **do.**	*No, I/we/you/they* **don't.**
Does he/she/it **have to/need to** *pay?*	*Yes, he/she/it* **does.**	*No, he/she/it* **doesn't.**

Have to and *need to* are different from most modal verbs. They change after *he/she/it* and use *do/does* in questions and negatives, like all main verbs.

2 *have to* or *need to*?

We use *have to*

- when it is important to do something because there is a rule or a law:
  You **have to put** *a card down.* (It's a rule of the game.)
  Cars **have to pay** *to cross the bridge.* **Do** *you* **have to be** *a member to use the gym?*
- when it is necessary to do something; we cannot choose not to do it:
  I **have to get up** *early tomorrow – the train leaves at 6.45 a.m.*

We use *need to*

- when we think something is necessary or a good idea:
  I **need to earn** *some more money.* *She* **needs to talk** *to her doctor.*
- when something is necessary for our body or health:
  I **need to go** *to bed early tonight – I'm very tired.* *You* **need to drink** *more water.*

NATURAL ENGLISH In everyday English we often use the short form *have got to* ('ve/'s got to). It means the same as *have to*:
I've **got to get up** *early tomorrow to catch the train.*

3 *don't have to* or *don't need to*?

We use *don't have to* and *don't need to* when it is NOT necessary to do something:
Cyclists **don't have to/need to pay** *to cross the bridge – there's no charge for bicycles.*
We **don't have to/need to get up** *early tomorrow – it's Sunday.*

⚠ It is possible to use *needn't* for *don't need to*. We use it with the infinitive without *to*:
✗ ~~You needn't to pay. I've got enough money.~~ ✓ *You* **needn't pay**. *I've got enough money.*

mustn't or *don't have to*? ➤ Unit 65.3

160

Practice

1 GRAMMAR IN USE **Read the information. Choose the correct answers, A, B or C. In one question, two answers are possible.** 🔊3.47 **Listen and check.**

Barton Cross Fun Run SUNDAY 13 APRIL

START 10 km

Please arrive at the meeting point no later than 8.30 a.m. You (0) .... register by 9.00 a.m. If you have pre-registered online, you (1) .... provide all your details again, but you (2) .... collect your personal number for the race. Everyone (3) .... wear their number at the start and end of the race so that we can be sure we have the correct times, but you (4) .... wear the number through the whole race.
The Fun Run is only 10km, but please remember that you (5) .... do some warm-up exercises before you start, to avoid injury. You (6) .... bring bottles of water with you – the organisers provide water at points along the route. Please don't stop at these points for more than a few seconds – everyone (7) .... keep moving during the race.
Finally, please remember that this is a very physical event and you (8) .... be fit and healthy. Good luck!

0 A need to (B) have to C don't have to
1 A have to B don't have to
   C do not need
2 A have to B needn't C don't have to
3 A has to B needs C doesn't need to
4 A has to B needs to C don't have to
5 A need to B don't need to
   C don't have to
6 A needn't B have to C don't need to
7 A needn't B has to C doesn't need to
8 A need to B needn't C has to

2 **Complete the sentences with a form of the verbs in brackets () and a verb from the box. Use short forms.** 🔊3.48 **Listen and check.**

become buy drink go ~~pay~~ stay

0 I'm a member of the club so I _don't have to pay_ to get in. (have to)
1 I .... shopping because we haven't got any food at all. (need to)
2 Tourists .... full-price metro tickets. They can get special discount cards. (have to)
3 Do you .... a member of the tennis club if you want to play? (have to)
4 Your friend .... at a hotel. She can sleep on the sofa. (need to)
5 It's a really tough aerobics class, so you .... lots of water. (need to)

3 **Find four more mistakes or missing words in the sentences and correct them. Tick (✓) the correct sentences.**

0 Sarah has to wear a uniform because she is a nurse. ✓
1 Harry needs wear reading glasses.
2 Caroline needs to do more exercise.
3 Raisa has to carry an identity card.
4 Peter have to start work at eight o'clock.
5 Do you have go to work on Sundays?
6 Have you to cook every night?

4 **Write sentences 3 and 4 from Exercise 3 again so they are true for you.**

....
....

65 *must/mustn't*

I mustn't hurry.
I must get it right.

1 *must*

Must is a modal verb.

Modal verb form ➤ Unit 61.1

We use *must* when we think it is important to do something.
It is our opinion, not a rule or law:
*I **must get** it right.*
(= I think it is important that
I get it right.)
*I **must go** now – I don't want to be late.*
(= I think it is important to be on time.)

We also use *must* in formal instructions, signs and notices. It means 'Do this!':
*Passengers **must wear** seat belts.*
(instruction on a plane)
*Candidates **must answer** six questions.*
(instructions on an exam paper)

NATURAL ENGLISH It is possible to ask questions with *must*, but it is more common to use *have to*:
***Must** you **leave** so soon?* → ***Do** you **have to leave** so soon?*

2 *must not* (*mustn't*)

We use *mustn't* when we think it is important NOT to do something:
*You **mustn't tell** anyone.* (= I think it is important to keep this secret.)
*Hurry up! We **mustn't be** late for Diana's party.* (= I think it is important that we aren't late.)

We use *must not* in instructions, signs and notices. It means 'Don't do this!':
*Visitors **must not smoke** in reception.*
*Students **must not take** food into the exam room.*

 Don't use *to* after *must* or *mustn't*:
✗ *I must to remember to phone the doctor.*
✓ *I **must remember** to phone the doctor.*

 Pronunciation ➤ 1.26

3 *mustn't* or *don't have to*?

- *Mustn't* means it is important not to do something; it means 'Don't do this!':
  *We **mustn't leave** the restaurant without paying – it's illegal.*
- *Don't have to* means something is not necessary (but you can do it if you want to):
  *We **don't have to pay** for the meal now. We can pay when we leave the hotel.*

Practice

1 Match the signs with the sentences. Then complete each sentence with *must* or *must not*.

0 You ..*must not*.. make any fires. ..*E*...

1 You .... put some coins in the meter. ....

2 You .... dive into the pool. ....

3 You .... wait behind this sign. ....

4 You .... walk on the left. ....

5 You .... bring your dog into the shop. ....

2 Choose the correct words in *italics*. 🔊 **3.49** Listen and check.

0 It's an important interview. You *don't have to* /(*mustn't*) be late.

1 The exam is finished. You *must / don't have to* stop writing now.

2 I've told you – you *must / mustn't* take sweets from people you don't know.

3 It's a very busy road so you *must / don't have to* cross carefully.

4 We *must / don't have to* go to the theatre – we can get the tickets on the Internet.

5 I've sent the company an email so you *mustn't / don't have to* phone them.

6 It's OK – we *must / don't have to* pay because I've got free tickets.

7 We *mustn't / don't have to* leave the party early – the taxi can come later.

8 You *mustn't / don't have to* be rude to Auntie Irene!

3 **GRAMMAR IN USE** Complete the conversation with the correct forms of *must* or *have to*. Use short forms. 🔊 **3.50** Listen and check.

ALICE I've never been to a TV quiz show before – it's really exciting!

TIM It's fun. I've been a few times.

ALICE What time does it start?

TIM The show starts at 8.00, but the audience (0) ..*has to*.. be there by 7.30.

ALICE Can we choose our seats or (1) .... we .... sit in specific seats?

TIM We can sit anywhere, but we (2) .... get there early to get good seats.

ALICE Can I take photos during the show?

TIM No, it says on the tickets that you (3) .... do that.

ALICE OK. What about clothes?

TIM Well, it's not formal so we (4) .... wear smart clothes, but we (5) .... wear anything with a name on it, you know, like Nike or Lacoste.

ALICE Oh, I see. By the way, how much are the tickets?

TIM Oh, we (6) .... pay. The tickets are all free.

4 Write about one thing that you have to do, don't have to do and mustn't do at school or work.

0 have to *I have to be at my desk by 9.00 a.m. every morning.*

1 have to ....

2 don't have to ....

3 mustn't ....

66 *had to, will have to*

Alex Zanardi was a Formula 1 racing
driver. He had a terrible accident in
2001 and **he had to stop** racing for a
long time. Any car he uses in the future
will have to have special controls.

1 *had to*

Had to/didn't have to is the past form of both
must and *have to*.

SUBJECT	POSITIVE	NEGATIVE
I/He/She/It/ We/You/They	had to stop.	did not (didn't) have to stop.

QUESTIONS	SHORT ANSWERS
Did I/he/she/it/we/ you/they **have to stop?**	Yes, I/he/she/it/we/you/they **did**. No, I/he/she/it/we/you/they **didn't**.

We use *had to* when we talk about things that were
necessary in the past:
*In 2010 she **had to go** to the USA to take part in competitions.*
*They **had to get** visas when they went to South America last year.*

We use *didn't have to* for something that wasn't necessary in the past:
*My uncle made a lot of money and he **didn't have to work** after he was fifty.*
*We **didn't have to show** our passports at the border between France and Germany.*

2 *will have to*

Will/won't have to is the future form of both *must* and *have to*.

SUBJECT	POSITIVE	NEGATIVE
I/He/She/It/We/You/They	will have to stop.	will not (won't) have to stop.

QUESTIONS	SHORT ANSWERS
Will I/he/she/it/we/you/they **have to stop?**	Yes, I/he/she/it/we/you/they **will**. No, I/he/she/it/we/you/they **won't**.

We use *will/won't have to* when we talk about things that are necessary/not necessary
in the future:
*We**'ll have to pay** more for petrol in the future because the price of oil is increasing.*
*Carol won two cinema tickets in a competition so we **won't have to pay** at the cinema tonight.*

Practice

1 Complete the sentences with a past or future form of *have to*. Use short forms.

0 When I was at school, we ....*had to*.... have sports lessons twice a week.

1 We .... carry cash in the future if we can use credit cards for everything.

2 We .... go shopping yesterday because we still had some food in the fridge.

3 .... I .... pay for the course when I arrive or can I pay at the end?

4 My computer stopped working last week; I .... go and buy a new one!

5 .... you .... queue to get on the bus this morning?

2 **GRAMMAR IN USE** Complete the conversation about becoming a football referee. Use the phrases from the box. ◀)**3.51** Listen and check.

all had to   ~~did you have to~~   didn't have to   had to   I had to   I'll have to   will have to   won't have to

ANNA   Hi, Lara, how are things? I haven't seen you for a long time.

LARA   Everything's fine. I've just finished a course to become a football referee.

ANNA   Really? Did you have lessons? I mean, what exactly (0) ...*did you have to*.... do?

LARA   Well, I (1) .... go to classes – we (2) .... learn the rules of the game, of course. And I had to take two exams.

ANNA   That's all?

LARA   Yes, but there's another class in four weeks' time and (3) .... go to that, but I (4) .... do any more exams.

ANNA   And then you can be a referee at matches?

LARA   That's right, but another referee (5) .... watch me at first, of course.

ANNA   Did the course cost a lot?

LARA   No, I (6) .... pay for the course, though (7) .... pay to do the exams. It wasn't much.

ANNA   So we'll see you at the next World Cup then!

LARA   I don't think so!

3 Use the words below to answer these questions. Use *had to* or *'ll have to*. ◀)**3.52** Listen and check.

0 Have you called your mother yet?   No, I / call her later   *No, I'll have to call her later.*

00 Has Neil sent in his university application form?   Yes, he / apply before yesterday
   Yes, he had to apply before yesterday.

1 Did you take the car to the garage today?   No, I / do it tomorrow

....

2 Was Joanna at work yesterday?   No, she / go to the dentist

....

3 I think the DVD player has broken.   Yes, we / buy a new one

....

4 Did you go to the bank yesterday?   Yes, I / get some money out

....

67 should, ought to, must

That looks fantastic! I'd love to try it.

I did it last year. It's really exciting. You **really must do** it.

You **ought to find out** how much it costs first.

No, it's too dangerous; **I don't think you should do** it.

1 should, ought to

Should and *ought to* are modal verbs.

Modal verb form ➤ Unit 61.1

We use *should* and *ought to* to say we think it is a good idea to do something:
*The sun is very strong – you **should wear** a hat.*
*You **ought to find out** how much it costs.*

We can ask for advice with *should*:
***Should** I **buy** the red dress or the blue one?*

We use *shouldn't* to say we think it is a bad or dangerous idea to do something:
*You **shouldn't eat** a lot of cakes; they make you fat.*
*You **shouldn't sit** outside in the sun at midday.*

 Don't use *to* after *should* or *shouldn't*:
✗ ~~Everyone should to learn another language.~~
✓ *Everyone **should learn** another language.*

When we are speaking, we often say *I (don't) think + should/ought to* and
do you think + should/ought to:
***We think you should study** maths at university.*
*It's too dangerous. **I don't think you should do** it.*
***Do you think we ought to get** a digital TV?*

NATURAL ENGLISH *Should* is more common than *ought to*. We usually say *you shouldn't* and *should I … ?* (not *you oughtn't to* or *ought I … ?*).

2 must

We can use *(really) must* to give strong advice or to recommend something.
It is stronger than *should* or *ought to*:
*You **really must try** snowboarding. It's great fun!*
*We **must see** the new Harry Potter film. Everyone says it's great.*

must / mustn't ➤ Unit 65

Practice

1 **Match the problems 1–5 with the advice A–F.
Then complete the advice with *should* or *shouldn't*.** 🔊 **3.53** **Listen and check.**

0 I always have a headache when
  I wake up.

1 I want to speak more Spanish to
  improve my conversation.

2 My mobile phone bills are huge!

3 I often have a stomachache
  when I go to bed.

4 My job is really boring and I
  don't like my boss.

5 My apartment's very untidy
  because I'm not often there.

A You .... look for something
  more interesting.

B You .... talk so much. Send text
  messages to your friends.

C You _should_ have the window open in
  your bedroom.

D You .... have private lessons with
  a teacher.

E You .... eat large meals late at night.

F You .... go out so often. Spend
  some time at home.

2 **Look at the pictures. Then complete the advice with the words from the box.**
🔊 **3.54** **Listen and check.**

~~must~~ must should (x3) shouldn't

0 You ..._must_... call
  the police!

1 I don't think you
  .... buy that jacket.

2 I think we ....
  call a taxi.

3 You .... go
  to bed early!

4 He .... eat
  so much.

5 I got this in Proxima. You
  really .... go
  there. It's so cheap!

3 **Write answers to these questions. Use *should*, *shouldn't* or *must* and your own ideas.**

1 Can you recommend a good book?
  Yes, you should read ....,
  but you shouldn't read .... – it's awful!

2 I haven't been to the cinema for a long time. Are there any good films on at the moment?
  Yes, I think you ....,
  but you shouldn't ....

3 I'd like to try some interesting new food. Do you have any ideas?
  Yes, you really ....

4 I'm feeling a bit bored at the moment. What should I do?
  ....

68 *might, may, must be, can't be*

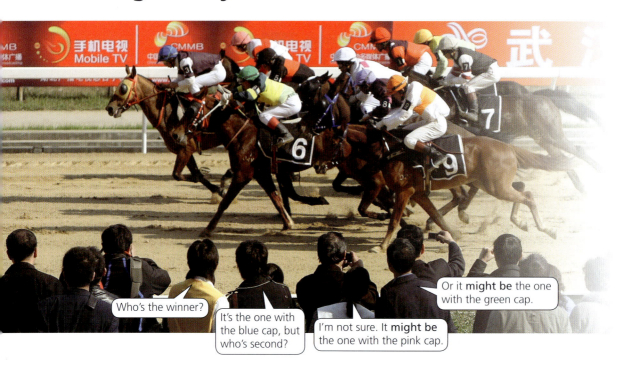

Who's the winner?

It's the one with the blue cap, but who's second?

I'm not sure. It **might be** the one with the pink cap.

Or it **might be** the one with the green cap.

1 *might* (*not*) and *may* (*not*)

We use *might* (*not*) when we think something is true or will be true but we aren't sure:
'*Who's second?*' '*It **might be** the one with the pink cap.*'
*Jenny **might be** at home now. Call her.*
*The parcel **might not arrive** tomorrow.*

In more formal English we can use *may* (*not*) when we aren't sure about something:
*Mr Clement **may be** with a client. I'll just check for you.*
*The order **may not arrive** next week.*

> **NATURAL ENGLISH**   We don't often form questions with *may* or *might*.
> We prefer to use *Do you think … ?*:
> ***Do you think** they've got any cheap trainers?*
> ***Do you think** the order will arrive this week?*

2 *must be* and *can't be*

If we are almost certain that something is true, we use *must be*:
*You're very late home. You **must be** tired.*
*I can't find the cat. She **must be** somewhere upstairs.*

If we are almost certain that something is not true, we use *can't be*:
*This ring was very cheap so it **can't be** gold.*
*That boy looks exactly like Sam but it **can't be** him – he's at school.*

Practice

1 Match the sentences. 🔊3.55 Listen and check.

0 There's nothing interesting on TV tonight. ⟶
1 That man's wearing a white coat.
2 I saw Julia at the sports centre yesterday.
3 Dario's looking much thinner.
4 The director isn't answering her phone.
5 My spelling isn't very good.
6 The house is completely dark.
7 We want to go skiing this winter.
8 It's snowing in New York.

A We might go to Switzerland.
B I might watch a DVD instead.
C Everyone must be out.
D That can't be right. She's in Milan.
E I might buy a dictionary.
F He must be on a new diet.
G Really? It must be colder than here.
H She may be in a meeting.
I He might be a doctor.

2 GRAMMAR IN USE Complete the conversation with phrases A–G below. 🔊3.56 Listen and check.

LIAM I see that Ellen MacArthur has entered another round-the-world yacht race.

STEVE Oh, yes. (0) ...E.... she'll win?

LIAM I think (1) .... win, but that Frenchman, Francis Joyon, won the last one, didn't he?

STEVE Yes, he did. So (2) .... be more confident than MacArthur at the moment.

LIAM Mmm, maybe. Do you think he's actually a better sailor than she is?

STEVE No idea – I don't know enough about it. I (3) .... be faster than her, but she's done some amazing things.

LIAM Mmm. Shall we go to watch the start of the race next weekend?

STEVE I'm not sure. My boss thinks (4) .... have to work next weekend, so (5) .... be free.

LIAM OK. (6) .... go anyway with some other friends. I'll let you know.

A I might
B he must
C we may all
D she might
E Do you think
F think he might
G I might not

3 Look at the pictures below and make two sentences about each one. Use *might be*, *must be* or *can't be* and some of the ideas in the box.

children's toys   colourful stamps   glasses for watching 3-D films   mobile clock   personal DVD player
something to put on the desk   special sunglasses   things for warming your hands   toy for pets

1 They might be ....   They can't be ....
2 They can't be ....   They must be ....
3 It ....   It ....

Review MODULE 9

1 UNITS 61, 62 AND 63 **Match the sentences 1–5 with the sentences A–F that have the same meaning.**

0 We could speak French when we were younger.

1 We will be able to speak French after the course.

2 Students may not speak French in their English class.

3 Can we speak French here?

4 We couldn't speak French when we were younger.

5 We could speak French in Tunisia.

A We didn't know how to speak French.

B We knew how to speak French.

C It was possible to speak French.

D The teacher said we can't speak French.

E May we speak French?

F We will know how to speak French.

2 UNITS 64, 65 AND 66 **Complete the text with the correct words or phrases, A, B or C below.**
🔊 **3.57** **Listen and check.**

Welcome to *SuperIce* Skating

You (0).......... be a good skater to use the SuperIce rink, but you (1) .... be twelve or older.

Please follow these rules for your own safety.

- You (2) .... take food or drinks onto the ice – they can be dangerous.
- You (3) .... wear skates at all times on the ice. You (4) .... to bring your own skates – we have skates in all sizes here.
- You (5) .... wear special clothes on the ice but we recommend that you wear strong gloves.

- We clean the ice every hour. When you hear the bell, you (6) .... leave the ice immediately: you (7) .... go near the ice-cleaning machine – it is very dangerous.
- All sports centres (8) .... follow strict health and safety rules. If you have an accident on the ice, you (9) .... tell us because we (10) .... report it to our main office.

0	A have to	B had to	C don't have to
1	A need	B must	C must not
2	A must not	B needed	C will have to
3	A need	B don't need to	C must
4	A must not	B needn't	C don't have
5	A needn't	B must not	C have to
6	A didn't have to	B must	C must not
7	A don't have to	B must	C must not
8	A need	B must not	C have to
9	A must	B had to	C needn't
10	A needed to	B will have to	C don't have to

3 UNITS 67 AND 68 **Complete the second sentences so they mean the same as the first ones.**

0 It isn't a good idea to eat it. It doesn't taste very good. You .... *shouldn't eat it* ....

1 It's a good idea to wear a suit to the interview.
   You ....

2 I'm not sure but I don't think he's going to finish the course.
   He ....

3 *Chicago* is a fantastic musical. Don't miss it!
   You really ....

4 I think he sounds a little bit Spanish.
   He ....

5 It isn't a good idea to leave school at sixteen.
   You ....

170

4 ALL UNITS Look at each picture. What does each sign mean? Choose A, B or C.

0 A You can stay with your bags.
  Ⓑ You must stay with your bags.
  C You don't have to stay with your bags.

1 A You can listen to music here.
  B You can't listen to music here.
  C You might listen to music here.

2 A You needn't walk on the grass.
  B You have to walk on the grass.
  C You mustn't walk on the grass.

3 A You can't bring your children.
  B You should bring your children.
  C You may bring your children.

4 A Your journey can't take a long time.
  B Your journey might take a long time.
  C Your journey will take a long time.

5 A You shouldn't go in the sea if you can't swim well.
  B You can go in the sea if you can't swim well.
  C You don't have to go in the sea if you can't swim well.

5 ALL UNITS Complete the note with the phrases A–I below.

A need to eat
B should eat it soon
C couldn't wait to see you
D could you get some milk
E have to recycle
F won't be able to have a shower
G don't have to stay here
H must be outside
I mustn't eat too much

Hi Tina,
Thanks so much for coming to look after our house and the cats while we're on holiday. Sorry we (0) ....C.... but the taxi is here now.

Just a few things to tell you –
The cats aren't a problem. They (1) .... twice a day but they (2) .... – they're both too fat! Just give them half a can of cat food a day. Of course, you (3) .... every day to feed them – you can put dry food out for them.
The men empty the rubbish bins on Thursday. They come early so the bags (4) .... by about 7.00. You can leave them outside the back door. We (5) .... glass and paper, so can you put the bottles and newspapers in the kitchen cupboard?
The hot water system isn't very good. Turn it on at least an hour before you need hot water or you (6) ....!
There's some chicken in the fridge. It's a day old now, so you (7) ....
Finally, we're coming back on Sunday evening, as you know, so (8) .... for us? We won't be able to get to the shops.
Thanks again,
Mary and Mike

Test MODULE 9
Modal verbs

Choose the correct answer, A, B or C.

1 Matt .... cook a fantastic curry!   ➤ Unit 61
  A can B cans C can to

2 We're sorry, but we .... come to your party on Saturday.   ➤ Unit 61
  A don't B don't can C can't

3 It's women only at the health club pool tonight. Men .... go.   ➤ Unit 61
  A can't B couldn't C can

4 Susanna was an amazing child – she .... speak before she was two.   ➤ Unit 62
  A did B could C can

5 When I get my new car, I .... drive to work.   ➤ Unit 62
  A can B will can C 'll be able to

6 Dad, ... I watch *Ugly Betty* on TV tonight?   ➤ Unit 63
  A am B can C do

7 'Could I come to your class today?' 'Yes, of course you ....'   ➤ Unit 63
  A can B could C will be able

8 Excuse me. This room is very cold. .... turn up the heating, please?   ➤ Unit 63
  A May you B Could you C Shall you

9 Where's your passport? You .... show it when you get off the plane.   ➤ Unit 64
  A have to B need C don't have to

10 I'm really tired today. I .... to drink some more coffee!   ➤ Unit 64
  A needn't B need C have to

11 I've told Jan about the sales at the shopping centre so you .... to call her.   ➤ Unit 64
  A needn't B don't have C have

12 .... to wear a uniform in your new job?   ➤ Unit 65
  A Do you must B Must you C Do you have

13 Passengers .... speak to the driver while the bus is moving.   ➤ Unit 65
  A must not B don't have to C must

14 Danuta .... learn English when she got the job with the American company.   ➤ Unit 66
  A had to B will have to C must

15 I've just bought a bike so you .... drive me to work any more.   ➤ Unit 66
  A won't need B won't must C won't have to

16 Chris just sits and watches TV every evening. He .... join an evening class.   ➤ Unit 67
  A must B should C ought

17 It's quite a formal party so .... wear jeans to it.   ➤ Unit 67
  A I don't think you should B you should C you must

18 I'm not very busy this weekend so I .... come to the football match.   ➤ Unit 68
  A might B may C might not

19 'That's $200 dollars, sir.' 'That .... right! Your website said $150.'   ➤ Unit 68
  A mustn't be B can't be C must be

20 The place we're visiting is in the mountains so your mobile .... work there.   ➤ Unit 68
  A must not B can C might not

⏻ Go online for a full exit test

Conditionals

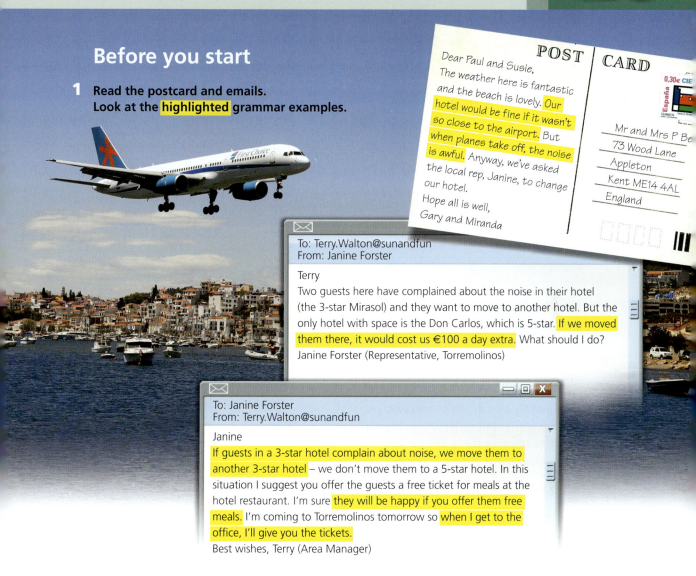

Before you start

1 **Read the postcard and emails.
Look at the <mark>highlighted</mark> grammar examples.**

> **POST CARD**
>
> Dear Paul and Susie,
> The weather here is fantastic
> and the beach is lovely. <mark>Our
> hotel would be fine if it wasn't
> so close to the airport.</mark> But
> when planes take off, the noise
> is awful. Anyway, we've asked
> the local rep, Janine, to change
> our hotel.
> Hope all is well,
> Gary and Miranda
>
> 0,30€ CIE
> España
>
> Mr and Mrs P Be
> 73 Wood Lane
> Appleton
> Kent ME14 4AL
> England

> To: Terry.Walton@sunandfun
> From: Janine Forster
>
> Terry
> Two guests here have complained about the noise in their hotel
> (the 3-star Mirasol) and they want to move to another hotel. But the
> only hotel with space is the Don Carlos, which is 5-star. <mark>If we moved
> them there, it would cost us €100 a day extra.</mark> What should I do?
> Janine Forster (Representative, Torremolinos)

> To: Janine Forster
> From: Terry.Walton@sunandfun
>
> Janine
> <mark>If guests in a 3-star hotel complain about noise, we move them to
> another 3-star hotel</mark> – we don't move them to a 5-star hotel. In this
> situation I suggest you offer the guests a free ticket for meals at the
> hotel restaurant. I'm sure <mark>they will be happy if you offer them free
> meals.</mark> I'm coming to Torremolinos tomorrow so <mark>when I get to the
> office, I'll give you the tickets.</mark>
> Best wishes, Terry (Area Manager)

2 **Now read the sentences. Choose the correct words in *italics*.
The <mark>highlighted</mark> grammar examples will help you.**

1 If hotel guests *have / had* small children, they usually want rooms on
   the ground floor.   ➤ Unit 69
2 When people arrive at a hotel, there *is / was* a form to fill in.   ➤ Unit 69
3 I'll be very pleased if we *get / got* a room with a view of the sea.   ➤ Unit 70
4 When we go down to reception we *would / 'll* ask for a bigger room.   ➤ Unit 70
5 We *would stay / stayed* in the hotel on the beach if it wasn't expensive.   ➤ Unit 71
6 If we *have / had* a lot of money, we would stay in a five-star hotel on our   ➤ Unit 71
   next holiday.

3 **Check your answers below. Then go to the unit for more information and practice.**

1 have 2 is 3 get 4 'll 5 would stay 6 had

69 Present conditions

If you **put** the card in, the lights **come** on.

1 Form

CONDITION (*if ...*) present tense	RESULT present tense
*If you **put** the card in,*	*the lights **come** on.*
*If you **look** directly at the sun,*	*it **damages** your eyes.*
*If plants **don't get** water,*	*they **die**.*
*If you **need** any help,*	***ask** the teacher.*

When we are talking about real situations in the present, BOTH verbs are in the present tense. Notice the position of the comma (,):
*If you **put** the card in, the lights **come** on.*

If we write the result first, a comma is not necessary:
*The lights **come** on if you **put** the card in.*
*Plants **die** if they **don't get** water.*

2 Use

We use *if* or *when* + present tenses
- to talk about real situations:
  *If you **turn** the key, the engine **starts**.*
- to say that one event always follows another:
  *When I **go** to bed late, I **feel** tired the next day.*
- to describe rules:
  *If a player **drops** the ball, he/she **is** out.*

NATURAL ENGLISH When we are speaking to someone, we often use the *if* part of the sentence alone:
*'Do you like curry?' 'Yes, **if it's not too spicy**.'*

We use *if* + the imperative to give instructions or advice:
*If it's **raining**, **take** an umbrella.*

 Notice that we don't repeat the subject:
✗ *If you want more information, you look on our website.*
✓ *If you want more information, **look** on our website.*

 We don't use *to* after *please*:
✗ *If you need anything, please to call reception.*
✓ *If you need anything, **please call** reception.*

Practice

1 **Complete the sentences. Use the words from the box.**
🔊 **3.58** **Listen and check.**

The Automatic House

0 When your car enters the drive, the garage doors ..... *open* ....

1 If you .... into a room, the lights come on.

2 When you .... on the sofa, the TV switches on.

3 When you .... the taps, water comes out.

4 .... it is hot, the windows open.

5 If it .... cold, the heating system turns on.

6 If you .... the house, the door locks itself.

> gets
> leave
> ~~open~~
> sit
> touch
> walk
> when

2 **Match the two parts of the sentences. Then choose the correct words in *italics*.**
🔊 **3.59** **Listen and check.**

0 If you turn the key,
1 When I drink too much coffee,
2 If you *stay / will stay* in the sun for a long time,
3 If you need more information,
4 My boss gets angry
5 If the machine doesn't start,
6 You *don't / didn't* need a passport
7 Phone this number

A your skin gets burnt.
B when I *am / will be* late for work.
C the engine (*starts*)/ *started*.
D if you *have / had* any problems.
E *press / you will press* the red button.
F I *get / will get* a headache.
G if you never travel anywhere.
H please *to visit / visit* our website.

3 **GRAMMAR IN USE** **There are five more grammar mistakes in the text. Find and correct them.**

Welcome to the
PENRITH HOTEL

+ All our rooms are non-smoking. If you ~~wished~~ *wish* to smoke, please use the balcony.

+ If you want breakfast in your room, please to phone reception.

+ We provide 24-hour room service. If you needing any items from our room service menu, please call 200.

+ Guests must leave their rooms by 12.00. Please contact reception when you plan to leave after 12.00.

+ If there is a fire, please leaving by the stairs; do not use the lift.

+ If there is anything we can do to make your stay more enjoyable, please told us.

70 First conditional

If you **give** me some money, I'll **get** some ice creams.

1 Form

CONDITION (*if ...*) present tense	RESULT *will* / *won't* + infinitive without *to*
*If you **give** me some money,*	*I'll (I will) **get** some ice creams.*
*If you **call** me before six o'clock,*	*I **won't** (I will not) be at home.*
*If you **don't work** hard,*	*you'll (you will) **fail** your exams.*

The first conditional describes a future situation.

 But we use the present tense after *if*, not *will* or *won't*.
✗ ~~If you will call me before six o'clock,~~ I won't be at home.
✓ *If you **call** me before six o'clock,*

2 Possible and certain future situations

We use the first conditional to talk about a POSSIBLE future action or situation:
*If you **give** me some money, **I'll get** some ice creams.* (You might give me some money.)
*If the tickets **are** too expensive, we **won't buy** them.* (The tickets might be too expensive.)
*Sue's parents **will give** her a car if she **passes** the exam.* (Sue might pass the exam.)

We can use *when* if a future action or situation is CERTAIN:
***When** I arrive at the airport, **I'll phone** you.* (I will arrive at the airport.)
*Jane **will start** work as a nurse when she **finishes** the course.* (She will finish the course.)

Future situations with *when*, *until*, *as soon as*, etc. ➤ Unit 94.2

3 Offers and warnings

We can also use the first conditional
- to offer or suggest something:
  ***If you get** the shopping, **I'll wash** the car.*
  ***I'll pay** for dinner **if you pay** for lunch.*
- to warn someone not to do something:
  ***If you arrive** late, **we'll go** without you.* (Don't arrive late.)
  ***If you make** any more noise, **I'll call** the police.* (Don't make any more noise.)

Practice

1 Use the words below to write sentences with *if* or *when*. 🔊**3.60** Listen and check.

possible future action	result
0 Dilip / pass the exam	he / go to university
If Dilip passes the exam, he'll go to university.	
1 you / get there early	you / get the best seats
2 I / need your help	I / phone you
3 the bus / not come	we / take you in our car
4 it / rain tomorrow	we / not go to the park

certain future action	result
00 Mary / get to Paris	she / send us an email
When Mary gets to Paris, she'll send us an email.	
5 Jo and Mike / arrive	I / offer them a drink
6 the train / stop	the doors / open
7 we / go into town	we / have lunch there
8 course / finish	I / go back to Japan

2 Choose the best answer, A or B.

0 I'll get some milk when I go to the shops.
  (A) I'll go to the shops soon. B I might go to the shops.

1 If I find the book you want, I'll send you a text message.
  A I'll definitely find the book. B I might find the book.

2 When your cousins arrive, we'll start cooking supper.
  A This is going to happen in the future. B This happens regularly.

3 When Neela finishes the course, she'll be a doctor.
  A I'm not sure if Neela will finish the course. B I'm certain Neela will finish the course.

4 I'll tell her the news if she comes to the party.
  A She's definitely coming to the party. B She might come to the party.

3 **GRAMMAR IN USE** Complete the email with forms of the verbs in brackets (). Use short forms if possible. 🔊**3.61** Listen and check.

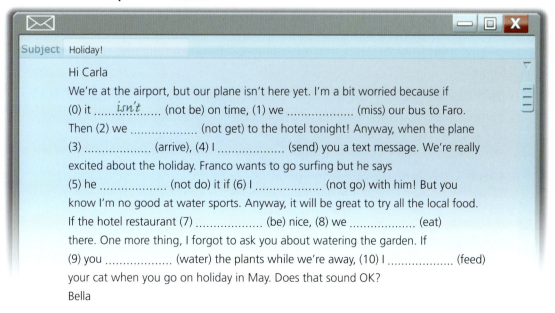

Subject | Holiday!

Hi Carla

We're at the airport, but our plane isn't here yet. I'm a bit worried because if
(0) it ......*isn't*...... (not be) on time, (1) we .... (miss) our bus to Faro.
Then (2) we .... (not get) to the hotel tonight! Anyway, when the plane
(3) .... (arrive), (4) I .... (send) you a text message. We're really
excited about the holiday. Franco wants to go surfing but he says
(5) he .... (not do) it if (6) I .... (not go) with him! But you
know I'm no good at water sports. Anyway, it will be great to try all the local food.
If the hotel restaurant (7) .... (be) nice, (8) we .... (eat)
there. One more thing, I forgot to ask you about watering the garden. If
(9) you .... (water) the plants while we're away, (10) I .... (feed)
your cat when you go on holiday in May. Does that sound OK?
Bella

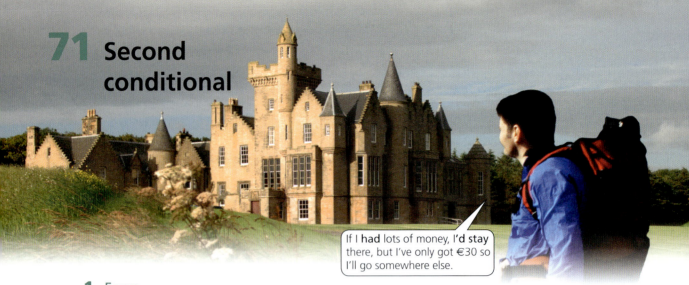

71 Second conditional

If I **had** lots of money, I**'d stay** there, but I've only got €30 so I'll go somewhere else.

1 Form

CONDITION (*if ...*) past simple	RESULT *would* (*not*) + infinitive without *to*
If I **had** lots of money,	I**'d** (I **would**) **stay** there.
If I **bought** a motorbike,	I **wouldn't** (I **would not**) take the bus to work.

We use the second conditional to describe a situation that we are imagining in the present or the future.

 We use the past tense after *if*:
✗ *If I have lots of money, I'd stay there.* ✓ *If I **had** lots of money, I'd stay there.*

NATURAL ENGLISH We use the short forms *'d* and *wouldn't* in spoken English and in informal written English.

2 Use

We use the second conditional

- for future situations that probably won't happen:
  *If I **won** the race, I**'d get** a prize.*
  *If Carla **got** the job, she **wouldn't be able to** live here anymore.*
- for present situations that are not possible:
  *If David **was** here, he**'d enjoy** this film.* (He isn't here.)
  *If I **had** wings, I**'d fly** all over the world.* (I don't have wings.)
  *What **would you do** if you **weren't** a student?* (You are a student.)

Compare:

FIRST CONDITIONAL	SECOND CONDITIONAL
for something that might happen: *If you **give** me some money, I**'ll get** some ice creams.*	for something that probably won't happen or is not possible: *If you **gave** me a million dollars, I**'d stop** work.*

After *if* + *I*/*he*/*she*/*it*, we can use *was* or *were*:
*If I **was/were** the president, I would reduce taxes. She**'d** love this place if she **was/were** here.*

3 if I were/was you ...

We often say *if I were/was you, I'd ...* to give advice:
*If I **were** you, I**'d send** him a text message.* (= I think you should send a text message.)
*There's always a big queue so I**'d get** there early if I **were** you.*
(= I think you should get there early.)

 Pronunciation ➤ 1.27

Practice

1 Look at the pictures. Use the words below to complete the sentences.

0 If I were ....*you, I'd lie down*............ .
   (you / I / lie down)

1 I'd buy ....
   (that dress / if / I / be / thinner)

2 If I were ....
   (you / I / put on / some sun cream)

3 If it was ....
   (sunny / I / take / the baby to the park)

4 If I had ....
   (some food / I / make / you a snack)

5 I'd ....
   (buy / some new shoes / if / I / be / you)

2 **GRAMMAR IN USE** Complete the conversation with forms of the verbs in brackets (). 🔊 **3.62** Listen and check.

MANDY   It would be nicer if this hotel room (0) ....*had*............. (have) a view of the sea.

DAVID   I know, but those rooms cost extra. So, what are our plans for the next few days?

MANDY   What about the diving course? It's rather expensive, but …

DAVID   Mmm. If we (1) .... (do) that, we wouldn't have any more money! What about the two-day trip to Granada?

MANDY   We've already paid for all our meals here. If we went on the two-day trip, we (2) .... (miss) dinner here. What else can we do?

DAVID   I'm not sure. I (3) .... (look) in the guidebook if I (4) .... (have) it here; but I left it at home. We can ask at reception …

MANDY   OK, I'll do that. Now what shall I wear for dinner? My new jacket?

DAVID   I (5) .... (not wear) that if I were you. It's very warm tonight.

3 Complete the second sentence so it means the same as the first. Use one, two or three words. 🔊 **3.63** Listen and check.

0 I can't come to the meeting because I'm ill.
   If I ....*wasn't ill*........, I'd come to the meeting.

1 They don't expect to win the match.
   They'd be surprised if .... the match.

2 You ought to ask for help.
   I .... for help if I were you.

3 I think you should call a doctor.
   If ...., I'd call a doctor.

4 Jack is too fat because he doesn't do any exercise.
   If Jack did some exercise, he .... fat.

5 I don't think I'll get a place at Harvard.
   I .... very happy if I got a place at Harvard.

Review MODULE 10

1 UNITS 69 AND 70 **Choose the correct words in *italics*.** 🔊 **3.64** **Listen and check.**

0 (When) / If you finish the test, give your question papers to the teacher.

1 When I stay up late, I *feel / will feel* tired the next morning.

2 If there is a fire, *you will use / use* the emergency exit.

3 If they get to the airport early, they *will get / get* good seats on the plane.

4 I'm sure we *find / 'll find* some good bargains if we go to the sales tomorrow.

5 If you don't go to the party, you *don't / won't* meet my new friend.

6 Press the red button if you *want / will want* to record the programme.

7 *You will wear / Wear* a smart suit if they ask you to an interview.

8 If Janice takes the earlier train on Friday, she *gets / 'll get* here by lunchtime.

2 UNITS 69 AND 70 **Write one word in each space.**

Instructions for use

1 First, choose your drink from the list.

2 If you want milk, (0) ......*press*...... the white button.

3 (1) .... you (2) .... sugar, press the grey button.

4 Now put in 50p. ((3) .... you don't have a 50p coin, the machine (4) .... accept 2 x 20p coins and 1 x 10p coin.)

5 Wait for ten seconds.

6 (5) .... the door opens, your drink will be ready.

IF YOU HAVE ANY PROBLEMS WITH THIS MACHINE, (6) .... 099032111.

3 UNITS 70 AND 71 **Read the email. Decide if the sentences 1–5 are true (T) or false (F).**

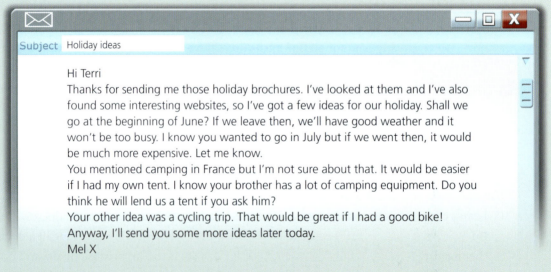

Subject Holiday ideas

Hi Terri

Thanks for sending me those holiday brochures. I've looked at them and I've also found some interesting websites, so I've got a few ideas for our holiday. Shall we go at the beginning of June? If we leave then, we'll have good weather and it won't be too busy. I know you wanted to go in July but if we went then, it would be much more expensive. Let me know.

You mentioned camping in France but I'm not sure about that. It would be easier if I had my own tent. I know your brother has a lot of camping equipment. Do you think he will lend us a tent if you ask him?

Your other idea was a cycling trip. That would be great if I had a good bike!

Anyway, I'll send you some more ideas later today.

Mel X

0 Mel isn't sure about the weather in June. ....*F*....

1 Mel wants to go on holiday at the beginning of June. ....

2 Mel expects to go on holiday in July. ....

3 Mel doesn't have a tent. ....

4 Mel thinks Terri is probably going to ask her brother about his camping equipment. ....

5 Mel has a good bicycle. ....

4 ALL UNITS Correct the grammar mistakes in the sentences below.

1 If you heat water, it
   ~~would boil~~. *boils*

2 If you will see a fire,
   break the glass.

3 If I were you, I'll take it
   back to the shop.

4 If I had a million pounds,
   I will buy that.

5 Be careful. If you touched
   the fire, you'll burn yourself.

6 Bye. I'd phone you when
   I get there.

5 ALL UNITS Complete the information with the correct word(s), A, B or C below.

DAILY ACTIVITY SHEET – TUESDAY

(0) ………. you need more information about any of the activities, please ask at reception.

AEROBICS CLASS 9.30–10.30
Beginners welcome.
Start your day with some exercise.

LOCATION: EAST TERRACE
(IF IT (1) ………., WE WILL HAVE THE CLASS IN ROOM A.)

CHILDREN'S ACTIVITIES 10.00–13.00
For children aged 5–12.
(If your children (2) ………. older, they can take part in the teenagers' theatre class in our other hotel, the Hallanford Vista.)
LOCATION: ROOM B

DANCING 14.00–16.00
Warning – this is a very popular activity!
If we (3) ………. a larger room, we would invite everyone; but we can only fit twenty-five people. So come early!
LOCATION: ROOM C

BEACH BALL GAMES 16.30–17.15
If you enjoy sports and sunshine, you (4) ……….
this. Adults only.
LOCATION: BEACH

KEEP FIT CLASS 17.00–18.00
Enjoy a one-hour keep fit class in our luxurious health club. (5) ………. the class ends, you (6) ………. full of energy.
LOCATION: HEALTH CLUB (GROUND FLOOR)

0 A When (B) If C For
1 A rained B rains C will rain
2 A are B would be C were
3 A have B had C will have
4 A loved B will love C would love
5 A When B If C For
6 A felt B would feel C will feel

Test MODULE 10

Conditionals

Choose the correct answer, A, B or C.

1 If you press the .... comes on.
A button if the light   B button, the light   C button the light
➤ Unit 69

2 If you .... the key, the car starts.
A turned   B turn   C will turn
➤ Unit 69

3 If people eat too much, they .... fat.
A get   B got   C are getting
➤ Unit 69

4 .... I eat very spicy food, I get a stomachache.
A When   B If that   C For
➤ Unit 69

5 Phone this emergency number .... your car breaks down.
A if   B when   C for when
➤ Unit 69

6 If it isn't sunny, we .... to the beach.
A went   B didn't go   C won't go
➤ Unit 70

7 If you take me to the shops, I .... some food for supper.
A 'll buy   B buy   C bought
➤ Unit 70

8 If the hotel receptionist .... us a better room, we'll give her
some money.
A gave   B will give   C gives
➤ Unit 70

9 When I .... at the hotel, I'll send you a text message.
A arrive   B 'll arrive   C arrived
➤ Unit 70

10 Jake .... a pay increase when he finishes the management course.
A got   B didn't get   C will get
➤ Unit 70

11 If you make lunch, I .... the dishes.
A 'll do   B do   C don't do
➤ Unit 70

12 If the restaurant is really expensive, we .... there.
A didn't eat   B ate   C won't eat
➤ Unit 70

13 My boss will check her messages when she .... back to the office.
A 'll get   B gets   C got
➤ Unit 70

14 If we had a garden, we .... a pet.
A got   B 'd get   C will get
➤ Unit 71

15 If I .... a million dollars, I'd spend the money on a fast car.
A have   B will have   C had
➤ Unit 71

16 If you went to the concert, you .... it.
A would enjoy   B had enjoyed   C will enjoy
➤ Unit 71

17 Marianne .... with us today if she wasn't at her sister's wedding.
A would be   B was   C is
➤ Unit 71

18 If it .... so cold, we'd go for a swim.
A isn't   B won't be   C wasn't
➤ Unit 71

19 If ...., I'd see a doctor as soon as possible.
A I were you   B I was me   C you were me
➤ Unit 71

20 .... buy the tickets online if I were you; they're much cheaper.
A You will   B I will   C I'd
➤ Unit 71

Word order and sentence patterns

Before you start

1 Read the texts. Look at the **highlighted** grammar examples.

WEATHER WARNING
Warning of a storm tonight from approximately 17.00. Expect 30mm rain. **Do not drive** unless necessary.

STORM AT BRIGHAM-ON-SEA

HEAVY RAIN AND WINDS at 125kmh caused problems in Brigham yesterday evening. The storm started in the early evening and continued for most of the night.

Dear Dad

I'm sending you this photo of the sea last night. We had an awful storm. I watched it all from the bedroom window – **it's great to be** so close to the sea, but it can be frightening, too! The storm started at about five o'clock and **it rained** heavily all evening. **There is a 150-year-old sea wall** in Brigham. **Have you ever seen it?** But luckily it was OK after the storm. I was lucky with that photo – **I waited for a really big wave,** and finally one came. I'm going to show it to my art class next week!

2 Now read the sentences. Choose the correct words in *italics*.
The **highlighted** grammar examples will help you.

1 We waited *the bus / for the bus* from 8.00 to 8.50! ➤ Unit 72
2 *Heavy rain caused difficulties / Difficulties caused heavy rain* on the roads. ➤ Unit 72
3 Rome is wonderful! *Have you / You have* ever been there? ➤ Unit 73
4 The storm will get worse tonight. *Do not / You do not* go out after midnight if you don't have to. ➤ Unit 73
5 My aunt sent *to me / me* a lovely box of chocolates. ➤ Unit 74
6 *A Victorian hospital is / There is a Victorian hospital* in this town. ➤ Unit 75
7 The weather was terrible yesterday. *It / There* snowed all day. ➤ Unit 76
8 It's great *meet / to meet* you after all these years! ➤ Unit 76

3 Check your answers below. Then go to the unit for more information and practice.

1 for the bus 2 Heavy rain caused difficulties 3 Have you
4 Do not 5 me 6 There is a Victorian hospital 7 It 8 to meet

⏻ Go online for a full diagnostic test

72 Word order in statements

1 Subject + verb (+ object)

A statement contains a subject and a verb. It can also contain an object and other phrases. We put a full stop (.) at the end of a statement.

SUBJECT	VERB	OBJECT
I	don't know.	
Paul	is reading	a magazine.
The dry weather	caused	a lot of problems.

If we change the position of the subject and the object, the meaning of the sentence changes:

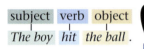  

subject verb object
The boy *hit* *the ball* .

subject verb object
The ball *hit* *the boy* .

A few verbs have adjectives after them instead of an object (e.g. *be, look, seem, smell, taste*):
*Melanie **is** very angry.*
*That **looks** delicious!*

Adjectives after verbs ➤ Unit 25.3

We often use the *-ing* form of a verb as the subject of the sentence. Here, it is like a noun:
***Swimming** is good for you.*
***Driving** in fog can be dangerous.*

2 Subject + verb (no object)

Some verbs never have an object
(e.g. *arrive, come, go, happen, rain, land, wait*).

SUBJECT	VERB
The taxi	is waiting.
Our friends	haven't arrived.
The plane	landed.

 Remember to put the subject BEFORE the verb:
✗ ~~Then arrived my friends and we had lunch.~~
✓ *Then **my friends arrived** and we had lunch.*

Other verbs can have an object, but do not always need one:
I'm reading a magazine. I'm reading.
Our team has just won the game! Our team has just won!

3 Building a sentence

NOUN (subject)	VERB	NOUN (object)	PLACE	TIME
We	are going to meet	our friends	outside the cinema	at 8.30.
The concert	will take place		in Beijing	in June.
The workmen	cleared	the snow	from the streets	early this morning.

This word order is the normal order for the parts of a sentence.
If there is an adverb of manner, too, we put it before place or time:

manner place time
He played *well* *at the game* *on Saturday* .

Adverbs and word order ➤ Unit 28 Word order in questions ➤ Unit 73.1

Practice

1 **Match the pictures with the correct sentences.**

0 The cat attacked the dog. ...C...
1 The dog attacked the cat. ....
2 The people waited for the bus. ....

3 The bus waited for the people. ....
4 Martin is watching Jane. ....
5 Jane is watching Martin. ....

2 GRAMMAR IN USE **Read the text. Write the <u>underlined</u> words in the correct order.** 3.65 **Listen and check.**

EXTREME WEATHER IN BRITAIN

In July 2005 there was a very bad storm in Birmingham.
It injured nineteen people and (0) <u>a lot of damage caused</u> to buildings.
This is what Cathy Mead, a teacher from Birmingham, said:

I work in Dudley Park School. I was (1) <u>on Thursday afternoon in the classroom</u>.
It was (2) <u>heavily raining</u> and then it went very dark. The wind became stronger
and the building started to shake. The children all (3) <u>scared looked</u>, so I moved
them into the middle of the classroom. Then I left them (4) <u>for a while alone</u>, and
I went (5) <u>for a few minutes outside</u>, to see what was happening. It was amazing –
(6) <u>a car lifted the wind</u> in the street and then it fell to the ground again, then
(7) <u>started a tree to fall</u>. I went back into the school, we closed the doors and
sat with the children. We waited until the storm passed, then we left
(8) <u>at about four o'clock the school</u>. I went home and, luckily, my house was OK.

Map	FAQ	Contact us

0 *caused a lot of damage*
1 ....
2 ....

3 ....
4 ....
5 ....

6 ....
7 ....
8 ....

3 **Write the words and phrases in the normal order. Then write a second sentence that is true for you.** 3.66 **Listen and check.**

0 ate for lunch Vicki a huge pizza
   Vicki ate a huge pizza for lunch.   *I had a cheese sandwich for my lunch.*

1 at the supermarket works Patrick on Saturday mornings
   ....

2 in my town rained yesterday it heavily
   ....

3 was when he got home very tired Joe
   ....

4 Andrea on holiday to Tunisia is going later this year
   ....

73 Word order in questions and imperatives

Have you seen that?

Quick! Drive!

1 Questions

Question forms can be

- *be* + subject: *Are you happy?   Was she late yesterday?*
- auxiliary/modal verb + subject + main verb: *Do you understand?*

Questions can also contain an object and other phrases. We usually put a question mark (?) at the end of a question.

AUXILIARY / MODAL VERB	SUBJECT	MAIN VERB	OBJECT
Can	*she*	*speak*	*French?*
Did	*it*	*snow*	*last winter?*

Modal verbs ➤ Module 9   More on questions ➤ Units 77 and 78

2 Imperatives

We use the infinitive form for imperatives. We use *don't* + infinitive to make a negative imperative. We sometimes put an exclamation mark (!) at the end of an imperative, to make it stronger.

POSITIVE	NEGATIVE
Come in!	*Don't worry.*
Take a seat.	*Don't forget your keys!*
Stop talking!	*Don't start writing yet.*

 ✗ ~~*You listen to me. I'm talking.*~~ (This is not polite.)
✓ *Listen to me. I'm talking.*

We use imperatives to:

- give orders: *Stand up!*
- give instructions: *Mix the eggs and milk together.*
- give warnings: *Don't go out in this weather. It's horrible.*
- offer something: *Have a biscuit.*
- ask for something: *Pass the salt, please.*

In public signs, we don't use imperatives:
✗ ~~*Don't smoke.*~~
✓ *No **smoking***
✗ ~~*Don't park.*~~
✓ *No **parking***

Practice

1 Write the words in the correct order to make questions or imperatives. Write ? or ! at the end of each one. 🔊 **3.67** Listen and check.

0 that don't do ..*Don't do that!*...

1 sit there don't ....

2 me that give knife ....

3 want you do an apple ....

4 see later me and come ....

5 silly be don't so ....

6 coming you the party to are ....

2 There is a mistake in each sentence. Correct the mistakes.

0 You have a piece of cake. ..*Have a piece of cake.*...

1 The cat's very gentle. Not to be afraid. ....

2 Passing me the dictionary, please. ....

3 Sign in exam room: no talk! ....

4 Not to use your father's computer! ....

5 Sign at swimming pool: don't dive! ....

6 You sit here next to me! ....

3 **GRAMMAR IN USE** Complete the conversation with the verbs in brackets (). Decide whether the sentences should be questions or imperatives. 🔊 **3.68** Listen and check.

BRIAN Hi, Eva. Kerry and I are going to visit your home country and I ...

EVA You're going to visit Iceland – that's great! (0) ....*Sit*............ (sit) down! When (1) .... (you / go)?

BRIAN We wanted to ask you. When are the best times to go, do you think?

EVA Well, (2) .... (you / want) to go to festivals, or to travel around?

BRIAN Travel around, really.

EVA Well, (3) .... (not / go) there in the winter! It's cold, it's rainy and it's dark nearly all the time.

BRIAN Mmm, (4) .... (the summer / be) quite warm?

EVA Oh, yes, it can be very warm in July and August.

BRIAN (5) .... (we / can see) any festivals then?

EVA Yes, (6) .... (go) in June and spend two or three weeks there, and (7) .... (make) sure you stay in Reykjavik on 17 June.

BRIAN Why (8) .... (June / be) so good?

EVA Because it's light 24 hours a day in June; it's wonderful. Also, Iceland's Independence Day is on 17 June. It's a very good time to be in Reykjavik, but (9) .... (book) a hotel!

BRIAN Thanks, Eva. That's really useful.

EVA You're welcome. Oh, another thing – (10) .... (not / forget) your camera when you go – there's some wonderful scenery.

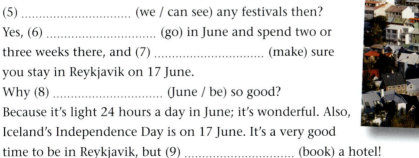

74 Verbs with two objects

We had a lot of heavy rain this year so we **bought the children some rubber boots**.

1 Person + thing

Some verbs can have two objects; one is usually a person and the other is usually a thing. Some verbs with two objects are: *bring, buy, give, make, lend, offer, pay, send, show, teach, tell, throw, write.*

We usually put the person object first:

SUBJECT	VERB	OBJECT (person)	OBJECT (thing)
We	bought	the children/them	some boots.
Harry	sent	Sally/her	some flowers.
Lianne	showed	Mike/him	her new laptop.
Jasmine	didn't tell	the students/them	a story.

 We don't use *for* or *to* when the person object comes first:
✗ *Harry sent to Sally/her some flowers.*
✓ *Harry sent Sally/her some flowers.*

2 Thing + person

We can also put the 'thing' object first. Then we need to use *for* or *to*:

SUBJECT	VERB	OBJECT (thing)	PREPOSITION + OBJECT (person)
We	bought	some boots	**for** the children/**for** them.
Harry	sent	some flowers	**to** Sally/**to** her.
Lianne	showed	her new laptop	**to** Mike/**to** him.
Jasmine	didn't tell	a story	**to** the students /**to** them.

We use *to* after most of the verbs in the list above, but we use *for* after *buy* and *make*.

 For some verbs (e.g. *explain*, *describe* and *translate*) we always put the 'thing' object first:
✗ *The teacher explained me the grammar.*
✓ *The teacher explained the grammar to me.*

Practice

1 Choose the correct words in *italics*. 🔊 **3.69** Listen and check.

0 We sent (her)/ *to her* the tickets.

1 Can you bring the dictionary *me / to me*?

2 Come in. I'll show *you / to you* our wedding photos.

3 Can you explain the answer *me / to me*?

4 The teacher translated the text *us / for us*.

5 I'll send *the hotel / to the hotel* an email to check the prices.

6 The café is giving a free cake *all its customers / to all its customers* tomorrow.

2 Change the sentences to use a different word order. Add the preposition *to* if necessary.

  0 Can you pay her the money?   *Can you pay the money to her?*

00 I haven't shown the photos to Dad yet.   *I haven't shown Dad the photos yet.*

  1 We're giving flowers to Mum for her birthday. ....

  2 Allan teaches engineers English literature. ....

  3 I'll buy a coffee for you after dinner. ....

  4 They've offered Alexis the job! ....

  5 Throw the baby a ball – she'll catch it. ....

  6 Alison told the children a story. ....

3 **GRAMMAR IN USE** Write five more missing words in this conversation. 🔊 **3.70** Listen and check.

SAM   I'm not sure about camping now. There's going to be heavy rain this weekend.

PAULA I can lend some warm coats *to* you, if you want.

SAM   Thanks. I'll have to buy some boots the children, too.

PAULA Don't worry, we can lend the children some boots.

SAM   Great. Oh, I don't have directions to the campsite.

PAULA That's OK. I can send them you now by email.

SAM   Can you give them Nina? My computer isn't working.

PAULA Yes, sure. Or I could tell the route now. It isn't very difficult.

SAM   No, email the directions to Nina. That's fine. Shall we bring a football?

PAULA Yes, good idea, and you can show your skills with the ball all the children!

4 Use the words below to complete the questions.
Then write full answers that are true for you.

0 when / you / last lend / money / someone?

When did you last lend *money to someone? I lent my friend ten euros last week* .

1 anyone / ever / send / you / flowers?

Has anyone ever ....

2 what / parents / give / you / for your last birthday?

What did your parents ....

3 who / teach / you / something useful / recently?

Who has taught ....

4 you / ever / tell a lie / a friend?

Have you ever ....

may need to cut a line?

75 *there + be*

There **was** a terrible flood in the UK last summer. There **was** water everywhere.

1 Form

We can use *there + be* in many tenses and forms, eg:

	SINGULAR COUNTABLE	UNCOUNTABLE	PLURAL COUNTABLE
present simple	*There's a flood.*	*There's water everywhere.*	*There are lots of storms.*
past simple	*There was a flood.*	*There was water everywhere*	*There were lots of storms.*

Look at those dark clouds. **There's going to be** *a storm.*
Have you heard the news? **There's been** *an accident on the motorway.*
I think **there will be** *about fifty people at the party.*

We also use the negative of *there + be*:
There isn't *any food in the fridge.*
There haven't been *any good programmes on TV for a long time.*

To form questions, we put *be* before *there*:
Is there *anyone you know here? Yes,* **there is**. */ No,* **there isn't**.

 We don't use *there + be* in continuous tenses:
✗ *There's being a concert in the park this weekend.*
✓ **There's** *a concert in the park this weekend.*

 We use *there + is* (a singular verb) with a list of singular nouns:
✗ *There are a film, a concert and a football match on TV tonight.*
✓ **There's** *a film, a concert and a football match on TV tonight.*

 Pronunciation ➤ 1.28

2 Use

We use *there + be*

- to say where something is:
  There's *a bank in the High Street.* **There's** *some salt in that cupboard.*

- to say when something happens:
  There was *a robbery in the town last night.*
  There'll be *another concert in the village hall on Friday.*

- to show something to someone:
  Look! **There's** *a bird in that tree.*

- to say how many:
  There are *three museums in the city.* **There have been** *five really bad storms in the last week.*

 We need the word *there* in these sentences:
✗ *Is a strange cat in the garden.* ✗ *It is a strange cat in the garden.*
✓ **There's** *a strange cat in the garden.*

✗ *Are three cash machines here.* ✗ *They are three cash machines here.*
✓ **There are** *three cash machines here.*

there and *it* ➤ Unit 76.4

Practice

1 GRAMMAR IN USE **Complete the conversation with a form of** *there + be.*
🔊 **3.71 Listen and check.**

A Hello, I'm calling about the advert in the newspaper, for offices.

B Ah, yes, you'd like to rent one of our offices?

A Yes, probably. How many (0) ...*are there* .. for rent?

B (1) .... two offices free at the moment. They're both the same size.

A Oh, good. (2) .... a kitchen in the building?

B Yes, (3) .... a kitchen on the ground floor.

A OK. (4) .... a photocopier and a fax machine?

B Well, (5) .... three photocopiers, one on each floor, but no fax machine, I'm afraid.

A Mmm. What about transport? (6) .... a station somewhere near the offices?

B No, (7) .... But there's a bus stop outside, and the bus goes to the town centre.

A OK, so (8) .... a car park?

B No, not at the moment, but (9) .... one soon – we're building one this year.

A Has there been a lot of interest in your advert?

B Yes, (10) .... over twenty calls.

A OK. Thank you. I'll think about it.

2 GRAMMAR IN USE **Choose the correct words in** *italics* **in the text.** 🔊 **3.72 Listen and check.**

Future Shock

Some people still say that our weather isn't changing, or that the problem isn't very serious, but there (0) *have* / *has* been a lot of signs of change in the last few years. It seems that every month there (1) *is* / *are* another terrible storm somewhere in the world. In fact, in the last twenty-five years, (2) *it has* / *there have* been twice as many storms as in the twenty-five years before that. (3) *Are* / *There are* also other problems which should worry us, for example, (4) *there were* / *it was* terrible floods in the United Kingdom in the summer of 2007, which is very unusual. In some places, (5) *it* / *there* isn't enough rain, for example, Australia is usually extremely dry. If we allow these weather changes to continue, (6) *there will be* / *will be* more and more problems of this kind in the future.

3 **Find five more mistakes in the sentences and correct them. Tick (✓) the correct sentences.**

There is
0 ~~Is~~ a really nice beach in the north of the island.

1 Are there lots of books for this course?

2 Weren't any new students in my class yesterday.

3 There are a bank, a post office and a supermarket here.

4 There will be a lot of building work in the town next year.

5 Are going to be a lot of people at the party?

6 Won't be any rice left for tomorrow if we eat it all now.

7 There was a Toyota and a Honda in the garage.

8 A really bad storm was last year.

⏻ Go online for more practice

76 *it* as a subject/object

It **snowed** all night and **it took** a long time to clear the roads in the morning.

1 *it* as a subject

We can use *it* as a subject pronoun, to talk about a noun we have already mentioned:

*There was an awful **storm** last night. **It** damaged the roof.*

But often *it* has no real meaning, e.g. ***It's** raining.* We use *it* + *be*

- with an adjective, to describe a general situation: *I love living in Cambridge. **It's** nice here.*
- to talk about time: *What time is **it**? **It's** ten o'clock. What time will **it** be when we arrive?*
- to talk about days and dates: *What day is **it**? **It's** Monday. **It** was my birthday yesterday.*
- to describe distances: ***It's** five kilometres from home to the station. **It's** 200 kilometres away.*
- to talk about the weather: ***It's** raining. **It** isn't cold.*

We say *it takes five minutes, two hours,* etc. when we talk about how long we need to do something:
*'How long **does it take** to get to the airport?' '**It takes** about an hour.'*
***It took** a long time to clear the roads in the morning.*

2 *it* as an object

We also use *it* as an object pronoun to talk about a noun we have already mentioned:

*There was a lot of **snow** yesterday. The children enjoyed playing in **it**.*

3 *it's* + adjective/noun + *to*

We often use an adjective or noun after *be* + infinitive with *to*:

It + be	ADJECTIVE	INFINITIVE
It's	nice	to see you.
It isn't	easy	to find our house.

It + be	NOUN	INFINITIVE
It was	a mistake	to accept this job.
It will be	a shame	to miss your wedding.

4 *there* and *it*

We use *there* + *be* to give new information. We use *it* to say more about that information.

***There's** somebody at the door. **It's** the postman.*

***There's** some soup on the cooker. **It's** tomato soup.*

⚠ We don't use *it* to say where something is or when something happened. We use *there*:
✗ *It's a swimming pool at the leisure centre.* ✓ ***There's** a swimming pool at the leisure centre.*
✗ *It was a lot of snow last night.* ✓ ***There was** a lot of snow last night.*

there + *be* ➤ Unit 75

192

Practice

1 Choose the correct word it *italics*. 🔊**3.73** Listen and check.

0 'When's your birthday?' '*Is /(It's)*on 30 May.'
1 Look out of the window – *it's / there's* snowing really heavily.
2 I'll do the dishes before we leave. *It won't / Won't* take long.
3 Mum gave me a scarf for my birthday. I *wear / wear it* all the time.
4 Have you seen the new building in the town centre? *It's / There's* really ugly.
5 We can go walking on the hill – *there isn't / it isn't* much wind today.
6 Gerry doesn't like being a shop assistant. *There's / It's* boring.
7 Paul is really happy these days – *it's / is* nice to see that.
8 How far *is there / it* to the station?

2 Match the two parts of the sentences. 🔊**3.74** Listen and check.

0 Hello. It's really nice   A to make new friends.
1 The show isn't full so it isn't necessary   B to see the director now.
2 When you move to a different town, it isn't easy   C to speak on a mobile phone.
3 We're away next weekend. It will be a shame   D to see you again.
4 I'm sorry but it isn't possible   E to book seats before we go.
5 When you're driving in the UK, it's a crime   F to have an extra pen.
6 In an exam, it's important   G to miss your party.

3 Match the questions with the pictures. Then write answers.

A Madrid 300km   B   C 23 APRIL   D   E QUICK CAR WASH ONLY TEN MINUTES

0 What's the weather like? ....D....   *It's really sunny.* ....
1 What time is it? ....
2 What's the date? ....
3 How far is Madrid? ....
4 How long does the car wash take? ....

4 GRAMMAR IN USE   Read the story. Then complete it with *it* or *there*.

MY WORST JOURNEY EVER

A few years ago, I had to go to Stuttgart Airport to meet some friends.
(0) ....*It*........ usually only takes about half an hour as (1) ....'s only about 25 kilometres from my house to the airport, but this day was totally different. (2) .... was some heavy snow in the night, but that isn't usually a problem in Germany – (3) ....'s usually easy to drive in snow because they clear the roads very quickly. Anyway, I left home a bit early because of the snow, as (4) .... was quite deep. Soon after I left, (5) .... suddenly started snowing again and the car in front of me stopped. Luckily, I didn't hit (6) ...., but I saw that (7) .... was a really long queue of cars ahead. I sat in that queue for about two hours – (8) .... was really boring, but I finally found out what the problem was – (9) .... was an accident at the front of the queue. (10) .... was really late when I finally got to the airport, and then I found out that my friends' plane had gone to Frankfurt because of the snow!

Review MODULE 11

1 UNITS 72 AND 73 **Change the negative sentences to make them positive. Put the words in brackets () in the correct place in the sentence.**

0 Don't tell your friends about the sale. (in January)
   Tell your friends about the sale in January.

1 We won't meet outside the cinema on Saturday afternoon. (you)

   ....

2 Don't get me a newspaper this afternoon. (at the shop)

   ....

3 The students haven't finished. (their homework)

   ....

4 The sun didn't shine all day yesterday. (brightly)

   ....

5 The 2008 Olympics didn't take place from 8–24 August. (in Beijing)

   ....

6 Annie didn't look very happy. (last night)

   ....

2 UNITS 72 AND 74 **Complete the email with the correct words and phrases, A or B below.**

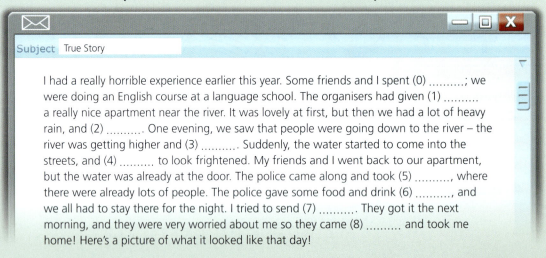

Subject True Story

I had a really horrible experience earlier this year. Some friends and I spent (0) ....; we were doing an English course at a language school. The organisers had given (1) .... a really nice apartment near the river. It was lovely at first, but then we had a lot of heavy rain, and (2) .... One evening, we saw that people were going down to the river – the river was getting higher and (3) .... Suddenly, the water started to come into the streets, and (4) .... to look frightened. My friends and I went back to our apartment, but the water was already at the door. The police came along and took (5) ...., where there were already lots of people. The police gave some food and drink (6) ...., and we all had to stay there for the night. I tried to send (7) .... They got it the next morning, and they were very worried about me so they came (8) .... and took me home! Here's a picture of what it looked like that day!

0 A in England the summer
   (B) the summer in England
1 A us B to us
2 A a lot of problems caused it
   B it caused a lot of problems
3 A it was watching everyone
   B everyone was watching it
4 A started everyone   B everyone started
5 A to a village hall us   B us to a village hall
6 A to everyone   B everyone
7 A my parents a text message
   B to my parents a text message
8 A a week later to England
   B to England a week later

3 UNITS 75 AND 76 **Complete the sentence for each piece of news.**
Use *There* or *It* and a suitable verb. (The word in brackets () shows you the tense.)

0 .....*There will be*..... a lot of snow tomorrow. (will)

Heavy snow tomorrow!

1 .... a new cinema
in the town centre by next June. (will)

New cinema in town by June

2 .... rain heavily next week.
(going to)

Three centimetres of rain next week

3 .... no British winners at
the Oscars last night. (past simple)

No British winners at Oscars!

4 .... a new road along the
south coast. (going to)

New road for South Coast

5 .... a bank robbery in the town
centre last night. (past simple)

LOCAL BANK ROBBED!

6 .... impossible to raise more money
for the new Olympic buildings. (present perfect)

No more money for Olympics

4 ALL UNITS **Write the words in the correct order. Make questions 0–3
and answers A–D. Then match the questions and answers.** ◀ 3.75 **Listen and check.**

0 meeting   yesterday   a   was there ?   *Was there a meeting yesterday?*   *C*

1 necklace   that   new   is   a ?   ....

2 on TV   a good film   is there   tonight ?   ....

3 a problem   the trains   was there   with ?   ....

A yes   for me   it   bought   Martin   ....

B yes   hit   a cow   a train   early this morning   ....

C yes   at 3.30   it was   in meeting room B   ....

D no   a good quiz show   but   there's   ....

5 ALL UNITS **Complete the second sentence so it has the same meaning as the first.
Use one, two or three words.**

0 Regular exercise is very important.
It is very .....*important to exercise*..... regularly.

1 There was eight hours of sunshine yesterday.
.... sunny for eight hours yesterday.

2 You need to allow at least ten minutes to read the exam paper.
It .... at least ten minutes to read the exam paper.

3 The children brought some really nice cakes for us.
The children brought .... some really nice cakes.

4 You're always tired. You really mustn't go to bed so late.
You're always tired. .... to bed so late!

5 Can you buy some chocolate for me and Joe at the shop?
Can you buy .... some chocolate at the shop?

6 Diving into the pool can be dangerous.
It can be .... into the pool.

Test MODULE 11

Word order and sentence patterns

Choose the correct answer, A, B or C.

1   .... cigarettes is very bad for your health.
    A Smoke   B Smoking   C You smoke
    ➤ Unit 72

2   They are arriving ....
    A 6.00 airport   B at 6.00 the airport   C at the airport at 6.00
    ➤ Unit 72

3   The keys should be in the kitchen. I left ....
    A them in the cupboard earlier   B in the cupboard them earlier
    C earlier them in the cupboard
    ➤ Unit 72

4   The drummer in the band was great. .... really well.
    A He played the drums   B The drums played he
    C The drums played him
    ➤ Unit 72

5   They've arrived! The plane has already ....!
    A landed it   B landed the airport   C landed
    ➤ Unit 72

6   What's wrong with Tracey? She looks ....
    A is angry   B angry   C like angry
    ➤ Unit 72

7   Rob's really upset because he played ....
    A in the match yesterday badly   B yesterday badly in the match
    C badly in the match yesterday
    ➤ Unit 72

8   .... forget to call the bank manager this afternoon.
    A You don't   B Don't   C Not
    ➤ Unit 73

9   '.......... busy at the moment?' 'Yes, very.'
    A You are   B Are   C Are you
    ➤ Unit 73

10 After our holiday we showed .... all the videos we'd taken.
    A our friends   B to our friends   C us our friends
    ➤ Unit 74

11 Can you buy some food .... at the supermarket?
    A the cats   B for the cats   C to the cats
    ➤ Unit 74

12 The police officer explained ....
    A us the problem   B the problem us   C the problem to us
    ➤ Unit 74

13 .... anyone you know at the swimming pool yesterday?
    A Was there   B Is there   C Was it
    ➤ Unit 75

14 .... going to be an election in France next year.
    A It's   B There's   C Is
    ➤ Unit 75

15 .... any interesting new clothes in the shops this spring.
    A It isn't   B Aren't   C There aren't
    ➤ Unit 75

16 There's going to be a new arts festival in the town. .... start in
    the summer.
    A It will   B There will   C Will
    ➤ Unit 76

17 .... very heavy snow in the Alps. Two skiers are missing.
    A It has been   B Has been   C There has been
    ➤ Unit 76

18 How long .... to get to the town centre by bus?
    A does it take   B it takes   C does it need
    ➤ Unit 76

19 It will be a pleasure .... your parents at the party.
    A meet   B to meet   C met
    ➤ Unit 76

20 .... a phone call for you. It's your daughter.
    A Is   B It's   C There's
    ➤ Unit 76

Before you start

1 Read the text. Look at the highlighted grammar examples.

WIN A NEW TV!

Just complete the questionnaire below and we will enter your name in our competition.

Do you watch a lot of TV?   YES ☐   NO ☐

Where do you usually watch TV?   LIVING ROOM ☐   KITCHEN ☐   BEDROOM ☐   OTHER ☐

When do you watch TV?   MORNING ☐   AFTERNOON ☐   EVENING ☐   WEEKENDS ☐

What time do you turn the TV on?   5.00 P.M. ☐   6.00 P.M. ☐   7.00 P.M. ☐   8.00 P.M. ☐

Who decides which programmes to watch?   MAN ☐   WOMAN ☐   BOTH ☐   CHILDREN ☐

How old is your present main TV?   UNDER A YEAR ☐   1–3 YEARS ☐   OVER 3 YEARS ☐

Whose is this TV? ☐

Which BBC channel is your favourite, 1, 2, 3 or 4? ☐

2 Now read the sentences. Choose the correct words in *italics*. The highlighted grammar examples will help you.

1 *Do / Are* you listen to music?   ➤ Unit 77
2 When *you / do you* listen to music?   ➤ Unit 78
3 *Where / Why* do you listen to music, e.g. in the car?   ➤ Unit 79
4 What type of music do you *to listen / listen to*?   ➤ Unit 79
5 *What / Which* music do you prefer, jazz or classical?   ➤ Unit 80
6 *Whose / Who's* music do you like best (i.e. which band / composer)?   ➤ Unit 80
7 *How old / How much old* is your music system?   ➤ Unit 81
8 Who *listen / listens* to music the most in your house?   ➤ Unit 82

3 Check your answers below. Then go to the unit for more information and practice.

1 Do 2 do you 3 Where 4 listen to 5 Which 6 Whose 7 How old 8 listens

77 *Yes/No* questions

Is it the newest one in the shops?

Was it expensive?

Can you watch films on it?

1 *Yes/No* questions

Yes/No questions ask if something is true or not:

'*Are you English?*'
'*Yes, I am.*' / '*No, I'm not.*'
'*Was it expensive?*'
'*No, it wasn't very expensive.*'
'*Has the post arrived?*'
'*Yes, it came early today.*'

In *yes/no* questions, we put the main verb *be*, an auxiliary or a modal verb BEFORE the subject:

- the main verb *be*

  STATEMENT   *It* *is* *cold outside.*

  QUESTION   *Is* *it* *cold outside?*

- auxiliary verbs *be*, *have* and *modal* verbs

  STATEMENT   *It* *is* *raining.*   *He* *has* *eaten.*   *Chelsea* *will* *win.*   *Laura* *can* *swim.*

  QUESTION   *Is* *it* *raining?*   *Has* *he* *eaten?*   *Will* *Chelsea* *win?*   *Can* *Laura* *swim?*

- the auxiliary verb *do/does* in the present simple, and *did* in the past simple

  STATEMENT   *Chris* *works* *here.*   *Chris* *worked* *here.*

  QUESTION   *Does* *Chris* *work* *here?*   *Did* *Chris* *work* *here?*

 We usually say *yes/no* questions with a rising intonation (⤴): *Are you hungry?*

 Pronunciation ➤ 1.29

2 Short answers

We can answer *yes/no* questions with a short answer:
'*Is it cold outside?*' '*Yes, it **is**.*'
'*Have you eaten?*' '*No, I **haven't**.*'
'*Can you watch films on it?*' '*Yes, you **can**.*'
'*Does Natalie live here?*' '*No, she **doesn't**.*'

We can also say only *yes/no* or *yes/no* with other words:
'*Is it the newest one in the shops?*' '*No. / No, it's about a year old.*'
'*Is Max in the office yet?*' '*Yes. / Yes, he **arrived** about ten minutes ago.*'

 Don't use *I'm, she's, it's*, etc. in positive short answers:

Are you busy?   ✗ *Yes, I'm.*
                  ✓ *Yes, **I am**.*

Is she ready?   ✗ *Yes, she's.*
                  ✓ *Yes, **she is**.*

 Don't use the main verb in short answers:

Do you like classical music?   ✗ *Yes, I like.*
                                 ✓ *Yes, I **do**.*

Does Marianne speak French?   ✗ *No, she doesn't speak.*
                                ✓ *No, she **doesn't**.*

Practice

1 Match the questions 1–8 and short answers A–J. 🔊 **3.76** Listen and check.

0 Is the office open on Saturdays?   A No, they haven't.
1 Have you got my email address?   B Yes, it does.
2 Does this DVD player also record programmes?   C Yes, it will.
3 Are you going to join the film club?   D No, you can't.
4 Were the police at the football match?   E No, it isn't.
5 Have the tickets arrived yet?   F No, we didn't.
6 Can I pay by credit card here?   G Yes, I have.
7 Did you go to France by plane?   H Yes, they were.
8 Will the weather be better tomorrow?   I Yes, I am.

2 You want to buy a new phone. Make *yes/no* questions from the words below.

0 use I Internet can it the on ?   *Can I use the Internet on it?*
1 number I my keep can phone ?
2 it voice does messages store ?
3 has reviews it had good ?
4 it use abroad I can ?
5 got it video camera has a ?
6 work immediately it will ?

3 **GRAMMAR IN USE** Now complete this conversation with questions from Exercise 2. Write the numbers of the questions. 🔊 **3.77** Listen and check.

A Can you tell me a bit about this phone, please? (0) ....1....?
B Yes, you can. You can add your number to the new SIM card.
A Oh, good. (1) ....?
B Yes, you can use it in most countries.
A And (2) .... ?
B Yes, it does. It stores about forty messages.
A That's good. (3) ....?
B Yes, it's very easy to go online.
A Wonderful! I'm not very good with new technology. (4) ....?
B Yes, it will.
A Good. (5) ....?
B Yes, it has, you can make videos and send them to your friends.
A And (6) ....?
B Yes, it has, very good ones. There's one here, in *Which Phone* magazine.
A Well, I think that's everything. Yes, I'll have one of those, please.

4 There are five more mistakes in the questions below. Find and correct them.

0 *Did you go?* ~~You went~~ to the play at the school last week?
1 Does Jane lives in the centre of town?
2 'Are you OK?' 'Yes, I'm. I'm fine.'
3 'Did you enjoy the film?' 'Yes, I enjoyed.'
4 Came everyone to the party last weekend?
5 Did the students stayed with families?

78 *Wh-* questions

Which way do you want to go?

1 Form and Use

Wh- questions always start with a *wh-* word
(*who, what, when, where, how, which, why, whose*):
Which *way do you want to go?*
Who *are you going to invite?*

statement	*The paper is here.*	*It starts at 8.00.*	*They ate a pizza.*	*They can see her.*
question	*Where is the paper?*	*When does it start?*	*What did they eat?*	*Who can they see?*

 We form simple *wh-* questions with *be*, an auxiliary verb or a modal verb BEFORE
the subject:
✗ *Where you live?*
✓ **Where do you** *live?*
✗ *Where you are going?*
✓ **Where are you** *going?*
✗ *When they will arrive?*
✓ **When will they** *arrive?*
✗ *How old he is?*
✓ **How old is** *he?*

Wh- questions ask for information:
'**Where** *does the bus stop?*' '*Outside the post office.*'
'**Which** *book are you reading?*' '*It's the new John le Carré book.*'

We can also use negative questions with *wh-* question words:
'*I don't understand this question.*' '**What don't you** *understand?*'
'*Rowan didn't come to my party.*' '**Why didn't he** *come?*'

 We usually say *wh-* questions with a falling intonation (↘): *What's the time?*

 Pronunciation ➤ 1.30

Practice

1 GRAMMAR IN USE Read the information about a new DVD recorder. Then complete the questions with the phrases from the box. 🔊 3.78 Listen and check.

How can   How many   What can   Where can   Why is   ~~Why should~~

Generation X

0 *Why should* I buy the **Generation X** DVD recorder?
– That's simple – because it's the most modern and best new DVD recorder!

1 .... the **Generation X** recorder more expensive than most of the others?
– Well, it's only a little more expensive ... and it is better than most others, for example, it can store more films.

2 .... films can the **Generation X** recorder store?
– About 100. It depends on how long the films are.

3 .... I use my old videos with this machine?
– If you have a video recorder, you can connect it to the DVD recorder and record your videos.

4 .... I do if something goes wrong?
– You can send it to us or take it back to the shop where you bought it.

5 .... I buy the **Generation X** recorder?
– In all good department stores and electrical shops.

2 Make questions from the statements.

0 I'm not sure where the nearest bank is. *Where is the nearest bank?*

1 I'm not sure where we're staying. ....

2 I'm not sure how we get to the station. ....

3 I'm not sure what time the plane arrived. ....

4 I'm not sure what kind of computer she wants. ....

5 You didn't phone me. I don't know why. ....

6 I'm not sure which class I'm in. ....

3 GRAMMAR IN USE Complete the job interview with questions. Use the words in brackets (). 🔊 3.79 Listen and check.

A Right. Do you have any questions about the job?

B Yes, I do, actually. (0) ...... *What time do you start* ...... (what time / you / start) in the morning?

A We open at 9.30 and the assistants have to be here at 9.00 or 8.30 on Thursdays.

B Oh, (1) .... (why / they / not start at 9.00) on Thursdays?

A Well, it's because we have staff training from 8.30 to 9.00.

B Oh, OK, thanks. And (2) .... (when / the shop / close)?

A It closes at 5.30 most evenings, but it's 6.00 on Friday and Saturday.

B (3) .... (how long / be / the lunch break)?

A It's an hour, with a 15-minute coffee break in the morning and afternoon.

B (4) .... (how much / be / the staff discount)?

A We give our staff a discount of 20% on all our clothes and shoes.

B That's good. If I get this job, (5) .... (who / be / my manager)?

A One of the senior staff will be your manager, and will train you.

B OK. (6) .... (when / you / tell me) if I've got the job?

A We'll try to contact everyone by the end of next week.

79 *who, when, where, why*

1 *who, when, where, why*

Wh- WORD	USE	EXAMPLE
who	asks about a person or people	*Who's your teacher this year?*
when	asks about time	*When did you get it?*
where	asks about place	*Where can we put it?*
why	asks for a reason	*Why do we need it?*

After *who, when, where* or *why* in questions, we need a verb:
***Who is** the best actor in the film?*
***Why did** the Romans come to Britain?*

 We cannot put a noun after them:
✗ *Where place does the president live?*
✓ ***Where** does the president live?*

2 *Wh-* questions + prepositions

If there is a verb + preposition in a statement, we often need to use the preposition at the end of a *wh-* question:
*They're talking **about** the director.* → *Who are they talking **about**?*

 *Angelo is writing **to** his friend.*   ✗ *Who is Angelo writing?*
✓ *Who is Angelo writing **to**?*

But with *when* and *where questions*, we don't usually put a preposition at the end of the question:
*I was born **in** London. Where were you born?*
*I was born **on** 30 August. When were you born?*
*I'm going **to** the cinema. Where are you going?*

 But we say: *'Where are you **from**?' 'I'm from Moscow.'*

Practice

1 [GRAMMAR IN USE] **Complete the questions in the conversation with a suitable _wh-_ word.**
🔊 **3.80 Listen and check.**

A I'm calling about your home cinema, Ms Jenkins.

(0) .....*Where*..... shall we deliver it? Is it the same address as on the receipt?

B Yes, that's right.

A And (1) .... is it best to deliver, morning or afternoon?

B Oh, afternoon, definitely.

A And (2) .... will be at the address to receive it?

B I'll probably be there.

A If no one is at home, (3) .... can our driver leave it?
Can he put it in the garage?

B Oh, no. If I know the date, I'll definitely be there.

A OK, so (4) .... would you like it? Would next Friday be OK?

B Yes, that's fine. Oh, (5) .... should I give the cheque to? Shall I give it to the driver?

A Yes, that's fine. Finally, for our records, (6) .... did you choose this product?

B Well, because it looks good and it wasn't too expensive.

2 Write a _wh-_ word in each question. Then match the questions and answers A– F.

0 .....*Who*..... was the first woman in space? ...*D*....

1 .... did dinosaurs live on the Earth? ....

2 .... did Arthur Conan Doyle write about? ....

3 .... did Christopher Columbus sail to America? ....

4 .... do giant pandas come from? ....

5 .... didn't Magellan finish his round-the-world journey? ....

A Sherlock Holmes.
B Because he died in a
   fight in the Philippines.
C From China.
D Valentina Tereshkova
E In 1492.
F Millions of years ago.

3 Write the questions for the <u>underlined</u> parts of the answers. Use the words below to help you. Use prepositions if necessary. 🔊 **3.81 Listen and check.**

0 (the film)   *When does the film start?*   It starts <u>at 8.15</u>.

1 (your manager)   ....   He works <u>in the office in the corner</u>.

2 (the kitten)   ....   It belongs <u>to my sister</u>.

3 (my address)   ....   <u>Because I need it for our records.</u>

4 (my homework)   ....   I want it <u>on Friday</u>.

5 (the letter)   ....   Send it <u>to the Managing Director</u>.

80 *what, which, whose*

Which button do I press?

What does this thing do?

Whose car is it?

1 *what, which, whose*

Wh- WORD	USE	EXAMPLE
what	asks about things or ideas	*What does it do?*
which	asks for a choice between a few things	*Which programme do you want to watch?*
whose	asks about possession/relationships	*Whose bag is this? Whose sister is she?*

2 *which* or *what*?

Which and *what* both ask about things and ideas.

- We use *which* when we are thinking of a small number of things:
  Which colour *do you want for the bedroom, blue, green or grey?*
  Which languages *do you speak?*

  We can also use *which* (but not *what*) to ask about people:
  Which member *of the band do you like most?*

  We do not need a noun if it is clear what we are asking about:
  'I speak four languages.' 'Really? **Which** *do you speak?'*

- *What* asks about more things than *which*. We often use *what* without a noun:
  What's *your favourite colour?* **What's** *on at the cinema this week?* **What** *does this thing do?*

  We can also use a noun after *what*: **What instrument** *do you play?*

3 Common uses of *what*

to ask about a person's work	*What + do + noun + do?*	*What does your husband do? He's a builder.*
to ask for a description	*What + be + noun + like?*	*What's the weather like? It's cold and rainy.* *What's Jonathan like? He's very clever and he's quite shy.*
to ask about likes and dislikes	*What + do + noun + like?*	*What kind of films does Jonathan like?* *He likes South American films.*

 We don't use *like* in the answer to *What is he like?*:
✗ *He's like very clever.* ✓ *He's very clever.*

4 *who* or *whose*?

We use *who* to ask about people: **Who** *did you see at the party last night?*

We use *whose* (with or without a noun) to ask about possessions and relationships:
Whose *is that bag on the table?* (= Who does the bag belong to?)
Whose sister *is she?* (= Who is her sister?)

 Who's and *whose* sound the same, but they are different. *Who's* means *who is* or *who has*:
Who's *washing up today?* (who is) **Who's** *seen the latest copy of 'Hello' magazine?* (who has)

Practice

1 These questions all come from a conversation at a party.
Choose the correct *wh-* word in each one.

0 (Who) / What was your favourite teacher?
1 What / Which did you study?
2 Which / What is your name?
3 Which / What do you do now?
4 Which / Who university did you go to?

5 Whose / What was she like?
6 What / Which year did you graduate, 2007 or 2009?
7 Who / Whose was your tutor for maths?
8 Whose / Who's group were you in for physics?

2 **GRAMMAR IN USE** Now complete the conversation with questions from Exercise 1.
■) **4.01** Listen and check.

JANE It's a good party, isn't it?
BETH Yes. Alison always has good parties.
JANE How long have you known her?
BETH For years. We met at university.
JANE Really? (0) ....4....
BETH Kent University.
JANE That's interesting. I went there, too. (1) ....
BETH Maths and physics.
JANE I studied physics, too. (2) ....
BETH Simone Allen's group.

JANE I didn't have her. (3) ....
BETH She was really good. (4) ....
JANE It was Jack Granger. I didn't like him.
BETH No, I had him, too. He wasn't very good. (5) ....
JANE I teach now – I work in a school in London. How about you?
BETH I write computer programs – mostly for games.

3 **GRAMMAR IN USE** Read about Penny Knight. Then write questions for the answers below. Use the *wh-* word in brackets (). ■) **4.02** Listen and check.

I'm Lucy and the person I admire most is Penny Knight.
She's my aunt but she's only five years older than me
– she's my grandparents' youngest daughter. She's great
– she's really friendly and lively, and she's very clever, too.
She works for the games company Nintendo and designs
computer games. She's married to Ryan – he's a sports
teacher so she keeps fit.

0 *Who is Penny Knight?* .... She's Lucy's aunt. (who)
1 .... She's Lucy's grandparents' daughter. (whose)
2 .... She's very friendly and clever. (what)
3 .... Nintendo. (which)
4 .... She designs computer games. (what)
5 .... A sports teacher called Ryan. (who)

4 Correct the mistakes in these questions. Then write true answers.

0 ~~Which~~ *What* do you do? *I'm a student.* ....
1 Who's class are you in? ....
2 Who school/college do you go to? ....
3 Which are you studying now? ....
4 Whose do you live with? ....
5 Which do you like doing? ....

81 *how*

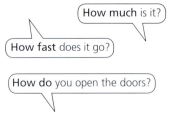

How much is it?

How fast does it go?

How do you open the doors?

1 *how*

The *wh-* word *how* can ask about a
lot of different things. We use it to ask about

- the way we do something:
  How do *I open this bottle?* **How do** *we get to your house?* **How do** *you open the doors?*

- other things, eg:

health (*how* + *be*)	*How are you?*	*I'm fine, thanks.*
	How's your father now?	*He's feeling better, thanks.*
opinion (*how* + *be*)	*How's the soup?*	*It's delicious.*
	How was the party?	*It was great. I enjoyed it.*
news about a person's life	*How's it going?*	*Fine, everything's OK.*
	How did the exam go?	*Fantastic! I passed!*

2 *how* + adjective

We use *how* before adjectives to ask about age, measurements and size:
How old *is Tracey? She's seven. / She's seven* **years old**.
How long *is the Nile? It's 6650 kilometres* **long**.
How tall *is the CNN Tower? It's 553 metres* **tall**.
How deep *is the swimming pool? It's two metres* **deep**.
How big *is the village? Not very* **big**, *only about 4000 people live there.*

 With exact measurements, we include the adjectives *tall, high, long, wide, deep* in
the answer. Look at the word order:
✗ ~~The CNN Tower is tall 553 metres.~~ ✓ *The CNN Tower is* **553 metres tall**.

 The answer to a question asking *How old ... ?* is different:
✗ ~~My daughter is seven old.~~ ✗ ~~My daughter is seven years.~~
✓ *My daughter is* **seven**. ✓ *My daughter is* **seven years old**.

3 Other common questions with *how*

We also use *how* to ask about:

length of time	*How long is the flight?*	*It's four hours.*
distance	*How far is the station from here?*	*It's half a mile.*
speed	*How fast does it go?*	*Very fast, 250 kilometres an hour!*
frequency	*How often should I take the medicine?*	*Twice a day.*
number	*How many people live on the island?*	*Three thousand.*
amount	*How much water is left?*	*Five bottles.*
price	*How much was the car?*	*It was really expensive!*

 We don't use adverbs (e.g. *fast, often*) after measurements in answers:
✗ ~~It goes at 250 kilometres an hour fast.~~ ✓ *It goes at 250 kilometres an hour.*

how much? or *how many?* ➤ Unit 8.3

Practice

1 Write questions for the answers. Use *how* + adjective and a place name from the box.

0 <u>How high is Mount Everest?</u> It is 8848 metres high.
1 .... It is 6400 kilometres long.
2 .... It is 300 metres tall.
3 .... It is 150 metres wide.
4 .... It is 1637 metres deep.
5 .... It is nearly six hundred years old.

the Amazon River
Lake Baikal
the Eiffel Tower
~~Mount Everest~~
Machu Picchu
the Panama Canal

2 **GRAMMAR IN USE** Complete this magazine interview. Use *how*, and add an adjective/adverb if necessary. **4.03** Listen and check.

GORDON LAWRENCE has worked on maglev trains for nearly 30 years.
In this interview he talks to *Chris Anderson*.

CA Gordon, everyone has heard of maglev trains, but we don't know much about them. (0) <u>How fast</u> can a maglev train go?
GL They can go at nearly 600 kilometres an hour.
CA And (1) .... does a maglev train actually work?
GL Well, it travels a few centimetres above the ground – it uses a new type of scientific technology.
CA (2) .... are there in use now?
GL Well, there's only one system in use – in Shanghai, China. It goes from the city to the airport.

CA So (3) .... is that?
GL Only about 30 kilometres.
CA And (4) .... does that take?
GL The train does that in about seven minutes.
CA Oh, that's fast! (5) .... do they leave?
GL There are four trains an hour.
CA I know it's new technology that quite a lot of countries are developing. (6) .... is the development going now?
GL It's going well. There are lots of plans for more maglev trains across the world.
CA Really? (7) .... does each train cost?
GL That's difficult to say. The Shanghai project cost over a billion US dollars.

3 Write questions starting with *How*. **4.04** Listen and check.

I want to know ...

0 if you are well. <u>How are you?</u>
1 the price of this book. ....
2 the age of your baby. ....
3 the length of the flight. ....
4 the distance to the airport. ....
5 if your interview went well. ....

82 Subject and object questions

1 Subject questions

SUBJECT	VERB	OBJECT
Who	*helped*	*Mandy?*
What	*happened?*	
Which band	*sang*	*'Take me out'?*
Whose mobile phone	*has*	*an MP3 player?*
How many friends	*called*	*you?*

In subject questions, the *wh-* word is the subject of the verb.
The order of the question is subject + verb + object.

Notice the answer: **Who *helped Mandy?* Robin. *or* Robin did.**

2 Object questions

OBJECT	AUXILIARY	SUBJECT	VERB (infinitive)
Who	*did*	*Robin*	*help?*
What	*do*	*you*	*do?*
Which band	*does*	*Alex Kapranos*	*sing with?*
Whose mobile phone	*has*	*the teacher*	*found?*
How many friends	*did*	*you*	*call?*

In object questions, the *wh-* word is the object of the verb.
The order of the question is object + auxiliary + subject + verb.

Notice the answer: **Who *did Robin help?* Mandy**

3 Subject and object questions

Compare these subject and object questions:

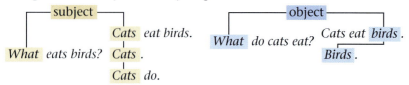

⚠ Don't confuse subject and object questions:
✗ ~~What means 'statement'?~~ ✓ **What does *'statement'* mean?**

⚠ We use a singular verb after *who*, *what* and *whose* in subject questions:
✗ ~~Who live in that old house?~~ ✓ Who **lives** *in that old house?*

Practice

1 Choose the correct words in *italics*. 🔊4.05 Listen and check.

0 What *happened* / *did happen* last night? I saw a robbery from my bedroom window.
1 Who *robbed* / *did rob* the shop? Two men.
2 What *stole they* / *did they steal*? They stole several TVs.
3 *What* / *Who* broke the window? The robbers.
4 Who *did you call* / *called you*? I called the police.
5 Who *did you call* / *called you*? The shop manager called me.
6 Who *recognised you* / *did you recognise*? I recognised one of the robbers.

2 Match the questions 1 and 2 with the answers A and B.

0 1 Who saw Amy? ─────────────→ A Matt saw Amy.
   2 Who did Amy see? ─────────→ B Amy saw Matt.

1 1 What do birds eat? A Cats eat birds.
   2 What eats birds? B Birds eat worms.

2 1 How many people saw him? A Ten people saw him.
   2 How many people did he see? B He only saw one person.

3 1 What book did Tolkien write? A *Lord of the Rings*.
   2 Who wrote *Lord of the Rings*? B Tolkien.

4 1 Who invited Isabel to the party? A Isabel invited James.
   2 Who did Isabel invite to the party? B Shelley invited Isabel.

5 1 Whose cousin did you call? A Mike's cousin called me.
   2 Whose cousin called you? B I called Mike's cousin.

3 GRAMMAR IN USE Complete the police interview with questions from the box.
There are three extra questions. 🔊4.06 Listen and check.

> which factory do you mean   who saw you   which factory makes cars
> what happened   whose face   who heard you   ~~what did you see~~   what did you frighten
> what did you hear   who did you see   what are you frightened of

OFFICER   So, Mr Lewis. (0) ....*What did you see*............ yesterday evening outside the club?

LEWIS   Well, there was a fight, a big fight.

OFFICER   (1) ....?

LEWIS   I'm not sure. I came out of the club to go home, and then I heard something ...

OFFICER   (2) ....?

LEWIS   Someone was shouting, then I heard other voices, so I turned round and saw them ...

OFFICER   Them? (3) ....?

LEWIS   The men who started the fight – the men from the factory. And I think they saw me.

OFFICER   I'm sorry – (4) ....?

LEWIS   Those men. The men who work at the factory.

OFFICER   (5) ....?

LEWIS   The car factory in Bolton. You see, I work there, too – and I saw his face!

OFFICER   (6) ....?

LEWIS   My boss's face – he was there, he was in the fight, and now I'm really frightened.

OFFICER   I'm not sure I understand – (7) ....?

LEWIS   Well, he knows I've told you everything. I'm frightened I'll lose my job.

Review MODULE 12

1 UNITS 77 AND 78 **Write the words in the correct order to make questions. Then match them with the answers A–I below.**

0 going to be   flight BA103   is   late ? — *Is flight BA103 going to be late?* ...H...

1 the film   started   has ? ....

2 working   is   the printer ? ....

3 does   stop   the bus   where ? ....

4 use   I   a pencil   should   a pen   or ? ....

5 rain   it   tomorrow   will ? ....

6 so hot   why   it   here   in   is ? ....

7 want   you   any breakfast   don't   why ? ....

8 prefer   apple juice   you   or   do   orange ? ....

A No, it won't.   D Orange juice.   G You should use a pen.
B I can't open the window.   E No, it hasn't.   H No, it's on time.
C It stops outside the bank.   F Because I'm not hungry.   I Yes, it is. But it needs paper.

2 UNITS 79, 80 AND 81 **Complete the question for each answer with one *wh-* word.**

0 '......*Why*...... are you having a party?' 'It's a birthday party.'

1 '.................. birthday is it?' 'It's my mother's birthday.'

2 '.................. old will she be?' 'She'll be fifty.'

3 '.................. is the party?' 'At a hotel near my parents' house.'

4 '.................. hotel is it at?' 'The Hilton, in Moorlands Road.'

5 '.................. date is it going to be?' '30 May.'

6 '.................. will it start?' 'At about 8.00 in the evening.'

7 '.................. time will it finish?' 'I don't know – probably at about 12.00.'

8 '.................. many people will be there?' 'Probably about seventy or more.'

3 UNITS 79, 80 AND 82 **Read the conversation. Use the words below to write questions.**
🔊 **4.07 Listen and check.**

JEREMY   Hi, Russell. (0) ...*What did you do last night?*... (what / do)

RUSSELL Oh, hello, Jeremy. We went to the cinema.

JEREMY   That's nice. (1) .... (what film / see)

RUSSELL We saw *Avatar*.

JEREMY   I've heard of that. (2) .... (who / be / in it)

RUSSELL Sam Worthington.

JEREMY   Oh, yes. (3) .... (who / go with)

RUSSELL I went with Rick, from the office.

JEREMY   Rick? I don't know him. (4) .... (what / like)

RUSSELL He's tall, with dark hair and a beard.

JEREMY   Oh. (5) .... (what / do)

RUSSELL He works in the computer department.

JEREMY   Oh. (6) .... (which / floor / work on)

RUSSELL He works on the third floor, with Matt and Steve.

4 ALL UNITS Complete the questions with the correct words or phrases, A, B or C below.

Bargain of the month the new Apricot III

FAQs

0) .... is the Apricot 111?
It's a new modern MP3 player.
(1) .... music only or videos, too?
It plays both.
(2) .... got a large screen?
Yes, the screen is quite big, so it's
good for watching films.
(3) .... do I get films for it?
It's very simple – you just download them from
the Internet. It's the same as for music.
(4) .... if I want to carry it around with me?
Well, it has a good battery, so you can take it
to places with you.

(5) Oh good, a battery.
..........?
A long time – 50 hours of
music or 10 hours of films.
(6) But most MP3 players
have these features. ....
so good?
Well, you can put it in one room in your home
and hear the music in every room – that's new.
And, of course, the price.
(7) ....?
Only £259.
(8) .... it?
It's a fantastic machine at a really low price!

0 (A) What   B Which   C Who
1 A Is it play   B It plays   C Does it play
2 A Does it   B Has it   C Does it have
3 A How   B How is   C How can
4 A What does happen   B What is happen   C What happens
5 A How does it work   B How long it works   C How long does it last
6 A Why is   B Why it is   C Why is it
7 A How much costs it?   B How much does it cost?   C How much it costs?
8 A Why should I buy   B Why I buy   C What should I buy

5 ALL UNITS **Read the conversation. Add six more missing words in the questions.**
◄)) 4.08 **Listen and check.**

A Excuse me. I'd like to open a bank account.

B Certainly. Is the account for you?

A No, it isn't.

B I see. Who is it *for*?

A It's for my son. You have a young person's account?

B Yes. You want to open the account now?

A Yes, because he's earning money now.

B Oh, OK. How is your son?

A He's sixteen.

B Oh, has left school?

A No, he just works at the weekend.

B That's nice. What does he?

A He works at the local car wash. Which forms does he need to open an account?

B Here. It's just this one.

A Thanks. Whose name you need for the account – mine or my son's?

B Only your son's if he's sixteen.

A OK. Thanks very much.

Test MODULE 12

Questions

Choose the correct answer, A, B or C.

1 .... live near here?
   A You do B Do you C You

   ➤ Unit 77

2 'Is it going to rain, do you think?' 'No, ...'
   A it isn't B isn't it C it is

   ➤ Unit 77

3 'Have you done the dishes?' 'Yes, ...'
   A I have B I've C I did

   ➤ Unit 77

4 What time ....?
   A the bus leaves B leaves the bus C does the bus leave

   ➤ Unit 78

5 'I didn't talk to her.' '.......... you talk to her?'
   A Why B Why did C Why didn't

   ➤ Unit 78

6 .... is the manager of this department?
   A Who B What C Who person

   ➤ Unit 79

7 There's no one in the room. Who ....?
   A she talking B is she talking C is she talking to

   ➤ Unit 79

8 Sue, I don't understand these sales figures. .... you get them from?
   A Where did B From where did C Where from did

   ➤ Unit 79

9 I didn't know you came from Brazil. Where ....?
   A were you born in B in were you born C were you born

   ➤ Unit 79

10 .... do you speak better, French or Spanish?
   A Whose B What C Which

   ➤ Unit 80

11 Someone has left a wallet here. .... wallet is it?
   A Whose B Who's C Who

   ➤ Unit 80

12 '.......... Sarah like?' 'Flowers – she loves roses.'
   A What is B What does C Who is

   ➤ Unit 80

13 'What's the new shop assistant like?' 'He ....'
   A likes reading B is like friendly C is friendly

   ➤ Unit 80

14 .... the journey from London to Paris?
   A Is long B How long is C How is long

   ➤ Unit 81

15 '.......... your sister's wedding?' 'It was lovely, thanks.'
   A How B What was C How was

   ➤ Unit 81

16 'How tall are you?' 'I'm ....'
   A tall 1.6m B 1.6m tall C tall

   ➤ Unit 81

17 'Who ....?' 'Sally did.'
   A invited Charlie B did Charlie invite C did invite Charlie

   ➤ Unit 82

18 'What ....?' 'He agreed to my idea.'
   A he said B said he C did he say

   ➤ Unit 82

19 'What ....?' 'It means "on the Internet".'
   A means "online" B does "online" mean C does mean "online"

   ➤ Unit 82

20 Who .... chemistry at the university?
   A teach B teaches C is teach

   ➤ Unit 82

Verbs with -*ing* forms and infinitives

Before you start

1 **Read the messages on the Internet. Look at the <mark>highlighted</mark> grammar examples.**

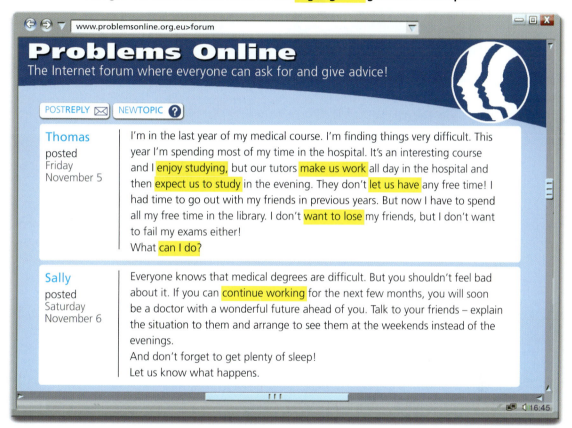

2 **Now read the sentences. Choose the correct words in *italics*. The <mark>highlighted</mark> grammar examples will help you.**

1 I enjoy *watch / watching* television in the evening.   ➤ Unit 83
2 You'll get fat if you continue *eating / eat* so many cakes.   ➤ Unit 83
3 He doesn't want *to work / working* on Saturday.   ➤ Unit 84
4 Excuse me. Can I *to take / take* your photograph?   ➤ Unit 84
5 My boss expects me *to work / working* on Saturday mornings.   ➤ Unit 85
6 You shouldn't let impolite people *annoy / to annoy* you.   ➤ Unit 85
7 The manager makes me *do / to do* all the photocopying in the office. ➤ Unit 85

3 **Check your answers below. Then go to the unit for more information and practice.**

1 watching 2 eating 3 to work 4 take 5 to work 6 annoy 7 do

---

83 Verb + *-ing* form

1 Verb + *-ing* form

	VERBS	EXAMPLES
likes and dislikes	*like dislike enjoy love hate prefer (not) mind*	Do you **like working** here? Children often **dislike going** to school. I **don't mind getting up** early in the morning.
ideas and opinions	*suggest consider imagine recommend*	Jack **suggested going** to the cinema. Can you **imagine living** without your mobile phone?
actions that start, stop or continue	*begin continue delay start stop finish*	He **began playing** in the second half of the game. **Stop making** all that noise!
other verbs	*avoid miss*	Do you **miss living** in a big city?

After *begin*, *start* and *continue*, we can use an *-ing* form or an infinitive with *to*.
The meaning is the same.

would + like/love/hate/prefer ➤ Unit 84.3

2 Verb + preposition + *-ing* form

	VERBS	EXAMPLES
verbs with prepositions	*give up* (= stop) *talk about* (= discuss) *think of* (= consider)	**I'm thinking of training** as a nurse. **She's talking about changing** her course at university.

Verbs with prepositions ➤ Unit 100

3 *go + -ing* form

We sometimes use *go + -ing* form to talk about doing sports and other activities:

	VERBS	EXAMPLES
sports and other activities	*go swimming go skating go horse-riding* *go running go skiing go shopping*	How often **do** you **go swimming**? Last year we **went skiing** in Colorado.

Spelling of *-ing* forms ➤ page 316

Practice

1 Complete the sentences with words from the box. There are three extra words. 🔊 **4.09** Listen and check.

0 Are you going to ....*continue*........ studying next year?

1 Do you miss .... in a big city?

2 The doctor .... staying in bed for three days.

3 We went .... in New York last December.

4 If you continue .... the medicine, you will feel better.

5 When did you give up ....?

6 I .... laughing – it's so funny!

> can't stop ~~continue~~ live living recommended shopping smoke smoking take taking

2 **GRAMMAR IN USE** Complete the advertisement with forms of the verbs in the box. 🔊 **4.10** Listen and check.

> become change earn ~~help~~ study work

Do you enjoy (0) ...*helping*... people?
Are you thinking of (1) .... your job?
Have you ever considered (2) .... a nurse?

Training as a nurse takes three years. As soon as you finish, you can start (3) .... good money.
Or you can continue (4) .... and learn more about special areas like child care.
If you want a job that is satisfying and you don't mind (5) .... long hours, then nursing is for you!

3 Write questions. Use the words in brackets () and *go* + an activity.

 0 (when?)
When do you go swimming?

 1 (how often?)
....

 2 (when?)
....

 3 (how often?)
....

 4 (when?)
....

 5 (how often?)
....

4 Complete these sentences with true information about you/your best friend.

0 He/She hates *going to the dentist* ....

1 I hate ....

2 I never go ....

3 He/She doesn't mind ....

4 He/She often goes ....

5 I began .... in ... .

6 I enjoy ....

7 I'm thinking of .... next year.

84 Verb + infinitive

So, you're a doctor at last. I can't believe it! Let's celebrate …

1 Verb + infinitive without *to*

We use the infinitive without *to* after modal verbs (e.g. *should*, *can*, *must*):
*I **can't believe** it!*
*We **should send** her an email.*
*You **must get** a job soon.*

We use *let's* + infinitive without *to* to make suggestions:
***Let's go** to the cinema this evening.*
***Let's celebrate** …*
*I don't like burgers – **let's have** a pizza.*

2 Verb + infinitive with *to*

We use the infinitive with *to* after some verbs:

> can/can't afford agree arrange ask choose decide
> deserve expect learn offer plan promise refuse seem want

*What a surprise! I **didn't expect to see** you here.*
*She **wants to find** a better job.*
*Where **did** you **arrange to meet** Danny and Laura?*

After *help* we can use an infinitive with *to* or without *to*; the meaning is the same:
*He **helped to carry** our bags.* or *He **helped carry** our bags.*

 With all the other verbs above we ALWAYS use *to*:
✗ *I want buy some new jeans.*
✓ *I **want to buy** some new jeans.*

3 *would + like/love/hate/prefer*

We use the infinitive with *to* after *would* (*'d*) *like/love/hate/prefer*:
*My parents **would love to meet** you.*
*I'd **hate to miss** Clara's party.*
***Would** you **like to come** with us on Tuesday evening?*

Look at the difference between *would like* and *like*:
*I'd **like to sail** around the world.* (= I want to do this in the future.)
*I **like sailing**.* (= I enjoy sailing.)

Practice

1 Match the two parts of the sentences. 🔊 **4.11** Listen and check.

0 I'm really bored. Let's ⟶ C   A   to eat some spicy food?
1 Do you feel like coming out this evening? I want   B   see a doctor.
2 Are you hungry? Would you like   C   go to the cinema.
3 I'm going to make an Indian meal. I hope you can   D   to see a doctor.
4 Mike's been feeling ill for days. He's decided   E   to go to the cinema.
5 If you've got a temperature, I think you should   F   eat spicy food.

2 **GRAMMAR IN USE** Complete this conversation in the supermarket.
Choose the correct words in *italics*. 🔊 4.12 Listen and check.

CARRIE   Hi, Zack. I didn't expect (0) *see /* to see you here.
ZACK   Well, I promised (1) *get / to get* some things for tomorrow evening.
CARRIE   Are you doing something special?
ZACK   We're going to have a barbeque in the garden. Would you like (2) *come / to come*?
CARRIE   Yes. I'd love (3) *come / to come*. But I'm not sure about my plans for tomorrow. I
        agreed (4) *help / to help* Dave with his homework, but that probably won't take long.
        I expect (5) *finish / to finish* it by eight o'clock. Is Isabel going to be there?
ZACK   I'm not really sure. She should (6) *be / to be* there, but she hasn't phoned yet ...
CARRIE   So, what are you buying?
ZACK   Well, I want (7) *get / to get* some burgers.
CARRIE   Oh, you know I'm a vegetarian. I can't (8) *eat / to eat* meat.
ZACK   Don't worry. I've already bought lots of salad.
CARRIE   Well, I must (9) *finish / to finish* my shopping. Let's (10) *talk / to talk* on the phone
        tomorrow. I hope I'll be able to come.

3 **GRAMMAR IN USE** Find eight more places in the email where *to* is missing.
Write *to* in the correct positions.

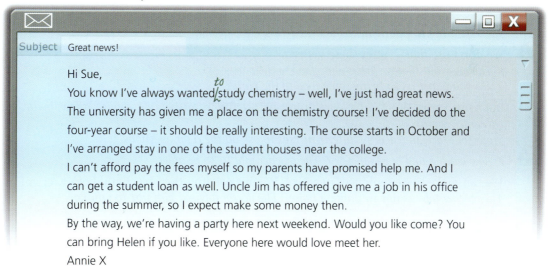

Subject   Great news!

Hi Sue,
                   to
You know I've always wanted study chemistry – well, I've just had great news.
The university has given me a place on the chemistry course! I've decided do the
four-year course – it should be really interesting. The course starts in October and
I've arranged stay in one of the student houses near the college.
I can't afford pay the fees myself so my parents have promised help me. And I
can get a student loan as well. Uncle Jim has offered give me a job in his office
during the summer, so I expect make some money then.
By the way, we're having a party here next weekend. Would you like come? You
can bring Helen if you like. Everyone here would love meet her.
Annie X

4 Write sentences about something that ...

0 you've arranged to do next week *I've arranged to meet my sister on Friday.*
1 you'd like to do in the future ....
2 you can't afford to do ....
3 you don't want to do ....

85 Verb + object + infinitive; *make* and *let*

Professor Maclean **teaches student nurses to ask** all the right questions.

1 Verb + object + infinitive

After some verbs, we can put an infinitive alone, or we can put an object before the infinitive:

SUBJECT	VERB	OBJECT	INFINITIVE WITH *to*
Lucy	wants		to go to university.
Carol	wants	her daughter	to go to university.
Carol	would like	her	to go to university.

Other examples of verbs like this are: *ask*, *expect*, *help* and *need*:
*She **asked me to phone** her. She **asked to see** the doctor.*

 We don't use *that* ... after these verbs:
✗ *Do you want that we bring some food to the party?*
✓ *Do you **want us to bring** some food to the party?*

But some verbs ALWAYS have an object before the infinitive (e.g. *advise*, *allow*, *invite*, *teach*, *tell*, *order*, *warn*):
*Professor Maclean teaches **student nurses** to ask all the right questions.*

 ✗ *The teacher told to be quiet.* ✓ *The teacher told **us** to be quiet.*

We can make these sentences negative. We put *not* after the object and before *to*:
*The teacher told us **not to make** a noise. The doctor advised him **not to smoke**.*

2 *make* and *let*

After *make* and *let*, we put an object + the infinitive without *to*:
*The cold weather **made the lake freeze**. (= The cold weather caused the lake to freeze.)*

 ✗ *Our teacher made us to do extra homework.*
✓ *Our teacher **made us do** extra homework. (= She forced us to do extra homework.)*

 ✗ *Our teacher let us to leave early.*
✓ *Our teacher **let us leave** early. (= She allowed us to leave early.)*

Look at the difference between *let* + object + infinitive and *let's* + infinitive:
*Our teacher **let us leave** early. (= Our teacher allowed us to leave early.)*
***Let's leave** early today. (= I suggest that we leave early today.)*

Practice

1 Choose the correct words in *italics*. ◄》**4.13** Listen and check.

0 My teacher made me (write) / *to write* a long report.
1 I asked *them / they* to give me the answers.
2 Would you prefer the children *go / to go* by train or by bus?
3 My teacher made me *take / to take* the test again.
4 The doctor told Gary *to not carry / not to carry* heavy suitcases.
5 The shop assistant advised *we / us* to keep our receipts.
6 Will they let me *bring / to bring* my dictionary into the exam?

2 GRAMMAR IN USE Complete the text with the words and phrases from the box.

help us ~~understand~~ his clients asks have would like lets them makes to talk

DANIEL FULTON is a special kind of doctor – his clients are people who have mental problems. He uses the ideas of the famous doctor and writer Sigmund Freud. Freud's ideas helped us (0) .....*understand*..... how the human mind works.

Daniel (1) .... people with mental problems to lie on a sofa and relax. Then he tells them (2) .... about their problems. He (3) .... his clients talk about their dreams as well as their real problems. He believes our dreams (4) .... to understand our feelings. Daniel also thinks bad experiences when we are young sometimes make us (5) .... mental problems

when we are adults, so he often asks (6) .... to talk about their childhood.

Daniel doesn't say very much to his clients. He (7) .... talk about anything – all their feelings and emotions, what they (8) .... to do and what they feel about other people. He thinks that talking about problems is the best way to solve them.

3 Complete the second sentence so it means the same as the first.
Use one, two or three words. ◄》**4.14** Listen and check.

0 The rain caused the river to flood.
   The rain ...*made the river*.... flood.
1 The customs officer forced me to open my suitcase.
   The customs officer .... my suitcase.
2 He said we shouldn't swim in the water because it was dangerous.
   He warned .... swim in the water.
3 Secretaries learn to type in Sean's class.
   Sean teaches .... in his class.
4 Our boss allowed us to go home early on Friday.
   Our boss .... home early on Friday.
5 Maria couldn't fill in the application form so I helped her.
   I helped Maria .... the application form.

Review MODULE 13

1 UNITS 83 AND 84 **Match 1 and 2 with A and B in each pair.**

0 1 This evening I'd like ⟶ A to go to a restaurant.
  2 Jemma loves ⟶ B going to Indian restaurants.

1 1 Caroline has decided   A studying history at school.
  2 The children have begun   B to study medicine at university.

2 1 On Saturday mornings I go   A to learn to ride a horse.
  2 One day I'd love   B riding.

3 1 Would you like   A dancing?
  2 How often do you go   B to dance?

4 1 I never expected   A to work in this office.
  2 Do you enjoy   B working here?

2 UNITS 84 AND 85 **Choose the correct words in** *italics*. 🔊 **4.15** **Listen and check.**

LUCY Hello, Alex. I didn't expect (0) *you to see* / *to see you* here at lunch time.

ALEX Oh, hi Lucy. I'm on my lunch break.

LUCY Right. So, how's the job going?

ALEX Not great. I'd like (1) *find* / *to find* a new job really.

LUCY I'm surprised. I thought you had a great job at the hospital …

ALEX Well, the job's OK but my boss is terrible. He's always telling (2) *to work* / *me to work* harder and he doesn't (3) *let* / *make* me have enough holiday. When I started, he promised (4) *to give me* / *to me give* a holiday after six months. But then he refused (5) *me to allow* / *to allow me* to go. He forced (6) *to work* / *me to work* all through the summer!

LUCY Perhaps you should (7) *to leave* / *leave*?

ALEX I can't afford (8) *to live* / *live* without my salary.

LUCY Well, I think it's very unfair. Everybody deserves (9) *have* / *to have* a holiday.

ALEX I know. Anyway, I must (10) *get* / *to get* back to the office now, it's almost two o'clock.

3 UNITS 83 AND 85 **Match the sentences with the pictures.**
Then complete the sentences. Use forms of the words and phrases in the box.

make me / wear
hate / go
tell us / not / take
mind / close the window
advise Henry / go on a
continue / read

0 'Excuse me. Do you ..... *mind closing the window* ......?' ..*D*....

1 The doctor .... diet. ....

2 Miranda sometimes .... all night long. ....

3 The security guard .... photos. ....

4 'It's so embarrassing. My mother .... them.' ....

5 Kyle .... to the dentist. ....

4 ALL UNITS **Complete the second sentence so it means the same as the first. Use one, two or three words.**

0 The bank wouldn't give me a new credit card.

The bank refused ....*to give me*........ a new credit card.

1 Pauline never wants to go to the dentist.

Pauline dislikes .... the dentist.

2 Everybody has to pay taxes.

Nobody can avoid ....

3 Danny doesn't have enough money to go skiing.

Danny can't .... skiing.

4 The doctor told me to take more exercise.

The doctor said I should .... more exercise.

5 My sister wouldn't give me her mobile phone.

My sister refused .... her mobile phone.

6 They made the last car at that factory in 1998.

They stopped .... at that factory in 1998.

7 Everyone has agreed – we're meeting at six o'clock.

We've arranged .... at six o'clock.

5 ALL UNITS **Complete the text with forms of the verbs in brackets ().**

International opportunities for young doctors and nurses

Doctors without Borders

Doctors without Borders or MSF (Médecins Sans Frontières) is an international organisation that gives medical help to people in emergency situations around the world. When there are terrible events such as floods or war, MSF arranges (0) ....*to send*.... (send) doctors and nurses to help the local people. Each year about 3000 MSF workers travel to more than 70 different countries.

MSF is an independent organisation so governments cannot (1) .... (control) it. As well as emergency help, MSF has an educational programme that teaches people about medical problems in poor countries. It also wants (2) .... (make) medicines cheaper around the world. It has a training programme for doctors who are planning (3) .... (travel) to foreign countries. Many MSF workers can (4) .... (teach)

local people to improve their own health. MSF also helps (5) .... (build) hospitals and it gives advice to local doctors.

IF YOU ARE A NURSE OR DOCTOR AND YOU WOULD LIKE

(6) .... (HELP) PEOPLE IN OTHER COUNTRIES, YOU CAN

(7) .... (DOWNLOAD) THE APPLICATION FORM HERE.

YOU MUST (8) .... (BE) 18 OR OLDER TO APPLY.

application form

Test MODULE 13

Verbs with *-ing* forms and infinitives

Choose the correct answer, A, B or C.

1 Excuse me. Do you mind .... the heater? It's cold in here.   ➤ Unit 83
   A to turn on B turn on C turning on

2 The company started .... the machines last year.   ➤ Unit 83
   A make B making C made

3 I love .... your emails.   ➤ Unit 83
   A receive B receiving C received

4 Harry says he will give up .... football when he's forty.   ➤ Unit 83
   A to play B play C playing

5 How often do you .... dancing?   ➤ Unit 83
   A go B do C going

6 Do you like .... to classical music?   ➤ Unit 83
   A listening B listened C listen

7 You must .... her new CD – it's fantastic.   ➤ Unit 84
   A buying B to buy C buy

8 I'm hungry. Let's .... something to eat.   ➤ Unit 84
   A get B to get C got

9 My brother is learning .... the electric guitar.   ➤ Unit 84
   A playing B play C to play

10 Thank you for the invitation. We'd love ....   ➤ Unit 84
    A to come B come C coming

11 I .... to study history next year.   ➤ Unit 84
    A like B liking C would like

12 It's hot today. We should .... to the beach.   ➤ Unit 84
    A going B to go C go

13 .... to buy some new jeans tomorrow.   ➤ Unit 84
    A I like B I'd like C I'm like

14 Would you like .... you some sandwiches?   ➤ Unit 85
    A Carol to make B that Carol makes C Carol make

15 I expect .... to pass the exam.   ➤ Unit 85
    A she B hers C her

16 The police officer told ....   ➤ Unit 85
    A to stop B us stopping C us to stop

17 Did your teacher .... grammar exercises?   ➤ Unit 85
    A make you do B make do C make you to do

18 My friend lets .... his car at the weekends.   ➤ Unit 85
    A me to use B use me C me use

19 I need .... my computer.   ➤ Unit 85
    A somebody repair B somebody to repair C repairing

20 Do you want .... you?   ➤ Unit 85
    A us to help B us helping C us help

Reported statements and indirect questions

Before you start

1 Read the two different conversations. Look at the <mark>highlighted</mark> grammar examples.

'I tried to return this dress to the shop yesterday and <mark>you advised me to go</mark> home and get the receipt. You said I could have my money back then.'

'Ah, I see, but I can't give you your money back, I'm afraid. <mark>We told you</mark> that we would give you your money back if the dress was in perfect condition, but it isn't.'

'But that isn't right. <mark>I said I hadn't worn</mark> it! It is in perfect condition!'

'Mr Bryant, we <mark>asked you to come</mark> for an interview because your qualifications are very impressive.'

'Thank you.'

'Now, could you tell us <mark>why you left</mark> your last job?'

'Of course. My manager <mark>said that he would</mark> give me a promotion after a year, but he didn't.'

2 Now read the sentences. Choose the correct words in *italics*.
The <mark>highlighted</mark> grammar examples will help you.

1 In your application, you said you *will / would* bring your certificates with you. ➤ Unit 86
2 Louisa said she *had / have* been a teacher before she had children. ➤ Unit 86
3 I told *you / to you* yesterday that I was going out this evening. ➤ Unit 87
4 The bank manager asked *me to / that I should* open a new account. ➤ Unit 87
5 We advised you *arrive / to arrive* early so we could copy your documents. ➤ Unit 87
6 Could you tell us how much *your train ticket cost / did your train ticket cost*? ➤ Unit 88

3 Check your answers below. Then go to the unit for more information and practice.

1 would 2 had 3 you 4 me to 5 to arrive 6 your train ticket cost

86 Reported statements

I have a gun. I'll use it!

What happened?

He said that **he had** a gun and that **he would** use it.

1 Verb changes in reported statements

We use reported statements when we tell someone what another person has said.
We usually use a past tense verb to report them:
I'm getting the 9.30 train. → *She **said** that she was getting the 9.30 train.*

After the past tense *said*, we usually change the tense of the person's words.

	THE PERSON'S WORDS		THE REPORTED STATEMENT
present simple	*'I'm really hungry.'* *'I have a gun.'*	past simple	*She said that she **was** really hungry.* *He said that he **had** a gun.*
present continuous	*'The team's playing badly.'*	past continuous	*He said that the team **was playing** badly.*
can *will* *must*	*'I can do that.'* *'I will use the gun.'* *'You must be quiet!'*	*could* *would* *must/had to*	*She said that she **could** do that.* *He said that he **would** use the gun.* *She said that we **must/had to** be quiet.*

Some verbs do not change in reported statements: *could, should, ought to, would, might*:
*'I **might** go shopping later.'* → *She said she **might** go shopping later.*

2 Reporting the past simple and present perfect

After the past simple and present perfect, we often use *had* + the *-ed* (past participle) form
of the verb, e.g. *had/hadn't finished*. (This is called the past perfect tense.)

	THE PERSON'S WORDS	THE REPORTED STATEMENT
past simple	*'It snowed a lot in the winter.'*	*They said that it **had snowed** a lot in the winter.*
present perfect	*'Anna hasn't arrived yet.'*	*He said that Anna **hadn't arrived** yet.*

Regular past participles ➤ page 316   Irregular past participles ➤ page 314

3 Pronoun changes in reported statements

		CHANGES TO	EXAMPLES
pronouns and possessives	*I*	*he/she*	*'I'm cold.'* → *Dave said that **he** was cold.*
	me	*him/her*	*'They need me.'* → *She said that they needed **her**.*
	my	*his/her*	*'That's my book.'* → *He said that it was **his** book.*
	ours	*theirs*	*'Those seats are ours.'* → *Alice said that those seats were **theirs**.*

Also: *we → they, us → them, our → their, you → I/we, you → me/us, your → my/our,
yours → mine/ours*

Practice

1 Complete the reported statements with verbs, pronouns or possessives. **4.16** Listen and check.

0 'I haven't got any money.' She said that she ......*hadn't*.... got any money.
1 'I work at the factory.' He said that he .... at the factory.
2 'We can't leave early.' They said that they .... leave early.
3 'The parcel hasn't arrived.' Jane said that the parcel .... arrived.
4 'We aren't going to stay long.' We said that we .... going to stay long.
5 'Jim lost his job a few weeks ago.' She said that Jim .... his job a few weeks ago.
6 'I'm not happy about the date.' He said that .... wasn't happy about the date.
7 'We can wait for you.' They said that they could wait for ....
8 'You've taken my coat.' The woman said that I had taken .... coat.

2 **GRAMMAR IN USE** Match the reported statements 1–7 in the conversation with the person's words A–H below. **4.17** Listen and check.

EMILY Mr Fellowes, could I ask you something?
MR F Yes, of course, Emily. What is it?
EMILY Well, in my interview they said that (0) *I wouldn't have to wait long for a promotion.* I've been here for two years and I think my work has been good. When I asked you about it last month, you said that (1) *you'd think about my promotion.*
MR F I did, but then two weeks ago you said that (2) *you were thinking about leaving.* I told you that (3) *I had thought about your promotion.* I said that (4) *I didn't think you were ready,* and, anyway, I said that (5) *I couldn't make the decision alone.*
EMILY Yes, I said that (6) *I had thought about leaving.* But that's because I'm beginning to think that I don't have a future here. Did you get my email last week? In it, I said that (7) *I thought I was ready* for a more difficult job. If you can't offer me one, I'll look for one with another company.

A 'I'm thinking about leaving.' ....
B 'I can't make the decision alone.' ....
C 'I'll think about your promotion.' ....
D 'I don't think you're ready.' ....
E 'You won't have to wait long for a promotion.' ....0....
F 'I think I'm ready ...' ....
G 'I've thought about leaving.' ....
H 'I've thought about your promotion.' ....

3 Make the words in the pictures into reported statements.

0 The robber said that he *wanted all the money* .
1 The assistant said that she ....
2 The other robber said that they ....
3 The assistant said that ....
4 The first robber said ....
5 The customer said ....

I want all the money!
I can't give you the money.
We forgot about the security guard!
He's already called the police.
We must get out quickly!
He doesn't have a gun – it's a banana!

87 *say, tell, ask, advise*

Jack **told the doctor** that he was still having headaches and she **advised him to see** a specialist.

> I'm still having headaches, Doctor.

> I think you should see a specialist.

1 *say* and *tell*

We use the verbs *say* and *tell* to report information.
Look at the differences between *say* and *tell*:

SAY	TELL
Jack **said that** he was still having headaches. Jack **said to me that** he was still having headaches.	Jack **told me that** he was still having headaches.

  ✗ ~~Jack said me that he was still having headaches.~~
✗ ~~Jack told that he was still having headaches.~~
✗ ~~Jack told to me that he was still having headaches.~~

> **NATURAL ENGLISH** In everyday English, we often use *say* and *tell* without *that*:
> Lucy **said (that) she'd meet** us at six o'clock.
> He **told me (that) he couldn't come** to the party.

🔊 Pronunciation ➤ 1.31

2 *tell*, *ask* and *advise*

When we report instructions, requests and advice, we can use *tell*, *ask* and *advise*.
With these verbs, we use the infinitive with *to*:
'Be quiet!' → She **told me to be** quiet.

 We put *not* BEFORE the infinitive with *to*:

'Don't touch the oven!' → 	✗ ~~She told me don't touch the oven.~~
	✓ She told me **not to touch** the oven.

- instructions:
  TEACHER *'Don't talk during the lesson!'* → Our teacher **told us not to talk** during the lesson.
- requests:
  MOTHER *'Please phone home, Anna.'* → Anna's mother **asked her to phone** home.
- advice:
  DOCTOR *'I think you should see a specialist.'* → Jack's doctor **advised him to see** a specialist.

Verb + object + infinitive ➤ Unit 85.1

Practice

1 Choose the correct words in *italics*. ◄)) **4.18** Listen and check.

0 I *said* / *told* the interviewer that I was really interested in the job.
1 He *said* / *told* me that a lot of people had applied for the job.
2 But he *said* / *told* that my qualifications were good.
3 I *told* / *said* him that I had studied part-time.
4 He *said* / *told* that my application was very impressive.
5 After the interview, he *said* / *told* me that I was perfect for the job.
6 And I *said* / *told* that I would love to work there.

2 Look at the pictures and complete the reported instructions, requests or advice for each one. ◄)) **4.19** Listen and check.

0 The teacher asked _the students to listen carefully_ .
1 He told them to ....
2 He told Carla ....
3 He told the students ....
4 He asked the class ....
5 He advised ....

3 Find six more mistakes in the sentences and correct them. Tick (✓) the correct sentences.

0 My mother ~~said~~ *told/asked* me to phone her from the airport.
1 Harry told that he was very happy.
2 The assistant asked me wait for a few minutes.
3 My lecturer advised me take the exam again in June.
4 The teacher told the children to not talk in class.
5 I said the assistant that I wanted a return ticket to Paris.
6 My boss asked me not to leave work early that day.
7 Sophie said that she was feeling really unhappy.
8 My friend asked me don't buy her a birthday present.

4 Think about the last time you had an interview: as part of an exam, for a job, or for a course of study. Write three sentences about it, starting *They / He / She asked me to / told me to / advised me to*.

At my last interview, they asked me to take a test.

88 Indirect questions

Just one more question. Could you tell me how often you go shopping in the town centre?

1 Use

We use indirect questions to ask for information in a polite way, eg:
Can/could you tell me …? Do you know …? I'd like to know … :
*Excuse me, **could you tell me** where the nearest bank is?*

2 *Wh-* questions

In indirect questions the subject of the verb comes after the *wh-* word and before the verb.

DIRECT QUESTION	INDIRECT QUESTION
What time is it?	*Do you know **what** time it **is**?*
Where is the English exam?	*Can you tell me **where** the English exam **is**?*
How much are these jeans?	*I'd like to know **how much** these jeans **are**.*
Who is that man?	*Do you know **who** that man **is**?*
When are they coming back?	*I'd like to know **when** they are coming back.*
Where has Neil gone?	*Do you know **where** Neil **has gone**?*

 ✗ ~~*Can you tell me where is the station?*~~ ✓ *Can you tell me **where** the station **is**?*

3 *Wh-* questions with *do, does* and *did*

In indirect questions, we do not use *do, does* or *did* after the *wh-* word.
We use the normal verb form for positive sentences:

DIRECT QUESTION	INDIRECT QUESTION
*Where **does** he live?*	*Do you know **where** he **lives**?*
*How often **do** you go shopping?*	*Could you tell me **how often** you **go** shopping?*
*Where **did** they go for their holiday?*	*I'd like to know **where** they **went** for their holiday.*

 ✗ ~~*I'd like to know what did he say.*~~ ✓ *I'd like to know **what** he **said**.*

4 *Yes/No* questions (*Is …? Do …? Have …? Will …?* etc.)

In indirect questions, we use *if* or *whether* + subject and the normal verb form for positive sentences:

DIRECT QUESTION	INDIRECT QUESTION
Is there a petrol station near here?	*Could you tell me **if** there **is** a petrol station near here?*
*Will he **be** at the party?*	*I'd like to know **if** he **will be** at the party.*
Has she seen that film?	*Do you know **whether** she **has seen** that film?*

🔊 Pronunciation ➤ 1.32

Practice

1 Choose the correct words in *italics*. 🔊 **4.20** Listen and check.

0 Can you tell me what (the time is) / is the time?
1 Could you tell me how *do I get / I get* to the bus station?
2 Could you tell me where *is the ticket office / the ticket office is*?
3 I'd like to know how often *runs the airport bus / the airport bus runs*.
4 Can you tell me how much *the journey costs / does the journey cost*?
5 Do you know if the airport bus *leaves / does leave* from here?
6 Do you know where *I get on / do I get on* the bus?
7 Can you tell me if *the bus has gone / has the bus gone*?
8 Could you tell me what time *the last bus is / is the last bus*?

2 Rosemary often forgets things. Complete the questions she is asking her friend. Use the verbs in brackets ().

0 'Do you know where ....*I put*............ my glasses?' (put)
1 'Can you remember if .... my handbag?' (pick up)
2 'Can you remember where .... the car?' (park)
3 'Oh dear. Do you know if .... the front door?' (lock)
4 'Can you tell me who .... to dinner this evening?' (come)

3 GRAMMAR IN USE Read the questions in the questionnaire and make them more polite. 🔊 **4.21** Listen and check.

INFOSYSTEMS

Our shopping habits

0 How often do you use the town centre shops?
1 Which shops do you like most?
2 How much do you usually spend in the town centre?
3 Do you use cash or credit cards?
4 Do you ever go out of town to shop?
5 Have you ever used the Internet for shopping?
6 Did you come by car or bus today?
7 Where did you park?
8 Will you continue to use the town centre for shopping?

0 Could you tell me how *often you use the town centre shops* .... ?
1 I'd like to know which ....
2 Can you say how .... ?
3 I'd like to know if ....
4 Could you tell me .... ?
5 I'd like to know ....
6 Can you tell me .... ?
7 Could you tell me .... ?
8 Finally, I'd like to know ....

Review MODULE 14

1 UNITS 86 AND 87 **The interviewer asked these people a question. Report their answers.**
🔊 **4.22** **Listen and check.**

What do you plan to do after university?

I want to travel to South America.

Daniel

I'm going to find a job for the summer.

Mariesa

I failed my exams so I'm staying for another year.

Iain

Nadia

I miss my home in Russia and now I can go back!

Interviewer

Andy and Liz

We're getting married in September!

Ines

I think I'll stay at home for the summer.

Joseph

I've just finished a politics course, so I might go home to Zambia and use it.

0 Daniel said that *he wanted to travel to South America* .
1 Mariesa said that she ....
2 Iain said that he ....
3 Nadia said ....
4 Joseph said ....
5 Ines said ....
6 Andy and Liz ....

2 UNITS 86 AND 87 **Choose the correct words in *italics* to complete the journalist's report.**

EMERGENCY LANDING AT AIRPORT – Nick Bowen reports

When I arrived at the airport, there was a lot of activity around the plane. The passengers were all in the airport building, waiting to talk to the police. It was a very lucky escape. Some of them described what had happened.

Joshua Otobo, from Nigeria, said that everything (0) *had* / *has* gone dark and some people (1) *start* / *had started* screaming. Several people said that the pilot had told them (2) *keep calm* / *to keep calm*, and that they (3) *are* / *were* going to land safely.

Tom Strachan, a company director, (4) *told me* / *told* that he just (5) *feels* / *felt* happy to be safe and that he (6) *is* / *was* going home to (7) *his* / *my* wife and children to celebrate.

New York singer, Samantha Allen, said that the airport doctor had advised them all (8) *talk* / *to talk* to him about the experience, but added that she (9) *was* / *is* flying on to the US so she (10) *will* / *would* have to talk to someone there.

3 UNIT 88 **Use Rowan's notes to write Sarah's questions to the sales manager.**

0 Can you tell me *how many bikes we sold last month* ?

1 I'd like to know if ....
....

2 Could you tell me how ....
.... ?

3 Do you know ....
.... ?

4 Can you tell me ....
.... ?

5 I'd like to know ....
....

Sarah
Can you call the sales manager for me?
I need to find out
0 how many bikes did we sell last month?
1 does he have a list of them all?
2 how much discount do we give to
   important customers?
3 are the sales increasing?
4 has he got enough salespeople in the shops?
5 when can he get to the office for a meeting?
Thanks,
Rowan

4 ALL UNITS **Complete the second sentence so it means the same as the first.
Use one, two or three words.**

0 The tourist guide said, 'Put your suitcases into the bus.'
   The tourist guide .... *told us to* .... put our suitcases into the bus.

1 She said, 'Please wait inside the bus.'
   She asked .... wait inside the bus.

2 She said to us, 'I hope you will have a good holiday in my country.'
   She said that she hoped .... a good holiday in her country.

3 She said to us, 'May is a lovely time of year.'
   She told .... May was a lovely time of year.

4 She said, 'But it can be very hot by the sea.'
   She said to .... be very hot by the sea.

5 She said to us, 'You should be careful in the hot sun.'
   She advised .... be careful in the hot sun.

5 ALL UNITS **Write the words in the correct order to make reported sentences or
indirect questions.**

0 advised smoking the doctor stop to me *The doctor advised me to stop smoking.*

1 where is you me could the nearest bank tell ?
   ....

2 the builder the stairs dangerous us were told that
   ....

3 asked to fill in the hotel receptionist me a form
   ....

4 the cinema full said the manager that was
   ....

5 like if marked to know my homework you've I'd
   ....

6 our teacher the exam said on Friday was us to that
   ....

⏻ Go online for more review exercises

Test MODULE 14

Reported statements and indirect questions

Choose the correct answer, A, B or C.

1 When they found the woman in the snow, she said .... freezing.
   A I was   B she is   C she was
   ➤ Unit 86

2 Dmitri said that he .... me that evening, but he didn't.
   A would call   B will call   C is calling
   ➤ Unit 86

3 Damon told me that he .... last weekend with his brother.
   A is spending   B was spending   C will spend
   ➤ Unit 86

4 Carol said that she .... the Marketing Director before.
   A didn't meet   B hasn't met   C hadn't met
   ➤ Unit 86

5 When I started my new job they told me that .... arrive at 8.30.
   A I had to   B I have to   C she must
   ➤ Unit 86

6 'I think mine was the best answer.' → Anna said she thought ....
   was the best answer.
   A hers   B her   C mine
   ➤ Unit 86

7 'We'll go in our car.' → Mum and Dad said we would go in .... car.
   A our   B your   C their
   ➤ Unit 86

8 'I'll show you the photos.' → She told me that she would show ....
   the photos.
   A you   B me   C her
   ➤ Unit 86

9 Shona told .... that she was leaving the company.
   A her manager   B to her manager   C it to her manager
   ➤ Unit 87

10 At the airport they .... that the flight was delayed.
    A said us   B told to us   C said
    ➤ Unit 87

11 My friend Sam .... that he wanted to leave home.
    A told his parents   B said his parents   C told to his parents
    ➤ Unit 87

12 My teacher advised .... harder for the exams.
    A me study   B me to study   C to me study
    ➤ Unit 87

13 We asked the window cleaner .... later.
    A come back   B to come back   C please come back
    ➤ Unit 87

14 The woman on the bus told the children ....
    A not to shout   B to not shout   C no shouting
    ➤ Unit 87

15 My neighbour asked .... play my music loudly.
    A to me not to   B me not to   C me don't
    ➤ Unit 87

16 Could you tell me .... here?
    A does Angela live   B if Angela does live   C if Angela lives
    ➤ Unit 88

17 Do you know ....?
    A where the post office is   B where is the post office
    C is where the post office
    ➤ Unit 88

18 I'd like to know what time .... last night!
    A you got home   B did you get home   C you did get home
    ➤ Unit 88

19 Can you tell me .... finished?
    A has the exam   B if the exam has   C the exam has
    ➤ Unit 88

20 Do you know where .... at night?
    A goes the cat   B does the cat go   C the cat goes
    ➤ Unit 88

Relative clauses

Before you start

1 Read the text from a film magazine. Look at the ==highlighted== grammar examples.

KING KONG

EVERYONE KNOWS this famous view. It shows ==the building which was once== the tallest in the world. The Empire State Building became famous around the world because of the movie *King Kong*. Clearly this is the 1933 film, not the one from 2005! In the movie, a film director can't find an actress for his new movie – ==a film he wants to make== on a mysterious island. Finally, he finds a young ==woman who agrees== to work for him, and they go to the island. When they get there, they realise that there is great danger – there is a huge gorilla on the island who kills people in ==the forest where he lives.==

But the gorilla takes the woman from the city and runs away with her, and protects her from other animals. ==The people who have come== from New York catch him and take him back there, ==which is very sad.== In the final scene he carries ==the girl that he ran away with== to the top of the Empire State Building. Of course, when you watch the film, you believe that he is going to kill the girl, but in fact he puts her down gently and then falls from the building and dies. The 1933 film was very successful – this was ==the reason why== they made another one in 2005.

2 Now read the sentences. Choose the correct words in *italics*. The ==highlighted== grammar examples will help you.

1 We live in a building *was once / which was once* in a film. ➤ Unit 89
2 My brother married the girl *who / which* lived next door to us. ➤ Unit 89
3 We're going to meet the people *who / who they* have come to look at the school. ➤ Unit 90
4 What's the name of that vegetarian dish *you made / that you made it*? ➤ Unit 90
5 San Francisco is the city *that / where* I spent the first five years of my life. ➤ Unit 91
6 Who was the man you were playing *tennis / tennis with* last night? ➤ Unit 91
7 Let me tell you the reasons *which / why* I don't want the job. ➤ Unit 91
8 I'm starting a great new job next week, *which / what* is very exciting. ➤ Unit 91

3 Check your answers below. Then go to the unit for more information and practice.

1 which was once 2 who 3 who 4 you made 5 where 6 tennis with 7 why 8 which

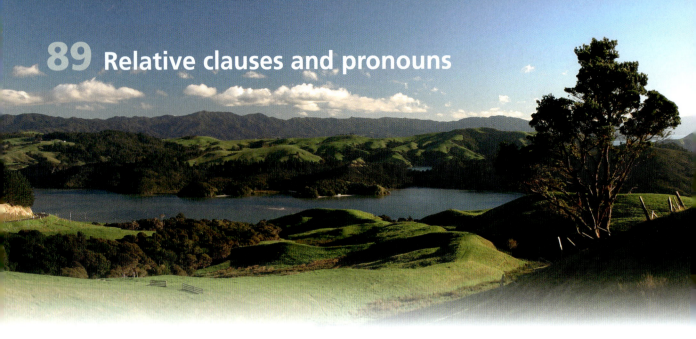

89 Relative clauses and pronouns

Director Peter Jackson filmed the three movies **which form the**
Lord of the Rings **series** in his home country, New Zealand.

1 Relative clauses

We can use relative clauses to make two sentences into one sentence:

TWO SENTENCES	
Sentence 1	**Sentence 2**
This is my brother.	*He lives in Japan.*
There are three movies.	*They form the 'Lord of the Rings' series.*
I've got a new mobile phone.	*It takes brilliant photos.*

ONE SENTENCE	
Main clause	**Relative clause**
This is my brother	*who lives in Japan.*
There are three movies	*which form the 'Lord of the Rings' series.*
I've got a new mobile phone	*that takes brilliant photos.*

The relative clause gives us more information about the person or thing in the main clause.

2 *who, which, that*

We introduce a relative clause with a relative pronoun (*who*, *which* or *that*).

- *who* is for a relative clause about people:
  Alexander Graham Bell was the man **who** *invented the telephone.*
  Do you know the woman **who** *works at the cinema?*
- *which* is for a relative clause about animals or things (but not people):
  The horse **which** *won the race has died. I've bought* a new computer **which** *cost £800.*
- we can use *that* for people, animals and things:
  I've contacted all the students **that** *took the exam. It's* a phone **that** *plays music.*

 In a relative clause, *who*, *which*, or *that* REPLACES *he, she, it*, etc, or a noun:
  ✗ ~~Jose is the man who he lives next door.~~
  ✓ *Jose is the man* **who** *lives next door.*
  ✗ ~~We don't go to restaurants which they serve meat.~~
  ✓ *We don't go to restaurants* **which** *serve meat.*

Practice

1 Choose the correct words in *italics*. In two of the questions, both words are correct.
◄)) 4.23 Listen and check.

0   We've just bought a DVD player (*that*)/ *who* can store over 100 films.
1   Do you know my friend *which* / *who* is a racing driver?
2   I got these shoes from the shop *who* / *which* has a sale at the moment.
3   This is an iPod *who* / *which* can also play films.
4   We had the teacher *who* / *that* speaks Japanese.
5   The woman *who* / *which* lives across the road saw the thieves.
6   China is the country *that* / *which* is growing fastest at the moment.
7   At the zoo we saw a tiger *who* / *which* only had three legs.
8   Green tea is a delicious drink *that* / *who* is good for your health.

2 Match the two parts of the sentences. Then write a relative pronoun.
◄)) 4.24 Listen and check.

0   Most people like films *which/that* ⟶
1   June is a month ....
2   Jennifer Lopez is an actor ....
3   Neil Armstrong was the astronaut ....
4   In 1918 there was an illness ....
5   Summerhill is a school in England ....
6   Mozart was a composer ....

A   allows students to choose their own classes.
B   is also famous as a singer.
C   make them feel happy.
D   died at the age of 35.
E   first walked on the moon.
F   often has very nice weather in the UK.
G   killed over 50 million people around the world.

3   GRAMMAR IN USE   Read the text. Complete it with a relative pronoun and one of the phrases A–F below.

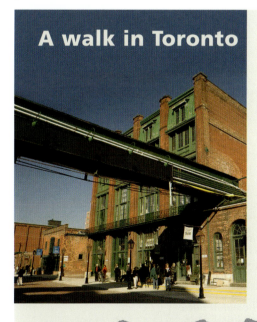

A walk in Toronto

TORONTO IS A MODERN CITY and it is not very popular with tourists, but there's a part of it
(0) ...*which B*... This area is full of buildings
(1) .... in the 1800s – it's the best example of Victorian industrial architecture in the country. This part of Toronto is now an area (2) ....,
– so it is full of cultural interest. Because it's an area (3) ...., you can walk round it without any traffic problems. But there is one thing
(4) .... It is the fact that it's the second most popular film location in the world, after Hollywood. Many successful films were made here, such as *Chicago* and *X-Men*, and on any day you might see film stars (5) ...., such as Renée Zellweger.

A   attracts artists
B   ~~is really worth a visit~~
C   were built
D   makes the area really famous
E   are very well-known
F   doesn't allow cars

90 Relative pronouns

Basildon Park is a house **which** often appears in films.
It's the house **which** they used in *Pride and Prejudice*.

1 Relative pronoun as subject

Look at these sentences:

Basildon Park is a house . Basildon Park often appears in films.

Basildon Park is a house **which often appears** in films.

Here, *which* = the subject of *appears*. It replaces the noun *Basildon Park* in the second sentence.

2 Relative pronoun as object

Now look at these sentences:

Basildon Park is a house . They used the house in 'Pride and Prejudice'.

Basildon Park is the house **which they used** in 'Pride and Prejudice'.

Here, *which* = the object of *used*.

We can also use *who* and *that* in this way:

The teacher **who** I like most is my music teacher.

Alex is the guy **that** I met yesterday.

> **NATURAL ENGLISH** We often use relative clauses without *which*, *who* or *that* when they are the object of the verb:
> *Basildon Park is the house they used in 'Pride and Prejudice'.*
> *The teacher I like most is my music teacher.*
> *Alex is the guy I met yesterday.*

 Don't repeat the noun or pronoun:
✗ *The house they used in the film it was called Basildon Park.*
✓ The **house** they used in the film **was called** Basildon Park.

 We need the relative pronoun when it is the subject:
✗ *Basildon Park is a house often appears in film.*
✓ *Basildon Park is a house **which** often appears in films.*

Practice

1 **Put a line through the relative pronoun if it is not necessary.** ◀♫4.25 **Listen and check.**

0 We've just sold the car ~~which~~ we bought two years ago.
1 Have you met Richard? He's the friend that I met in Bangkok.
2 Have you got any pens which I can use on the whiteboard?
3 I don't like coffee which tastes really bitter.
4 Did you see the doctor who examined you last time?
5 Harrison's? Is that the tour company which you used for your last holiday?
6 Is James McAvoy the actor who was in *Atonement*?

2 **GRAMMAR IN USE** **Complete the conversation with relative pronouns, but only if they are necessary.**

TOURIST Excuse me. Can you tell me something about the Harry Potter tour?
OFFICIAL Of course. It's a fascinating tour (0) ....*which*..... lasts all day. It starts in London and you visit a lot of the places (1) .... the director chose when he filmed the Harry Potter movies.
TOURIST Oh, so the tour isn't only around London?
OFFICIAL No, there were several places in and around Oxford (2) .... they used in the filming.
TOURIST That's interesting. Is there a guide?
OFFICIAL Oh, yes, there's a guide with every tour (3) .... can give you a lot of interesting information.
TOURIST Right. Where does the tour go in London?
OFFICIAL It goes to St Pancras Station – that's the station (4) .... has the famous Platform 9¾ in the film. Then it goes to London Zoo – you know, you see that in the part of the film (5) .... shows Harry with the animals. You have lunch in London and after lunch the tour goes to Oxford. There are several places in the University (6) .... you visit.
TOURIST It all sounds good. Now, how much are the tickets ...?

3 **Join the sentences. Use a relative pronoun if necessary.** ◀♫4.26 **Listen and check.**

0 I've never eaten at my cousin's restaurant. He opened it last year.
   I've never eaten *at the restaurant my cousin opened last year* ....
1 Here's the book. I promised to give it to you.
   Here's the book ....
2 Have you seen the technician? He repairs the computers.
   Have you seen .... ?
3 That's the film. I described it on the phone.
   That's ....
4 Have you been to the hotel? It was in *The Italian Job*.
   Have you been .... ?
5 Sally's just bought a car. It goes really fast.
   Sally's just bought ....
6 We saw the woman. We met her at Ginny's party last year.
   We saw the woman ....

91 Relative clauses and prepositions

Gandhi is a famous film from 1982. It was filmed in the UK and India, and the actor Ben Kingsley played Mohandas Gandhi, the Indian lawyer **that** the film is **about**. It was a remarkable film with a lot of famous actors in it, and for the scene of Gandhi's funeral, there were over 300,000 people, **which** is amazing.

1 Prepositions in relative clauses

Verbs often have prepositions after them (e.g. *look **for**, talk **about**, go **to***). In relative clauses, we usually put the preposition at the end of the clause:

*I'm looking **for** a book.* → *This is the book (that) I'm looking **for**.*
*I was talking **about** Maria.* → *Maria is the woman (who) I was talking **about**.*
*We went **to** that beach.* → *That is the beach (which) we went **to**.*

2 *when, where, why*

We can also use *when, where* and *why* for relative clauses

* *When* is for a relative clause about time, days, years, etc:
  *We met **on the day when** I passed my final exam.*
* *Where* is for a relative clause about places:
  *That's **the bank where** Joan works.*
* *Why* is for a relative clause about reason:
  *She's working. That's **the reason why** she can't come.*

There is always a subject after *when, where* or *why*. It is a different subject from the one in the main clause:

main clause subject   relative clause subject

*That's **the building** where **we** do our exams.*

 When the relative clause begins with *when* or *where*, we do not include a place or time preposition:

✗ ~~September 20th is the day when we got married on.~~
✓ *September 20th is the day when we got married.*
✗ ~~That's the house where we spent our childhood in.~~
✓ *That's the house where we spent our childhood.*

3 Using *which* to make a comment

We can use *which* to make a comment on the idea in a clause:
*For the scene of Gandhi's funeral, there were over 300,000 people, **which** is amazing.*
(The fact that there were over 300,000 people is amazing.)

*We took the children to the seaside on Sunday, **which** was really relaxing.*
(Taking the children to the seaside was really relaxing.)

With these relative clauses we need a comma (,) before *which*.

Practice

1 Choose the correct words in *italics*. ◄))**4.27** Listen and check.

0 The reason *which / why* I can't come with you is that I don't have enough money.
1 It was really sunny on the day *when / where* we had our last exam.
2 2007 was the year *when / which* there were a lot of floods.
3 Have you chosen the date *on when / when* you want to have your party?
4 I've just read the new book by Orhan Pamuk, *that / which* I really enjoyed.
5 I'm sure this is the place *when / where* we agreed to meet.
6 Mrs Coles, I've got the DVD *for which / which* you were looking for.

2 Match the two parts of the sentences.

0 Last weekend I saw my first football match,	A which was very tiring.
1 David's grandmother died last week,	B which was fantastic news!
2 We had to drive 800km in one day last week,	C which was really boring.
3 My cousin in Canada called last night,	D which was very sad.
4 We had to wait in the queue for two hours,	E which was exciting.
5 We won the top prize of 10,000 euros,	F which was a real surprise.

3 **GRAMMAR IN USE** Complete the conversation with the phrases from the box. ◄))**4.28** Listen and check.

A Excuse me. I'm looking for Jeremy Trent.
B I'm the person (0) ......*you're looking for*........ .
 Why do you want me?
A I've got lunch for some people, some sandwiches.
B Oh, right. Well, put the box down there.
A Where?
B There! On the chair where (1) ....!
 OK, who are the sandwiches for?
A This is for Carol Holmes.
B She's the woman over there (2) .... and a black jacket.
A OK. And these are for Peter Davis.
B That's him – the man (3) ....
A And the salad is for Alicia Keane.
B Alicia's the woman (4) .... that boy over there.
A OK, and finally, George Andropoulos.
B George is the boy (5) ....
A And I've got the bill. Are you the person (6) ....?
B Yes, I'll pay it.
A Are you the director?
B Yes, I'm the director, (7) ....!

> I should give it to   I'm pointing
> who's wearing a leather skirt
> which means I pay for everything
> that Alicia's shouting at
> who's shouting at
> who's got a red beard
> ~~you're looking for~~

4 Use the ideas below to write sentences. Add a comment using *which*.

0 something you did last week *I went to the cinema, which wasn't very exciting.*
1 something you did last weekend ....
2 your last holiday ....
3 a recent piece of news ....
4 a recent celebration ....

Review MODULE 15

1 UNITS 89 AND 90 **There are five more mistakes in the email. Find and correct them.**

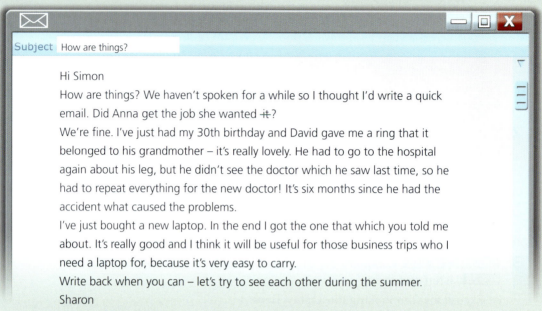

Subject How are things?

Hi Simon

How are things? We haven't spoken for a while so I thought I'd write a quick email. Did Anna get the job she wanted ~~it~~?

We're fine. I've just had my 30th birthday and David gave me a ring that it belonged to his grandmother – it's really lovely. He had to go to the hospital again about his leg, but he didn't see the doctor which he saw last time, so he had to repeat everything for the new doctor! It's six months since he had the accident what caused the problems.

I've just bought a new laptop. In the end I got the one that which you told me about. It's really good and I think it will be useful for those business trips who I need a laptop for, because it's very easy to carry.

Write back when you can – let's try to see each other during the summer.

Sharon

2 ALL UNITS **Complete the sentences. Use a relative pronoun if one is necessary.**

0 Here's a list of books. You need them for the course.
   Here's the list of books ...._you need_......... for the course.

1 Have you seen the flowers? Max sent them to me.
   Have you seen the flowers .... to me?

2 I haven't seen the man for two weeks. He lives upstairs.
   I haven't seen the man .... for two weeks.

3 I visited a house. Jane Austen grew up there.
   I visited the house ....

4 Have you heard about that woman? She won a million pounds.
   Have you heard about that woman .... a million pounds?

5 Do you remember that day last summer? We went to the beach then.
   Do you remember that day last summer .... to the beach?

6 Did you find that CD? You were looking for it.
   Did you find that CD ....?

7 I left my job. Let me tell you the reason why.
   I'll tell you .... my job.

8 Have you got any of that liquid? It covers mistakes.
   Have you got any of that liquid .... mistakes?

240

3 ALL UNITS Complete the conversation with the phrases from the box. 🔊**4.29** Listen and check.

A Did you do anything interesting last night?

B Yes, I went to the cinema,

(0) *which was the first time in weeks*.

I saw *The Ghost Writer*.

A I don't know that. Was it good?

B No, not really. It's by a director (1) .... a lot of good films, but this was disappointing.

A What's it about?

B Well, it's a thriller (2) .... by Robert Harris. I expected a film

(3) .... to be great, as he's such a good actor, but it's quite boring,

(4) .... But the person (5) .... enjoyed it.

A Oh, who did you go with?

B Julia – the friend of mine (6) .... at Sandra's party.

A Oh, yes. I remember. She was the girl (7) .... and jeans, wasn't she?

B Yes, that's right.

A Where was the film on?

B At the Regent. It's the cinema (8) .... on the way to the station.

> that was wearing a leather jacket   you met
> that's from the novel   I went with
> which is a real pity   that you pass
> ~~which was the first time in weeks~~
> who's made   that Ewan McGregor acts in

4 ALL UNITS Complete the text with the correct words or phrases, A, B or C below.

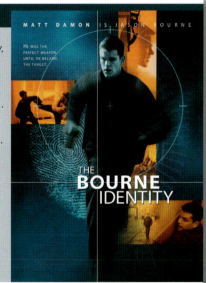

FAMOUS LOCATIONS IN FILM   PART 7

THIS WEEK we're going to look at the locations in *The Bourne Identity*. The film, with Matt Damon (as Jason Bourne) and Franka Potente (as Marie) was a huge success in 2002, the year (0) ...*A*... it first appeared in the cinemas. The story of Jason Bourne, a man (1) .... can't remember anything about his life, is interesting, but the locations (2) .... the film uses were also main features. The sea (3) .... some fishermen find Bourne and pull him into their boat is near the coast of northwest Italy, and the apartment (4) .... is in Paris. Bourne first meets Marie in the US Embassy in Zurich (5) .... is interesting because the building was actually in Prague! A lot of the film takes place in Paris, in or near places (6) .... are very well-known, such as the Louvre. The film ends on a Greek island (7) .... Marie has made a new life – this is the famous holiday island of Mykonos.

0 Ⓐ when B which C where
1 A who he B which C who
2 A who B that C whose
3 A where B which C whose
4 A Bourne lives B that Bourne lives C Bourne lives in
5 A which B , which C , that
6 A where B who C that
7 A which B where C when

⏻ Go online for more review exercises

Test MODULE 15

Relative clauses

Choose the correct answer, A, B or C. Sometimes two answers are correct.

1 Mr Robbins is the teacher .... taught me French.
   A who   B which   C has
   ➤ Unit 89

2 Samson is the horse .... the biggest race of the year.
   A who won   B that won   C what won
   ➤ Unit 89

3 Janice is my neighbour .... works for the BBC.
   A who   B what   C which
   ➤ Unit 89

4 I met the architect .... designed the shopping centre in the town.
   A that   B which   C who
   ➤ Unit 89

5 Is Arthur C Clarke the author .... wrote *2001: A Space Odyssey*?
   A who he   B who is   C who
   ➤ Unit 89

6 They're opening a shop .... is going to sell old books and records.
   A it   B which   C which it
   ➤ Unit 89

7 I'm going to try to replace the phone .... in the street.
   A that I dropped   B I dropped   C who I dropped
   ➤ Unit 90

8 Karen's working with the man .... at the party last week.
   A I met   B who I met him   C I met him
   ➤ Unit 90

9 That's the house ....
   A we're buying it   B we're buying the house   C that we're buying
   ➤ Unit 90

10 Is this the CD ....?
   A you wanted   B wanted   C that you wanted
   ➤ Unit 90

11 Did you see the man .... leather trousers?
   A who was wearing   B was wearing   C he was wearing
   ➤ Unit 90

12 We're meeting at the restaurant ....
   A Fran told us   B Fran told us about   C Fran told us about it
   ➤ Unit 91

13 Who was the woman .... at the party?
   A to you were talking   B you were talking to   C you were talking
   ➤ Unit 91

14 I've looked everywhere but I can't find the DVD ....
   A I'm looking for   B that I'm looking   C that I'm looking for
   ➤ Unit 91

15 Kevin Black is the man .... all afternoon.
   A John played tennis with   B with John played tennis
   C who John played tennis
   ➤ Unit 91

16 Venice was the town .... I met my wife.
   A where   B which   C what
   ➤ Unit 91

17 The reason .... so much is that she's so friendly.
   A for I like her   B why I like her   C which I like her
   ➤ Unit 91

18 We visited some of the places in the United States .... *Star Wars* was filmed.
   A which   B when   C where
   ➤ Unit 91

19 Lara came to visit us last night, ... was a nice surprise.
   A what   B that   C which
   ➤ Unit 91

20 Lots of people laughed at the children, ... made me very angry.
   A it   B which   C that
   ➤ Unit 91

Linking words

Before you start

1 Read the police report. Look at the highlighted grammar examples.

Police Report
June 10 2007 East 46th Street Apt 217
Watching Al Padrone
9.30 Police officer Haynes and I arrived at 9.30 and set up the equipment. We had to watch carefully **because** Apartment 217 is about 30 feet away across the street. No action.
13.15 Woman X arrived at Apartment 217. She rang the bell but no one opened the door. **While** she was waiting, she smoked a cigarette, then she made a call on her mobile. **In the end,** she walked away.
18.30 Al Padrone and woman X arrived at the apartment, but from different directions. **Before going in,** the woman pointed up at the window where we were sitting. Haynes waved at her, **so** I think they know we are here.
20.00 There was a knock at our door. Haynes opened it and came back with two pizzas. **When** I looked across at Apartment 217, **both Al and the woman** were waving at us and laughing. I think we have a problem.

Boss, please see report. Is the job finished, **or** shall we continue until Al **leaves** again?

2 Now read the sentences. Choose the correct words in *italics*.
The highlighted grammar examples will help you.

1 We can stay at this hotel *and / or* we can look for a better one.	➤ Unit 92
2 Both Sony *and / or* Philips produce electrical goods.	➤ Unit 92
3 I left my job *so that / because* I was getting bored with the work.	➤ Unit 93
4 The camera didn't work properly *so / because* we got a refund.	➤ Unit 93
5 *While / When* we turned on the light, we noticed the broken window.	➤ Unit 94
6 Please wait here until the dentist *will be / is* ready for you.	➤ Unit 94
7 *During / While* we were having dinner at the restaurant, it started snowing.	➤ Unit 94
8 You have to buy a ticket at the machine before *getting / get* on the bus.	➤ Unit 95
9 We got up really late. Then we missed the bus and had to wait for the next one. *In the end, / At first,* we arrived at the wedding ten minutes late.	➤ Unit 95

3 Check your answers below. Then go to the unit for more information and practice.

1 or 2 and 3 because 4 so 5 When 6 is 7 While 8 getting 9 In the end,

92 *and, but, or*

1 *and, but* and *or*

We can use *and, but* and *or* to join two clauses. We put them between the clauses:

SENTENCE 1	LINKING WORD	SENTENCE 2
I've washed up	*and*	*I've put the dishes away.*
I've washed up	*but*	*I haven't put the dishes away.*
I can wash up	*or*	*I can put the dishes away.*

After *and* and *or* we don't need to repeat the subject (*I, he, you*, etc.) or the auxiliary/modal verb:
*I've washed up **and** (I've) put the dishes away.*
*I can wash up **or** (I can) put the dishes away.*

We don't need to repeat the verb if it is the same in both clauses:
*I've made a cake **and** (I've made) some biscuits.*
*Would you like tea **or** (would you like) coffee?*

We repeat the subject (*I, he, you*, etc.) after *but*:
*I'd like to come **but** I haven't finished my homework yet.*

🔊 Pronunciation ➤ 1.33

2 *both … and, either … or*

We use *both … and* and *either … or* to make *and/or* stronger.

- *both … and* is for two similar ideas:
  Hilary speaks French and Japanese.
  *Hilary speaks **both** French **and** Japanese.*
  We can go shopping and see the film. We've got time.
  *We can **both** go shopping **and** see the film. We've got time.*

- *either … or* is for two choices:
  We can watch TV or we can listen to music.
  *We can **either** watch TV **or** (we can) listen to music.*

Practice

1 **Complete the sentences with *and, but* or *or*.** 4.30 **Listen and check.**

0 I've booked the flights ..*and*.. I've found a great hotel!
1 I've booked the flights .... I couldn't find a hotel.
2 I'm afraid I haven't booked the flights .... found a hotel. I've been too busy.
3 I haven't booked the flights yet .... I've found a really good hotel.
4 We visited Mum in hospital .... took her a huge bunch of flowers.
5 Did you visit Mum in hospital .... did you just phone her today?
6 We visited Mum in hospital .... we couldn't bring her home today.

2 GRAMMAR IN USE **Complete the text with linking words from the box.**

and (x 3) both but either ~~or~~ or

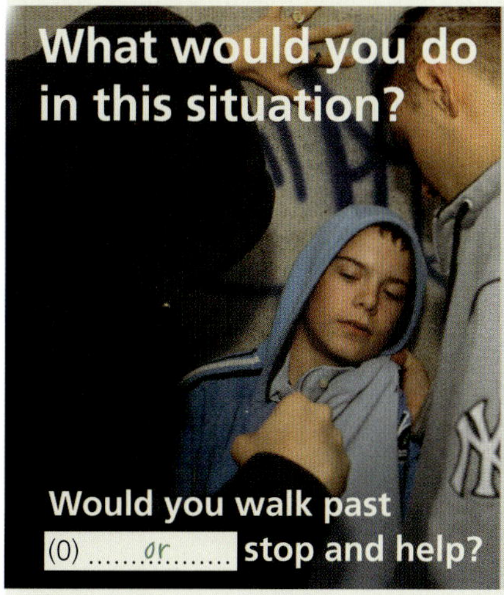
What would you do in this situation?
Would you walk past
(0) ......*or*...... stop and help?

Do something special – become a special police officer.

- Do you want to do something to help people (1) .... you don't know what?
- Are you (2) .... young with free time (3) .... retired from full-time work?
- Being a special police officer can (4) .... give you a new interest (5) .... provide some extra money for you.
- We train you (6) .... provide your uniform and equipment – we do this because we need people like you.

Become a special police officer (7) .... find a new life today.

3 **Write sentences 1–3 with *both* ... *and*. Write sentences 4–6 with *either* ... *or*.** 4.31 **Listen and check.**

0 Julie / swim / dive very well ...*Julie both swims and dives very well.*...
1 John / ride a motorbike / drive a car
....
2 Samantha / work part-time / look after the baby
....
3 Our cleaner / clean the house / wash the clothes
....
00 we can / watch TV / go to the cinema ..*We can either watch TV or go to the cinema.*..
4 we can / have a sandwich / go out for lunch
....
5 after lunch / the children / play in the garden / watch some cartoons
....
6 Carl / drive / take the train / when he visits customers
....

93 because, so, so that

Why do you want to join the police, Andrew?

Because I think it's a very interesting job.

Any other reasons?

Yes, **so that** I can help people.

1 because

Because joins two sentences and explains *why*:
Everyone loves Johnny Depp. He's a brilliant actor.
*Everyone loves Johnny Depp **because** he's a brilliant actor.*

We use *because of* + noun:
*All the trains are late **because of the bad weather**.*

 But we cannot use *because of* + noun and verb:
✗ *All the trains are late because of it is snowing.*
✓ *All the trains are late **because of the snow**.*

We can use *because* and *because of* at the beginning of a sentence. When we do this, we put a comma (,) after the first clause:
***Because** he's a brilliant actor, everyone loves him.*
***Because of** the bad weather, all the trains are late.*

2 so

So gives the result of something:
*Lucia didn't work hard **so** she failed her Spanish exam.*
*Summers are getting hotter **so** different types of plants are growing.*

3 so that, to + infinitive

We use *so that* to say why a person does something. *Can* and *could* often come after *so that*:
*Andrew wants to join the police **so that** he **can** help people.*
*She worked really hard **so that** she **could** go to university.*

We can also use *to* + infinitive instead of *so that*:
*I'm joining the police **so that** I can help people.*
*I'm joining the police **to help** people.*

NATURAL ENGLISH In everyday English, *to* + infinitive is more common than *so that*:
*Liz has gone to the shops **so that** she can buy some bread.*
→ *Liz has gone to the shops **to buy** some bread.*

Practice

1 Match the two parts of the sentences to tell Antonio's story. 🔊 **4.32** Listen and check.

0 Antonio went to Mexico to ⟶   A save money.
1 He stopped work for a year so that   B he could get married to Maria.
2 He arrived in the city and went to a   C Antonio moved in with him.
   hotel because   D he could spend a long time there.
3 After three days he left the hotel because   E it was too expensive.
4 He moved into a student hostel to   F study Mexican history.
5 But he didn't like it there because of   G Antonio talked to her a lot.
6 A friend had a free room in his house so   H the loud noise every evening.
7 His friend's sister was nice so   I it was late and he needed a room.
8 In the end Antonio stayed in Mexico
   so that

2 GRAMMAR IN USE Complete the conversation. Use one word only for each question.
🔊 **4.33** Listen and check.

ART   Sorry I'm late, Sonia. The police stopped me (0) ..*because*.. I was driving too fast.

SONIA   Not again! So you were driving fast (1) .... get here on time, were you?

ART   No, (2) .... I was trying to catch the car in front. The driver dropped his wallet
at the petrol station and I wanted to give it back to him, (3) .... I followed
him. I was driving fast so (4) .... I could catch him.

SONIA   Did you catch him?

ART   No, I didn't, (5) .... the police stopped me before I could catch him.

SONIA   But why didn't they stop the other man?

ART   I don't know!

SONIA   It's probably because (6) .... your silly fast car.

ART   Anyway, they took me to the police station (7) .... that they could interview me.

SONIA   What – for driving too fast?

ART   No ... it was also (8) .... of the wallet. They thought that I'd stolen it!

3 Write each sentence again so the second sentence means the same as the first.
Use the linking words in brackets ().

0 Janet left London because she wanted to live in the country. (to)
   Janet left London to live in the country.

00 Dmitri didn't come with us because he didn't have enough money. (so)
   Dmitri didn't have enough money so he didn't come with us.

1 We didn't go to the zoo because it was raining. (because of)
   ....

2 Terry went to prison because he stole a car. (so)
   ....

3 Josh wanted a bigger garden so that he could grow vegetables. (to)
   ....

4 Marion was really tired so she went to bed early. (because)
   ....

5 I can't hear anything because of your loud music. (because your)
   ....

94 Linking words for time

1 Common linking words for time

We use linking words (e.g. *when, before, after, until, while*) to talk about time.

- We use *when, before, after* to show the order of events:
  *I'll call you **when** we get back from our holiday.*
  *I locked the back door **before** I went to bed.*
  *I went to bed **after** I locked the back door.*

- We can also use *when, while* and *until* to talk about a period of time:
  *We heard the news **when** we were in France.*
  *Wait here **until** I get back.*

  *I broke my arm **while** I was playing tennis.*

  Look at the difference between *while* and *during*:
  *I broke my arm **while** I was playing tennis.* (*while* + verb)
  *I broke my arm **during** a game of tennis.* (*during* + noun)

- *as soon as* means 'immediately when':
  *Please call us **as soon as** you arrive.*

after and *before* + *-ing* ➤ Unit 95.1   *when* and *while* + past continuous ➤ Unit 48.2

2 Future time

When we are talking about the future, we use a PRESENT tense after *when, before, after, until, as soon as*. We don't use *will* or *going to*:

FUTURE TENSE	LINKING WORD	PRESENT TENSE
I think I'll get a good job	when	*I finish this course.*
She will come and see us	before	*she leaves.*
We're going to have a long holiday	after	*he gets out of hospital.*
Will you wait	until	*I come home?*
They'll call us	as soon as	*they have any news.*

 ✗ *They'll call us as soon as they will have any news.*
✓ *They'll call us **as soon as** they **have** any news.*

3 Commas

If a linking word begins the sentence, we use a comma. We don't use a comma if the linking word is in the middle of the sentence:
As soon as they have any news, they'll call us. (comma)
They'll call us as soon as they have any news. (no comma)

Practice

1 Which action comes first in these sentences? Which comes second?
Write 1 or 2 in the brackets ().

0 Mariam *went travelling* (2) after she *finished her university course* (1).
1 I always *have a shower* ( ) before I *brush my teeth* ( ).
2 We'll *have dinner* ( ) this evening as soon as you *get home* ( ) from work.
3 We *had a big party* ( ) after I *passed my driving test* ( ).
4 Don't worry about washing the dishes – we can *do that* ( ) after you *leave* ( ).
5 *Wait for me* ( ) in the café until I *finish the shopping* ( ).

2 Look at the pictures and complete the sentences below.
Use the linking word under the picture and a phrase from the box. ◀))4.34 Listen and check.

before   while

| I was having a shower |
| she left the supermarket |
| his mother called him |
| ~~the postman came~~ |
| the taxi arrived |
| we left home |

after   as soon as

until   when

0 We had to go out *before the postman came* .

1 The phone rang ....
   ....

2 Her shopping bags broke ....
   ....

3 It began to rain ....
   ....

4 He slept ....
   ....

5 We were still packing our bags ....
   ....

3 Join the two sentences. Use the linking words in brackets (). ◀))4.35 Listen and check.

0 We had lunch. Then we watched a DVD. (after) *We watched a DVD after we had lunch.*

00 I'll finish the report. I'll email it to you. (when)
    When I finish the report, I'll email it to you.

1 I was driving. I fell asleep. (while)
   ....

2 My friends waited at the airport. My plane arrived. (until)
   ....

3 I won't try to find a job. I'll finish my course. (before)
   ....

4 The interview finished. I called my wife. (as soon as)
   ....

5 You finish using the CD. Remove it from the computer. (after)
   ....

⏻ Go online for more practice   **249**

95 Linking words for stories and instructions

'Well, you see officer, **first** a rabbit ran across the road and I stopped quickly.

Then the car behind me stopped and almost hit me, but **after that**, another car came up really fast and hit the car behind me.

That hit my car and pushed it into the tree.

Then another car came up too fast and another, and **in the end**, there were six cars there!'

1 Describing events in the past

When we describe the order of events in the past, we use the linking words *first*, *then*, *after that* and *in the end*.

- We use *first* for the first event:
  ***First** a rabbit ran across the road ...*
- We use *then* and *after that* for more events. We usually use *then* before *after that*:
  *... **then** the car behind me stopped ... **after that**, another car ...*
- We use *in the end* for the last event of many, or to mean after a long time:
  ***In the end**, there were six cars there. **In the end**, we got our luggage back from the airline.*

In writing we often use *after + -ing* and *before + -ing* to describe the order of events.

Compare:
*I went to bed **after I locked** the back door.*
→ *Mycroft went to bed **after locking** the back door.*

*I decided to travel **before I went** to university.*
→ *Many school leavers travel **before going** to university.*

 Don't use the infinitive *to* after *before* and *after*:
✗ *Always check the oil in your car before to drive a long way.*
✓ *Always check the oil in your car **before driving** a long way.*

before and *after* ➤ Unit 94.1

NATURAL ENGLISH Don't use too many linking words together because it can sound unnatural:
✗ *First I got up, then I had a shower. After that I had breakfast and then I went to get the bus ...*
✓ ***First** I got up and had a shower. **Then** I had breakfast and went to get the bus ...*

2 Giving instructions

We often use the linking words *first*, *next*, *then*, *finally* to give instructions:
***First**, take six eggs, ... **Next**, put a little butter in a pan.*

We use *finally* for the last instruction, not *in the end*:
***First**, boil some milk in the pan. **Then** add the chocolate powder to the milk and mix.*
***Finally**, pour it into a cup and enjoy it!*

Practice

1 **GRAMMAR IN USE** Choose the correct words in *italics* in the story. 🔊**4.36** Listen and check.

Last night I was driving home along an empty motorway. Suddenly, I saw a car behind me – it came quite close. (0) *Then* / *After* it started flashing its lights. (1) *First* / *In the end*, I decided not to stop but (2) *first* / *then* I saw signs for a petrol station, so I decided to stop there. (3) *After that* / *After* driving into the petrol station, I parked in front of the restaurant. (4) *In the end* / *Then* I noticed the other car again, so I waited (5) *after* / *before* opening my car door. A man and a woman got out of the car and I could see they were police officers, so (6) *in the end* / *first* I got out and spoke to them. They explained that one of my back lights wasn't working and that's why they were following me.

2 Look at the pictures. Then complete the instructions for booking train tickets on the Internet.

It's easy to book your train tickets online now – just follow these simple steps.

0 Go to *our website Train tickets online* . 3 ....

1 First, choose .... 4 ....

2 Then, ... 5 ....

3 **GRAMMAR IN USE** Read the story below. Then put the words in 1–5 in the right order and add a linking word or phrase. 🔊**4.37** Listen and check.

0 *First, a letter came in the post* .... 3 ....

1 .... 4 ....

2 .... 5 ....

This really happened to my aunt and uncle. (0) *in the post/a letter/came* one day. It said that a taxi would collect them at 6.00 the next Saturday evening. (1) *to a show/arrived/with tickets/another letter*. They thought it was a bit strange, but my uncle is a lawyer, with lots of important clients, and they thought the tickets came from one of them. So the next Saturday evening they took the taxi into the town. But, (2) *going/into the theatre/phoned/my uncle/a friend* who works for the police. (3) *went/the show/to see/they* and had a great time. (4) *went home/they/in the taxi*. They were worried when they arrived home, because the front door was open, but (5) *was/OK/everything*, because my uncle's friend was in the house, with two other police officers and the man who had tried to rob their house while they were at the show.

Review MODULE 16

1 UNITS 92 AND 93 **Read the email and choose the correct answers in *italics*.**

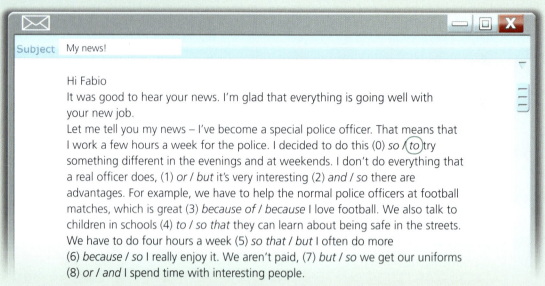

Subject My news!

Hi Fabio

It was good to hear your news. I'm glad that everything is going well with
your new job.

Let me tell you my news – I've become a special police officer. That means that
I work a few hours a week for the police. I decided to do this (0) *so / to* try
something different in the evenings and at weekends. I don't do everything that
a real officer does, (1) *or / but* it's very interesting (2) *and / so* there are
advantages. For example, we have to help the normal police officers at football
matches, which is great (3) *because of / because* I love football. We also talk to
children in schools (4) *to / so that* they can learn about being safe in the streets.
We have to do four hours a week (5) *so that / but* I often do more
(6) *because / so* I really enjoy it. We aren't paid, (7) *but / so* we get our uniforms
(8) *or / and* I spend time with interesting people.

2 UNITS 94 AND 95 **Complete the conversation with linking words from the box.**
🔊 **4.38 Listen and check.**

> after   after that   before   first   in the end   then   until   ~~when~~   while

SUE   I'm bored with studying. Let's go out now.

BRIAN   I want to do a bit more. Let's go out (0) ....*when*.... Dan arrives.

SUE   Dan isn't coming this evening. I told you that (1) ....
you were preparing lunch.

BRIAN   Really? I didn't hear you. Why isn't he coming?

SUE   He got home from Poland really late last night.

BRIAN   Oh? I thought he was landing at about 6.00.

SUE   Yes, he landed at 6.00 but everything went
wrong (2) .... the plane landed.
(3) ...., everyone had to sit on the
plane for over an hour (4) .... they
could get off. (5) .... one of Dan's
bags didn't arrive from the plane, and he had
to complete a lot of different forms.
(6) ...., he had to wait a long
time for a train. (7) ...., he got home
at about 1.00 a.m.

BRIAN   Oh no! But Dan never goes to bed early anyway, so why can't he come out with us?

SUE   The problem is that the airline has found his bag, and he has to wait at home
this evening (8) .... they deliver it.

3 ALL UNITS **Do the sentences in A and B have the same (S) or different (D) meanings?**

0 A I left the party early because I was feeling sick. .....S......
   B I was feeling sick so I left the party early.
1 A She can both go to the cinema and go skating. ....
   B She can either go to the cinema or go skating.
2 A The weather is cold, but my grandparents don't put the heating on. ....
   B The weather is cold, so my grandparents don't put the heating on.
3 A I decided not to take the job because it didn't pay very well. ....
   B The job didn't pay very well so I decided not to take it.
4 A I went to the bank to get some money out. ....
   B I went to the bank so that I could get some money out.
5 A Look after the children until I get back from the cinema. ....
   B Look after the children while I'm at the cinema.
6 A We were so tired we fell asleep while we were watching the match. ....
   B We were so tired we fell asleep during the match.
7 A I'll call you as soon as the train arrives at the station. ....
   B I'll call you before the train arrives at the station.

4 ALL UNITS **Complete the second sentence so it means the same as the first. Use one, two or three words.**

0 Lawrence went to drama school to become an actor.
   Lawrence went to drama school .....because he..... wanted to become an actor.
1 I finished reading my book before I went to sleep last night.
   I went to sleep last night .... finished reading my book.
2 Lock the door immediately after you get home.
   Lock the door .... you get home.
3 We didn't go on holiday last summer because we didn't have enough money.
   We didn't have enough money last summer .... didn't go on holiday.
4 My passport was stolen while I was travelling to Moscow.
   My passport was stolen .... the journey to Moscow.
5 Remember to wash your hands after using the toilet.
   Remember to wash your hands .... use the toilet.
6 Kylie learnt English so that she could travel around the world.
   Kylie learnt English .... around the world.

5 ALL UNITS **Complete the text with the correct words or phrases, A, B or C below.**

0 (A) when   B so   C as soon as
1 A but   B so   C and
2 A because   B because of
   C so that
3 A and   B but   C or
4 A so that   B so   C to
5 A so that   B because   C to
6 A While   B When   C During
7 A because   B so that
   C because of
8 A then   B first   C in the end

A HAPPY ENDING

On the evening of 20 March, Marina Portman was cycling down a hill to a friend's house (0) .... a car came very close to her and hit her bike. Marina was a very good cyclist, (1) .... she couldn't control her bike (2) .... she was on a hill. She fell off and hit a wall. She was able to stand up (3) .... she couldn't walk. A police car passed and saw her, (4) .... they took her to hospital (5) .... she could see a doctor. (6) .... her stay in hospital, one of the police officers came to see her – he told her that she was in trouble (7) .... there were no lights on her bike that evening. Then he got to know Marina's family, and (8) ...., Marina and the young police officer got married.

Test MODULE 16

Linking words

Choose the correct answer, A, B or C.

1 I remembered his face .... I couldn't remember his name.   ➤ Unit 92
   A and B but C or

2 Do you want to stay at home this evening .... go out for a walk?   ➤ Unit 92
   A and B but C or

3 I was invited to Jane's party .... I decided not to go.   ➤ Unit 92
   A so B but C or

4 You can choose two languages for this course so you can study ....   ➤ Unit 92
   French and Spanish.
   A and B both C either

5 You can study .... maths or history, but you can't do both of them.   ➤ Unit 92
   A or B both C either

6 I really enjoy working here .... the lovely people.   ➤ Unit 93
   A because B because of C to

7 There was a lot of traffic on the motorway .... we missed our plane.   ➤ Unit 93
   A so that B because C so

8 I'm going to join a gym .... get fitter.   ➤ Unit 93
   A because B to C so that

9 .... we travel a lot, we decided not to get a pet.   ➤ Unit 93
   A So that B Because of C Because

10 .... Martin passed his exams, he could go to Oxford University.   ➤ Unit 93
   A And B But C Because

11 We enjoyed the film club, ... we decided to go every week.   ➤ Unit 93
   A so B but C because

12 We bought the car .... it was a very good price.   ➤ Unit 93
   A but B because C so that

13 I'm expecting a parcel, so don't leave .... the post comes.   ➤ Unit 94
   A after B when C before

14 The children are waiting in the car .... we get back.   ➤ Unit 94
   A until B when C while

15 Please don't interrupt me .... I'm talking!   ➤ Unit 94
   A until B while C during

16 They'll phone us as soon as they .... any news.   ➤ Unit 94
   A have B will have C had

17 As soon as you .... at the airport, change this money into euros.   ➤ Unit 94
   A will arrive B arrived C arrive

18 First, the plane was late, then we had to wait a long time for our   ➤ Unit 95
   bags. After that, we waited half an hour for a bus. ...., we arrived at
   the hotel three hours late and they didn't have a room for us.
   A First B After C In the end

19 Check that you have your passport .... leaving for the airport.   ➤ Unit 95
   A before B before you C then

20 To make this soup, ... chop all the vegetables into small pieces ...   ➤ Unit 95
   A first B next C finally

Passive forms

Before you start

1 Read the magazine article. Look at the highlighted grammar examples.

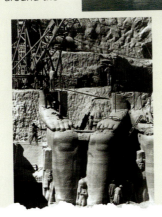

ABU SIMBEL

THE TEMPLE OF ABU SIMBEL is more than three thousand years old. The king of Egypt, Ramesses II, **had the temple built** in 1265 BC after he won a battle. The huge building was cut from the side of a mountain next to the River Nile.

For many centuries the temple **was buried** under sand until it **was discovered by Europeans in 1813.** In the 1960s the river water around the temple began to rise. People thought it might flood the temple. So in 1964 the United Nations Educational, Scientific and Cultural Organisation (UNESCO) started a project to save the temple. A team of international engineers was formed. The engineers **had the building cut into small pieces by local workers.** Then the stone pieces **were taken** to a new place high above the river and they were put into position.

Now the pieces of stone **have been joined** together and the temple **has been saved** from the rising water. Today it **can be visited** by anybody who is interested in Ancient Egypt and the amazing achievements of modern engineering.

2 Now read the sentences. Choose the correct words in *italics*.
   The highlighted grammar examples will help you.

1 The Taj Mahal was *built / building* in the eighteenth century.   ➤ Unit 96
2 Those old leather suitcases *was / were* used by my grandparents.   ➤ Unit 96
3 The telephone was invented *of / by* Alexander Graham Bell in 1876.   ➤ Unit 96
4 My mobile phone *has / have* been stolen from my bag.   ➤ Unit 97
5 For some reason all my emails have *sent / been sent* back.   ➤ Unit 97
6 This watch can *using / be used* in water.   ➤ Unit 97
7 Michael *had / made* his camera repaired last week.   ➤ Unit 98
8 He had it *repaired by the mechanic / by the mechanic repaired*.   ➤ Unit 98

3 Check your answers below. Then go to the unit for more information and practice.

1 built 2 were 3 by 4 has 5 been sent 6 be used 7 had 8 repaired by the mechanic

96 The passive (1)

Santiago Calatrava designed the Alamillo Bridge in Seville. It **was opened** in 1992.

1 Present simple and past simple

We make the passive of the present and past simple with *is/are/was/were* + the past participle. The object of an active sentence becomes the subject of the passive sentence:

They **opened** *the bridge in 1992.* (active, *bridge* = the object)

The bridge **was opened** *in 1992.* (passive, *bridge* = the subject)

	ACTIVE	PASSIVE
present simple	*We make cheese from milk.* *The farmer grows wheat crops in this field.* *We don't allow children in the restaurant.* *Does anyone ever wash these windows?*	*Cheese is made from milk.* *Wheat crops are grown in this field.* *Children aren't allowed in the restaurant.* *Are these windows ever washed?*
past simple	*Europeans found the temple in 1813.* *They didn't open the bridge until 1992.* *Did the postman deliver the letters yesterday?* *When did they discover it?*	*The temple was found in 1813.* *The bridge wasn't opened until 1992.* *Were the letters delivered yesterday?* *When was it discovered?*

 We don't make passives from verbs that don't have objects (e.g. *come, arrive, happen, wait*):
✗ ~~I was grown up in a small village.~~ ✓ *I **grew up** in a small village.*

 Born is always passive:
✗ ~~My brother born in 1995.~~ ✓ *My brother **was born** in 1995.*

2 Use

We usually use an active verb when we are interested in the person who does the action:
*Santiago Calatrava **designed** the Alamillo Bridge.*

We use a passive verb

- when we are more interested in the action than the person who did it:
  *The bridge **was opened** in 1992.*

- when we don't know the person:
  *Julia's handbag **was stolen**.* (We don't know who stole it.)

- when the action is a law or rule:
  *Smoking **is not allowed** in this building.*

3 Passive + *by*

We can say:
***Santiago Calatrava designed** the bridge.* or *The bridge **was designed by Santiago Calatrava**.*

Practice

1 Write the sentences and questions again. Use passive forms only. 🔊**4.39** Listen and check.

A I'd like to ask you some questions about the house I'm renting from
Mr and Mrs Garcia this summer.

B OK.

A Do the owners heat the swimming pool?   0 _Is the swimming pool heated_ .... ?

B No, they don't heat it.   1 No, ...

A How often does the maid clean   2 How often ....
the bedrooms?   .... ?

B She cleans them every day.   3 The bedrooms ....

A Do you include meals in the rent?   4 .... ?

B No, we don't include them.   5 No, meals ....

A When did they build the house?   6 When .... ?

B They built it four years ago.   7 It ....

A Did the owners sign the agreement   8 ....
on Friday?   .... ?

B No, they didn't sign the agreement.   9 No, it ....

A But I paid the deposit on time!   10 But the deposit .... !

2 **GRAMMAR IN USE** Choose the correct words in *italics* in the article. 🔊**4.40** Listen and check.

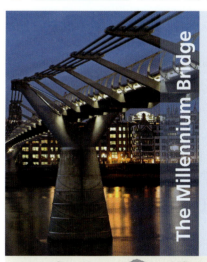

The Millennium Bridge

THIS IS THE FAMOUS MILLENNIUM BRIDGE which (0) *crosses* / *is crossed* the River Thames in London. Every day the bridge (1) *be* / *is* used by thousands of people. Many of them do not know that when the bridge first opened, there was a serious problem and it (2) *was* / *were* closed again for almost two years.

The bridge was designed (3) *by* / *from* the famous British architect, Sir Norman Foster. It (4) *opened* / *was opened* by Queen Elizabeth II on 9 May 2000 but members of the public were only allowed to use the bridge on 10 June. Over 90,000 people (5) *were used* / *used* the bridge on that first day. All the people walking on the bridge (6) *made* / *was made* it move slowly from side to side. It was a strange experience and some of the people were very frightened. The next day the same thing (7) *happened* / *was happened* again, so the bridge was (8) *closed* / *closing* until they fixed the problem.

3 Complete the second sentence so it means the same as the first.
Use one, two or three words.

0 They make cars there. Cars _are made there_ .

1 Tommy Hilfiger designed her dress. Her dress .... Tommy Hilfiger.

2 Somebody stole my dictionary yesterday. My dictionary ....

3 She cleans the windows once a week. The windows .... once a week.

4 They didn't accept your offer. Your offer ....

5 The teacher doesn't mark our homework every day. Our homework ....
every day.

97 The passive (2)

The beautiful castle at Chenonceaux **has been owned** by the Menier family since 1913.

1 Present perfect

We make the passive of the present perfect with *has/have been* + the past participle.
The object of the active sentence becomes the subject of the passive sentence:

*The Menier family **have owned** the castle since 1913.* (active, *castle* = the object)

*The castle **has been owned** by the Menier family since 1913.* (passive, *castle* = the subject)

	ACTIVE	PASSIVE
present perfect	*Scientists **have discovered** a new planet.* *They **haven't fixed** the computers yet.* ***Have** they **emptied** the bins?*	*A new planet **has been discovered.*** *The computers **haven't been fixed** yet.* ***Have** the bins **been emptied**?*

2 Modal verbs

We make the passive form of modal verbs with the modal verb + *be* + past participle:

ACTIVE	PASSIVE
*You **can wash** this shirt at 40 degrees.*	*This shirt **can be washed** at 40 degrees.*
*You **must switch off** mobile phones.*	*Mobile phones **must be switched off.***
*They **will fix** the TV tomorrow.*	*The TV **will be fixed** tomorrow.*
*You **should not wash** this dress.*	*This dress **should not be washed.***
*They **had to delay** the flight.*	*The flight **had to be delayed.***

We often use modal passives for written instructions and rules:
*Answers **must be written** in ink.*
*Mobile phones **cannot be used** during the flight.*

 Don't use *to* after *can, must, will* or *should* in active or passive sentences:
✗ *All the questions must to be answered.*
✓ *All the questions **must be answered**.*

Irregular past participles ➤ page 314

Practice

1 Choose the correct words in *italics*. 🔊 **4.41** Listen and check.

0 Julia's bag (*has*)/ *have* been stolen.
1 *Did* / *Has* your mobile phone been repaired yet?
2 An amazing new medicine has *been* / *be* discovered in America.
3 Cameras must not *be* / *to be* used inside the theatre.
4 Where is the cleaner? The beds haven't been *make* / *made* yet!
5 Money and passports can be *leave* / *left* in the hotel safe.
6 *Are* / *Have* those letters been delivered?

2 ▐GRAMMAR IN USE▌ Read the email from Judy to her boss.
Then use the information to complete the sentences below.

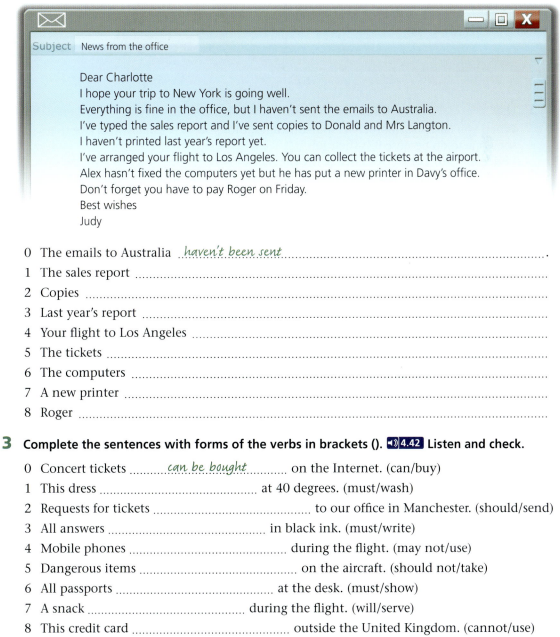

Subject | News from the office

Dear Charlotte
I hope your trip to New York is going well.
Everything is fine in the office, but I haven't sent the emails to Australia.
I've typed the sales report and I've sent copies to Donald and Mrs Langton.
I haven't printed last year's report yet.
I've arranged your flight to Los Angeles. You can collect the tickets at the airport.
Alex hasn't fixed the computers yet but he has put a new printer in Davy's office.
Don't forget you have to pay Roger on Friday.
Best wishes
Judy

0 The emails to Australia *haven't been sent* ....
1 The sales report ....
2 Copies ....
3 Last year's report ....
4 Your flight to Los Angeles ....
5 The tickets ....
6 The computers ....
7 A new printer ....
8 Roger ....

3 Complete the sentences with forms of the verbs in brackets (). 🔊 **4.42** Listen and check.

0 Concert tickets .... *can be bought* .... on the Internet. (can/buy)
1 This dress .... at 40 degrees. (must/wash)
2 Requests for tickets .... to our office in Manchester. (should/send)
3 All answers .... in black ink. (must/write)
4 Mobile phones .... during the flight. (may not/use)
5 Dangerous items .... on the aircraft. (should not/take)
6 All passports .... at the desk. (must/show)
7 A snack .... during the flight. (will/serve)
8 This credit card .... outside the United Kingdom. (cannot/use)

98 *to have something done*

> I **have my house painted** once every five years. I use a local company. They're very good.

1 Use

When you *have something done*, someone does it for you. It is usually a service that you pay someone to do because it is their job.

*I **have my hair cut** every six weeks.* (by the hairdresser)
*Carol **has her house painted** once every five years.* (by professional painters)
*How often **do you have your car checked?*** (by the garage)

We don't usually say who does the action. But if we say this, we use *by*:
*Paula has her hair cut **by Sergio** at the hairdresser's in the high street.*

NATURAL ENGLISH In everyday English, we can also say *get something done*:
*I'm going to **get** my hair **cut** tomorrow.*
*Don't forget to **get** the car **checked**.*

2 Form

We use *have* + object + the past participle of the verb:

AFFIRMATIVE AND NEGATIVE					
present simple	I/We/You/They	have	don't have		
	He/She/It	has	doesn't have		
past simple	I/He/She/It/We/You/They	had	didn't have	the house	painted.
present perfect	I/We/You/They	have had	haven't had		
	He/She/It	has had	hasn't had		

We can also use *will, can, must* and *should* + *have something done*:
*I **must have** the windows **cleaned** soon.*
*The college **will have** a new library **built** next year.*

We can ask questions:
*How often **do you have** your hair **cut?***
***Did you have** the house **painted** last year?*
***Should we have** the car **checked** before we drive to Scotland?*
***Will you have** the TV **repaired** soon?*

Practice

1 Choose the correct words in *italics*. 🔊 **4.43** Listen and check.

0 The car's very dirty. Shall I *make* /(*have*) it cleaned next time I go to the garage?
1 Mrs Aziz always *has / have* her hair done before a big party.
2 Davina's wedding photos were fantastic. She *had taken / had them taken* by a famous photographer.
3 Your computer's making a strange noise. I think you should *it have / have it* checked.
4 My neighbours have a beautiful garden. They *have / are having* the grass cut twice a week!
5 Don't forget to *get / got* my suit cleaned when you go to the dry cleaner's.
6 It was a special party so we had *prepared the food / the food prepared* by a professional chef.

2 Melinda is a film star. She has a big house and lots of people do things for her. Study the information. Then answer the question. Use the words in brackets (). 🔊 **4.44** Listen and check.

MELINDA'S STAFF:
* The gardener cuts the grass
* The cleaner makes the beds and washes the clothes
* A famous chef prepares the meals
* A professional hairdresser cuts Melinda's hair
* Her assistant organises her diary
* Her secretary types Melinda's letters

What does Melinda have done for her?
0 *She has her letters typed by her secretary.* .... (letters)
1 .... (meals)
2 .... (clothes)
3 .... (hair)
4 .... (beds)
5 .... (grass)
6 .... (diary)

3 GRAMMAR IN USE There are six more mistakes in the letter. Find and correct them.

Dear Mr Hanshaw,

Thank you for agreeing to advertise our house for sale.

We had a lot of things ~~do~~ *done* to the house and garden last year. Here is a list:

* We had the roof it repaired. Most of the roof is completely new.
* Last summer we have the outside of the house paint. We also had the kitchen and bathroom painting.
* We the new heating system had put in last winter.
* There were some improvements to the garden: we have some new trees planted and we had the walls repaired.

Review MODULE 17

1 UNITS 96 AND 97 **Read about Hampton Court Palace, then use the information to complete the sentences below. The information you need is <u>underlined</u>.**

THE STORY OF
Hampton Court Palace

In 1514 <u>Thomas Wolsey</u>, King Henry VIII's most important and richest minister, <u>bought</u> a large piece of land in Hampton Court on the River Thames, just west of London. Over the next ten years he <u>built</u> an enormous palace on the land. In 1525 <u>Wolsey gave</u> the palace to the king and since that time the palace has belonged to the kings and queens of England. Henry's daughter

<u>Queen Elizabeth I used</u> the palace during the later sixteenth century.
In 1689 King William III decided the palace was too old-fashioned and he <u>asked</u> Sir Christopher Wren to design a new section. William was Dutch and he <u>created</u> a Dutch garden in front of the new part of the palace.

Queen Victoria didn't like the palace and she didn't want to live there. So in 1838 she <u>opened</u> the palace for ordinary people to visit.
The government <u>repaired</u> the palace and gardens in the 1990s. Today the royal family doesn't use Hampton Court, so the public <u>can visit</u> the palace.

1514 – A piece of land in Hampton Court (0) ...*was bought*... by (00) ...*Thomas Wolsey*...

1514 –1524 – An enormous palace (1) .... on the land.

1525 – The palace (2) .... to the king (3) .... Thomas Wolsey.

LATER 16TH CENTURY – The palace (4) .... by (5) ....

1689 – Sir Christopher Wren (6) .... to design a new section.

1689 – A Dutch garden (7) .... in front of the new palace.

1838 – The palace (8) .... to the public by Queen Victoria.

1990s – The palace and gardens (9) .... by the government.

TODAY – The palace (10) .... by the public.

2 UNITS 97 AND 98 **Choose the correct words in *italics*.** 🔊4.45 **Listen and check.**

PEDRO Your hair looks nice.

CAROL Thank you. I (0) *have / had* it cut yesterday. I had (1) *it done / done it* at that new place on the High Street. You know, next to the Ford garage.

PEDRO Oh yes. I (2) *had my car checked / was checked my car* at that garage last month.

CAROL Have you (3) *found / been found* a new flat yet?

PEDRO No. But I saw a nice one yesterday. It's got a garden and it's just (4) *painted / been painted*, but the rent's quite expensive. What about you? You had some work (5) *done / did* at your house last month, didn't you?

CAROL Yes. We (6) *had / have* a new hot water system put in. The work is almost finished but the water in the bathroom hasn't (7) *connected / been connected* by the builders yet, so we can't have showers. Anyway, they're going to do it today.

PEDRO Your brother's a builder, isn't he? Did he (8) *do / have done* the work?

CAROL No, we (9) *had it done / was done* by someone else. My brother isn't working at the moment. He (10) *had / was had* a car accident last month and he broke his leg, so he can't do very much.

PEDRO That's awful!

3 ALL UNITS **Complete the second sentence so it means the same as the first. Use one, two or three words.**

0 They've repaired your computer.

Your computer ....*has been repaired*............

1 The driver will collect you from the station.

You .... from the station.

2 Somebody has stolen my credit card!

My credit card ....!

3 You must clean this shirt professionally.

This shirt must .... professionally.

4 Marianne cleans Michael's house.

Michael has .... by Marianne.

5 Children under the age of twelve should not take this medicine.

This medicine should .... by children under the age of twelve.

6 How often does Jenny cut your hair?

How often .... your hair cut by Jenny?

4 ALL UNITS **Complete the article with the correct words or phrases, A, B or C below.**

The Mile High Tower

This is Jeddah in Saudi Arabia, the city where the new Mile High Tower (0) .... The building will be one mile (1.6 kilometres) high and it (1) .... 375 floors. When it (2) ...., it will be the tallest building in the world.

   The company that plans to build the tower is Kingdom Holdings, which (3) .... by Prince Al-Waleed bin Talal, a nephew of the Saudi Arabian king. In a recent magazine article the Prince (4) .... as the 19th richest person in the world. He (5) .... part of EuroDisney in Paris and the Savoy Hotel in London. The famous old hotel was bought by the Prince in 2005 and he has recently (6) .... and improved.

   The Mile High Tower is the Prince's most exciting project. Many people think that such a tall building (7) ...., but the Prince is confident. He (8) .... by the American architects Pickard Chilton.

0 A will built (B) will be built   C will be build
1 A will have   B will be had   C will has
2 A are finished   B is finished   C is finish
3 A is owned   B be owned   C is own
4 A are described   B be described   C was described
5 A is owned   B owns   C be owned
6 A have repaired   B had it repaired   C had repaired it
7 A cannot build   B be cannot built   C cannot be built
8 A had plans prepared   B plans had prepared   C have plans prepared

Test MODULE 17

Passive forms

Choose the correct answer, A, B or C.

1 Our classroom .... cleaned every day.
   A are B is C being
   ➤ Unit 96

2 Every customer is .... a receipt when they pay.
   A give B gave C given
   ➤ Unit 96

3 .... the rubbish bins emptied this morning?
   A Is B Did C Were
   ➤ Unit 96

4 The *Mona Lisa* was painted .... Leonardo da Vinci.
   A to B by C of
   ➤ Unit 96

5 I can't send any emails because my laptop .... last week.
   A stolen B was stolen C had stolen
   ➤ Unit 96

6 Those films .... in Hollywood.
   A are making B was made C were made
   ➤ Unit 96

7 That ring is very old. ....
   A It was made in 1850. B In 1850 somebody made it.
   C Somebody made it in 1850.
   ➤ Unit 96

8 .... those houses been sold?
   A Have B Has C Are
   ➤ Unit 97

9 .... to Linda's birthday party?
   A Who has been invited B Has been invited who
   C Who has invited been
   ➤ Unit 97

10 Has your mobile phone .... yet?
    A been repaired by somebody B been repaired C is repaired
    ➤ Unit 97

11 I'll email you because the new phone line .... been put in yet.
    A haven't B hasn't C don't have
    ➤ Unit 97

12 Your exam results ....!
    A have arrived B have been arrived C were arrived
    ➤ Unit 97

13 The application form must .... in before the end of the month.
    A be sent B to be sent C sent
    ➤ Unit 97

14 Your order .... next Thursday.
    A will delivering B will to be delivered C will be delivered
    ➤ Unit 97

15 James has his car .... twice a year.
    A check B checking C checked
    ➤ Unit 98

16 We will probably .... by a professional company.
    A have the party organised B have organised the party
    C organised the party
    ➤ Unit 98

17 .... the bedroom painted or will you do it yourself?
    A Will you B Will have you C Will you have
    ➤ Unit 98

18 They had the photos taken .... a professional photographer.
    A from B by C of
    ➤ Unit 98

19 I must .... cleaned – it's very dirty.
    A got my car B the car C get my car
    ➤ Unit 98

20 My mobile isn't working. I need to ....
    A have it repaired B have repaired C it repaired
    ➤ Unit 98

Words that go together

Before you start

1 Read the job advertisement and the letter. Look at the <mark>highlighted</mark> grammar examples.

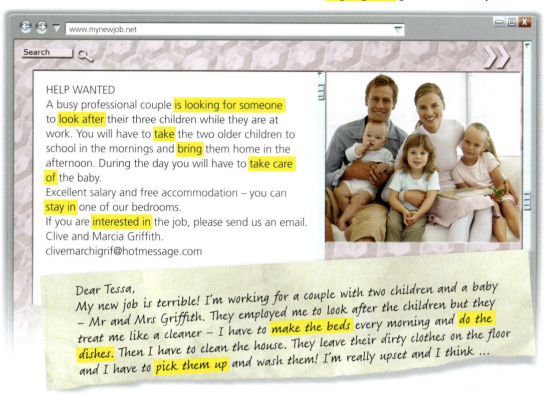

www.mynewjob.net

Search

HELP WANTED
A busy professional couple <mark>is looking for someone</mark> to <mark>look after</mark> their three children while they are at work. You will have to <mark>take</mark> the two older children to school in the mornings and <mark>bring</mark> them home in the afternoon. During the day you will have to <mark>take care of</mark> the baby.
Excellent salary and free accommodation – you can <mark>stay in</mark> one of our bedrooms.
If you are <mark>interested in</mark> the job, please send us an email.
Clive and Marcia Griffith.
clivemarchigrif@hotmessage.com

Dear Tessa,
My new job is terrible! I'm working for a couple with two children and a baby – Mr and Mrs Griffith. They employed me to look after the children but they treat me like a cleaner – I have to <mark>make the beds</mark> every morning and <mark>do the dishes.</mark> Then I have to clean the house. They leave their dirty clothes on the floor and I have to <mark>pick them up</mark> and wash them! I'm really upset and I think …

2 Now read the sentences. Choose the correct words in *italics*.
The <mark>highlighted</mark> grammar examples will help you.

1 I'm not really interested *of* / *in* business.	➤ Unit 99
2 My boss is away so I'm going to *take* / *have* care of that project.	➤ Unit 99
3 Are you looking *a new job for* / *for a new job*?	➤ Unit 100
4 Don't worry. I'll look *at* / *after* the pets while you're away.	➤ Unit 101
5 Are you staying *in* / *with* a hotel?	➤ Unit 101
6 Don't leave paper on the floor. *Pick up it* / *Pick it up* and put it in the bin, please.	➤ Unit 102
7 You will be able to *take* / *bring* the prize away at the end of the competition.	➤ Unit 103
8 Can you lend me your umbrella? I forgot to *bring* / *take* one when I came here.	➤ Unit 103
9 I usually cook the meal and my wife *makes* / *does* the dishes.	➤ Unit 104
10 Mrs Lombard has a cleaner so she never has to *do* / *make* the beds herself.	➤ Unit 104

3 Check your answers below. Then go to the unit for more information and practice.

1 in 2 take 3 for a new job 4 after 5 in 6 Pick it up 7 take 8 bring 9 does 10 make

99 Words that go together

1 Verb + noun

Here are some common examples of verbs and nour
that go together:

VERB	NOUN
do	the housework the dishes the cleaning your homework an exercise
make	dinner a mistake a noise the beds friends
take	an exam a test a photo
pass/fail	an exam a test
play	a sport a game
drive	a car
ride	a bike a horse

*I often listen to the radio while I **do the dishes**.*
*Can you **ride a bike**?*
*I haven't **taken my** driving **test** yet.*

A few verbs and nouns that go together usually have
a preposition after them (e.g. *take care of, take part in
make friends with*):
*Have you **made friends with** anyone in your new class?*
*Can you **take care of** the baby while I go to the shops?*

More examples of *make/do/take* + noun ➤ Unit 104

Carla was **good at** cleaning.
The hotel manager was always
pleased with her work.

2 Adjective + noun

Some adjectives and nouns go together:
*a **strong** swimmer* = a person who can swim very well
*a **good** driver* = a person who can drive very well (**✗** *a strong driver*)

Here are some common examples:
*smart clothes, a smart suit, a tall building, a high wall, a heavy smoker, heavy rain,
a light meal/lunch/dinner, a strong smell, a hard worker*

*I usually have **a light meal** at lunchtime.*
*You should wear **a smart suit** for that job interview.*

These are often different in other languages, so it is best to check in a good dictionary.

3 Adjective + preposition

We often use a preposition after an adjective and before the noun that follows it:

FEELINGS	ABILITIES	BEHAVIOUR	OTHERS
afraid of angry with excited about interested in pleased with worried about	good at bad at	kind to nice to	different from famous for

*Carla was **good at** cleaning. The hotel manager was always **pleased with** her work.*
*Paris is **famous for** its beautiful buildings.*

When we put a verb after the preposition we use the *-ing* form:
*I'm really **bad at cooking**. Are you **excited about going** on holiday?*

Prepositions + nouns, e.g. *at home, on time, for sale* ➤ Unit 24

Practice

1 **Match the two parts of the sentences.** 🔊 **4.46 Listen and check.**

0 1 I recently learnt how to ride ——→ A a car.
    2 I don't know how to drive ——→ B a bike.

1 1 Have you taken   A the exam?
    2 Did you do   B your homework?

2 1 She's very good   A for delicious food.
    2 France is famous   B at cooking.

3 1 Kristof is a hard   A swimmer.
    2 Lizzie is a strong   B worker.

4 1 I'm very excited   A in the news.
    2 I'm not very interested   B about the news.

5 1 Sue's worried   A of the dark.
    2 Sally's afraid   B about her job.

2 **GRAMMAR IN USE** **Complete the conversation with words from the box. There are three extra words.** 🔊 **4.47 Listen and check.**

about at done for from hard in made of pass smart strong ~~taken~~ with

SOPHIE How are the children, Anna?

ANNA Oh, fine. Steven's just (0) ..... _taken_ ..... a science exam.

SOPHIE Did he (1) .... it?

ANNA Yes, he got 88 percent. He's always been good (2) .... science.

SOPHIE And how's Carrie? How's she getting on at her new school?

ANNA Very well. Of course, it's very different (3) .... her old school, but she seems very interested (4) .... the lessons and she's (5) .... friends with lots of the other children.

SOPHIE That's good.

ANNA What about you? Are you still working with children?

SOPHIE Yes. I'm taking care (6) .... three young children at the moment. By the way, that's a very (7) .... suit you're wearing. Are you going somewhere special?

ANNA Yes, I'm going for a job interview. I'm really excited (8) .... it.

SOPHIE I'm sure you'll get it. Everyone knows you're a (9) .... worker. Well, I must hurry. I haven't even (10) .... the dishes yet!

3 **Complete the second sentence so that it means the same as the first. Use one, two or three words.**

0 That building has many floors.   It's .... _a tall_ .... building.
1 Jim can swim very well.   Jim is .... swimmer.
2 Mandy doesn't eat much for lunch.   Mandy prefers .... lunch.
3 John didn't pass the exam.   John ....
4 Uncle Leroy smokes a lot.   Uncle Leroy is ....
5 Sara's boss made her angry.   Sara was .... her boss.
6 Your book isn't the same as mine.   Your book .... mine.

100 Verb + preposition (1)

Jim phoned the electrical shop and **spoke to the manager**.
He **complained about his new vacuum cleaner**.

1 Verb + preposition + object

After some verbs (e.g. *complain*, *look*) we need a preposition BEFORE the object:

verb	+	object		verb	+	preposition	+	object
Jim phoned		*the shop*	*and*	*complained*		*about*	*his*	*new vacuum cleaner* .
Sue ate		*a sandwich*	*and*	*looked*		*at*		*a magazine* .

Look at the word order in questions:
*Are you **complaining about** the camera? Which camera are you **complaining about**?*
*What are you **looking at**?*

2 Verb + preposition

Here are some common verbs + prepositions:

verb + *to*	belong to explain to listen to speak to talk to write to
verb + *about*	complain about read about speak about talk about think about
verb + *for*	apply for look for pay for wait for work for
verb + *in*	arrive in believe in get in live in succeed in stay in
verb + *of*	approve of think of
verb + *on*	depend on decide on
verb + *at*	arrive at laugh at look at stay at
verb + *with*	agree with stay with

*We've been **waiting for** half an hour! What are you **listening to**?*
*Maria is right. I **agree with** her.*

 If there is a verb after the preposition, we use the *-ing* form:
✗ *I'm thinking of buy a new car.* ✓ *I'm thinking **of buying** a new car.*

 We don't use *to* after the verbs *ask, answer, call, phone* and *thank*:
✗ *Please phone to me later.* ✓ *Please **phone me** later.*

 We don't use *about* after *discuss*:
✗ *We discussed about the weather.* ✓ *We **discussed the weather**.*

3 Verb + *to/about*

We often use *to* before people and *about* before things:
*I saw Lucy **talking to** Jake. They were **talking about** Jake's party.*

A verb can be followed by more than one preposition + noun in a sentence:
*I complained **to the manager about the vacuum cleaner**.*

Practice

1 **Match the two parts of the sentences.**

0 That book belongs   A in luck.
1 She often complains   B to the library.
2 You have to apply   C at your visa.
3 Let me look   D on other people.
4 I don't believe   E about the weather.
5 She doesn't approve   F of my friends.
6 You should never depend   G for a visa.

2 **GRAMMAR IN USE** Choose the correct words in *italics* in the text. ◀))4.48 Listen and check.

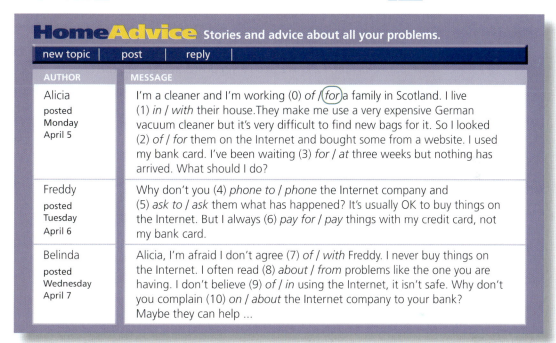

Home Advice Stories and advice about all your problems.

| new topic | post | reply | |

AUTHOR	MESSAGE
Alicia posted Monday April 5	I'm a cleaner and I'm working (0) *of / for* a family in Scotland. I live (1) *in / with* their house. They make me use a very expensive German vacuum cleaner but it's very difficult to find new bags for it. So I looked (2) *of / for* them on the Internet and bought some from a website. I used my bank card. I've been waiting (3) *for / at* three weeks but nothing has arrived. What should I do?
Freddy posted Tuesday April 6	Why don't you (4) *phone to / phone* the Internet company and (5) *ask to / ask* them what has happened? It's usually OK to buy things on the Internet. But I always (6) *pay for / pay* things with my credit card, not my bank card.
Belinda posted Wednesday April 7	Alicia, I'm afraid I don't agree (7) *of / with* Freddy. I never buy things on the Internet. I often read (8) *about / from* problems like the one you are having. I don't believe (9) *of / in* using the Internet, it isn't safe. Why don't you complain (10) *on / about* the Internet company to your bank? Maybe they can help ...

3 **GRAMMAR IN USE** Complete the phone conversation with prepositions. Write (–) if you do not need a preposition. ◀))4.49 Listen and check.

AGENT Good morning. Apex Cleaning.

MARTA Hello. I'm looking (0) ..*for*.... some part-time cleaning work.

AGENT OK. First, I need to ask (1) .... you – do you have any experience?

MARTA Yes. I'm working for SuperClean at the moment, but I'm thinking (2) ....
changing my job.

AGENT How long have you worked there and why do you want to change?

MARTA I've worked (3) .... them for about six months. But I live outside the city now and
SuperClean doesn't pay (4) .... my transport. Your office is much closer to my house.

AGENT I see. Which area do you live (5) ....?

MARTA Solihull.

AGENT Have you applied (6) .... a job with us before? Or spoken (7) .... a member
of staff?

MARTA Well, I phoned (8) .... your office last week but nobody answered ...

101 Verb + preposition (2)

You **look after** the baby – I'll **look for** the milk.

1 Verb + preposition + object

After some verbs, the preposition we use depends on the object:

arrive	arrive *in* (a town or country)	*When did you **arrive in** England?*
	arrive *at* (any other place)	*The train **arrived at** Victoria Station at six o'clock.*
pay	pay (a person or a bill) (no preposition)	*My mother **paid** the bill/the waiter.*
	pay *for* (a thing)	*I haven't **paid for** the tickets yet.*
stay	stay *in/at* (a place)	*She **stayed at** the Hilton Hotel last month.*
	stay *with* (a person)	*I'm **staying with** my cousins for the holidays.*

2 Different preposition, different meaning

The meaning of some verbs changes with the prepositions, eg:

- *look at* = turn your eyes towards something or someone:
  '**Look at** the clock. We're late!'
- *look for* = try to find something:
  *Excuse me. I'm **looking for** Dr Watson's office. Do you know where it is?*
- *look after* = take care of someone/something:
  *A friend **looks after** the children while Emily is at work.*
- *look like* = have a similar appearance:
  *Michael **looks like** his grandfather. They are both tall and slim.*

3 Verb + object + preposition

With some verbs (e.g. *ask, thank, invite, tell*) we need a preposition AFTER the object:

verb   object   preposition

I *asked* *the stranger* *for* *directions to the post office.*

ask somebody for something	*Did you **ask the doctor for** some advice?*
thank somebody for something	*The manager **thanked the staff for** their hard work.*
invite somebody to something	*I **invited Carla to** my party.*
tell somebody about something	*Have you **told your parents about** your new job yet?*

Practice

1 Complete the sentences with the correct prepositions.

0 Grandma loves looking ....*at*.... her old photos.

1 'He looks .... his father!'

2 I've just arrived .... the station.'

3 Caroline's looking .... her earring.

4 'Have you told your parents .... your exam result?'

5 'Excuse me. You haven't paid .... your meal!'

2 Write the words in the correct order. 🔊 **4.50** Listen and check.

0 about have told you Karel your new job ? *Have you told Karel about your new job?*

1 pay how much the meal did you for ?

....

2 at those people me are looking

....

3 to have your party you invited my brother ?

....

4 my teacher I some extra homework for asked

....

5 thanked for Sandra the birthday present her mother

....

3 **GRAMMAR IN USE** Complete the email. Use a verb from A and a word or phrase from B for each space. 🔊 **4.51** Listen and check.

A ~~arrived~~ collecting invited look pay staying told   B after ~~at~~ him me the bill us with

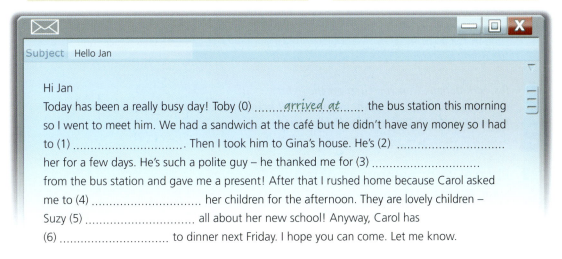

Subject Hello Jan

Hi Jan
Today has been a really busy day! Toby (0) ....*arrived at*........ the bus station this morning so I went to meet him. We had a sandwich at the café but he didn't have any money so I had to (1) .... Then I took him to Gina's house. He's (2) ....
her for a few days. He's such a polite guy – he thanked me for (3) ....
from the bus station and gave me a present! After that I rushed home because Carol asked me to (4) .... her children for the afternoon. They are lovely children – Suzy (5) .... all about her new school! Anyway, Carol has (6) .... to dinner next Friday. I hope you can come. Let me know.

102 Phrasal verbs

We should **take** our shoes **off** before we go in.

In Japan visitors usually remove their shoes before they enter a house.

1 Verb + adverb

A phrasal verb is a verb + an adverb/preposition, e.g. *take* + *off* (= *take off*).
It usually has a different meaning from the verb alone:
*It's cold. You should **take** a jumper with you.*
*It's warm. I'm going to **take off** my jumper.* (*take off* = remove)

In formal English we often use a different verb with the same meaning as the phrasal verb:
*Why don't you **take off** your shoes?* (informal) = *Please **remove** your shoes.* (formal)

2 Phrasal verbs with an object

Many phrasal verbs have an object:
*Please take off **your shoes**.*

> **put on** (put something on) to put clothes on your body:
> Put your coat on – it's cold outside! | Let me put on my
> glasses – I can't read this. > opposite TAKE OFF.

If the object is a noun, we can put it before or after the adverb/preposition:
*Please **put your jacket on**. Please **put on your jacket**.*

⚠ But we always put pronoun objects (e.g. *it, him, them*) between the verb and
adverb/preposition:
✗ *Put on it.* ✓ *Put **it** on.*

Here are some common phrasal verbs that have an object:

bring/give/put something back	*pick somebody up*
fill something in (= complete a form)	(= collect somebody and take them somewhere)
find something out (= get information)	*put something down*
give something up	*put something on*
(= stop a habit, activity or job)	*switch/turn something on/off*
let somebody in	*take something away*
look something up	*take something off*
(= find in a book, etc.)	*turn something down* (= reduce the sound)
pick something up	*write something down*

*It's dark in here. Can you **turn on** the lights?*
*I'll **take** your computer **away** today and I'll **bring** it **back** on Friday.*
*Liz is on a diet so she's **giving up** chocolate.*

 Pronunciation ➤ 1.34

3 Phrasal verbs without an object

Some phrasal verbs have no object:

*come back come in get out get up go away go back go in go out grow up hurry up
lie down look round look out* (= be careful) *sit down stand up turn around wake up*

Hurry up! *We're late. I usually **wake up** early. **Look out!** A car's coming.*

Practice

1 Match the two parts of the sentences. ◀)) **4.52** Listen and check.

0   It's dark in here. You should turn   A   a jacket on.
1   Your TV is too loud, please turn   B   it in.
2   It's hot in here – why don't you take   C   on the lights.
3   Here's the application form – please fill   D   your jacket off?
4   It's a formal meeting, you should put   E   down.
5   I'm quite tired. I think I'm going to lie   F   it down.

2 Match the sentences with similar meanings. Then decide which sentences
are formal (F) and informal (I).

0   I can find that out for you. ....*I*....   A   Do not remove the book's cover. ....
1   Our representative will collect   B   Look out! ....
    you from the airport.   C   I can get the information
2   You have to bring them back. ....   you need. ....*F*....
3   Please be careful. ....   D   They have to fill it in. ....
4   Don't take it off. ....   E   Readers must return all the
5   Please ask your parents to complete   books. ....
    the form. ....   F   We'll pick you up. ....

3 GRAMMAR IN USE Complete the conversation. Use one word only for each question.
◀)) **4.53** Listen and check.

JACKIE   Hurry (0) ...*up*..., you two! You'll be late for school.
         It's cold – you should both put (1) .... your coats.

EMMA   Where's my coat, Jackie?

JACKIE   I (2) .... it back in the hall cupboard yesterday.

EMMA   Are you picking us (3) .... from school today?

JACKIE   No, Emma. Mrs Stevens is going to bring (4) ....
         back. Now what's that on Harry's coat? (5) ....
         around, Harry. Oh, it's only a piece of paper.

HARRY   Jackie, can I borrow your camera for my geography trip?

JACKIE   All right. But be careful with it. Don't forget to give it
         (6) .... to me later.

HARRY   OK. I'll (7) .... it back this afternoon. Oh, how do you turn (8) .... on?

JACKIE   You press the red button. And to turn it (9) .... you press the black one.

HARRY   I see. Are we going swimming on Saturday?

JACKIE   I don't know but I'll find (10) .... for you. Now come on, we're late ...

4 Complete the sentences. Use a verb from A and a pronoun from B.

A   give back   let in   look up   ~~put on~~   take away   turn down   B   him   it (x 3)   me   ~~them~~

0   My grandmother wears glasses – she ....*puts them on*.... when she's reading.
1   If you don't want your old fridge, I'll ....
2   John's at the door – can you ....?
3   Please .... my dictionary – I need it.
4   I don't know the answer but I'll .... on the Internet.
5   Your music's too loud! Can you ....?

103 Confusing verbs

Karel –
The delivery men are **bringing** the new fridge at 11. Make sure they **take** the old one with them!
Jenny

1 *bring/come* or *take/go*

bring/come (movement towards or with the speaker)	*Will you **bring** your camera?* (when you come here) *Are you **coming** to the cinema tonight?* (= Are you coming with me?)
take/go (movement away from or without the speaker)	*Will you **take** your camera?* (when you go away on holiday) *Are you **going** to the cinema tonight?* (= I'm not going.)

2 *live* or *stay*

We use *live* to talk about permanent situations or long periods of time:
*Most British people **live** in towns. I've **lived** in Cape Town since 2002.*

We use *stay* for temporary situations:
*We went to Holland on holiday and **stayed** in Amsterdam. How long are you **staying** here?*

stay + with/in/at ➤ Unit 101.1

3 *do the cooking/cleaning*, *go swimming/dancing*, etc.

We use *do + the + -ing* for some activities, usually jobs around the house.
We use *go + -ing* for activities that we enjoy, usually sports or leisure:

do the	*cleaning, washing, cooking, gardening*, etc.
go	*swimming, dancing, skiing, camping, riding, hiking*, etc.

We can use *do* or *go* with *shopping*:
*Have you **done the shopping** yet?* (for food)
*We're **going shopping** this afternoon.* (for food or other things, e.g. clothes)

 ✗ *I want to do camping this summer.*   ✓ *I want to **go camping** this summer.*

4 *get*

We often use *get*:

to mean *buy, bring*, or *receive*	*Can you **get** some coffee?* (buy) *I'll **get** the dictionary for you.* (bring) *Did you **get** a letter from the bank?* (receive)
to mean *become*	*The weather's **getting hotter**.* *I hope you **get better/well** soon.* (become well again after an illness)
in common phrases, e.g. *get married, get dressed, get wet, get lost*	*They **got married** last April.* *Take an umbrella or you'll **get wet**.*
to talk about going or arriving somewhere	*How do you **get to** the airport from here?* *What time do you usually **get home**?*

Phrasal verbs with *get*, e.g. *get up* ➤ Unit 102.3

Practice

1 Complete the sentences with a form of *come*, *go*, *take* or *bring*.

 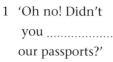   

1 'Oh no! Didn't you .... our passports?'

2 Barbara didn't .... to her neighbours' party. They didn't invite her.

3 'This year we're .... the children camping for the first time.'

4 'We're going to the concert now. Are you .... with us?'

2 GRAMMAR IN USE **Jane looks after Zara's children. Read Zara's note to Jane and choose the correct <u>underlined</u> words. ◀)4.54 Listen and check.**

Jane,
Here is the list of things I'd like you to do today after I've (0) <u>come</u> / gone to work:
- (1) <u>Take</u> / <u>Bring</u> Jake to the dentist. His appointment is at 10.15. His teeth are (2) <u>making</u> / <u>getting</u> better, but tell me what the dentist says.
- Please (3) <u>do</u> / <u>make</u> the washing – the dirty clothes are on top of the washing machine.
- I (4) <u>took</u> / <u>brought</u> some fresh vegetables from the market yesterday – please use them to make lunch for the children.
- When you do (5) <u>shopping</u> / <u>the shopping</u>, don't forget to (6) <u>get</u> / <u>do</u> my mother's medicine from the chemist's – she is (7) <u>living</u> / <u>staying</u> here at the weekend and she will need it.
- I'm (8) <u>going</u> / <u>coming</u> home at about six o'clock today, so you don't have to prepare dinner.
Thanks! Zara

3 GRAMMAR IN USE **Complete the conversation with the words from the box. There are three extra words. ◀)4.55 Listen and check.**

come do doing ~~done~~ get getting go going got live make stay took went

MIKE Have you (0) .....*done*..... the shopping yet?

DAVE Yes, I (1) .... lots of food this morning. It's all in the fridge.

MIKE Are you (2) .... the cooking this evening?

DAVE No, I'm (3) .... ice skating with Alex. He's really good at it. Of course I'm not as good as him – but I'm (4) .... better all the time.

MIKE Why don't you (5) .... at home tonight? I hate eating alone.

DAVE I don't like being at home every evening. I (6) .... bored. Listen, why don't you (7) .... to the ice rink with us?

MIKE No thanks! I (8) .... skating with my brother when I was ten. He (9) .... me to a frozen lake – I fell over and broke my arm!

DAVE Mmm. Well, if you're not going out, you could (10) .... the cleaning ...

104 *make* or *do*, *have* or *take*?

Miranda is **making clay pots and dishes**. David is **doing the dishes**.

1 *make* or *do*?

We often use the verb *make* to talk about creating or producing something:
*Mercedes cars **are made** in Germany.*
*Who**'s making** lunch today?*

We often use *do* to talk about any activity:
*What **do** you usually **do** at the weekends?*
*I'm afraid I **haven't done** the report yet.*

Here are some common words we use with *make* and *do*:

make	*a meal breakfast lunch dinner a phone call a noise a mistake an appointment an arrangement a suggestion a plan the bed a copy*
do	*the shopping the gardening your homework an exercise a test an exam the housework the cleaning the washing the cooking the dishes*

***Don't make** any noise – **I'm doing my homework**.*
*On Saturday mornings I **do the cleaning** and my wife **makes lunch**.*

2 *have* or *take*?

We can describe some actions with either *have* or *take*:

have or take	*a bath a shower a break a holiday a rest a seat (= sit down)*

*Have you **taken your break** yet?*
*Yes, I **had a break** at eleven o'clock.*

But for some actions we only use *take*:

take	*an exam a test care (of) medicine drugs a message part in a photo*

*Mrs Carshaw isn't here. Can I **take a message**?*
*You aren't allowed to **take photos** in the museum.*

We usually use *take*, not *have*, to talk about time (days, hours, etc.):
*That letter **took three days** to get here.*
***How long does** it **take** to boil an egg?*

have for doing things, e.g. *have breakfast, have a party* ➤ Unit 43.3

Practice

1 GRAMMAR IN USE **Choose the correct words in *italics* in the advertisement.**
🔊 **4.56 Listen and check.**

HouseMate *X2*
The robot that (0) *makes* / ~~does~~ all your housework!

The **HouseMate** *X2* is a new kind of robot.
It (1) *makes* / *does* all the jobs that you hate!
It can (2) *make* / *do* the beds every morning and then (3) *make* / *do* the washing.
Then it will (4) *make* / *do* your lunch for you.
And afterwards it will (5) *make* / *do* the dishes!
It can even (6) *make* / *do* phone calls,
(7) *make* / *take* messages and
(8) *make* / *take* appointments. And, believe it or not, it can (9) *make* / *take* care of children!
The **HouseMate** *X2*
is (10) *made* / *done* in Japan.

Only $495

2 **Answer the questions. Use *make*, *do* or *take* in each answer.**

0 What do carpenters do? *They make things from wood.*
1 What do photocopiers do? ....
2 What do gardeners do? ....
3 What do telephone answering machines do? ....
4 What do cooks do? ....
5 What do photographers do? ....
6 What do washing machines do? ....

3 GRAMMAR IN USE **Complete the article with forms of *make*, *do*, *have* or *take*.**

Local Hero Alison Doughty

ALISON DOUGHTY RETIRED last year. She didn't want to stay at home and (0) ......*do*...... nothing, so she decided to become a home help. Each day she visits old people in their homes and helps them.

Some of the old people can't (1) .... housework so Alison has to (2) .... their beds and (3) .... the cleaning. If they have problems with walking, she will go out and

(4) .... their shopping. Sometimes she even (5) .... lunch for the old people – Alison says that is her favourite part of the job. A lot of the old people have health problems so Alison checks that they (6) .... the correct medicines at the right time of the day. If they need to see a doctor or dentist, she can phone and (7) .... an appointment for them.

Alison tells us she really enjoys (8) .... care of old people.

4 **Find four more mistakes in the sentences and correct them. Tick (✓) the correct sentences.**
🔊 **4.57 Listen and check.**

0 How long does it ~~have~~ *take* to get to the station?
1 Did you have a shower this morning?
2 It had three hours to get here today!
3 Kyle has just taken his driving test.
4 I'm sorry. I've done a silly mistake.
5 Sue did a good suggestion tonight.
6 We're very tired. Shall we take a break?
7 I'm going to make the shopping – do you need anything?

Review MODULE 18

1 UNITS 99 AND 100 **Match the two parts of the sentences.**

0 Are you excited ⎯⎯⎯⎯⎯   A for a better job?
1 Is this job different   B in getting that job?
2 Are you looking   C from the old job?
3 Is Roger good   D of his job?
4 Did she succeed   ⎯⎯→ E about your new job?
5 What does Tim think   F at his job?

2 UNITS 99, 100 AND 101 **Write the second sentence so it has a similar meaning to the first.
Use the word in brackets ().**

0 Mandy smokes a lot. (smoker) ...... *Mandy is a heavy smoker.* ....

1 I don't have the same opinion as Jim. (agree) ....

2 Gerry doesn't drive very well. (driver) ....

3 My brother likes his new car. (pleased) ....

4 Alicia said I could come to her party on Friday. (invited) ....

5 Your MP3 player isn't the same as mine. (different) ....

6 Who bought the tickets? (paid) ....

7 I'm trying to find the post office. (looking)..

8 When will you get to the railway station? (arrive) ....

3 UNITS 101 AND 102 **Put the words in brackets () in the correct order.
Then complete the conversation.** 🔊 **4.58** **Listen and check.**

DANIEL   Hello, Helen. When did (0) ...*you arrive in town*...... (arrive/town/you/in)?

HELEN   I got here yesterday. I'm (1) .... (my parents/with/staying).

DANIEL   Is this your new baby? She's lovely. She (2) ....
         (like/you/looks).

HELEN   Thanks. My mother's helping me to (3) .... (look/her/after).

DANIEL   That's nice of her. But she has a job too, doesn't she?

HELEN   No. She's (4) .... (it/up/given). She (5) ....
         (her boss/for/asked/a promotion) but she didn't get it.

DANIEL   That's a pity. But of course it means she can (6) ....
         (home/at/stay) and help you with the baby.

HELEN   Yes.

DANIEL   Can I (7) .... (her/up/pick)?

HELEN   Of course. But be careful, she's sleeping. By the way, (8) ....
         (the/present/you/thank/for) you sent. That was really nice of you.

DANIEL   Oh, it's nothing ... Have I (9) .... (about/told/my new job/you)
         yet?

HELEN   No. What is it?

DANIEL   I'm working at the art gallery. I check people's tickets and (10) ....
         (them/in/let) to the exhibitions.

HELEN   That's interesting. What exhibition is on at the moment?

4 UNITS 103 AND 104 **Complete the text with the best words or phrases, A, B or C below.**

Dear Laura,

Here's some information about your new job.

We would like you to wake the children up and (0) .... their breakfast in the morning, then you can (1) .... them to school. (You don't have to (2) .... to the school in the afternoons because the children (3) .... home on the school bus.) We don't expect you to (4) .... any cleaning but we would like you to (5) .... the beds. I'm afraid I don't have time to go (6) .... so I will give you money and you can (7) .... everything you need at the supermarket; it only (8) .... a few minutes to drive there.

Please remember to (9) .... your driving licence and passport with you. We would like to (10) .... copies of them.

Best wishes,

Helen Matherson

0	A do	B make	C have
1	A take	B bring	C get
2	A come	B go	C bring
3	A come	B go	C take
4	A do	B make	C take
5	A do	B make	C get

6	A the shopping	B shop	C shopping
7	A shop	B get	C have
8	A takes	B has	C makes
9	A take	B do	C bring
10	A do	B make	C bring

5 ALL UNITS **Complete the crossword.**

ACROSS

2 Jane looks ... our children when we're at work.
4 Are you ... to the party with us?
5 It's cold outside. You should ... your coat on.
6 Venice is ... for its canals and beautiful buildings.
8 Can you ... a bicycle?
9 I'm not very hungry so I only want a ... meal.
10 Have you ... the washing yet?
11 My best friend ... married last week.
12 Can you ... me to the airport tomorrow?
14 The traffic was terrible; It ... an hour to get here.
15 Shall I take ... of the baby while you do the shopping?
16 Tell me about your new friend. What does she look ... ?

DOWN

1 I don't know if I want it; it ... on the price.
3 Zara's a ... swimmer; she's in the school team.
5 Are you going to take ... in the charity race?
7 We're really worried ... the test tomorrow.
9 Someone's at the door. Can you ... them in?
11 Sorry about your illness – I hope you ... better soon.
13 You're right; I ... with you.

Test MODULE 18

Words that go together

Choose the correct answer, A, B or C.

1 How many exercises did you .... at the gym this morning?
A have B take C do
➤ Unit 99

2 I'm busy. Can you take care .... the baby for a minute?
A of B for C with
➤ Unit 99

3 Dharma will pass her test. She's a .... driver.
A good B strong C well
➤ Unit 99

4 My brother's very excited .... his new job.
A of B about C for
➤ Unit 99

5 Philip went to the hotel reception and ....
A about the room complained B complained about the room
C complained the room about
➤ Unit 100

6 Hurry up. I've been waiting .... hours!
A of B at C for
➤ Unit 100

7 I think you're wrong. I don't agree .... you.
A with B of C at
➤ Unit 100

8 My grandmother is thinking of .... for a whole week.
A to stay B stay C staying
➤ Unit 100

9 How much did you .... your motorbike?
A pay B pay of C pay for
➤ Unit 101

10 Justin is very handsome – he looks .... a film star.
A after B like C for
➤ Unit 101

11 After the lesson I asked .... some advice.
A my teacher for B to my teacher C for my teacher
➤ Unit 101

12 It's hot now. I think I'll .... my jacket.
A take B take on C take off
➤ Unit 102

13 I don't eat chocolate any more. I've ....
A given it up B given up it C it given up
➤ Unit 102

14 When I say your name, please ....
A stand up B stand up you C stand you up
➤ Unit 102

15 Hi, Steve, it's me. Are you .... here this evening or not?
A going B taking C coming
➤ Unit 103

16 In my country a lot of people .... in small villages.
A live B stay C get
➤ Unit 103

17 I think the weather is .... colder.
A getting B making C being
➤ Unit 103

18 Be quiet. I need to .... an important phone call.
A do B have C make
➤ Unit 104

19 People don't believe me but I actually enjoy .... the cleaning.
A doing B making C getting
➤ Unit 104

20 Mrs Bradley isn't here. Would you like me to .... a message for her?
A take B make C do
➤ Unit 104

Forming words

Before you start

1 Read the advertisement. Look at the highlighted grammar examples.

SALE starts 2 SEPTEMBER!!!

BLAKE'S
Home & Garden Centre

- Special prices on comfort**able** leather sofas and armchairs.
- A large range of **in**expensive garden tools and garden furniture.
- **Dining room** furniture at low, low prices.
- A wide range of kitchen equipment from **well-known** makes such as Miele and Siemens.
- 20% discount for professional build**ers**.
- Experienced and help**ful** staff.
- Free car parking for all visit**ors** to the store.

For more inform**ation** visit our website: www.blakeshomeandgarden.net

2 Now read the sentences. Use the words and ideas in brackets () to complete them. The highlighted grammar examples will help you.

1 Young .... have more accidents than older ones. (a noun from *drive*)	➤ Unit 105
2 Who is your favourite ....? (a noun from *act*)	➤ Unit 105
3 When is your next ....? (the noun from *examine*)	➤ Unit 105
4 Carla's sister is very .... (an adjective from *beauty*)	➤ Unit 106
5 Is long hair .... at the moment? (an adjective from *fashion*)	➤ Unit 106
6 I'm afraid that answer is .... (not correct)	➤ Unit 106
7 The flat has two bedrooms and a large .... (a room you live in)	➤ Unit 107
8 I have a .... job with an IT company. (I get paid a lot of money)	➤ Unit 107

3 Check your answers below. Then go to the unit for more information and practice.

1 drivers 2 actor 3 examination 4 beautiful 5 fashionable 6 incorrect 7 living room 8 well-paid

105 Forming nouns

I asked for a **cook**, not a **cooker**!

1 Nouns that end in *-er*, *-or*, *-ant/-ent* and *-ist*

These nouns are often people and their jobs
(e.g. *a teacher*, *a dentist*):

VERB OR NOUN	+	= PERSON/JOB
teach drive build	-er	*teacher driver builder*
visit act	-or	*visitor actor*
assist study	-ant/-ent	*assistant student*
art journal cycle	-ist	*artist journalist cyclist*

Some nouns that end in *-er* are things, not people:
cooker = a machine that cooks things
photocopier = a machine that makes copies

2 Nouns that end in *-ese*, *-(i)an* and *-ish*

These nouns are often nationalities and/or languages. They are also used as adjectives:

COUNTRY	+	= NATIONALITY/LANGUAGE/ADJECTIVE
China Japan Portugal	-ese	*Chinese Japanese Portuguese*
Italy Russia Hungary	-(i)an	*Italian Russian Hungarian*
England Spain Poland Sweden	-ish	*English Spanish Polish Swedish*

⚠ The names of some languages and nationalities do not follow these patterns
(e.g. *The Netherlands* → *Dutch*, *Greece* → *Greek*, *Thailand* → *Thai*).

3 Nouns that end in *-ment*, *-(t)ion*, *-ation* and *-sion*

We make these nouns from verbs:

VERB	+	= NOUN
move argue govern	-ment	*movement argument government*
communicate educate	-ion	*communication education*
produce	-tion	*production*
examine invite inform	-ation	*examination invitation information*
discuss decide	-sion	*discussion decision*

4 Nouns that end in *-ness*, *-ity* and *-ance/-ence*

We make these nouns from adjectives:

ADJECTIVE	+	= NOUN
happy dark ill	-ness	*happiness darkness illness*
able active national	-ity	*ability activity nationality*
important distant	-ance	*importance distance*
independent different silent	-ence	*independence difference silence*

The spelling often changes when we add letters to a word that ends with a vowel or *-y*:
cycle → *cyclist, study* → *student, decide* → *decision, argue* → *argument, happy* → *happiness*

Practice

1 Match the words in A with the letters in B to make ten more nouns.
You need to change the spelling in some of them.

A <del>visit</del> active art China dark drive educate examine govern Poland study

B -<del>or</del> -ation -ent -er -ese -ion -ish -ist -ity -ment -ness

0	*visitor*	3	....	6	....	9	....
1	....	4	....	7	....	10	....
2	....	5	....	8	....		

2 Complete the sentences. Use nouns formed from the words in brackets ().
◀)) **4.59** Listen and check.

0 Elizabeth is studying ..*Japanese*... at university. (Japan)

1 Is Billy better after his .... yet? (ill)

2 The bus hit a .... as it was turning the corner. (cycle)

3 Misha speaks Polish and .... (Hungary)

4 We need to buy a new .... for the kitchen. (cook)

5 I heard a really interesting .... on the radio. (discuss)

6 When did your country get its ....? (independent)

7 I can understand .... but I can't write it very well. (Portugal)

8 What is the .... between New York and Los Angeles? (distant)

3 GRAMMAR IN USE Complete the notice with nouns from this unit.
The first two letters of each noun are given. ◀)) **4.60** Listen and check.

Tranley Adult (0) Ed..*ucation*.. Centre   CURRENT JOBS

- **Art (1) Te**.............. Are you a good (2) ar..............? We need someone to teach art on our painting course (Tuesday and Thursday evenings).

- **(3) Ex**.............. **manager.** We need someone to organise tests and examinations at the centre. We have more than 600 (4) st.............. here, so there are a lot of exams to organise each year. You should have at least five years' experience in adult education.

- **Teaching (5) As**.............. This job involves helping teachers on our (6) co.............. course. The course helps people to communicate in writing and speech and to discuss different topics (You will have your own (7) di.............. group). Good (8) En.............. is necessary for this job.

- **Bus (9) Dr**.............. We need someone to drive people to swimming classes at the local swimming pool. You should have a driving licence.

  For more (10) in.............. about hours, salary, etc., please ask at reception.

4 Complete these sentences. Use nouns from this unit.
Change the words in brackets () if necessary, so they are true for you.

0 I think watching television is (<del>an interesting</del>) ....*activity*.... *a boring*

1 I think .... is (a beautiful) language.

2 My favourite .... is (Picasso).

3 In my country, shop .... are usually (polite and friendly).

106 Forming adjectives

These shelves are going to be very **useful**.

These instructions are **useless**!

1 Changing nouns or verbs into adjectives

NOUN OR VERB	+	= ADJECTIVE
centre music nation	-al	central musical national
beauty care help pain use	-ful	beautiful careful helpful painful useful
care pain use	-less	careless painless useless
comfort fashion	-able	comfortable fashionable
dirt health rain wind	-y	dirty healthy rainy windy
danger fame	-ous	dangerous famous
act attract expense	-ive	active attractive expensive

The spelling often changes when we add letters to a word that ends with a vowel or -*y*:
fame → famous
expense → expensive
beauty → beautiful

 Pronunciation ➤ 1.35

Adjectives with -*ed* and -*ing*, e.g. *interested/interesting* ➤ Unit 26

2 Making adjectives negative

in-, *un-* and *im-* mean 'not':
unhappy = not happy
informal = not formal

	+ ADJECTIVE	= ADJECTIVE WITH NEGATIVE MEANING
un-	comfortable happy healthy helpful lucky tidy usual	uncomfortable unhappy unhealthy unhelpful unlucky untidy unusual
in-	complete correct expensive formal	incomplete incorrect inexpensive informal
im-	patient perfect polite possible	impatient imperfect impolite impossible

 If the adjective begins with the sound /p/ we use *im-*, not *in-* to make it negative:

polite → ✗ *inpolite*
       ✓ **im**polite

perfect → ✗ *inperfect*
       ✓ **im**perfect

Practice

1 Match the words in A with the letters in B to make nine more adjectives.
You need to change the spelling in some of them. 🔊 **4.61** Listen and check.

A ~~music~~ act beauty care comfort
fame formal happy health possible

B -al -able -ful im- in-
-ive -less -ous un- -y

0 *musical*   1 ....   2 ....   3 ....   4 ....

5 ....   6 ....   7 ....   8 ....   9 ....

2 Write an adjective under each picture. Some of the adjectives are negative.
Use the words in the box.

comfort correct danger expense ~~happy~~ health pain rain

0 *unhappy*   1 ....   2 ....   3 ....

4 ....   5 ....   6 ....   7 ....

3 Complete the second sentence so it means the same as the first.
Use adjectives from this unit. Use one, two or three words. 🔊 **4.62** Listen and check.

0 Cotton is a material you can use for many things.

   Cotton is a ...*useful material*....

1 That sofa costs a lot of money. It is .... sofa.

2 Don't worry; the operation won't give you any pain.

   Don't worry; the operation ....·

3 I want a hotel in the centre of the city. I want .... hotel.

4 You shouldn't eat food that is bad for your health.

   You shouldn't eat ....·

5 Some people never have any luck. Some people ....·

6 My sister helps people all the time. My sister is .... person.

7 Everyone in my family is good at music. I come from .... family.

8 In autumn there are a lot of days when it rains all the time.

   There are a lot of .... in autumn.

9 I hate people who don't behave in a polite way. I hate ....·

10 Two of the answers in the exercise are not correct.

   There are two .... in the exercise.

107 Forming compound nouns and adjectives

1 Compound nouns

A compound noun is a noun made from two words. The first noun is usually singular.

We sometimes write compound nouns as one word (e.g. *newspaper*, *supermarket*) and sometimes as two separate words (e.g. *car park*, *ice cream*). It is best to check the correct form in a dictionary.

We can make compound nouns by adding a noun, verb or adjective to a noun:

noun + noun	*bedroom clothes shop furniture shop record shop* *pizza restaurant traffic jam history teacher credit card*
noun + verb-*er*	*DVD player dishwasher taxi driver*
noun + verb-*ing*	*ice-skating snowboarding horse-riding*
verb-*ing* + noun	*shopping centre washing machine living room swimming pool*
adjective + noun	*best friend grandfather supermarket whiteboard*

The stress is usually on the first syllable:
***living** room*, ***traffic** jam*, ***horse**-riding*, ***grand**father*

 Pronunciation ➤ 1.36

The first word usually gives more information about the second word. It can tell us:

- What kind of thing?
  a bathroom (= a room with a bath)
  a clothes shop (= a shop which sells clothes)
- What kind of person?
  a history teacher (= a person who teaches history)
  a taxi driver (= a person who drives taxis)
- What is its purpose?
  a washing machine (= a machine for washing clothes)
  a tennis ball = (a ball for playing tennis)

2 Compound adjectives

Compound adjectives are made from nouns, adjectives, verbs and adverbs.
They usually have a hyphen (-) between the two words when they come before a noun:

number/measurement + noun	*three-hour two-day two-kilometre* *16th-century 250-gramme 600-dollar half-price* *half-hour full-time part-time ten-year-old*
adjective + noun	*high-quality high-speed low-price low-calorie*
adverb + participle verb	*well-known well-paid centrally-heated*
self + verb/adjective/noun	*self-employed self-confident self-service*

A compound adjective gives us information about the noun that follows it:
*We had a **three-hour** exam.* (an exam that lasted for three hours)
*We went on the **high-speed** train.* (the train that travels at high speed)
*I'd like a **well-paid** job.* (a job which pays me a lot of money)

 The noun in these adjectives is always singular:
✗ *He's a ten-years-old boy.*   ✓ *He's a ten-**year**-old boy.*
✗ *It was a three-hours film.*   ✓ *It was a three-**hour** film.*

Practice

1 Match the two parts of the sentences. 🔊 **4.63** **Listen and check.**

0 Our neighbours have got a swimming   A calorie diet.
1 Why don't you ask the taxi   B known actress?
2 Is there a washing   C pool in their garden.
3 Last year we went snow   D speed train to Madrid?
4 Zoe got a job as a French   E machine in your house?
5 She's on a special low-   F boarding in Switzerland.
6 Did you catch the high-   G teacher at the local school.
7 Is she related to that well-   H driver for directions?

2 `GRAMMAR IN USE` **Choose the correct words in *italics* in the text.**

The story of IKEA

IKEA is one the most famous (0) *shops of furniture* / (furniture shops) in the world. It has more than 300 stores and employs over 100,000 people. It was started by Ingvar Kamprad in Sweden in 1943.

The store is (1) *well-known* / *very known* for its (2) *cheap-price* / *low-price* furniture which customers have to put together at home. This is much cheaper than ordinary furniture. IKEA sells about 12,000 products; it has something for every room in the house – for (3) *livings* / *living* rooms, kitchens, bathrooms, dining rooms and (4) *bedrooms* / *sleeping rooms*.

All the stores are very large and (5) *self-service* / *serving-yourself*. They have enormous (6) *car* / *cars* parks. Shopping at IKEA is popular with families because every store has a safe place for children to play and a cheap restaurant. So if you get tired of shopping you can get a cup of coffee or an (7) *ice cream* / *ices cream*. It's like a huge (8) *central-shopping* / *shopping centre* inside one shop!

3 **Each sentence contains a part of a compound word, but the other part is missing. Find the incomplete words. Then write the whole compound word.** 🔊 **4.64** **Listen and check.**

0 Can you go to the (super) and buy me some bread? ....*supermarket*....
1 Uncle Gerald doesn't work for a company – he's self ....
2 Coca-Cola is a well company throughout the world. ....
3 Our teacher wrote the answer on the white ....
4 Can I pay by credit in this restaurant? ....
5 We were late because there was a bad traffic on the motorway. ....
6 Glenda is one of our part workers, so she isn't here on Tuesdays. ....
7 How do you set the washing for a 40-degree wash? ....
8 Johnny can afford a big house; he's got a very paid job. ....
9 If you need to buy a new coat, there's a good clothes near me. ....
10 I'm on a low diet because I want to get fitter. ....

Review MODULE 19

1 UNITS 105 AND 106 **Complete Charts A and B with nouns. Complete Chart C with adjectives.**

A

adjective	ill	active	important	silent	happy	able	different
noun	illness						

B

verb	dicuss	argue	educate	inform	decide	move	produce
noun	discussion						

C

noun	health	music	danger	expense	nation	beauty	fashion
adjective	healthy						

2 UNITS 105 AND 106 **Complete the sentences about the pictures. Use some of your answers from Exercise 1.**

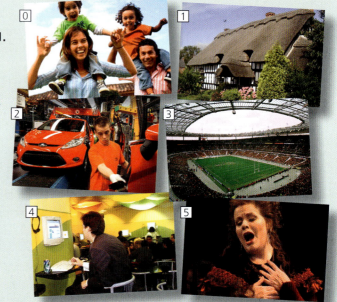

0 Health and ...happiness... are the most important things in life.

1 Mel lives in a .... house in the country.

2 One of Germany's main industries is the .... of cars.

3 The Stade de France is France's .... sports stadium.

4 The Internet is a great place to get ....

5 The .... to sing well is very rare.

3 UNITS 105 AND 106 **Complete the conversation. Use the words in brackets () to make nouns or adjectives.** 🔊4.65 **Listen and check.**

SUSAN   Hi, Samir. How are things?

SAMIR   Oh, life is always busy when you're a (0) ...builder... (build)!

SUSAN   I can imagine. How are the kids?

SAMIR   Well, Suzy has finished school now. She's working as a shop (1) .... (assist) at that big furniture store in Crownley. She rides her bike there every day – she's a keen (2) .... (cycle).

SUSAN   But that's quite a long (3) .... (distant) from home, isn't it? And it's a very busy road – it sounds (4) .... (danger)!

SAMIR   Well, I worry about it sometimes, but she loves her (5) .... (independent) so she doesn't want to go on the bus. We had a big (6) .... (argue) about it a few days ago!

SUSAN   What about Danny? Has he finished his (7) .... (educate) yet?

SAMIR   No, he's still at school. He's very (8) .... (music) so he's thinking about going to the Royal College of Music ...

288

4 UNITS 106 AND 107 **Complete the second sentence so it means the same as the first. Use one, two or three words.**

  0 The journey lasted for six hours. It was a *six-hour journey*.

00 Did Philip help you? Was *Philip helpful*?

  1 Don't wear formal clothes to the party. Wear .... clothes.

  2 There was a lot of wind last Thursday. Last Thursday was a ....

  3 He only works two days a week. He has a .... job.

  4 Sam always has a lot of luck. Sam is never ....

  5 Is there a restaurant that sells pizza near here?

     Is there a .... near here?

  6 His clothes are always covered in dirt. He always wears ....

  7 I like buildings that were built in the 18th century. I like ....

  8 We stayed in a hotel that nobody knows about.

     We didn't stay in a ....

5 ALL UNITS **Do the sentences in each pair have the same (S) or different (D) meanings? Write S or D.**

0 A	Does Penny teach geography?	B Is Penny a geography teacher?	*S*
1 A	Did it hurt a lot?	B Was it painless?	....
2 A	You don't see that colour very often.	B That's an unusual colour.	....
3 A	My father has a well-paid job.	B My father earns a lot of money.	....
4 A	Zack is a driving examiner.	B Zack is learning to drive.	....
5 A	We had a political discussion.	B We talked about politics.	....
6 A	We need a self-confident person for this job.	B This job isn't suitable for someone who is shy.	....

6 ALL UNITS **Complete the crossword.**

ACROSS
  1 Not possible.
  4 I think ice ... is delicious.
  6 A person who works for the answer to 12 across.
  8 The adjective from *danger*.
10 Your father's father.
12 Something you can read every day.
13 The opposite of *painless*.
14 The noun from *communicate*.
15 The noun from *decide*.

DOWN
  2 The language spoken in Portugal and Brazil.
  3 The adjective from *beauty*.
  5 The adjective from *attract*.
  7 The noun from *independent*.
  9 Not expensive.
11 The noun from *happy*.

Test MODULE 19

Forming words

Choose the correct answer, A, B or C.

1 Does your town have a lot of foreign ....? ➤ Unit 105
   A visitings B visiters C visitors

2 Jan is ....: he's from Amsterdam. ➤ Unit 105
   A Netherlands B Dutch C Hollander

3 Did Ali send you an .... to his party? ➤ Unit 105
   A invitation B inviting C invitement

4 I don't like my sister; we are always having .... with each other. ➤ Unit 105
   A argues B arguments C argumations

5 Who won? Have the judges made a .... yet? ➤ Unit 105
   A decision B decide C deciding

6 I have no .... to sing – I just can't do it. ➤ Unit 105
   A ableness B able C ability

7 What is the .... between silver and white gold? ➤ Unit 105
   A difference B differ C differance

8 If I have a .... headache, I usually lie down. ➤ Unit 106
   A pain B painless C painful

9 Have you seen Helen's older sister? She's very .... ➤ Unit 106
   A attractive B attraction C attracting

10 This phone doesn't send text messages – it's completely ....! ➤ Unit 106
   A useful B useless C used

11 Debbie's very old-fashioned – she doesn't like .... clothes. ➤ Unit 106
   A fashionable B fashionist C fashionive

12 That DVD's very .... – only three euros! ➤ Unit 106
   A expensiveless B inexpensive C unexpensive

13 If customers are .... to me, I just put the phone down. ➤ Unit 106
   A inpolite B impolite C unpolite

14 I don't like those chairs; they're really .... ➤ Unit 106
   A discomfortable B uncomforting C uncomfortable

15 You can buy CDs at the .... ➤ Unit 107
   A records shop B record shop C shop of records

16 Is there a chemist's at the ....? ➤ Unit 107
   A centre's shopping B centre of shopping C shopping centre

17 Caroline used to be my sister's .... ➤ Unit 107
   A most friend B best friend C best of friend

18 There's a .... dining table in the January sale. ➤ Unit 107
   A half-price B price half C price low

19 There are no waiters here; it's a .... restaurant. ➤ Unit 107
   A service yourself B self serving C self-service

20 She's the daughter of a .... TV actress. ➤ Unit 107
   A much known B well-known C very-known

Spoken English

Before you start

1 **Read the conversation. Look at the highlighted grammar examples.**

Elaine and Mariusz Novak
invite you to celebrate
Elaine's 50th Birthday
on 15 June
at 73 Grovelands Close
From 7.30 p.m.
RSVP

JIM You went to Elaine's party, **didn't you?** Was it good?

GABY Yes, it was excellent. It was in their garden and the weather was great. The food was great too. And she got lots of presents.

JIM **Did she?** I'm not surprised, really. She's very popular.

GABY Mmm. The only problem was that Paul **wasn't** there, you know, their son. He refused to come.

JIM **That's** awful! Why?

GABY **Don't know.** Elaine didn't want to talk about it. But I've never liked Paul really.

JIM No, **neither** have I. He always seems unfriendly. Anyway, I'm glad the party went well.

GABY I am, **too.** Now, you're coming to dinner tomorrow evening, **right?**

2 **Now read the conversation between Ellie and Olivia. Choose the correct words in *italics*. The highlighted grammar examples will help you.**

ELLIE Hi, Olivia. You've had an invitation to Hanna's 21st birthday party, (1) *have / haven't* you? ➤ Unit 108

OLIVIA Yes, I have. I thought Hanna was younger than that, though.

ELLIE (2) *Didn't / Did* you? Yes, she's a bit older than us. Well, it's a pity, but I can't go to the party. ➤ Unit 108

OLIVIA No, (3) *neither / so* can I. I'm on holiday that weekend. ➤ Unit 109

ELLIE Yes, I am, (4) *too / so.* Anyway, did you know that she's invited everyone from the History Department at the university? ➤ Unit 109

OLIVIA No! (5) *That's / It's* crazy! That's over 100 people! ➤ Unit 110

ELLIE Well, I'm sure they (6) *will not / won't* all go. ➤ Unit 112

OLIVIA Mmm, (7) *don't know / not know* about that. Those guys like parties! ➤ Unit 112

ELLIE True. Listen, you'll be in college tomorrow, (8) *no / right*? I want to ask ... ➤ Unit 112

3 **Check your answers below. Then go to the unit for more information and practice.**

1 haven't 2 Did 3 neither 4 too 5 That's 6 won't 7 don't know 8 right

108 Question tags

You **aren't coming** to Uncle Pete's wedding in those jeans, **are you?**

1 Form

There are two main types of question tag.

- Negative statement + **positive** tag:

  Mr Connors **doesn't work** here anymore, **does** he? Cats **don't eat** chocolate, **do** they?

- Positive statement + **negative** tag:

  Mr Connors still **works** here, **doesn't** he? Cats only **eat** meat, **don't** they?

VERB FORM	STATEMENT	QUESTION TAG
to be	Sorry, I'm really late, Trevor**'s going to be** late,	aren't I? isn't he?
there is	There **isn't** a bus after 11.00,	is there?
present simple	You **prefer** tea to coffee,	don't you?
past simple	He **didn't phone**,	did he?
present continuous	They**'re building** a new sports centre,	aren't they?
past continuous	It **wasn't raining** last night,	was it?
present perfect	There **hasn't been** another accident,	has there?
will	I**'ll be** on time if I leave now,	won't I?
can	We **can finish** this work tomorrow,	can't we?

Question tags always use short forms: ... *isn't he?* ... *don't you?*

 We always match the tag with the statement:
✗ *He's English, no?* ✗ *He's English, isn't it?* ✓ *He's* English, **isn't he?**

 We can't make a question tag with *am*, so we use *are*:
✗ *amn't I* ✓ **aren't I**

2 Use

We add a question tag to change a statement into a question (➤ Unit 77.1).
We can use question tags:

- to ask for information. We say these tags with a rising intonation (➚):
  I can get a bus from here, can't I? (I don't know the answer – I haven't taken a bus from here.)
  You aren't coming to the wedding in those jeans, are you? (I don't know, but I hope not.)

- to ask for agreement, when we think we know the answer. We say these tags with a falling intonation (➘):
  It's really hot today, isn't it? (I think it's hot and I want you to agree.)
  You haven't seen that film yet, have you? (I think you haven't.)

We answer question tags with *yes/no*, a short answer and other information if necessary:
'I can get a bus from here, can't I?' 'Yes, you can. The next one is in ten minutes.'
'The bus leaves at six o'clock, doesn't it?' 'Yes, that's right.'

 Pronunciation ➤ 1.37

Practice

1 Match the sentences with the question tags. ◀» 4.66 Listen and check.

0 You take sugar in coffee,
1 Steve's going to sell his car,
2 Juliet can't run faster than you,
3 The cat's had its food,
4 You don't work at Smith's,
5 Emma can give us a lift to the airport,
6 You will remember to talk to Adam,
7 It hasn't rained here today,
8 Clive isn't back from Australia yet,

A do you?
B won't you?
C has it?
D is he?
E don't you?
F can she?
G hasn't it?
H can't she?
I isn't he?

2 GRAMMAR IN USE Complete the conversation with question tags. ◀» 4.67 Listen and check.

MIKE   It was your cousin's wedding last weekend, (0) .... *wasn't it* ....?

CARA   That's right, in a five-star hotel with fantastic gardens.

MIKE   But it rained on Saturday, (1) ....?

CARA   Yes, a bit. But it was sunny when they took the photos.

MIKE   That's good. Were there many guests?

CARA   More than a hundred, and Annabel and her husband paid for everything.

MIKE   Oh! But they're very young, (2) ....?
How could they afford it?

CARA   Annabel was my grandfather's favourite grandchild. He left her all his money.

MIKE   That's a bit strange, (3) .... ? So no one else in the family got any money?

CARA   No, but we don't mind. Anyway, how was your weekend? You went to see the tennis at Wimbledon, (4) ....?

MIKE   Yes, we did. You haven't been, (5) ....?

CARA   No, I'm not interested in tennis. Anyway, you can't get tickets very easily, (6) .... ?

MIKE   No, you can't – we were lucky ... Oh, nearly two o'clock! It's late, (7) .... ? We should get some lunch.

CARA   Good idea. That new sandwich shop in the High Street has opened now, (8) ....?

3 Change the questions into statements and question tags. ◀» 4.68 Listen and check.

0 Did Paul tell you about the party?   Paul didn't *tell you about the party, did he* ?
1 Were you at the same school as Paul?   You weren't .... ?
2 Is there going to be food at the party?   There isn't .... ?
3 Am I included in the invitation?   I am .... ?
4 Will you come home by twelve o'clock?   You will .... ?
5 Did you tell Fran about the party?   You didn't .... ?

109 *too* and *so* … ; *either* and *neither* …

1 too, so …

We use *too* after a positive verb to agree with someone or to add information:
'*I'm cold.*' '*I am,* **too.**'
'*Sophie passed the exam!*' '*Nat did,* **too.**'

We can say the same thing with *so*, but *so* comes before the verb and the verb comes before the subject:
'***I'm** cold.*' '*So **am I.**'
'***We love** skiing.*' '*So **do we.**'
'***He went** to Greece.*' '*So **did she.**'
'***I've** got an interview.*' '*So **have I.**'
'***I'd** love to try that restaurant.*' '*So **would I.**'

 We always put the verb before the subject, and we don't repeat the main verb:
'*I passed the exam!*' ✗ *'So did I pass!'* ✗ *'So I passed!'* ✗ *'So I did!'*
  ✓ '*So **did I!**'

2 either, neither …

We use *either* after a negative verb to agree with someone or to add information:
'*I'm not getting up yet.*' '*I'm not **either.**'
'*My mum doesn't like that programme.*' '*My mum doesn't **either.**'

We can say the same thing with *neither*, but *neither* comes before a positive verb and the verb comes before the subject:
'***I'm** not getting up yet.*' '*Neither **am I.**'
'***I don't** like this cold weather.*' '*Neither **do I.**'
'***She can't** swim yet.*' '*Neither **can he.**'
'***We've** never been to Egypt.*' '*Neither **have we.**'
'***I mustn't** be late again.*' '*Neither **must I.**'

 Pronunciation ➤ 1.38

3 Disagreeing with people

We can disagree or say that something is different with short answers like this:

POSITIVE	'*This music's too loud!*'	'*No, it **isn't!**'*
	'*I **like** spicy food.*'	'*Oh, I **don't.**'*
NEGATIVE	'*I **haven't** finished my homework yet.*'	'*Oh, I **have.**' (not *I've*)*

NATURAL ENGLISH We often use *Oh* before we disagree. It sounds a little more polite:
'*I want to go sightseeing today.*' '***Oh, I don't.** Let's go to the beach again.*'

294

Practice

1 Choose the correct reply to each statement. ◄)) **4.69** Listen and check.

0	I can't believe that story.	*Neither do I. /* (*Neither can I.*)
1	Jade's cousin has been to Australia.	*So has mine. / Neither has mine.*
2	The sports centre is closed today.	*The pool is, too. / The pool is either.*
3	We didn't really enjoy that meal.	*Neither did we. / So did we.*
4	My legs really hurt after that walk!	*Mine do either. / So do mine.*
5	Our holiday was fantastic!	*Neither was ours. / Ours was, too.*
6	I didn't hear the news until this morning.	*So did we. / Neither did we.*

2 GRAMMAR IN USE The students want to be in the college band.
Look at the information and complete the conversations. ◄)) **4.70** Listen and check.

STUDENT	LIKES	DOESN'T LIKE	CAN	CAN'T
ELENA	classical music	jazz	sing	play an instrument
ANDREAS	jazz	classical music	play the violin	sing
BRIGITTE	jazz	classical music	sing	play an instrument
MAREK	popular and classical music	jazz	play the guitar	sing

0 LEADER OK, who can sing in your group?
ELENA Well, I can sing.
BRIGITTE *So can I.*
ANDREAS *I can't.*
MAREK *Neither can I.*

1 LEADER What about instruments?
ELENA I can't play an instrument.
BRIGITTE ....
ANDREAS ....
I can play ....
MAREK ....
I can play ....

2 LEADER What kind of music do you like Brigitte?
BRIGITTE Well, I really like jazz.
ANDREAS ....
MAREK Oh, I don't.
ELENA ....

3 LEADER Do you all like classical music?
ANDREAS Well, I don't really.
BRIGITTE ....
MAREK ....
ELENA .... I love it!

3 Write sentences that are true for you.

0 I drink a lot of tea. *I don't. I drink a lot of coffee.*
00 I don't drink a lot of milk. *Neither do I.*
1 I live with my wife and children. ....
2 I don't like jazz. ....
3 I love driving fast. ....
4 I have blond hair. ....
5 I went out last night. ....
6 I can't play an instrument. ....

110 Expressing surprise, shock, pleasure, etc.

Look at this watch. **How** horrible!

That's crazy!

What a waste of money!

1 That's/How + adjective

We can use *That's* + an adjective when we think something is very good, very bad or very surprising:
'Jeremy has just asked me to marry him!'
'That's wonderful!'

'My mobile phone was stolen yesterday.'
*'Oh, **that's awful!**'*

	GOOD
That's	*wonderful! great! fantastic!*

	BAD
That's	*awful! terrible! horrible!*

	SURPRISING
That's	*crazy! amazing! incredible!*

We can also use *How* + an adjective:
'Last night we heard a knock at the door, but there was no one there.'
***'How strange!** Was it the wind?'*

'She's angry and she's not speaking to me.' ***'How silly!'***

2 What a/an + (adjective) + noun

We use *What a/an* + (adjective) + noun when we are disappointed, annoyed, surprised or very pleased:
*'We can't come to your party next week, I'm afraid.' 'Oh, **what a pity!** I'm sure you'd enjoy it.'*
*'Karen phoned to say she's coming home for the summer.' **'What a lovely surprise!'***

	POSITIVE	NEGATIVE
What	*a (lovely) surprise! a (fantastic) idea! a (wonderful) day!*	*a pity! an (awful) shame! a pain! (= That's annoying!)*

We need a noun in exclamations with *what*. We don't use *what* + adjective; we use *That's* or *How*:
✗ ~~What fantastic!~~ ✓ *That's fantastic!*

3 Really?, No!, Wow!

There are also some single words which we use when something is surprising:
                                                          ***'Wow!** That's fantastic!'*
'I've just got a pay rise of €2,000 a year.' ***'No!** What a surprise!'*
                                                          ***'Really?** Lucky you.'*

⚠ We use *Wow!* only for something good. *No!* and *Really?* can be used for good or bad news:
                                                          ✗ ~~Wow! I'm really sorry.~~
'I failed my final university exams.' ✓ *'**No!** I'm really sorry.'*
                                                          ✓ *'**Really?** I can't believe that …'*

 Pronunciation ► 1.39

Practice

1 **Complete the sentences with *That, How* or *What*.** 🔊**4.71** **Listen and check.**

0 'Jacob didn't get on the university course he wanted.' '.....*What*..... a shame!'

1 'I've just passed my driving test!' '...................'s great!'

2 'There's been another bank robbery in the city.' '................... awful!'

3 'We decided to sell our house and we sold it to the first person who looked at it.'
   '...................'s amazing!'

4 'Mum, Jane's expecting a baby!' '................... a lovely surprise!'

5 'The doctor says that I must stop drinking coffee.' '................... a pity!'

6 'I think we should all join together to buy Lucy a really good present.'
   '................... a fantastic idea!'

7 'Our car has been stolen again.' '...................'s terrible!'

8 'The engineers are working on the railway this weekend, and it's the
   busiest weekend of the year.' '................... silly!'

2 **GRAMMAR IN USE** **Choose the correct words in *italics* in the conversation.**
   🔊**4.72** **Listen and check.**

GREG   Holly – have you heard about the office party?
        It's going to be at the Norfolk Hotel this year.

HOLLY   How (0) *awful* / *wonderful*! It's a really good hotel.

GREG   Yes, but we can't stay the night. We'll all have to get taxis home.

HOLLY   Oh, that's (1) *nice* / *a pity*. What's happening? Is there a meal?

GREG   A really expensive meal, but we don't have to pay for it, of course.

HOLLY   (2) *Wow!* / *That's crazy!* When is it?

GREG   December 20th – it's a Saturday.

HOLLY   What a (3) *surprise* / *shame*! I'm going away that weekend to visit my parents.
        They're having a party.

GREG   (4) *Really?* / *That's awful.* What's the party for?

HOLLY   It's because they've been married for forty years. All the family will be there.

GREG   (5) *What fantastic!* / *How fantastic!* How many people will there be?

HOLLY   Only fifteen, but my brother is coming from Canada – and my parents don't know.

GREG   What a (6) *lovely surprise* / *pain* for them. Oh, I'd better go. I've got a meeting in
        two minutes!

3 **Look at the pictures. Which of the ideas below do you think go with each one?**

A Oh, that's awful!
B What a silly little thing!
C How disgusting!
D How fantastic!
E That's really nice.
F Wow! Lovely place!
G What a horrible photo!

4 **Now write your own ideas for each picture.**

Picture 1: ....

Picture 2: ....

111 Weak forms

1 Weak vowels

Weak vowels are vowels that we do not stress (say strongly).
The two weak vowels are /ə/ and /ɪ/:

	WEAK	STRONG
a/an	/ə/ /ən/	/eɪ/ /æn/
the	/ðə/	/ðiː/
of at	/əv/ /ət/	/ɒv/ /æt/
can	/kən/	/kæn/
was	/wəz/	/wɒz/
been	/bɪn/	/biːn/

We usually use weak vowels in 'grammar' words, e.g. *the, a, an*, prepositions and
auxiliary verbs.

2 Weak forms in prepositions

Most short prepositions are weak when we are speaking:
I'm going to /tə/ the cinema. Dimitri is from /frəm/ Greece. He's at /ət/ the doctor's.

We usually use the weak form of *to* /tə/ in *going to* and *used to*:
Are you going to /tə/ phone the cinema?
We used to /tə/ get the school bus at 8.00 in the morning.

 Pronunciation ➤ 1.40

3 Weak forms in other words

- *a/the*: We usually pronounce *a/an* and *the* with /ə/:
  a book, an apple, the garden

  But when a vowel sound comes after *the*, we pronounce *the* with /iː/:
  the apple

- *was/were* /wəz/ /wə/:
  Was it hot in Corfu? There were a lot of insects.

- *that* /ðət/:
  Do you think that everyone's ready?

  But when we use *that* to ask about something or choose something, it is always strong:
  What's that? I'd like that one, please.

- *than* /ðən/: We also use weak forms in comparative and superlative adjectives:
  cheaper /-ə/ cheapest /ɪst/
  The restaurants are cheaper here than in London.
  But the cheapest restaurants are in the country.

- *been* /bɪn/: We usually pronounce *been* with the weak form /ɪ/:
  We've been to the theatre. Have you ever been to India?

- *can* /kən/: We usually pronounce *can* as /kən/ in statements and questions.
  Karen can play the piano. Can Karen play the piano?

  We use the strong form /kæn/ in short answers:
  *Yes, she **can**.*

  The negative *can't* is usually strong /kɑːnt/ in most varieties of British English:
  *Karen **can't** play the guitar.*

 Pronunciation ➤ 1.41

Practice

1 Write the words in the correct place below.

~~an~~ ~~ball~~ been cat from hand leave stay that the to train wait was

vowel usually weak	*an*						
vowel usually strong	*ball*						

2 Some words with weak vowels are <u>underlined</u>. Put a circle around the other words with weak vowels. The number in brackets () tells you how many other words there are. 🔊 **4.73** Listen and check.

0 Would you like ⓐ cup <u>of</u> tea? (1)

1 Louise comes from <u>the</u> United States. (1)

2 We <u>were</u> always very busy in the mornings. (1)

3 I told you <u>that</u> I'd <u>been</u> to France. (1)

4 They <u>are</u> going to repair the car. (2)

5 Let's go <u>to</u> the park – we can do our English homework tonight. (2)

6 June 21st is the long<u>est</u> day of <u>the</u> year. (2)

7 <u>The</u> black jeans are cheaper than <u>the</u> blue ones. (3)

8 I can play <u>the</u> piano at the show. I can't play <u>the</u> guitar. (3)

3 **GRAMMAR IN USE** Read the conversation. Then put a circle around the weak forms of *can*. <u>Underline</u> the strong forms, including *can't*. 🔊 **4.74** Listen and check.

FRAN It's nearly the end of our last year at university. We should organise a party.

ZOE Yes, you're right. Where (0) ⓒⓐⓝ we have it, do you think?

ALEX We (1) can probably use the student union building.

ZOE (2) Can you check?

ALEX Yes, I (3) can. No problem. I'll do that tomorrow.

FRAN What about food? (4) Can we do the food ourselves?

ALEX No, we (5) can't. The university cooks will have to do it. But I'm sure they (6) can do it for a good price.

FRAN OK. What about music? I suppose we (7) can't organise that, either.

ALEX Yes, we (8) can. We just bring the CDs we want and play them on the system there.

ZOE Great. Look, I'll do an invitation tomorrow and show it to you. Then we (9) can decide who to invite. OK?

ALEX Yes, but I've got a class in the morning, so I (10) can't meet you until after lunch.

ZOE Let's meet at about 2.00, then.

FRAN Good idea.

112 English in conversation

GRANDFATHER	So, we're ready for your birthday dinner now, right?
DAD	I think so, don't you Jonas?
JONAS	Oh, yeah.
MUM	You having beans, Jonas?
JONAS	Mmm … don't really like them, Mum.
GRANDMOTHER	Really? Some beans for you, Selina?
SELINA	Not sure … yeah, I'll have some.

1 Speaking

There are a lot of differences between the way we speak English and the way we write it.

- We usually use short forms when we are speaking:
  So, we're ready for your birthday dinner now.
  I think so, don't you?
  Yeah, I'll have some beans.

- We don't always use pronouns (*I*, *you*, etc.) or auxiliary verbs (*do*, *is*, etc.):
  I don't know, Mum. → ***Don't know**, Mum.*
  Are you coming to the party? → ***You coming** to the party?*
  It's hot today, isn't it? → ***Hot today**, isn't it?*

  We only do this when we are talking to people we know very well.

  We don't do this in writing.

- We can use an extra word, (*right?* or *OK?*) when we want to check something:
  *We're ready for dinner now, **right?***
  *We'll order the taxi for seven o'clock, **OK?***

  We usually use *right?* to check that what we are saying is correct.

  We usually use *OK?* to check that an arrangement is good for the person we are speaking to.

2 Listening

When we are listening to someone speaking, we often make noises or say things to show we are listening:
'You know your friend Jake …' 'Mmm …'
'I've got tickets for the match on Saturday …' 'Really?' 'Yeah. Do you want one?'

NATURAL ENGLISH *Yeah* is a very informal way of saying *yes*.

Practice

1 **Find and write the words that are usually short forms. There are two in each sentence.** 🔊 **4.75** **Listen and check.**

0 I <u>do not</u> understand why <u>you are</u> so unhappy.　　　　　 ....*don't*.... 　....*you're*....

1 I have not had curry for years. I will enjoy this.　　　 ....　 ....

2 There is a bus stop on the corner. We will meet you there.　 ....　 ....

3 Jack and Alice can not join us because they are busy.　 ....　 ....

4 You must not leave your shoes there. It is dangerous.　 ....　 ....

2 **Decide which words are missing from these conversations and add them.** 🔊 **4.76** **Listen and check.**

Have you
0 A / Seen Jason recently?　　　　　　3 A Ready?

B No, / don't know where he is.　　　　　　B Not sure ... I can't find my passport.

1 A Awful weather, isn't it?　　　　　　4 A Hi. Want a quick coffee before we go?

B Yes, really bad for the time of year.　　　　B Mmm, great idea.

2 A OK, then, call you later.　　　　　　5 A More potatoes, Jen?

B Right. Speak to you then.　　　　　　B Mmm, love some, and some carrots, too.

3 **Complete the conversation with** *Mmm, Really, Yeah, right* **or** *OK*. 🔊 **4.77** **Listen and check.**

DYLAN Hi, Eddie. Coming to the match tonight?

EDDIE (0) .....*Mmm*....., not sure. I might have to work late.

DYLAN (1) ....? That's unusual. You don't often stay late.

EDDIE (2) ...., I know. You've got the tickets for the match, (3) ....?

DYLAN (4) ...., but my brother will come if you can't, so don't worry.

EDDIE Good. Look, I'll call you at about 6.00, (5) ....?

4 GRAMMAR IN USE **Write lines 1–3 again with short forms. Then complete lines 4–6 to make the conversation more informal.** 🔊 **4.78** **Listen and check.**

0 DENISE Hi, Lynne. I have not seen you for a long time. Have you been away?

1 LYNNE We have been to Australia. We went to Sydney for the New Year celebrations.

2 DENISE I did not know you were going away. How long were you there?

3 LYNNE We were not there for long – only two weeks. Did you do anything for New Year?

00 DENISE We didn't do much. Your daughter lives in Australia, doesn't she?

4 LYNNE Yes, she does, in Perth. We went there for a week before we went to Sydney.

5 DENISE Do you want a coffee? I'm not too busy right now.

6 LYNNE I'd love one. I'll be with you in ten minutes.

0 *Hi, Lynne. I haven't seen you for a long time.* .... Have you been away?

1 .... We went to Sydney for the New Year celebrations.

2 .... How long were you there?

3 .... only two weeks. Did you do anything for New Year?

00 *Not much. Your daughter lives in Australia, right?* ....

4 ...., in Perth. We went there for a week before we went to Sydney.

5 .... a coffee? I'm not too busy right now.

6 .... with you in ten minutes.

Review MODULE 20

1 UNITS 108 AND 109 **Choose the correct words in _italics_ to complete the conversation.**
🔊 **4.79** **Listen and check.**

CHLOE Only three months to our wedding. We should book our holiday soon,
(0) _should we /_(_shouldn't we?_)

ANDY Yes, you're right. Well, I'd like to go somewhere really relaxing.

CHLOE Oh, (1) _so / neither_ would I! The next three months are going to be very difficult,
so I don't want any problems on our holiday.

ANDY (2) _So / Neither_ do I. Well, you prefer beach holidays, (3) _don't / aren't_ you?
So how about Egypt? I love Egypt.

CHLOE Mmm, I do, (4) _so / too_, but we're getting married in late July, and that's the hottest
time in Egypt. I think it'll be too hot.

ANDY Yeah, you're right. We could go further away, (5) _couldn't we? / no?_ How
about Thailand?

CHLOE I don't know. Thailand will be hot, too, and we've only got two weeks. I'm not happy
about spending days travelling.

ANDY No, I'm not (6) _too / either_. We haven't thought about Europe, (7) _have / haven't_ we?

CHLOE True. I'd like to visit Bulgaria, or Romania, perhaps.

ANDY Yes, (8) _so I would / so would I_, but I don't know anything about those countries.
I don't know anyone who's been there.

CHLOE But (9) _I do / do I_! Laura from my office has been to Bulgaria.
I can ask her about it, (10) _do I? / can't I?_

ANDY Good idea.

2 UNITS 110 AND 112 **Complete the conversation. Use the words and phrases from the box.**
🔊 **4.80** **Listen and check.**

What	right
Really	Want
Wow	how
~~Everything OK?~~	
Yeah	That's
that's awful	

MARTA Hi, Karen. (0) ...._Everything OK?_....

KAREN Fine, thanks. (1) .... a coffee? I've got something to tell you.

MARTA Oh, what's that?

KAREN Well, I've got a new job.

MARTA (2) ....? I didn't know you were looking for a new job.

KAREN I wasn't. The company came to me!

MARTA (3) .... a surprise! (4) .... fantastic!

KAREN Thanks. It's a great job – better salary, a company car, and even an apartment ...

MARTA (5) ....! More money and a car – (6) .... wonderful!
But ... you said there was an apartment, (7) ....?

KAREN (8) ...., that's the only problem. The job's in New York.

MARTA New York! But (9) ....! I'll hardly ever see you.

KAREN Yes, you will. I'll be back quite often, and you can come and visit me – it isn't that far.

MARTA No, you're right, and I'd love to see New York.

3 UNITS 111 AND 112 **In each sentence below, put a circle around the weak form(s)
and make short forms where you can.**

0   ~~I have~~ ^{_I've_} never been ⊙to⊙ Africa.

1   The train has not arrived yet.

2   They did not want to go to the beach.

3   I used to study the history of art.

4   It is very hot there during the summer.

5   There are hundreds of people outside.

6   Alissa can play the piano, but she can
not read music.

4 ALL UNITS **Look at the signs and notices. Choose the best answer.**

0 A That's not English, no?
   (B) That's not English, is it?
   C That's not English, isn't it?

1 I love Scottish dancing!
   A So I do!
   B Neither do I!
   C I don't!

2 I don't have a ticket.
   A Neither do I.
   B So do I.
   C I don't, too.

3 A That terrible!
   B What terrible!
   C How terrible!

4 A Wow! That's good.
   B Right! That's good.
   C So! That's good.

5 They can't do that! It's against the law to put an age in a job advert.
   A Neither can I!
   B Really? I didn't know that.
   C Mmm. That's good.

Scottish dancing
Saturday 5th June
11 am to 6 pm
on Thistle Fields

Plane crashes in Andes
By Simon Harding
News Correspondent

SEVERE weather in the area has hampered the search for survivors, following the crash of a small passenger plane in the early hours today. It is feared that over 100 travel... Relatives are waiting for information on their loved ones, but are unlikely to hear anything today, as torrential rain has been falling since Monday. The weather have played a part

FESTIVAL
Friday – Sunday
Free entry all day Sunday!

Contact Mr C. Winston 0800 246246

Assistant wanted
for mens clothes shop.
Must be under 40.
Good communication skills are wanted but previous experience not needed
Contact Janette on 0800 123123

5 ALL UNITS **Complete the conversation with the correct words and phrases, A, B or C below.**
🔊 **4.81** **Listen and check.**

JOHN Are you going to a fireworks party on November 5th?
PILAR (0) ...., I think so. (1) .... one by the river.
JOHN Mmm. It's usually a good one. You'll enjoy it.
PILAR Yes and (2) .... I prefer to go to an organised event.
JOHN (3) ...., actually. We usually do something at home for the children.
PILAR Oh, what do you do?
JOHN We make a fire in the garden and buy fireworks.
PILAR (4) .... But you can't have as many fireworks, (5) ....?
JOHN Maybe not, but we make soup and bake potatoes in the fire. (6) .... really good fun.
PILAR (7) ...., I can see that.
JOHN Look, why don't you come along? You haven't bought tickets for the other one yet, (8) ....?
PILAR No, we haven't. (9) .... of you!
JOHN Right. Come over to our place at about 6.00, (10) ....?
PILAR Thanks. That's great.

0 A No (B) Yeah C Right
1 A There's B Is C There is
2 A so the children B so the children will C so will the children
3 A I do B I don't C So I do
4 A Wow! B Really? C No?

5 A can you B you can C can't you
6 A It is B Is C It's
7 A Oh B Mmm C No
8 A no B is it C have you
9 A It's nice B How's nice C That's nice
10 A is it B yes C OK

Test MODULE 20

Spoken English

Choose the correct answer, A, B or C.

1 You've been to Monaco, ...?
   A have you   B haven't you?   C isn't it?   ➤ Unit 108

2 There .... many people at the shops, were there?   ➤ Unit 108
   A were   B aren't   C weren't

3 I'm going to meet your new classmates tonight, ...?   ➤ Unit 108
   A aren't I   B am not I   C are not I

4 We can park the car here for an hour, ...?   ➤ Unit 108
   A can we   B no   C can't we

5 There isn't much time, ...?   ➤ Unit 108
   A is it   B is there   C are we

6 We won't be late, ...?   ➤ Unit 108
   A will we   B are we   C is it

7 'My boss makes me work really hard.' '..........'   ➤ Unit 109
   A So mine, too.   B So mine does.   C So does mine.

8 'Our daughter won't eat meat.' '..........'   ➤ Unit 109
   A Neither my son.   B Neither will my son.   C So will my son.

9 'I really like Friday evenings, when I can relax.' '..........'   ➤ Unit 109
   A We do, too.   B So we, too.   C We too do.

10 'Carla never puts her books away in the evening.' '..........'   ➤ Unit 109
   A Luke either.   B Luke doesn't, too.   C Luke doesn't either.

11 'I didn't enjoy the party.' 'Oh, ...! It was great.'   ➤ Unit 109
   A I didn't   B I did   C I don't

12 'All the people in Germany live in flats.'   ➤ Unit 109
   '........... Some German people live in houses.'
   A Don't   B We do   C They don't

13 'I'll give you a lift to the airport in the morning.' 'Oh, ... so kind!'   ➤ Unit 110
   A what's   B that   C that's

14 'They're closing the station car park.' '.......... annoying!'   ➤ Unit 110
   A How   B That   C What

15 'I felt really ill so I couldn't go to the concert.' '.......... pity!'   ➤ Unit 110
   A What   B That   C What a

16 'My father has bought me a Ferrari!' '..........! That's amazing!'   ➤ Unit 110
   A OK   B Wow   C So

17 You really .... spend all your money on expensive clothes!   ➤ Unit 112
   A do not   B not should   C shouldn't

18 'We're all ready now. Hurry up!' '..........! I'll be with you in a minute.'   ➤ Unit 112
   A Am coming   B I come   C Coming

19 'I had an awful time yesterday evening.' '..........? What happened?'   ➤ Unit 112
   A Really   B Did   C Wow

20 I'll call you later this evening, ...?   ➤ Unit 112
   A when   B no   C OK

Grammar check

This section will help you with your work on the practice exercises; it will help you with revision for exams, too.

APPENDIX 1

QUICK CHECK 1 MODULE 2 **Pronouns**

	SUBJECT PRONOUNS	OBJECT PRONOUNS	POSSESSIVE ADJECTIVES	POSSESSIVE PRONOUNS	REFLEXIVE PRONOUNS
singular	I	me	my	mine	myself
	you	you	your	yours	yourself
	he	him	his	his	himself
	she	her	her	hers	herself
	it	it	its		itself
plural	we	us	our	ours	ourselves
	you	you	your	yours	yourselves
	they	them	their	theirs	themselves
UNIT	11	11	13	13	15

QUICK CHECK 2 MODULES 5, 6, 7 AND 8 **Verb tenses**

TENSE	USE	EXAMPLE	UNIT
present simple	facts/permanent situations	Water boils at 100°C.	37.2
	thoughts/feelings	I think New York is exciting.	37.2
	regular activities and habits	David goes to work by bus. We usually start at eight o'clock.	38.2
	with verbs that do not use the continuous	I don't agree with you.	41.2
present continuous	actions happening now	The taxi's waiting outside.	39.1
	temporary situations	My computer isn't working.	39.2
past simple	finished actions in the past	I went to the dentist yesterday.	45.2
	repeated actions in the past	She phoned her parents every day.	45.2
	a series of past actions	We arrived at the airport and then took a taxi to the hotel.	46.2
	past situations	Did men have long hair in the 1960s?	46.2
past continuous	an action at and around a time in the past	I was watching TV at nine o'clock yesterday.	47.2
	temporary situations in the past	She was living in Paris when she had her first baby.	47.2
	a scene in the past	The sun was shining when we arrived.	47.2
	an action you did until something interrupted you	I was watching TV when the phone rang.	47.2

TENSE	USE	EXAMPLE	UNIT
present perfect	actions and experiences in our lives until now	*My parents have visited Austria once.*	50.2
	with superlative adjectives	*This is the worst food I've ever had.*	50.3
	a recent action with present results	*I've broken my leg so I can't play football.*	51.2
	giving news	*The president has arrived in London.*	51.2
	with *just*, *already*, *yet*	*The train has just arrived.*	52.1
		He's already got off.	52.2
	with *for*, *since*, etc.	*I've known Sami for thirty years.*	53.1
	with *this morning*, *this week*, etc.	*I've worked forty hours this week.*	53.2
present perfect continuous	for actions/situations until now	*I've been training for six months.* *We've been waiting since three o'clock.*	55.2
	to explain a present situation	*I'm hot because I've been running.*	55.2
future with *going to*	future plans	*What are you going to do this evening?*	57.2
	things we expect to happen	*I'm in a traffic jam so I'm going to be late.*	57.2
future with *will*	certain future	*My mother will be fifty in May.*	58.2
	things we think will happen	*You should go to the gym – you'll enjoy it.*	58.2
	immediate decisions	*I'm tired. I think I'll go to bed.*	58.3
future with present continuous	future arrangements	*I'm giving a talk at the sales meeting on Wednesday.*	59.1
future with present simple	future events on timetables and programmes	*The train leaves London at 10.25 and arrives in Bristol at 11.50.*	59.2

QUICK CHECK 3 MODULE 9 **Modal verbs**

VERB	USE	EXAMPLE	UNIT
can/can't	present ability	I can speak Spanish well.	61.2
	present possibility	You can get cheap tickets on the Internet.	61.2
	arrangement	The doctor can see you tomorrow.	61.2
	not allowed	We can't wear jeans in the office.	61.2
	permission	Can we borrow the car this evening? I'm sorry, you can't. I need it.	63.1
can	request	Can you help me with these bags?	63.2
can't be	almost certain	That can't be Ed in the café – he's at school at the moment.	68.2
could/ couldn't	past ability	Mozart could write beautiful music.	62.1
	past possibility	Children could play in the streets years ago.	62.1
	permission	Could I use your bathroom, please?	63.1
	request	Could you open the window, please?	63.2
have to/ don't have to	necessary/ not necessary	I have to get up early tomorrow to catch the train.	64.2
	necessary in the present	You don't have to get a licence to ride a bicycle.	64.3
had to/ didn't have to	necessary/ not necessary	They had to get visas when they went to South America.	66.1
	necessary/ not necessary in the past	We didn't have to show our passports.	66.1
may/may not	permission	You may start writing now.	63.1
	not allowed	Students may not take coats or bags with them into the exam.	63.1
	not certain	Mr Clement may be with a client. The order may not arrive next week.	68.1
might/ might not	not certain	I might work in my uncle's shop during the holidays. The parcel might not arrive tomorrow.	68.1
must/ must not	instructions, signs and notices	Passengers must wear seat belts. Visitors must not smoke in reception.	65.1 65.2
(really) must	recommending something	You really must try this salad – it's delicious!	65.2
must be	almost certain	They must be out – there are no lights on in the house.	68.2
need to/ don't need to	necessary/ not necessary	I need to earn some more money. We don't need to take our jackets – it's warm outside.	64.2 64.3

VERB	USE	EXAMPLE	UNIT
ought to/ ought not to	advice	*You ought to find out how much it costs.* *You ought not to sit in the sun all day.*	67.1
should/ should not	advice	*You should see the doctor.* *You shouldn't eat a lot of sugar.*	67.1
will/won't be able to	future ability	*I won't be able to drive for weeks.*	62.2
	future possibility	*We'll be able to swim every day at the hotel.*	62.2
will/won't have to	necessary/ not necessary in the future	*I'll have to wait until tomorrow.* *We won't have to pay at the cinema tonight.*	66.2

QUICK CHECK 4 MODULE 10 **Conditionals**

CONDITIONAL	USE	EXAMPLE	UNIT
present conditions	real situations that can happen at any time	*If you water the plants, they grow.*	69.2
	giving instructions or rules for a situation	*If it doesn't work, bring it back to the shop.*	69.2
first conditional (future conditions)	possible future situations	*If the tickets are expensive, we won't buy them.*	70.2
	certain future situations	*When I arrive at the airport, I'll phone you.*	70.2
	offers and warnings	*If you arrive late, we'll go without you.*	70.3
second conditional (unlikely/unreal conditions)	unlikely future conditions	*If we had a lot of money, we'd buy a big house.*	71.2
	unreal present conditions	*If David was here, he'd enjoy this film.*	71.2
	advice	*If I were you, I'd get there early.*	71.3

QUICK CHECK 5 MODULE 13 Verbs + *-ing* form and infinitive

	VERBS	EXAMPLE	UNIT
verb + *-ing* form	*like dislike enjoy (not) mind love hate prefer suggest consider imagine recommend begin delay start stop finish avoid miss*	*After you finish eating, you can wash the dishes.*	83.1
verb + preposition + *-ing* form	*give up* (= stop a habit or activity) *talk about* (= discuss) *think of* (= consider)	*I'm thinking of training as a nurse.*	83.2
go + *-ing* form	*go swimming/skating/dancing*, etc.	*Let's go shopping on Saturday.*	83.3
verb + infinitive without *to*	*should can can't must let's*	*You should send her an email.*	84.1
verb + infinitive with *to*	*can/can't afford agree arrange ask choose decide deserve expect learn offer plan promise refuse seem want*	*I want to buy some new jeans.*	84.2
	would like/love/hate/prefer, etc.	*I'd love to come to your party.*	84.3
verb (+ object) + infinitive with *to*	*ask expect help need want*	*He asked me to call again later. He asked to see the manager.*	85.1
verb + object + infinitive with *to*	*advise allow cause force invite teach tell order warn*	*They told us to leave.*	85.1
verb + object + infinitive without *to*	*make let*	*The cold weather made the lake freeze.*	85.2

QUICK CHECK 6 MODULE 16 **Linking words**

TYPE OF LINKING	LINKING WORDS	EXAMPLES	UNIT
joins two sentences	*and* *but* *or*	*I've washed up and I've put the dishes away.* *I've washed up but I haven't put the dishes away.* *I can wash up or I can put the dishes away.*	92.1
makes *and/or* stronger	*but ... and* *either ... or*	*Hilary speaks both French and Japanese.* *We can either watch TV or listen to music.*	92.2
explains why something happens	*because* *because of*	*The match is delayed because it's raining.* *The match is delayed because of the rain.*	93.1
gives a result	*so*	*It's raining, so the match is delayed.*	93.2
explains why you do something	*so that* to + infinitive	*I studied languages so that I could become a translator.* *I studied languages to become a translator.*	93.3
gives a time	*when* *after* *before* *while* *until* *as soon as*	*I'll call you when we get back.* *I went to bed after I locked the back door.* *I locked the back door before I went to bed.* *He saw the accident while he was waiting for the bus.* *I waited with the children until she got home.* *I'll call you as soon as the plane lands.*	94.1
gives the order of events in a story	*first* *then* *after that* *in the end*	*First the bus was late.* *Then there was a lot of traffic.* *After that, there was a long queue at the ticket office.* *In the end, we got on a train, but we were very late.*	94.1
gives instructions	*first* *next* *then* *finally*	*First, enter the number of your car.* *Next, put the coins in the machine.* *Then press the green button.* *Finally, take your ticket and put it inside your car.*	95.2

QUICK CHECK 7 MODULE 18 **Verbs + prepositions**

COMMON VERBS + PREPOSITIONS		UNIT 100.2
verb + *to*	belong to explain to listen to speak to talk to write to	That house belongs to my uncle.
verb + *about*	complain about read about speak about talk about think about	British people often complain about the weather.
verb + *for*	apply for ask for look for pay for wait for work for	We've been waiting for half an hour!
verb + *in*	arrive in believe in get in live in succeed in stay in	Do you believe in luck?
verb + *of*	approve of think of	What do you think of her new friend?
verb + *on*	decide on depend on	I decided on studying chemistry.
verb + *at*	arrive at laugh at look at stay at	We're staying at a small hotel.
verb + *with*	agree with stay with	Maria is right. I agree with her.

VERBS + DIFFERENT PREPOSITIONS		UNIT 101.1 AND UNIT 101.2
arrive	arrive in (a town or country)	When did you arrive in England?
	arrive at (any other place)	The train arrived at Victoria Station at six o'clock.
pay	pay (a person or a bill)	My mother paid the bill.
	(no preposition)	She paid the waiter at the end of the meal.
	pay for (a thing)	I haven't paid for the tickets yet.
stay	stay in/at (a place)	She stayed at the Hilton Hotel last month.
	stay with (a person)	I'm staying with my cousins for the holidays.
look	look at somebody/something	Look at the clock. We're late!
	look for somebody/something	Excuse me, I'm looking for Dr Watson's office. Do you know where it is?
	look after somebody/something	A nanny looks after the children while Emily is at work.
	look like somebody/something	Michael looks like his grandfather. They are both tall and thin.

VERB + OBJECT + PREPOSITION	UNIT 101.3
ask somebody for something	Did you ask the doctor for some advice?
thank somebody for something	The manager thanked the staff for their hard work.
invite somebody to something	I invited Carla to my party.
tell somebody about something	Have you told your parents about your new job yet?

QUICK CHECK 8 MODULE 18 **Phrasal verbs**

COMMON PHRASAL VERBS WITH AN OBJECT		UNIT 102.2
bring	*bring* something *back*	*Did you bring those books back?*
fill	*fill* something *in* (= complete a form)	*Please fill in this application form.*
find	*find* something *out* (= get information)	*Did you find out her phone number?*
give	*give* something *back* *give* something *up* (= stop a habit, activity or job)	*We gave the books back at the end of the lesson.* *He broke his leg and had to give up running.*
let	*let* somebody *in*	*There's somebody at the door. Please let them in.*
look	*look* something *up* (= find information in a book or computer, etc.)	*I don't know the address but I can look it up on the Internet.*
pick	*pick* something *up* *pick* somebody *up* (= collect somebody and take them somewhere)	*Don't leave your towel on the floor. Pick it up!* *I'll pick you up at six o'clock.*
put	*put* something *back* *put* something *down* *put* something *on*	*Have you put the book back on the shelf?* *She put the letter down on the table.* *It's cold outside. You should put on your warm coat.*
switch	*switch* something *on/off*	*Did you switch the heating on?*
take	*take* something *away* *take* something *off*	*I've finished this soup. You can take it away.* *Take your shoes off at the door.*
turn	*turn* something *down* *turn* something *on/off*	*Can you turn your music down?* *Don't forget to turn off the TV.*

COMMON PHRASAL VERBS WITHOUT AN OBJECT		UNIT 102.3
move towards or away from something/somewhere	come back come in get out go away go back go in go out	*He turned round and went out.*
move your body	lie down look round sit down stand up turn around	*I'm tired. I think I'll lie down for a few minutes.*
others	get up grow up hurry up look out (= be careful) wake up	*Hurry up! We're late.* *Look out! A car's coming.* *I usually wake up early.*

APPENDIX 2
Common irregular verbs (1) A–Z list

INFINITIVE	PAST TENSE	PAST PARTICIPLE	INFINITIVE	PAST TENSE	PAST PARTICIPLE
be	was/were	been	keep	kept	kept
beat	beat	beaten	know	knew	known
become	became	become	learn	learnt/learned	learnt/learned
begin	began	begun	leave	left	left
break	broke	broken	lend	lent	lent
bring	brought	brought	let	let	let
build	built	built	lose	lose	lost
burn	burnt/burned	burnt/burned	make	made	made
buy	bought	bought	mean	meant	meant
catch	caught	caught	meet	met	met
choose	chose	chosen	pay	paid	paid
come	came	come	put	put	put
cost	cost	cost	read	read	read
cut	cut	cut	ride	rode	ridden
dig	dug	dug	ring	rang	rung
dive	dived	dived	rise	rose	risen
do	did	done	run	ran	run
draw	drew	drawn	say	said	said
dream	dreamt/dreamed	dreamt/dreamed	see	saw	seen
drink	drank	drunk	sell	sold	sold
drive	drove	driven	send	sent	sent
eat	ate	eaten	shine	shone	shone
fall	fell	fallen	show	showed	shown
feel	felt	felt	sing	sang	sung
fight	fought	fought	sit	sat	sat
find	found	found	sleep	slept	slept
fly	flew	flown	speak	spoke	spoken
forget	forgot	forgotten	spell	spelt/spelled	spelt/spelled
forgive	forgave	forgiven	spend	spent	spent
freeze	froze	frozen	stand	stood	stood
get	got	got	steal	stole	stolen
give	gave	given	swim	swam	swum
go	went	gone	take	took	taken
grow	grew	grown	teach	taught	taught
have	had	had	tell	told	told
hear	heard	heard	think	thought	thought
hide	hid	hidden	throw	threw	thrown
hit	hit	hit	understand	understood	understood
hold	held	held	wear	wore	worn
hurt	hurt	hurt	win	won	won
			write	wrote	written

Common irregular verbs (2) list of forms

1 Past tense form = past participle

INFINITIVE	PAST TENSE	PAST PARTICIPLE
buy	bought	bought
say	said	said
send	sent	sent
sleep	slept	slept
tell	told	told
win	won	won

2 Infinitive + (e)*n*

INFINITIVE	PAST TENSE	PAST PARTICIPLE
beat	beat	beat**en**
draw	drew	draw**n**
eat	ate	eat**en**
know	knew	know**n**
see	saw	see**n**
take	took	take**n**

3 Past tense form + (e)*n*

INFINITIVE	PAST TENSE	PAST PARTICIPLE
break	broke	broke**n**
choose	chose	chose**n**
forget	forgot	forgot**ten**
hide	hid	hid**den**
speak	spoke	spoke**n**

4 No change

INFINITIVE	PAST TENSE	PAST PARTICIPLE
cost	cost	cost
hit	hit	hit
hurt	hurt	hurt
put	put	put
read	read	read*

* For *read*, the spelling doesn't change, but the pronunciation does: /riːd/ /red/ /red/

5 Vowel change

INFINITIVE	PAST TENSE	PAST PARTICIPLE
beg**i**n	beg**a**n	beg**u**n
dr**i**nk	dr**a**nk	dr**u**nk
r**i**ng	r**a**ng	r**u**ng
sw**i**m	sw**a**m	sw**u**m

6 Two participle forms

INFINITIVE	PAST TENSE	PAST PARTICIPLE
burn	burn**t**/burn**ed**	burn**t**/burn**ed**
dream	dream**t**/dream**ed**	dream**t**/dream**ed**
learn	learn**t**/learn**ed**	learn**t**/learn**ed**
spell	spel**t**/spell**ed**	spel**t**/spell**ed**

APPENDIX 3

Spelling rules

1 Spelling of nouns/verbs + s

(plural nouns and present simple verbs after he/she/it)

most nouns and verbs	add -s	cat → cats house → houses eat → eats sleep → sleeps
nouns and verbs that end in -ch, -s, -sh, -x, -o	add -es	church → churches bus → buses dish → dishes box → boxes potato → potatoes teach → teaches miss → misses wash → washes go → goes
nouns and verbs that end in consonant + -y	take away -y and add -ies	city → cities family → families carry → carries fly → flies
nouns and verbs that end in vowel + -y	add -s	holiday → holidays key → keys enjoy → enjoys play → plays
nouns that end in -f or -fe	take away -f(e) and add -ves	wife → wives loaf → loaves (BUT roof → roofs)

2 Spelling of -ing forms of verbs

most verbs	add -ing to the infinitive form	eat → eating go → going sleep → sleeping
verbs that end in -e	take away -e and add -ing	take → taking use → using
verbs that end in -ie	take away -ie and add -ying	die → dying lie → lying
verbs of one syllable that end in a short vowel + consonant	double the consonant and add -ing	sit → sitting swim → swimming
verbs with more than one syllable that end in a stressed short vowel and consonant, e.g. begin.	double the consonant and add -ing (We don't double the consonant if the final syllable is not stressed: visit → visiting)	begin → beginning forget → forgetting

3 Spelling of regular verbs

(past simple endings and past participles)

verbs that end in -e	add -d	die → died like → liked live → lived
verbs that end in a stressed vowel and one consonant (except y, w or x)	double the consonant and add -ed (We don't double the consonant if the final syllable is not stressed)	plan → planned rob → robbed stop → stopped (visit → visited open → opened)
verbs that end in a consonant + -y	remove -y and add -ied	carry → carried study → studied
verbs that end in a vowel + -y	add -ed	enjoy → enjoyed play → played

4 Spelling of comparative adjectives

most short adjectives	add -er	rich → richer tall → taller
most short adjectives that end in e	add -r	late → later nice → nicer
short adjectives that end in one vowel + one consonant (except w)	double the consonant and add -er	big → bigger hot → hotter (slow → slower low → lower)
short adjectives that end in consonant + -y	change y to i and add -er	dry → drier funny → funnier

5 Spelling of superlative adjectives

most short adjectives	add -est	rich → rich**est** tall → tall**est**
short adjectives that end in -e	add -st	late → late**st** nice → nice**st**
short adjectives that end in one vowel + one consonant (except w)	double the consonant and add -est	big → big**gest** hot → hot**test** (slow → slow**est** low → low**est**)
short adjectives that end in consonant + y	change y to i and add -est	dry → dr**iest** lucky → luck**iest**

APPENDIX 4

British and American English

at/on the weekend ➤ Unit 21.1

BrE: **at** the weekend
*What are you doing **at** the weekend?*

AmE: **on** the weekend
*We're visiting our cousins in Ohio **on** the weekend.*

to/through ➤ Unit 21.3

BrE: **from** (day/date) **to** (day/date)
*The shop will be closed **from Wednesday to Friday**.*

AmE: (day/date) **through** (day/date)
*The shop will be closed **Wednesday through Friday**.*

have/have got ➤ Unit 42

We can use *have got* in American English but *have* is more common.

BrE: **Has** your house **got** a garden?
AmE: **Does** your house **have** a garden?

have/take a shower ➤ Unit 43.3

BrE: **have** a shower/bath/holiday
*Jack can't come to the phone; he's **having** a shower.*

AmE: **take** a shower/bath/holiday
*Jack can't come to the phone; he's **taking** a shower.*

just/already/yet ➤ Unit 52

In British English we usually use the present perfect with *just*, *already* and *yet*. We don't use the past simple.

*We've **just finished** eating.*   ~~We just finished eating.~~
*Graham's train **has already arrived**.*   ~~Graham's train already arrived.~~
***Have** you **seen** that film **yet**?*   ~~Did you see that film yet?~~

In American English we can use the present perfect OR the past simple.

*We've **just finished** eating.*   *We **just finished** eating.*
*Graham's train **has already arrived**.*   *Graham's train **already arrived**.*
***Have** you **seen** that film **yet**?*   ***Did** you **see** that film **yet**?*

Index

PICTURE CREDITS

The publisher would like to thank the following for their kind permission to reproduce their photographs:

(Key: b-bottom; c-centre; l-left; r-right; t-top)

4Corners Images: Johanna Huber 255t, Fantuz Olimpio 258; **Alamy Images:** 6, 16, 132l, 160, 178l, 206, 291, 299, Roger Bamber 183, Blend Images 104t, Peter Brown 236, Bubbles Photolibrary 199, China Images 207, Chris Howes / Wild Places Photography 228, David Cook 22, Elizabeth Whiting & Associates 77b, Greece photo library 173, Jeremy Hoare 126l, Image Source Pink 104c, INTERFOTO Pressebildagentur 117, Jeff Morgan 12 54, Jupiterimages 91, Kenneth Dyer 263 (realia), Eddie Linssen 37, Mike Kipling Photography 176r, Mira 281, Mirrorpix 70r, MIXA Co., Ltd. 142r, Nic Cleave Photography 272r, Jeremy Pardoe 204r, Bob Pardue 226, PCL 63cr, PhotoAlto 141t, Pictorial Press Ltd 203l, Jason Politte 186, Matthew Richardson 200b, Alex Segre 72r, Leonid Serebrennikov 9b, Friedrich Stark 288cl, Steve Allen Travel Photography 303, Tetra Images 156r, Arthur Turner 204c, UpperCut Images 205, vario images GmbH & Co.KG 198; **Axiom Photographic Agency Ltd:** 262; **Bridgeman Art Library Ltd:** Staatliche Kunstsammlungen Dresden 96b; **Camera Press Ltd:** 118l, Rossi - Benainous / Gamma / Eyedea Presse 296; **Corbis:** 2, 12, 219, 270, 277, B.S.P.I. 297l, Bettmann 120, Manuel Blondeau 68, Cultura 128l, Fancy / Veer 223t, Andrew Fox 204l, Image100 66, Moodboard 293, Roy Morsch 62, José Fuste Raga 256, Patrick Robert 221, Sunset Boulevard 108b; **Europa Park:** 74r; **FremantleMedia:** 114; **Getty Images:** 96t, 153t, AFP 154r, 161, 255b, AFP 154r, 161, 255b, Peter Cade 189, Chris Clinton 126r, John Coletti 297r, Gregg DeGuire 90r, Goodshoot 28, Jean Heguy 235, Dan Kenyon 260r, Glyn Kirk 128r, Knauer / Johnston 153b, Serge Krouglikoff 99, Bruce Laurance 176l, Melissa McManus 82, Kazuhiro Nogi 74c, Yo Oura 38, Photographers Choice 72l, Alberto E. Rodriguez 87r, Ezra Shaw 169t, Bob Stevens 36, Taxi 25, Edmond Terakopian 188r, The Image Bank 187, WireImage 100; **iStockphoto:** Garret Bautista 166, Mike Bentley 288tr, Tammy Peluso 83; **Jupiterimages:** 265, FoodPix 15; **Kobal Collection Ltd:** 55, 144, 241, 243, MGM / United Artists / Sony 110, 111, Paramount / Universal 116, Warner Bros 107t; **Lonely Planet Images:** 178r; **Masterfile UK Ltd:** 274, 300, Digital Vision 272l; **Moviestore Collection Ltd:** 238; **Panos Pictures:** Abbie Trayler-Smith 246; **Photofusion Picture Library:** Paul Baldesare 245; **Photolibrary.com:** 80, 162, 223b, 252, 273, 276l, Atlantide SN.C 288bl, Banana Stock 150, 154l, Bilderloung 30, Blend Images 64, Corbis 63r, Digital Vision 92, 103, Nick Dolding 132r, ERproductions Ltd 218, Dennis Gilbert 18, Peter Higgins 1, Rainer Holtz 261, i love images 216, Jon Arnold / Peter Adams 118r, Julian Love 257, Jose Luis Pelaez Inc 230, Kate Mitchell 89, Monkey Business Images Ltd 70l, Martin Moxter 40, Duane Osborn 215, Photodisc 136, Maurizio Polverelli 123, Stockbyte 39, Steve Vidler 75, Walter Zerla 14; **Photoshot Holdings Limited:** 43; **Press Association Images:** 74l, 90l, 104b, 129, 165, 168, 192, 288br, Evan Agostini 87l, AP 156l, Sean Dempsey 157, Vadim Ghirda 102, Peter Hatter 134, Jeff Moore 47, Matt Sayles 86; **Reuters:** Jason Lee 139, Max Whittaker 119; **Rex Features:** 13, 59, 85, 88, 108t, 109, 190, 233, 237, 260l, 276r, 287, 288cr, Riccardo Schito 164, SNAP 52, 107b, Westend61 61; **Shutterstock.com:** 4, 8tl, 8c, 8r, 8bl, 56, 63cl, 77t, 93, 142l, 149, 188l, 191, 203r, 211, 234, 288tl; **Thinkstock:** 63l, 266, iStockphoto 9t, Pixland 128c, Thinkstock Images 124; **TopFoto:** Ann Ronan Picture Library 29; **courtesey of www.iwantoneofthose.com** : 169b

All other images © Pearson Education

Every effort has been made to trace the copyright holders and we apologise in advance for any unintentional omissions. We would be pleased to insert the appropriate acknowledgement in any subsequent edition of this publication.

Pearson Education Limited
Edinburgh Gate
Harlow
Essex CM20 2JE
England
and Associated Companies throughout the world.

www.pearsonelt.com

First published 2012
Third impression 2013

ISBN: 9781408299135 (with key)
ISBN: 9781408299142 (without key)
ISBN: 9781408299272 Class audio CDs

Set in Frutiger and ITC Stone Serif

Printed in China
SWTC/03

Illustrated by Joanna Kerr, Lucy Truman, Paul Boston,
Colin Whittock, Douglas Ingram, Glyn Goodwin, Ian
Baker, Kath Walker, Kathy Baxendale, Mark Duffin, Ben
Scruton, and Roger Penwill